RISK TRAFFICKERS

THE STORY OF HOW OUR BANKERS BECAME BANK ROBBERS

BY

CHRISTOPHER J BRICKHILL

Risk Traffickers

O ur bankers are bank robbers.

Risk Traffickers tells the story of how deregulation, moral hazard, financial roulette, fraud, theft, financial "innovation", and the banking oligarchy enabled ludicrous bonuses at the time that our largest banks became *too big to fail*.

The decades after World War I were years of falling inequality, but from 1980, the gap between the haves and the have-nots began to widen dramatically. The rent seeking top 1% made enormous gains at the expense of everyone else. The *too big to fail* mega banks raped clients by resorting to fraud and theft. They eschewed traditional lending and engaged in high risk financial roulette. Moral hazard shielded their profits, and bonuses, and armed with high risk products, treated clients as exploitable, sheep for slaughter. Fleecing the public was part of the business model. Clients were no longer partners.

Risk Traffickers begins with a short history of banking in the US. The Roosevelt New Deal helped us recover from the Great Depression, but the FED's actions did not. The US regulators are described, and various financial risk management tools. The pernicious exotic derivatives and subprime mortgages are explained with arbitrage, conduits, securitizations, credit derivatives and their deficient risk models. The exotic products were sold to unsuspecting clients, and with securitizations, became the pathway to fraud. The changes in financial services after 1980, together with the first dice rollers, are identified. The Millennium arrived with more financial innovation, less regulation, and a strengthened banking oligarchy. The housing bubble burst in the race to the bottom, and the financial system imploded. Then came the 2008 Crisis. The financial system had become dysfunction and *Risk Traffickers* says what needed to be done. Finally, the products that enabled fraud, with the individuals that committed it, those who stole from us, are identified.

Risk Traffickers will help you understand why the financial system imploded, why the top 1% have done exceedingly well at our expense, why we need strong financial services' regulation and supervision, and why we must reform our banks.

Christopher Brickhill

C hris read philosophy, mathematics, logic and computer science at the Universities of Oxford, Essex and Melbourne, taught at each, and lectured in risk in South East Asia. He has numerous publications.

He has advised the largest twenty banks and numerous smaller financial institutions, in New York, London, Beijing, Singapore, Hanoi and Kuala Lumper. Chris formed STORM Technology in New York in 1982. STORM, a treasury and risk management system re-shaped the business of risk management. He is concerned with levels of capital, exotic derivatives, the banking oligarchy, the low level of banker expertise and integrity, and today's risk management metrics. Capital is not expensive!

Chris is a strong and effective communicator. He is a Past Patron of the Metropolitan Opera, New York, a member of the Oxford and Cambridge Society, a Balliol College fund raiser, a past President of the Balliol JCR, and a Balliol Pathfinder host. He was a Director of Martha Graham, and is an avid tennis player. He is a native British English writer and speaker with a good command of Brazilian Portuguese, and speaks some French and Mandarin. He is an Australian citizen, and married.

Copyright

Thank You

Terry Boehm, Peggotty Graham, Derek Kelly, Professor Douglas Kirsner, Dr. Theodora Lee Shuk Yee, Doug McClymont, Professor Stuart Forbes Macintyre, Michael Prideaux, Nigel Harvey, Justice Ross Robson, Sebastien Roussotte, and Benjamin Todd.

Dedication

To my partner, Antonio

Table of Contents

Preface

Bankers Must Not Play With Fire

In an address to Scottish Business Organizations in Edinburgh in October 2009, Mervyn King, the Governor of the Bank of England referred to what Sir Walter Scott had said after the failure of the Ayr bank in 1772. The majority of bankers, Scott said, were "good men" but "there may have been, among so numerous a body, men of a different character, fishers in troubled waters, capitalists who sought gain not by the encouragement of fair trade and honest industry, but by affording temporary fuel to rashness and avarice". King described the unsustainable capital inflows into the Western economies in the 2000s as fuel, inadequate regulation as the flint that ignited it, and concluded that we cannot let bankers play with fire, that we must keep the financial sector on a tight leash.

King did not mention something important. Since the 1980s, the banking sector had become increasingly engaged in activities that broke the law, and by the 1990s, law breaking was the norm. Until the 2008 crisis, the Crisis for short, action by law enforcement authorities had been limited for reasons we will go into, but by 2015, larger and larger fines were being assessed. The behaviour that led to them had not abated, and this behaviour contributed to the Crisis.

Many factors contributed to the raging financial storm in 2008 that brought an economic 9/11 to the globe. Crises are not new, but the destruction of this Crisis was unlike anything since the Great Depression. The banking oligarchy had taken control and Alan Greenspan[1] led a Wild West regulatory free-for-all, shelved ethics and abrogated his responsibilities. The *too big to fail* behemoths followed the reversal of the separation of the utility functions of banking from high-risk investment banking activities. Products that had no economic value, which served only to enhance profits, and which were poorly risk assessed, were sold. Malfeasance, moral hazard,[2] ludicrous compensation schemes justified with arguments devoid of reason, and nanosecond computers with instantaneous global reach all played a part.

After the Crisis, we suffered a global recession, the Great Recession. Worldwide unemployment soared, businesses collapsed, millions lost their homes, families were evicted and trillions of dollars in wealth evaporated. A few banks became megabanks and paid bonuses of millions of dollars at our expense. Monopolies emerged. Some financial services employees, already rich, became fabulously wealthy, some billionaires. To pay for it all, taxpayers all over the globe paid for massive bailouts, guarantees and stimulus packages.

Given the destruction of the Great Recession, you might think that we would have learned some lessons. We did not. The band played on. Banks continued to defraud us and although we saw more frequent and larger fines, there were few, if any, consequences. Fines are paid by shareholders, not the culprits, so are ineffective and simply a cost of doing business. Importantly, we have done nothing to reduce the likelihood of the next crisis, and we have not changed the banking system.

This book is about the banking oligarchy that enabled the Crisis, and bank malfeasance, a long overlooked, but egregious problem. Fines and penalties have exceeded $100 billion in recent years, and make FIFA's bribery, graft and corruption problems appear kindergarten like. It is entrenched, and continues unabated. We will begin by looking at the emergence of banks in the US, and then derivatives and see how they became exotic products. We will look at the factors that contributed to the Crisis and Great Recession, and then the oligarchy and malfeasance. Our discussion will be focused by two lenses, income and wealth distribution, and policies where the insured shares in the pay outs. If bank deposits are insured, then banks can invest them taking less heed of the risks. Banks that are *too big to fail* know that they can rely on government support when in trouble and are thus incentivised to take greater risks as greater risks give rise to greater profits and greater compensation for senior executives. There is little downside as the government, hence taxpayers pick up the losses. Moral hazard arises when market participants take risks assuming that they will be bailed out or otherwise avoid the consequences of reckless risk taking behaviour, how we go about providing housing.

Thomas Piketty shows inequality in the US graphically, from the beginning of the 20th century as a U-curve.[3] Inequality prior to World War II was relatively high. It decreased and remained lower until the 1980s when it began to increase, and it continues to increase today. This coincides with the time that banks began trading for their own accounts. The increased inequality in the US and Europe was exacerbated by the Crisis, and has returned to pre-World War I levels.

It is easy to drown in facts; bear with me. In the USA, in 1978, 34 million persons owned 1 billion acres of private land, 45% of the total land, and 1.7 million of these persons, 5% of landowners, owned 75% of this land. So, at the time when inequality was much lower, a small number of individuals controlled the land on which we build houses. Globally, from 1988 to 2008, the highest 1% of income earners saw their incomes increase by 60%, while those in the bottom 5% suffered no increase in income. In 2008, half of the globe's personal income went to those in the top 8%.[4] In 2010, the richest 20% of people on the globe consumed 80% of the world's food and energy while the poorest 20% consumed only 1.3% of these resources. In 2013, the combined wealth of the world's richest 85 individuals was $1.7 trillion, equal to the wealth of the poorest 3.5 billion, half of humanity. This gave the richest individuals $20 billion each, and the others $485. Moreover, things got worse. The rich got richer. In 2014, the riches of the top 67 individuals matched the wealth of the poorest half on the planet.[5]

"In the first four years of the Obama administration, the top 1% of Americans made real income gains of 31% and the bottom 99% of just 1%" *The Economist* reported, "short of the return to serfdom, conditions could hardly have been more favourable for the US business elite."[6]

In the closing weeks of 2014, Bloomberg told us that the net worth of the 400 richest people on the planet was $4.1 trillion, $10 billion on average. This galloping deterioration in wealth equality matters. If we divide the wealth of these top 400 among everyone else, each would receive $1,175. It would more than double the average wealth of the lowest half, and move them out of poverty for a year! Is it any wonder that almost 330 million children under the age of five in 2014 were severely handicapped by malnutrition?[7] That year 500,000 of these children died from malnutrition.

Danny Dorling[8] opens *All That Is Solid: The Great Housing Disaster*: "If people hoarded food on the basis that its value was sure to go up when others began to starve and would pay anything, we would stop their hoarding". Shelter is also an inalienable human right[9] and Dorling writes about the conflict between housing as shelter and housing as a store of value, as an investment. Housing is a right, he says, not something to be sold freely and bought by the highest bidder to the detriment of everyone else. We need to find an acceptable approach to financing it, so all of us can buy shelter.

For decades, individuals and families have jumped on the housing ladder, and acquired a home by mortgaging it. Mortgages mean low down payments, and for most are the only way to buy a home. The expectation is that the value of homes appreciate, so homeowners benefit from an investment. However, it's a Ponzi scheme, and the unprecedented increase of the US population from 3 million, two hundred years ago, to 350 million today, has made this possible in the US. In Europe, during this period, populations have doubled. There are two issues here. Will the appreciation in housing values continue, and if they do, what can be done to limit this? Many will find this controversial. Asset appreciation invites speculation, and speculation on housing, a basic human right, is unacceptable.

Something is clearly very wrong. There is a deep fault line between the top 1% and the rest of us, between the global financial services oligarchy and us. The oligarchy, a plutocracy, continues to enrich itself by taking from the bottom 99%, and what they take includes housing.

Bank malfeasance oiled the Crisis and Great recession. The financial system is a money generating tool for those who provide it. They are rent seekers. They enrich themselves not by making the size of the economic pie larger, but by manipulating the system in order to take a larger slice for themselves. It is now global and we need to change this, and replace the banking system with responsible bankers, and non-dysfunctional banks that are accountable, and effectively regulated. We need to destroy the system that compensates flagrant egregious behavior. Clearly we need to eliminate criminal behavior. We need to halt the move from democracy to a plutocracy, and destroy the banking oligarchy. We need a banking system, but not this one.

1

An Orgy of Delusion and Greed

T he Crisis, triggered by the downturn in the US housing market, resulted in a complete collapse of the financial markets in September 2008. The global financial system ground to a halt and mushroomed into the Great Recession, the second Great Depression. Despite some signs of recovery, the Great Recession remains with us today, and its magnitude is underplayed. Moreover, we have done nothing to prevent a repeat.

Since the 1990s, law enforcers have eschewed prosecution of white-collar crime. However, as we said in the opening remarks, the nefarious, criminal behaviour is on the uptake. Almost all of those responsible for this behaviour in the recent events have escaped unscathed, notwithstanding that the magnitude of the crime rivals the magnitude of the Great Recession itself. Today, powerful, self-serving interests continue to fudge integrity and leave the global financial system intact. We need to return to prosecuting white-collar crime.

The 2000s and Cheap Money

In the early 2000s, the US central bank, the Federal Reserve Bank, the FED, orchestrated cheap money to stimulate the economy and sidestep any looming recession. It expected to see investments in business assets like software, machinery and personnel. However, despite the lower cost of funds, business investments grew more slowly than in the prior decades as the cheap money was siphoned off into mortgages, consumer borrowing and spending. In addition, foreign money, popularly identified as savings, but in reality funds looking for a safe home after the Asian crises of the 1990s, poured into Western economies. These capital flows from the emerging markets into the developed world were unprecedented. China, then the long side of an enormous trade imbalance with the US, invested trillions internationally, mostly in the US, and this fuelled the cheap credit carnival.[10] Americans were not shy in their spending habits. In 1980, they saved 12% of their income, when private sector debt was 123% of GDP[11] and household debt 52%, but twenty-five years later, the savings rate was negative. Household debt had risen eight and a half times, from $1.5 trillion to $12.7 trillion[12], and against GDP had doubled. Private sector debt was 290% of

GDP at the time of the Crisis. Americans had borrowed $4 trillion in home equity loans and another $4 trillion on credit cards.[13] They were, however, generous, donating 14% of their incomes to charity.[14]

At the same time, the price difference between less and more risky investments, the risk premiums, had narrowed, and low interest rates, drove conservative investors like pension funds to the higher returns offered by investment funds, OTC derivatives and securitizations.[15] This led to a demand for mortgage backed securitizations, MBSs, which are built by packaging mortgages together. They were sliced into smaller packages or tranches, before being sold to investors, they offered good yields, and were attractive. Furthermore, they could be credit wrapped, that is insured against default, and made more attractive.[16] Demand for them from investors was insatiable.

Securitizers, usually the megabanks, did the packaging, and gorged on them too, stuffing their portfolios, and trading them. Each MBS needed thousands of mortgages. So the demand for the building blocks, mortgages, was also insatiable and drove a frenzy of mortgage origination. Wall Street.[17] Securitizers vacuumed mortgages from mortgage originators (banks, brokers and mortgage companies that provided mortgages to consumers) with little concern for quality, and in the frenzy, lending standards collapsed, and were eventually ignored. The volume of securitizations increased dramatically from 2000 until the Crisis, and 2010 data shows that the US was responsible for more than 80% of the market, Europe for 15% and Asia the balance.[18] The US was the cradle that nurtured the toxin.

What had developed was a shocking abrogation of responsibility and integrity as politicians, regulators and bankers exploited or ignored regulation, and shelved ethics. Mortgage originators issued millions of mortgages to people who could not afford them. Irresponsible and predatory lending fuelled a housing boom, and the cost of housing rose as did mortgage costs. Individuals incentivized by quick profits, engaged in speculative home flipping and bought and sold houses like stocks and shares. Lending became divorced from payment default risk,[19] which was now borne by the investors in MBSs, and the mortgage business became volume driven. The more mortgages, the more MBSs, the more revenue, revenue that was without default risk, the greater the profits and the larger the bonuses. Thus, the frenzy was fed. The housing market was out of control.

Property developers bought more and more houses onto the market, but eventually the supply of housing outstripped demand, residential property prices fell, and the property markets collapsed, first in the US, and then globally. The supply of mortgages dried up, which meant that there were not enough mortgages to securitize. Wall Street had made huge bets against an event it considered so unlikely that it could be ignored, that the value of US residential property would decline. The bankers were wrong, even though it was blindingly obvious that if the value of residential real estate did not continue to rise, the kinds of mortgages that were being sold meant that there had to be extensive mortgage defaults.

This was so because most mortgages were subprime, with adjustable rates,[20] and upward price resets followed a year or two after origination. Many borrowers could not afford the resets, and when the housing market collapsed and home prices fell, these owners could not sell their homes and repay the mortgages, or refinance them, so defaulting on mortgage repayments became the only option. Mortgage defaults occurred in droves and the MBSs collateralized by them lost value and investors, including securitizers, suffered large losses. The MBS market became illiquid, and their value as collateral evaporated. The short-term funding markets contracted, credit froze and the financial system neared collapse. The unlikely event had occurred!

The First Signs

HSBC disclosed a profit warning in 1Q 2007. Its US subprime mortgage portfolio had suffered extensive losses. It was a gross underestimate. In June 2007, two Bear Stearns hedge funds failed because their US mortgage collateralized products had lost substantial value. High leverage put them out of business, and they were liquidated within a month, with a staggering cost to Bear of $3.2 billion. Then a UBS sponsored fund failed, and a few months later, on 9 August, the French banking giant BNP Paribas blocked withdrawals from three of its money market funds. The funds were small with combined assets of €1.6 billion, had invested in US mortgage debt, and the market was illiquid. To bolster liquidity, the European Central Bank, the ECB, and the FED, injected more than $90 billion, and fifty European banks borrowed. More was to come. The Bank of England, the BoE, the Bank of Canada and the Bank of Japan soon followed suit.

In September, the German Finance Minister announced that the recent problems were US problems, but within a few days, the Germans had to bailout Hypo Real Estate and IKB. Both had extensive exposure to US real estate assets. Then Countrywide, the biggest mortgage originator in the US stumbled. A large UK bank, a major mortgage lender, Northern Rock, suffered a run, the first in the UK in 150 years. It was later nationalized. The Union Bank of Switzerland, UBS, Citigroup and Merrill Lynch announced staggering subprime mortgage losses. The FED, the BoE and the ECB pumped more money into their economies, but globally stock markets collapsed and the US and European housing markets disintegrated.

Why did the problems go global? Half the real estate collateralized securitizations had been sold to foreign investors. By the year-end 2007, there was extensive global contamination with a toxin born and nurtured in the domestic $11 trillion[21] US housing market. The toxin had been trafficked.

Larry Elliot, the Economics Editor of The Guardian, likened this time when liquidity evaporated to the turning point between the Edwardian summer of prosperity and tranquillity, and the outbreak of the First World War and the horrors of trench and chemical warfare.[22]

Then the Unimaginable

In March 2008, Bear Stearns, the fifth largest investment bank in the world, collapsed. It had assets of $350 billion, 15,500 employees in 25 offices, and a truly global footprint. Bear could not roll over its short-term debt, the loans which funded its day-to-day operations. Bear's trading partners questioned its viability because it was heavily exposed to US real estate and could only offer these assets as collateral. As there was no liquid market, they had been marked down. They were toxic. Lenders to Bear demanded good collateral, but Bear had none. To avoid bankruptcy, the New York FED engineered its sale to JP Morgan Chase for a song. It had been the weakest and most leveraged of the *Big Five* investment banks and the deal had to be backed by a $29 billion Washington guarantee[23] against losses from Bear's $30 billion toxic asset portfolio. Bear's failure rocked the global financial markets, but the disruptions and the market turmoil that followed paled into insignificance compared to the problems that would arise later in the year.

IndyMac failed in July. It was a mortgage lender and a Savings and Loan Association bank, or S&L.[24] They base their business on deposit taking and mortgage lending. IndyMac had been spun off from Countrywide in 1997 and was heavily into subprime mortgages. It had a very small deposit base, and therefore relied upon the short-term markets for funds. Indy, like Bear, could not find lenders. It was the fourth largest US bank failure.

During the summer of 2008, the fragility of the markets increased, and the US and European governments tried to find ways to soften the blows coming from the housing markets. Everything connected to these markets had taken a hit, including mortgage originators in the US, building societies in the United Kingdom and Europe, the German Landesbanken and all kinds of investors around the globe. Credit had contracted, some financial institutions raised capital, but things got worse.

The Meltdown

In September 2008, the Crisis hit, and the financial systems in the US and Europe went into meltdown. On the seventh, the two mortgage giants, Freddie Mac and Fannie Mae[25] were forced into conservatorship, a form of bankruptcy. On the 15th, Lehman Brothers, the fourth largest investment bank, on the edge and without a buyer, declared bankruptcy. At the same time, Merrill Lynch, the third largest investment bank, was sold to Bank of America in order to avoid a similar fate. A few days later, American International Group, AIG, the largest insurer in the world, was de facto nationalized, and on the 26th, JP Morgan Chase acquired Washington Mutual, WaMu, the sixth largest bank in the US and the largest S&L, in a fire sale. Wachovia, the fourth largest US bank, then suffered a run, and Wells Fargo acquired it a week later. The problem? Toxic US mortgage products.

By mid-October, the US taxpayer had become a part owner of each of the nine largest US banks. Goldman Sachs and Morgan Stanley, the only two remaining of the *Big Five* investment banks, swapped access to FED funds for tighter regulation and became commercial banks, ending the age of US investment banking. By early 2009, Citigroup had received two bailouts, as had Bank of America and the US taxpayer owned a third of the New York City financial disaster.

Europe was not immune, and Northern Rock's failure in the UK was soon followed by Bradford & Bingley and HBOS, both building societies. Bradford and Bingley was broken up and many of the pieces sold to the Spanish giant Banco Santander. HBOS received a bailout so that it could be sold to Lloyds. The Royal Bank of Scotland, RBS, once a regional bank, had grown its balance sheet to £2.2 trillion and become the largest bank in the world. Its assets were larger than the UK and Spanish GDPs combined. But after a disastrous, failed takeover of the Dutch ABN AMRO in October of 2007, it had to be bailed out. By 2009, the UK taxpayer had invested £40 billion and owned 81% of the bank, after which it announced the all-time largest loss for a UK company, £24.1 billion!

And it continued to lose money. After further years of losses culminating in a £9 billion loss, the bank retreated to UK regional banking. The RBS bailout was the largest banking takeover of all time. Toxic US mortgage products again the problem. Today, the UK banking system remains sick. It is too concentrated and too interconnected.

During all the fun and games, the banking systems in Iceland and Ireland collapsed. The Benelux giant Fortis was broken up and its pieces sold or nationalized. Fortis had been the 20th largest company on the globe. The Franco-Belgian Dexia Group collapsed and was bailed out on its way to its complete demise a few years later. Commerzbank, Hypo Real Estate, and many of the Landesbanken, notwithstanding rescues, all played with insolvency. More bailouts and the German government ended up owning a large part of its financial sector! No bank in Europe escaped.

After AIG, the money market funds stopped buying commercial paper, that is lending, and the hedge funds closed their brokerage accounts. Banks that relied on the short-term markets skidded into the rails. Between March and September 2008, nine major US financial institutions failed, seven in September alone. Ben Bernanke, the chairman of the FED, reported to the Financial Crisis Inquiry Commission[26] "out of maybe ... 13 of the most important financial institutions in the United States, 12 were at risk of failure within a period of a week or two".[27] Corporations that depended on the commercial paper markets could not sell their paper and fund their day-to-day expenses, including salaries. Global trade deteriorated and economies froze. By year-end 2008, the Great Recession had hit the wider economy.

Paul Krugman said that the Crisis was like:

> ... nothing we've seen before. But [it was] like everything we've seen before, all at once: a bursting real estate bubble comparable to what happened in Japan at the end of the 1980s; a wave of bank runs comparable to those of the early 1930s (albeit mainly involving the shadow banking system rather than conventional banks); a liquidity trap, in the United States, again reminiscent of Japan; and, most recently, a disruption of international cash flows and a wave of currency crises all too reminiscent of what happened to Asia in the late 1990s.[28]

Another Great Depression

When Barack Obama became the US President in 2009, the Great Recession had assumed the proportions of the Great Depression. Globally, financial systems were dysfunctional, stock markets were disasters, national housing markets had collapsed, there was no credit, and economic activity was at a near standstill. Worldwide unemployment had jumped sharply upwards, following extensive corporate and banking failures.[29]

There were many similarities between the Crisis and the Great Depression. Get rich quick schemes were promoted using fraudulent products, inexperienced investors were given large credit lines collateralized by these products, and the assumption was that their value would go up, forever. Widespread Ponzi schemes were supported by widespread fraud and collusion. Unemployment soared and banks failed.

Central banks and governments provided financial institutions and corporations with trillions in massive bailouts, funding programs and guarantees. They had no choice. In addition to the destruction and rescues in the US, Europe, provided 20 guarantee programs, 15 bank recapitalization programs and rescued 44 large banks. Many governments ended up with significant ownership in their financial sectors, and between October 2008 and October 2011, the European Commission committed €4.5 trillion, 37% of the European Union's[30] GDP, to the European financial sector.[31] The Commission commented in 2012:

> The financial crisis highlighted that public authorities are ill equipped to deal with ailing banks operating in today's global markets. In order to maintain essential financial services for citizens and businesses, governments have had to inject public money into banks and issue guarantees on an unprecedented scale. ... This averted [more and continued] massive banking failure[s] and economic disruption, but has burdened taxpayers with deteriorating public finances and failed to settle the question of how to deal with large cross-border banks in trouble. ... [If a bank's critical functions are rescued the costs of restructuring and resolving failing banks must fall upon the bank's owners and creditors and not on taxpayers].[32]

Why a Bubble Became a Disaster

Mortgage delinquencies were disastrous for borrowers, lenders, investors and securitizers alike, but when the housing bubble burst, what resulted should have been similar to the downturn after the dotcom bubble in 2001: a short, mild recession. Why then was the Crisis so destructive and why did the Great Recession follow?

Crisis are white swans and occur regularly,[33] and severe, systemic crises do not result from something as inconsequential as member states (at the time of writing) subprime mortgages and misguided, fraudulent risk takers. Structural changes in the financial system meant that fault lines formed over time. The changes began in the 1980s. The US current account deficit had grown, the shadow banking system[34] came into existence, leverage and debt ballooned and the property boom, both an asset and credit bubble, was built on these fault lines. Amazingly, at the time of the Crisis, the spread between Treasuries and high-risk junk bonds hovered between 2% and 3%. The whole system was subprime.

The collapse of the overheated property market exposed the fault lines and the fragility of the US and global financial sectors: ineffective regulation, too much debt with much of it hidden off balance sheet, too much leverage, too much short-term funding, too much risk, *too big to fail* megabanks, ineffective ratings agencies, interconnectivity, insufficient capital, toxic products, unconscionable, misaligned compensation, extensive, unchecked malfeasance, and so on, and all glued together by a disingenuous global banking oligarchy. Consequently, banks were in no way capable of absorbing losses and their interconnectedness meant that when one bank suffered losses, others did too. The outdated regulatory system was strangled by incompetence and a lack of integrity. The lower floor of a house of cards collapsed and a financial firestorm engulfed the globe.

The US was not the only country with a fragile economy to experience a housing bubble. In the early 2000s, The UK (housing increased 150%), Australia (115%), New Zealand, Dubai (226%), Iceland, Ireland (190%), Spain (145%), Hungary, Turkey, Estonia, Lithuania, Latvia, Vietnam, Thailand, China, Singapore (250%) and South Africa all saw dramatic housing price increases. From 2000 to 2005, the value of homes in the developed economies doubled an increase of $40 trillion.

How did the banking oligarchy escape accountability, responsibility and regulation and build a financial system ripe for self-destruction? The oligarchy had had few constraints for more than two decades and was assisted by compliant regulators, and lobbyists, auditors and lawyers in its service, and it purchased policy makers. It also had history on its side. A year before the Crisis, financial services in the US and Western Europe had been a wealth creation machine, generating 40% of all US corporate profits. London was alive. Wall Street had embraced a new and exportable model of free enterprise financial services. Sandy Weill, who put Citigroup together from Travelers and Citibank, reflected: "Not having American financial institutions that really are at the fulcrum of how these countries are converting to a free enterprise system would really be a shame".[35] Wall Street believed that freed from regulation, free markets would usher in a new financial era. This did not, of course, happen. Once freed from regulation, the global economy collapsed and taxpayers all over the world found themselves on the hook! This legacy, the inability of the financial system to cope, remains with us today, years after the Crisis.

Not only was history on their side, but many of those with responsibility denied there was an issue. The Crisis was just "one of those things". Notwithstanding that crises reappear all too often, Wall Street portrayed the Crisis as a once-in-a-lifetime event. They told us that it would be wasteful to put in place preventative measures to forestall events that happen very rarely, perhaps once every 100 or so years. However, the Crisis was not a once-in-a-lifetime event. Moreover, even for rare events, like encountering the poliovirus, there is no excuse for not being inoculated! It benefits us and prevents the spread of the disease.

Alan Greenspan, told us:

> ... that to put in place reform would be putting
> up an umbrella to protect one from a storm
> that is going to occur once in 100 years.
> Furthermore, it would be excessively
> expensive and would dampen growth.[36]

What planet was Greenspan on? An umbrella would have saved trillions of dollars, allowed millions of families to keep their homes, and tens of millions to remain employed.

The American Dream was already on its last legs, and the Crisis pounded the final nail into its coffin. The elderly middle classes had benefited from employment, retirement benefits, health and social entitlements and good investment returns. Now, the millions who had worked hard and behaved responsibly saw their life dreams eroded by greed, and irresponsible and criminal behaviour. We experienced a "reckless endangerment of the entire nation by people at the highest levels of Washington and corporate America"[37] ... [and in the United Kingdom and Europe].

Disaster Capitalism in Numbers

The size and destruction of the Crisis distinguishes it from any downturn since the Great Depression, and it did not need a war or external economic shock to kick it off. So let's look at the numbers.

Economies

The economic downturn began in 4Q 2008.[38] The DJIA, which had hit a high of 14,164 in October 2007, had fallen by almost 50%, by March 2009, to 7,555. By April 2009, the US economy had contracted 4% and the other developed economies 3.2%. Global output contracted by 2.7%[39] in 2009, contrasting saliently with an average annual growth of more than 4% for the immediately preceding years. Fifty-two countries had declines in per-capita income.[40] Looking to the future, Better Markets[41] estimated that for the years 2008 to 2018 losses would be a minimum of $12.8 trillion, 90% of the 2012 US GDP. Andrew Haldane at the Bank of England estimated the global economic loss would be between $60 trillion and $200 trillion; in the UK alone, it would be between £1.8 trillion and £7.4 trillion.[42]

Sovereign Debt

Governments funded bailouts, stimulus packages and guarantees, so sovereign debt increased dramatically. Tax revenues fell, and essential services were cut. By 2009, Washington had extended more than $7 trillion in bailouts, guarantees and loans,[43] half the US GDP that year. The FED's balance sheet, $940 billion before Lehman swelled to $2 trillion afterwards. It had lent for just about anything and provided offshore dollars by Eurodollar swaps with European central banks and the ECB. The national debt of the UK rose to just short of £1 trillion, nearly two thirds of its GDP. Generations to come will need to pay.

Lost Wealth

When President Barack Obama took office in January, $5 trillion in US household wealth had already evaporated since the Crisis.[44] By late 2009, the loss had become $19 trillion, a drop in wealth of 26%.[45] The Crisis had wiped out two decades of wealth accumulation. Retirement accounts had lost $3.4 trillion, 40% of their value. Adjusting for inflation, US household income had fallen from $52,600 in 1999 to $50,300 in 2008.[46]

Unemployment

In 2009, global unemployment had risen 15%, to 205 million and the US broad unemployment rate, U-6[47] hit 16.2%. The fully unemployed rate, U-3, was 9.3%. Throughout the 1990s, U-6 had been under 5%. By 2012, 23 million remained out of work or were part-timing it while looking for a job.[48] Wages stagnated, the unemployment lines stretched, and careers were destroyed. Long-term unemployment meant that savings were decimated and retirement provisions slashed. On top of this, 9.3 million Americans lost their health insurance.[49] The US poverty levels soared from 12.5% in 2007 to 15.1% in 2010, the highest rate in the 52 years that the US Census Bureau had recorded poverty levels. By 2010, 46.2 million Americans were living in poverty.[50]

By 2012, there were 13 million jobless in the European Union, the EU, the unemployment rate in the UK reached 10%, in France it was 12%, in Spain 23%, in Portugal 12% and in Greece 22%.[51] Notably, Goldman Sachs had sold derivatives to Greece so it could disguise its deficits and gain entry to the EU. Goldman profited, but the Greeks suffered 30% pay cuts, high unemployment and increased poverty. More telling than undifferentiated unemployment numbers are the data for the under 30s. In the UK, youth unemployment stood at 19%, in Ireland it was 17% and for each of Greece, Spain and Portugal it was 50%.[52] There were riots and in Greece, some were violent. The young of Greece, Spain and Portugal emigrated when they could, and continue to do so today. Contrary to what our bankers would have us believe, it is a disaster and horrific.[53] Imagine that you are lucky enough to get a university place, and can afford to accept it, but you have only a one in two chance of getting a job, any job, when you graduate!

Nicolas Sarkozy at Davos in 2011, alarmed by the losses, noted that the global job losses were in the tens of millions.[54] Eventually, we would see 14 million US jobs permanently lost.[55]

Housing

Housing was not seen primarily as shelter, but as a financial roulette wheel and speculation become a pastime. Fraud appeared in many guises. Appraisals overstated the values of homes, and black Americans in Detroit were 70% more likely to be given a subprime loan than whites in the same financial situation.

There were extensive foreclosures and the US and European mortgage markets destructed. The gasoline that fuelled the US housing bubble also fuelled property bubbles globally.

In the UK, homeownership fell from 69% to 64%, reversing a 50-year trend, and homelessness rose 17%. Deposits for home mortgages rose from 9 month's salary to 3 year's salary. In 2011, the value of residential property rose to £5.5 trillion, twice the size of the UK equity market when 69% of the land in the UK was in the hands of 0.6% of the population.[56]

In the US, it was worse. Homelessness reached 600,000, an all-time high. For most of the 2000s, repossessions and foreclosures hovered around 400,000, but by 2011, foreclosures had risen to 3.9 million. By 2012, 16 million homeowners or 31.4% of all homeowners with a mortgage were under water. Taken together, they owed $1.2 trillion more than their houses were worth. As a result of the Great Recession, 3.5 million Americans lost their homes.

Global Trade and Corporate Losses

By early 2009, direct corporate losses were greater than $4.1 trillion, $2.7 for the US and $1.4 trillion for the EU.[57] In 3Q 2007 corporate profits fell 10% from $1.67 trillion to $1.51 trillion as trade contracted globally. The Cap Gemini global trade index, 1,621 in 4Q 2008, dropped 16% to 1,366 in 1Q 2009.[58] At this time, a number of insurance companies specializing in financial insurance and thousands of home construction companies failed. Although the Detroit carmakers were rescued, thousands of their distributors failed. There were no bank failures in the three years prior to 2007, 3 in 2007, 25 in 2008, and 389 more between 2009 and 2011.

Not all banks continued to suffer after the Crisis. Some megabanks were back to profitability in less than a year. Goldman earned record profits of $5.2 billion for the first half of 2009. It made money from the miseries of others and from the FED's bailouts. Even the meagre attempts at recovery had created opportunities for abuse and profit for those in a position to take advantage.

Obscene Compensation

There was a bright side for a very small number of those employed in the financial services sector. Wall Street compensation packages were out of control, and the executives that caused the problems received outlandish compensation, hundreds of billions of dollars.

Compensation for the financial sector in New York City in 2007 was $53 billion, or $178,000 per individual.[59] Goldman alone paid its employees an average of $661,000. Almost $20 billion. The firm's CEO, Lloyd Blankfein took home $68.4 million. Hedge fund manager John Paulson bet against the housing bubble and pocketed $4 billion! The top 1% of US income earners increased their share of income and wealth to their highest levels since the 1920s.[60] By mid-2009, while Main Street[61] was continuing to suffer, some Wall Street organizations had returned to minting money, with record profits and compensation.

UK Conservative MP Jessie Norman stated, "… no reputable study has found a significant correlation between senior executive pay and long-term corporate performance".[62] The underachieving top 1% are grossly overpaid. Thomas Piketty called it meritocratic extremism.[63]

Compensation does not align with ability, nor performance, but with size. In addition to the Goldman numbers, for 2007 John Thain, the CEO of Merrill earned $84 million, John Mack, CEO of Morgan Stanley $41 million[64] and Jamie Dimon CEO of JP Morgan Chase $28 million.[65] By contrast, John Gutfreund, CEO of Salomon in 1988, earned, in 2009 dollars, a mere $5.8 million.

Absurd compensation also aligns with inequality. The Gini index places the US and the UK at numbers 1 and 2 in the inequality listing in the developed world. It took divine intervention via the Pope to remind us that Thatcher and Reagan trickle-down economics has no evidential basis. He reminded us that the poor are still waiting! The economist Kuznets' view, that growth is a rising tide that lifts all boats, seems to have found only the boats with gaping holes in their hulls.

Absurd financial sector compensation is concentrated in the US and UK. In 2012, 2,188 commercial and investment bankers in the UK received an average of €1.95 million, up 35% from 2011. In Sweden, only 11 investment bankers earned more than €1 million, in Spain there were 37, in Germany 100, and in France 117. In most other countries, this number was zero.[66] The top 1% of Swiss earners takes home half as much as their UK colleagues.

How is it that salaries and bonuses are so high? That is an easy question to answer. They are high because they are determined by their shameless recipients. Executives earn bonuses when profits are made, but do not suffer when losses are declared. This incentivizes them to take near term profits and push losses into the future. It's theft by any other name.

Obama Care: Banking Must Change

Shortly after Barack Obama assumed the Presidency, he met with the CEOs of thirteen of the largest US banks. It was the last Friday in March 2009.[67] The Great Recession had taken a vice like grip and the financial services industry needed Washington to continue its substantial support.

The US government had unprecedented power over the banks. TARP[68] and the other stimulus packages, bailouts, loans and guarantees meant that Washington was in a position to force the hand of Wall Street. Now also, Goldman Sachs and Morgan Stanley, the two remaining investment banks, had become bank-holding companies and subject to regulation.

The Obama message was clear: "How can I help you? We are all in this together". The bankers agreed. They needed Washington, and Washington needed banks, but the question was, did Washington need *these* banks? He said:

> But the old ways that led to this crisis cannot stand. And to the extent that some have so readily returned to them underscores the need for change and change now. History cannot be allowed to repeat itself.[69]

Obama knew that the business of banking had to change. The public had recently learned that AIG, the recipient of a $180 billion bailout, and which was now 80% owned by the US taxpayer, had just paid the executives that had caused its problems $165 million in bonuses. Then we learned that it had paid $440,000 for a retreat for its independent insurance agents at the St. Regis Monarch Beach resort in Dana Point, California, and another $86,000 for a partridge-hunting trip in the UK.[70] The public, Capitol Hill and Obama's administration were stunned. Morals and common sense were badly out of line. Obama was right; the excesses had not been curbed.

Notwithstanding their agreement in March to address the problems, the banks did nothing except pay more Washington lobbyists to oppose the newly invigorated fight for tighter regulation. So in December 2009, President Obama said:

> The people on Wall Street still don't get it. They don't get it. They're still puzzled: Why it is that people are mad at the banks? Well, let's see. You guys are drawing down ten-, twenty-million dollar bonuses after America went through the worst economic year that it's gone through in decades, and you guys caused the problem. And we've got ten percent

unemployment. Why do you think people might be a little frustrated?[71]

Obama needed to fix the problems in the banking system, the markets and the economy, and he needed to quell public anger. In March, he had asked the culprits, to mend their ways and to buy into a White House recovery program. He kept his side of the bargain, approved $787 billion in tax cuts, and increased Washington spending to offset the weak domestic and overseas demand. Nevertheless, no change. By December, the banks had done nothing but continue the practices that had brought the Crisis on. Malfeasance continued. The LIBOR and foreign exchange and other frauds had increased.[72]

Some US Bank CEOs Confess

The CEOs admitted a few problems, but denied that there was anything fundamentally wrong. They wanted the status quo, especially the compensation status quo. John Mack, the CEO of Morgan Stanley at the time of the Crisis and its Chairman in 2011, testified before the Financial Crisis Inquiry Commission in 2010. He said:

> ... Fundamental flaws in our financial system ... many firms were too highly leveraged, took on too much risk and *did not have sufficient resources to manage those risks* [my emphasis]... the regulators simply did not have the visibility, tools or authority to protect the stability of the financial system as a whole.[73] ... no firm should be considered 'too big to fail' ... the complexity of financial markets – and financial products - has exploded in recent years, but regulation and oversight have not kept pace ... many of the complex products were designed to spread out risk, they often had the opposite effect ... today's financial markets are global and interconnected ... our regulatory regime needs to be as well.[74] ... Leverage was a crucial factor ... Capital is important and the leverage of the investment banks was untenable.[75]

Mack argued for the status quo. Admit and fix a few problems like leverage, poor risk management and the obvious inadequacies of the regulators, and the big problems will be overlooked. In

Mack's eyes, wealth creation via excessive compensation, and leaving the taxpayers to pick up the downside were just fine.

Brian Moynihan, the CEO and president of Bank of America at the time of the Crisis was critical of bank risk management: "... at its core, our job is to manage risk ... many banks ... managed risk poorly".[76] They did not of course risk their own compensation! In his testimony before the Commission, he said, "the issues are complex and our views continue to develop as we learn more".[77] He continued:

> ... We, the industry caused a lot of damage. Never has it been clearer how mistakes made by financial companies can affect Main Street and we need to learn the lessons of the past few years ... the lessons are not simple ones; this crisis had multiple causes .... We have seen four crises: (1) a mortgage crisis in the US and abroad; (2) a capital market crisis; (3) a global credit crisis; and (4) a severe global recession.[78] ... It is difficult to understand how markets and regulators could tolerate leverage of 40-1 or even 60-1 in our largest investment banks.[79]

Again, Moynihan glossed over the real issues. Let the status quo remain and fix a few problems.

Jamie Dimon, the CEO of JP Morgan Chase testified before the Commission, and glossed over the issues:

> Let me be clear: No institution, including our own, should be 'too big to fail'[80]... I believe that the key underlying causes of the crisis [were] excessive leverage [and the] dramatic growth of structural risks and the unanticipated damage that they could cause; [and] regulatory lapses and mistakes.[81]

Lloyd Blankfein, the CEO of Goldman Sachs said:

> Factors from both Main Street and Wall Street contributed to today's circumstances. ... any examination ... must begin with an understanding of some of the global economic and financial dynamics of the last two decades. ... the roots of the damage to our financial system are broad and deep. ... the resulting under-pricing of risk led to massive leverage

across wide swaths of the economy … the overdependence on credit ratings coincided with the dilution of the coveted triple A rating. In January 2008, there were 12 triple A-rated companies in the world. At the same time, there were 64,000 structured finance instruments, like CDO tranches rated triple A…. models were too often allowed to substitute for judgment … risk monitoring and activities often failed to capture the risk inherent in off-balance sheet activities, such as Structured Investment Vehicles. During and before the crisis banks behaved badly, the financial system was mismanaged and was poorly regulated[82] … [We have] participated in things that were clearly wrong and … have reasons to regret and apologize for.[83]

In November 2009, Blankfein declared: "I'm doing God's work." Several days later he apologised, said he had intended it as a joke. The press went for his throat. This statement however, represents his actual views, and in line with Goldman's Brian Griffiths, who thinks that: "The injunction of Jesus to love others as ourselves is a recognition of self-interest … We have to tolerate the inequality as a way to achieving greater prosperity and opportunity for all."

Fundamental Change

The bankers that had met with Obama all agreed that reform was needed, but vigorously resisted it. Wall Street did not want reform. It would be prohibitively expensive. It was unnecessary, and would target an event that would occur once every hundred years, they told us. Importantly, it would limit compensation!

However, there is an urgent need for reform, and to hold Wall Street accountable for the wreckage that it inflicted on the globe. The costs of the Crisis and Great Recession are in the tens of trillions, but Wall Street has fought tooth and nail to hinder, weaken and dismantle reform and regulation. It has spent huge amounts of money on lawyers, lobbyists, PR firms, campaign contributions and academic research to achieve its goals.

The Thatcher government sowed Crisis seeds in the UK in 1979 when a nation of shopkeepers became shareholders. Many paid twice for the privilege. Taxes paid for the creation of the companies that were then sold to the public. A few years later, the US Reagan administration began an intensive deregulation process and at the turn of the Millennium the Glass Steagall Act, the GSA, was repealed. The eight years between the repeal of the GSA and the Crisis are strikingly similar to the years that led to the 1929 crash. Extensive fraudulent behaviour, extensive losses while a few made fortunes.

The Financial Crisis Inquiry Commission determined that the Crisis was avoidable. As well as the fault lines we have listed, the Commission added markets, especially the OTC markets, paid-for academic research, and finance ministries as making contributions to the Crisis. Furthermore, moral hazard needs to be addressed. We add to the list of issues, malfeasance.

The regulators and rating agencies colluded with Wall Street and its political supporters to build an unregulated profit-generating machine that was bound to collapse. Wall Street executives enriched themselves in the process and taxpayers picked up the tab. The biggest financial institutions received billions in handouts and the smaller institutions, individuals, and homeowners were left to fend for themselves. Wall Street raged against the Dodd-Frank Act, the act that was to enable reform, and told us that deregulation was good for us. It is not, and the claim is disingenuous, and results from the self-interest of individuals with records of accomplishment of reckless economic destruction driven by personal gain.[84] With rare exceptions, the academic economists supported the politicians, regulators and the banking executives and extolled the benefits of deregulation, and the wonders of financial innovation. Nouriel Roubini, Raghuram Rajan and Pablo Triano were dissenters. The academics should have known better. They were paid to know better. But, they were paid by Wall Street.

Reform will mean lower profits and drastically reduced compensation for bankers. The lavish campaign contributions provided by the financial sector must not contest political probity. Severe penalties that cannot be passed on to stockholders must be imposed on offenders, and must include incarceration and clawbacks.

Are all bankers to blame? Clearly not. The CEOs and top management, yes. Then there are the traders and their salespeople, who entered the picture when trading activities became the major source of bank profits. Anyone else? Yes, for sure. While traders manipulated markets and colluded in price fixing, money laundering, tax evasion, hiding assets and selling PPI involve customer facing individuals.

According to Robert Shiller, the greed of the top economic 1% has had worse effects than the Crisis:

> Today's trillion-dollar deficits are a direct result of the recent financial crisis. ... an innovative, predatory, and powerful financial sector convinced officials in Washington [and the other developed economies] to look the other way as it nearly wrecked the global economy.[85]

Michael Lewis, an ex-Wall Streeter and now a journalist tells us:

> I was telling people what to do with their money, but it was bullshit. Wall Street floats on bullshit. At the bottom of it is the belief that someone can tell you what's going up and what is going down. They can't. I knew what I was saying was without value. And yet they were throwing money at me to say it. It was mad. I began to think, if the market can miss-value me this way, what else can it miss-value?[86]

Frank Partnoy in FIASCO[87] described the trading floor at First Boston in the early 1990s during his tenure:

> First Boston was so plagued with harassment and discrimination problems that it hired a consultant to train salesmen and traders not to sexually harass female interviewees. Training was hopeless. ... during one training session, a male employee opened a mock interview: 'So babe, do you want to fuck? ... [When entertainment was lacking] a manager would pay a junior female employee to perform some obscene act on the trading floor. One senior mortgage trader paid a notably attractive sales assistant $500 to eat.

Organised Reactions

The Occupy Movement's first significant action, Occupy Wall Street, was successful, and drew attention to the Crisis. The Movement became an international protest movement concerned with social and economic equality and its concerns have received global recognition. It has focused on large corporations and the Western financial oligarchy that benefits an affluent minority and undermines democracy. It demands a democratic awakening and the elimination of plutocracy. Occupy Wall Street began in mid-September 2011 in a small park off Wall Street in New York City and a month later there were demonstrations in 950 cities in 80 countries and in a further 600 communities in the US. Some established organizations, public and private, like the Los Angeles City Council and the Bank of England have recognised its contributions, and Gartner says the movement is not over. Malfeasance, however, while an issue, remained low on the horizon.

Academics and Journalists

Louis Brandeis was the first to identify the relationship between Washington and the US Financial Sector as an oligarchy.[88] Simon Johnson and James Kwak[89] expanded. Bankers use invalid arguments and blatantly false statements, for example, that capital is expensive, to support a case for an unregulated and unconstrained banking system. They want to preserve the obscene compensation levels. Anat Admanti and Martin Hellwig[90] address a number of the absurd claims. For example, they show that capital is not expensive. Numerous journalists disenfranchised ex-financial sector and public sector employees are now being heard.

Malfeasance and Fraud

Prosecutors and the policymakers fear opening a Pandora's Box and disclosing extensive wrongdoing, and have pushed many problems under the carpet. Today, however, we are prizing the lid off the box.

Bank of America, Citigroup, JP Morgan Chase, Goldman Sachs, Morgan Stanley, Wells Fargo, HSBC, Barclays, BNP Paribas, UBS and Credit Suisse have continued with nefarious behaviour. Between 2010 and 2012, these institutions paid more than $100 billion in fines for fraud, theft, tax evasion, sanctions breaking, accounting fraud, earnings manipulation, insider trading, market manipulation, predatory lending, price fixing and money laundering. And this is the tip of the iceberg! The JP Morgan crime ring, for example, has incurred a further $60 billion in fines and penalties. Despite the mountain of undisputed evidence of wrongdoing, only a few banks have admitted so. In 2014, BNP Paribas, pleaded guilty to concealing billions of dollars in money transfers made on money laundering on behalf of South Sudan, Iran and Cuba, in violation of US sanctions laws, and agreed to a fine of $8.9 billion. Credit Suisse has admitting guilt. To date, however, there has been only one significant conviction of an employee, that of Goldman's Fabulous Fab.

The Story

We begin with an historical account of the US banking system. Then we look at banking in the US as it was at the beginning of the 1980s. We look at the world of exotic products, what the uncontrolled financial sector *innovated*. It's disgraceful, but all true! Then we see how banking changed between 1980 and 2000, how megabanks came about, how deregulation became de-rigueur and how toxic products were sold. It was at this time that malfeasance took a grip and became par for the course. We will review the events after the Millennium that enabled the Crisis, and the subsequent destruction, and how the individuals who operated the financial sector brought the financial world back to the realm of the Neanderthals. They were homesick? We will conclude by looking at malfeasance, and how the largest banks have continued their bad behaviour.

Bangsters

Some individuals committed fraud, stole from us or otherwise acted badly. Many helped the Crisis and the Great Recession develop, so we will build an Al Capone Bangster[91] Award Table. To receive an Al Capone Bangster Award you must be a financial gangster. The awards are for those who will go down in history as causing destruction and theft.

There are others that limited the problems, or at least tried to do so. They opposed the Bangsters. They get Gold Stars.

2

The Stage and Props

The Declaration of Independence

O n 4 July 1776, the US Declaration of Independence was adopted, and the issue of how to form a state became paramount. There were many debates, and one was over how large and how influential banks should be allowed to become. Thomas Jefferson, the author of the Declaration and third president, was adamant: "I sincerely believe, with you, that banking institutions are more dangerous than standing armies".[92] Jefferson believed in a decentralized political organization where its institutions would have limited economic power and influence. His nemesis, Alexander Hamilton, at the time President Washington's Secretary of the Treasury, was a supporter of a strong federal government with a strong federal bank. The envisaged First Bank of the United States would manage the federal government's funds, address fiscal stability, enable trade and lead the economy. Hamilton wanted to make sure that there was sufficient credit to fund economic development so that the US would become a prosperous country.

So from the very beginnings of the independent United States of America, we saw conflicting ideals: a centralized and strong financial system, which would perhaps impose no limits on the size, power and influence of the nation's financial institutions, versus a decentralized structure, that would limit political power, and influence.

When the First Bank of the United States came into existence in 1791, the US lacked a modern financial system. However, by the 1820s, a centralized financial system had taken shape, and the *culture and legal setting*[93] for a national market economy was in place. The US economy had developed. Investment in corporate America had been spawned.

The First Bank was both the biggest bank and the biggest corporation in the US. It was headquartered in Philadelphia and had seven branches. It issued a stable currency and regulated the banks, all state chartered. Bank capital increased and the equity markets developed sufficiently to attract foreign capital. When the

Industrial Revolution came to the US,[94] there was ample credit to apply technology to the production of goods. The First Bank was in many ways a success.

Not until the Banking Act of 1863 did national banks come into existence, and hundreds of banks received federal charters. Investment in federally chartered banks was facilitated by new ideas, innovations. For example, a proportion of shareholders could invest with limited liability, risking only their investment and not the entirety of their personal assets. A consequence of federal charters was that the banking system gained political power. It established considerable control over corporate credit, control that remains today, and as a result, control of industry. Today the banking system controls the short-term credit on which today's corporations rely for their operating expenses, including payroll, and longer-term debt enables investments in plant, machinery and technology.

One of Thomas Jefferson's concerns about the First Bank was that the interests of the northern states would unfairly dominate those of the southern states. And, indeed, the southern states came to distrust both the bank and Alexander Hamilton. The rise of the financial oligarchy in the last twenty years shows the acuteness of Jefferson's thinking.

However, Jefferson's major issue was that banks provided the nation's credit and controlled the payment systems. This meant banks decided who received credit and who did not and this gave banks power that they could and would use for their own benefit. Again, Jefferson's views were prescient. But it was a Catch 22: he realized that without a strong banking system, commerce and industry could not develop, but with it, undue power was funnelled into the hands of a few.

The conflict between the benefits of a strong banking system and the control of influence and emergence of abuse that could undermine economic prosperity has remained since the days of Jefferson and Hamilton. Many politicians have felt compelled from time to time to constrain unbridled capitalism, and the events that led from the First Bank of the United States to the Second Bank of the United States, and eventually to the FED, illustrate the tussle.

The Second Bank of the United States

The Second Bank of the United States came into existence in 1816. The First Bank had not survived, as Congress had refused to renew its charter. It had become unpopular because it had restrained bank lending. But the Second War of Independence, which began in

1812, resulted in financial chaos and Congress backtracked and decided that a central bank was indeed needed. The Second Bank regulated the money supply, issued bank notes, and provided credit for the public and private sectors and private individuals. It developed the capital markets and provided a coordination point for state and local banks. Nicholas Biddle was its chief.

Andrew Jackson, the 7th President, was elected in 1828, and vehemently opposed the Second Bank and its monopoly over Washington's finances. But Biddle provided retainers, credit and made advances to members of Congress and other influential professionals. He paid newspapers to publish his articles anonymously. In other words, Biddle bought power, influence and support from Congress. This power and influence soon became a corrupting force and handicapped the development of democracy in the US.

To further counter Jackson's opposition to the Second Bank, Biddle teamed with Henry Clay, a soon-to-be presidential candidate, and attempted to renew its charter four years before its time. Clay then made the Second Bank a campaign issue when he ran for the presidency against Jackson in the next election, and Biddle expanded the Second Bank's lending in order to gain popularity and political gain. When Congress voted and renewed its charter, Jackson vetoed it, and defeated Clay in the election in1832. Jackson moved Washington's deposits out of the Second Bank and into state banks where unfortunately they stimulated speculation. Biddle retaliated by demanding that the states repay their loans and curtailed credit, which resulted in a contraction of the money supply. Interest rates doubled to 12% and a recession ensued. Biddle wanted to damage Jackson by damaging the economy. Jefferson and Jackson were proven right and their concerns vindicated. Biddle had used financial might to achieve his ends. The receivers of Biddle's largesse provided support for the bank, conditional of course on receiving their retainers.[95]

The Second Bank had become a corrupting influence that undermined the democratic process, demonstrated how financial power could become political power, and be misused. Private power, translated into power over democratically elected power, could constrain economic development, increase its own financial returns, and hinder competition.

Year	Approximate closings
1893	100
1884	35
1890	15
1893	500

1907	80
1914	145

Figure 1: Bank Closings in the Banking Panics 1873 to 1914[96]

When the power of Biddle and the Second Bank was eliminated, it did not mean that there were no problems. From the 1830s until the Great Depression, the US had been plagued by financial crises, panics and runs. A problem occurred about every 15 to 20 years: in 1819, 1825 (the first global financial crisis), 1819, 1837, 1857, 1866, 1873, 1884, 1890, 1893, 1907, 1914 and then 1929.

The 1907 panic and crisis was severe, one of the worst financial crises in the US, with extensive bank runs and multiple failures. For some, it was the last straw.

Prior to the Great Depression, insider trading and market manipulation were par for the course and not illegal. If you could not manipulate the stock markets, how could an honest broker make a living? A routine attempt by insiders and their bankers to manipulate the stock price of the United Copper Company failed and resulted in a bank run. The run spread to some of the largest banks, including the Knickerbocker Trust Company, a large and influential bank in New York City. This in turn resulted in more bank runs. Banks in need of cash to pay depositors sold assets in fire sales, lowered prices, and a vicious circle of more asset sales at lower prices ensued. Banks called in loans to stockbrokers and stock prices fell further. The large trust companies were badly hit. Many banks failed, and the New York bankers concluded that the financial system had grown too big and too complex. Both politicians and the public wanted to reign in the trusts.

With no central bank or a lender of last resort, the financial industry itself needed to arrest the problem. The JP Morgan banking empire had grown very large, and provided, and controlled 40% of the capital raised by US industry.[97] Morgan himself stepped in and helped the federal government resolve the crisis. After the 1907 crisis, the writing was on the wall. The US needed a central bank.

Trust Busting in the US and the Arrival of the FED

Industrialization by the late 1890s had created powerful economic and political elites that influenced the president, the administration and both houses on Washington's Capitol Hill. Money bought influence, power and political support, typical of the politics of the era. Technology had enabled significant industrial developments for agriculture, communications, steam and coal power, iron and steel, and railroads. The railways hauled freight, including oil and steel, agricultural machinery and related products, livestock and building materials across the US, opening up the national markets. Coal, and then oil, fuelled the railroads. The nationwide markets were serviced with new economies of scale. Consolidation, including in the financial sector, eliminated competition, and trusts and monopolies evolved.

A trust was a conglomeration of business interests and corporations. In many ways they bore resemblances to the *too big to fail* banks we would see just prior to the Crisis. Between the late 1890s and the early 1900s, more than 4,000 organizations consolidated into about 250 conglomerates and trusts. Trusts could accept deposits and hold less capital than banks. They paid higher returns. In 1904, 318 trusts controlled 40% of US manufacturing[98]. Investment banking flourished as companies consolidated and expanded and a single individual, J. Pierpont Morgan emerged as a major player in the US financial sector. By 1900, railroad and steel industrialists controlled the Senate. It is important to note that commercial banks took consumer deposits and engaged in investment bank activities, putting the deposits at risk by doing so. However, most banks held far more capital than they do today, up to 40% of their assets. Also until the 20th century, most shareholders in banks were shareholders with unlimited liability. This meant that shareholder liability was not limited, and the full extent of an investor's assets were exposed. So if a bank failed, depositors could turn to its shareholders for restitution. In 1878, the City of Glasgow bank failed and 100% of its depositors were made whole, but over 80% of its shareholders were bankrupted. This meant that wealthy individuals would not want to be shareholders in banks, nor many others for that matter. So limited liability share ownership became the norm, and much later, prior to the end of the Great Depression, most banks had become limited liability shareholder companies.

J. Pierpont Morgan created giants from previously rival companies like US Steel and General Electric. He was adamant that competition was evil and was heavily involved in the mergers and consolidations of the time. He exemplified the moneyed northeast bankers and industrialists. The rest of the country hated them. For workers and farmers, they were robber barons.

Theodore Roosevelt's views were similar to those of Thomas Jefferson and Andrew Jackson. Large private concentrations of power and wealth were bad for society, democracy and prosperity. Americans needed to be protected and so monopolies must be curtailed and broken up. The associated abuse must be abolished.

He managed to build a consensus in Congress, and his trust busting efforts in the first days of the 20th century resulted in the breakup of many industrial monopolies. Soon gone were the days of concessions and subsidies and all industries, except the financial services industry, became tightly regulated. Excessive profits were eliminated. There were greater economic benefits for consumers and democracy was safeguarded from the rich and elite power brokers, the robber barons. But, although some huge conglomerates, for example Standard Oil that was broken up in 1911, Roosevelt was not successful in breaking up the financial sector and its concentration of power. What remained after the trust busting was a lightly regulated financial sector serving a more fragmented, but still concentrated, industrial base with no central bank. This created the stage for the problems of October 1929.

There was clearly a need for some kind of central bank. The Pujo Committee determined in 1912 that the control of credit was concentrated in a small group of large banks, and that a few men had used this control to amass enormous financial power. A future Supreme Court Justice, Louis Brandeis in *Our Financial Oligarchy* demanded that banks be constrained.[99] The investment banks used customer deposits to take control of industrial companies and promote the interests of the companies and themselves. With their commercial banking hats on, banks took deposits and made loans, but under their investment banking umbrella (advising, underwriting and investing), the same banks used the loans they had extended. Companies became a front for the bank's commercial pursuits. Brandeis told us that the "dominant element in our financial oligarchy is the investment banker." [100] For those trying to formulate what the US central bank should look like, a central concern was moral hazard. If a central bank was a lender of last resort, it incentivized excessive risk taking. The central bank would then have to manage moral hazard by regulation and supervision. Brandeis was not convinced. "No... regulation... can be devised to remove the menace inherent in private monopoly and overweening commercial interests."[101] Brandeis' views were before his time, prescient. He wanted to break up large financial and industrial conglomerates. Distrust of a central authority and moneyed, out of touch elites shaped the FED.

These concerns, together with a need to establish economic and financial stability motivated President Woodrow Wilson and Congress to create the FED.[102] It was composed of a Federal Reserve Board in Washington and a dozen regional Federal Reserve Banks. It opened its doors in January 1914 with marching orders to establish a safe, flexible and stable monetary and financial system with a sound banking system. The gold standard had been restored in the US in 1879 and its maintenance had caused problems, so the FED was tasked with managing the US Dollar gold relationship. The problems that led to the FED's creation were real and the costs of the panics substantial. These costs in themselves provided a strong financial justification for both the FED and banking regulation.

The Great Depression

In the 1920s, the economy boomed in the US, and goods and services were readily available. Europe was recovering from the First World War.

The War resulted in enormous social and ethnic problems, particularly in Czarist Russia and the former Habsburg and Ottoman Empires. The Allies split the conquered lands, marginalized ethnic minorities and the poor. Mass migration from Russia and Central Europe to Western Europe and the US resulted in local resentment, particularly in Germany and France, but the wealthier immigrants contributed to rebuilding Western Europe. Bankers and brokers, with newly augmented funds and investments thrived. They enjoyed renewed power, but eventually the politically driven demands for reparations and economic imbalances contributed to the Second World War.[103]

During this period, the US enjoyed an era of prosperity with little sentiment in the financial sector for regulation. The 1920s was an era of rampant speculation in an unregulated free for all. Foreshadowing what we would see in the 2000s, investors had little protection and were inveigled into a world of promised secure returns from investments they did not understand. They were provided with credit, leveraged in order to invest more, usually well beyond their means. Interest rates were low, so companies and individuals borrowed to excess and invested in the stock market and other financial assets. Not surprisingly, a few employed in financial services made fortunes. Jerry Markham tells the story of Charles Mitchell, who enjoyed an outstanding salary for its time of $25,000 per annum and bonuses between 1927 and 1929, of $3.5 million. [104]

The FED was not concerned with the excessive debt based investments and its safety net encouraged moral hazard. Speculation, excessive risk taking and debt driven investments had driven up stock market prices. Investors accrued enormous paper wealth, but finally on 29 October 1929, the New York Stock market, at an all-time high, crashed. The bubble had burst. It was unexpected. Investors had to repay their loans, the money they had used to buy stocks, but as stock prices had collapsed, they could not do so. Just as in 1907, what followed were fire sales. Billions in paper wealth was destroyed, and small and large investors were wiped out. The October crash was the first step in a prolonged and unprecedented global depression, the Great Depression. There had never been anything like it before, and since, until 2008.

The US problems soon became global. The Austrian bank Credit-Anstalt failed in 1933 and triggered many other European bank failures. The European economies and banks relied on the US markets and trade. There was a fundamental trade imbalance, exacerbated by the fixed exchange rates based on the gold standard.[105] The linked economies and the trade imbalances created contagion. The Great Depression lasted until the Second World War, when recovery was bootstrapped by the expenditure incurred by supporting combatant armies.[106]

During the Great Depression, economic output and prices fell in all developed countries. Businesses failed and stock markets collapsed. There was widespread financial uncertainty. Bank failures resulted in depositors withdrawing their deposits from sound banks. No one could predict what would happen, so to conserve money, consumers stopped buying durable goods. The reduction in demand resulted in the scaling down of industry and production. Workers in production lines were laid off and unemployment increased. Businesses downsized and failed, including 9,000 banks, 40% of all US banks. There was no credit. Living conditions fell dramatically, and many families lost their homes. Soon large numbers of individuals did not know from day to day whether they and their families would eat. Soup kitchens appeared. The stock markets continued to fall and by the early 1930s, the loss in market capitalization reached 90%. Although in 1929, the economy grew by 5%, from 1929 to 1933, GDP contracted by a third. In 1933, the contraction reached 14% and unemployment hit 25%. There was extreme deflation, reaching 45% for many consumables. The nation was suffering, and desperate.

From January 1933 through March 1933, deposits fell by a sixth, so to halt withdrawals, the FED closed the banks for eight days from 6 March. Of the 18,000 banks that closed, 5,000 did not reopen.

There are parallels between the Great Depression and Great Recession eighty years later. Although there was a stock price bubble, the Great Depression was not simply the result of a stock market crash. The financial system was fragile with extensive weaknesses: the economic repercussions of World War I, the stresses imposed by reparations, the retention of the gold standard, financial panic and instability, too much private debt, with too much leverage, too much risk, misaligned compensation, and so on, all glued together by a banking oligarchy. The failure of more and more financial institutions exacerbated the problems and the Depression.

The FED failed its first test. Its policies to deal with the Great Depression were simply wrong. Its monetary policy and financial stability efforts failed. To curtail stock market speculation and maintain the gold standard, instead of lowering interest rates it raised them! It wanted to make US investments attractive to prevent money flowing out of the country. The gold standard meant fixed exchange rates, which meant that the problems in the US were transmitted to other countries. Almost all farms and businesses depended on incomes that had become deflated. For example, the prices of farm produce fell and lowered farmers' incomes, but farmers and farm related businesses had entered the Great Depression with fixed cost outgoings especially mortgages. They failed in droves. Loans to farmers became near worthless. The FED's monetary policy resulted in a sharp drop in output, deflation and increased unemployment. It should have thrown money at the banks. Moreover, the FED was not an effective lender of last resort. This exacerbated the banking failures that swept the country. There were bank runs in 1930, 1931 and 1933. Banks that remained solvent suffered severe liquidity problems. The banking crises turned a terrible recession into the Great Depression.

Ben Bernanke's analysis was that the severity of the Great Depression was a result of the FED's poor performance. It occurred because Washington stood by as the financial system imploded:

> Much of the worldwide monetary contraction of the early 1930s ... was ... the largely unintended result of an interaction of poorly designed institutions, short sighted policy making, and unfavourable political and economic preconditions.[107]

As there was no control over the banking industry, it's "appetite for risk had led to a massive boom and monumental bust"[108]. Should the FED bailout the country's banks and promote another round of moral hazard, or should it let the system collapse into a US economic disaster? The Great Recession asked this question a second time.

Roosevelt, the New Deal and the Road to Recovery

The severity of the Great Depression empowered the political reformers to stand up against the financial sector. The Senate Banking Committee's Pecora Commission hearings, from 11 April 1932 to 4 May 1933, uncovered extensive abusive practices by the financial sector, including the underwriting of unsound securities in order to repay loans, and inflating asset prices artificially to benefit insiders. The Commission's exposure of the National City Bank, later Citibank, resulted in the resignation of its president. The bank had paid enormous bonuses to its sales staff for selling high-risk stocks.

The Commission's efforts galvanized an already angry public's support and resulted in the passing of the Glass Steagall Act of 1933, the Securities Act of 1933 and the Securities Exchange Act of 1934, and in the creation of the Securities and Exchange Commission, the SEC. These acts were designed to protect the public, but their passing also empowered President Franklin Delano Roosevelt. He was concerned that private interests, unless controlled, would undermine the economy, democracy and the political system. He spoke in January 1936: "Our enemies today are the forces of privilege and greed within our borders … Andrew Jackson sought social justice; Jackson fought for human rights in his many battles to protect the people against autocratic or oligarchic aggressions."[109]

We saw all of this again in the 2000s, but unfortunately, we did not have a Roosevelt. As we will see, the financial sector and its institutions were not reigned in.

The commercial banking system services three of society's needs. It provides a safe house for the savings of its citizens, it provides loans to businesses, thus turning savings into capital, and it enables payments to be made. Normal savings must be readily accessible at all times, but loans are often long term so that they can be used to buy fixed assets, to finance inventory and to fund ongoing cost commitments like salaries. This means that commercial banks are vulnerable to illiquidity. Savers may withdraw their deposits at any time, but loans cannot be reclaimed until they are due. This vulnerability had resulted in runs on banks even when they were sound. To be sound means that assets (far) exceed liabilities, so that in the long run, when all loans are repaid all deposits can be returned. But this does not mean that there is always sufficient cash available to meet the demands of depositors who wish to withdraw their money.[110] Commercial banks are thus required to maintain a capital base as a cushion against withdrawals and losses, governments regulate banks in order to ensure that their capital levels are sufficient, and that their management practices are safe and sound, and governments provide facilities for banks to borrow from central banks if liquidity, the ability to fund depositor withdrawals, but not solvency, becomes an issue.

President Franklin Delano Roosevelt came to the nation with the New Deal. The GSA separated commercial banking from investment banking and the SEC provided assurances to investors that the stock markets would no longer be rigged. Only commercial banks, deposit takers, could accept savings and business deposits. The separation protected deposits because banks had been using *other people's money* to generate higher profits for themselves, but when losses occurred this meant that deposits were compromised and often lost. So the separation meant that the nation's savings could not be used to fund high-risk investment banking activities. The new investment banks used their partners' capital and they could undertake whatever risks they saw fit. After all, it was their money.

The GSA was focused on safety and soundness, the SEC on enabling investors to invest wisely by requiring disclosure by public companies of essential information, and fraud detection. Notably, the separation of commercial, deposit taker banks and investment banks applied in the US only, so in Europe and elsewhere, *universal* banks remained intact. They engage in both deposit taking and investment banking.

President Roosevelt's New Deal also abandoned the US dollar gold standard, and this resulted in the expansion of the money supply as the dollar floated freely. He protected deposits with deposit insurance by setting up the FDIC. If savings were safe, depositors would make deposits, banks could then lend and this would enable the economy to function. It would get individuals and companies spending again. This measure eliminated bank runs and bank failures for forty years! Public projects got people back to work, and drove a renewed demand for goods and services.

Roosevelt also won the right from Congress to approve trade treaties and tariffs decreased from 45% to 10% in two decades. Trade flourished.

The actions of Congress were major, comprehensive and far-reaching. They made significant changes to the US financial landscape. It was clear that tightened financial sector regulation was necessary. Besides providing safeguards for individuals and businesses, the GSA stimulated recovery. The economy rebounded in 1933 and 1934 as Roosevelt had done what the FED had failed to do.

Any form of lending bears the risk that borrowers may default, or may not repay the principal borrowed or the interest. If a borrower defaults, the cash flow consequences can seriously impede a bank's ability to repay depositors. In addition, as commercial banks lend to each other, they face systemic risk, which means that risks can be contagious. The risks encountered by one financial market participant may spread and disrupt other participants, and the rest of the market.

In order to minimize default risk, regulators insisted that commercial, deposit taker banks complied with stringent safety and soundness regulations. This was part of the price paid for deposit insurance and the FED's lender of last resort facility open only to them. Investment banks, on the other hand, were to be far less regulated, and could engage in any lawful financial activities, including underwriting, selling and trading securities. There was no need to protect deposits if you did not have any! So the regulation of the new investment banks was handed to the SEC, which focused on disclosure and fraud.

In order to ensure that the barrier was watertight, commercial banks could not affiliate with investment banks, and their directors and employees could not hold positions in investment banks, and vice versa. The influences on each sector on the other were very constrained.

Then, as a further initiative to help the nation, Fannie Mae was created in 1938 to support and be the engine behind the mortgage markets. Fannie Mae was the first of the Government Sponsored Enterprises, the GSEs. Fannie Mae did not offer mortgages, but bought mortgages from mortgage originators, creating a mortgage secondary market. This meant that originators would always have sufficient funds to lend to mortgage borrowers. Mortgages became freely available.

Regulation was also put in place to limit what commercial, deposit taker banks could do. They were constrained by location, by limiting branches to a city or state, and by a cap on the interest they could pay for deposits. Regulation Q capped it at 6%. Deposit takers would always have to earn more on loans than they paid for deposits, so by capping deposit rates, what needed to be earned was capped. The consequence was that deposit takers were not forced into taking on high-return and high-risk investments in order to be profitable.

Prior to FDIC deposit insurance, leverage was around five to one. With FDIC guarantees, leverage doubled to around ten to one. An increase in moral hazard, yes. Higher leverage meant a higher risk of failure, but despite the increase in risk, the separation of deposit takers from investment banks, stringent regulation and deposit insurance, the safety of the banking sector was dramatically transformed and strengthened. From the time of the FDIC's inception until the beginning of deregulation in the early 1980s, the US had a safe and sound banking system and US depositors were protected from a powerful and exploiting banking oligarchy.

President Roosevelt targeted privilege. He fought against greed and championed human rights and social justice. A major enemy was the banking oligarchy and its economic and political power. He also promoted FED reforms, including ensuring that Washington's appointees were given more authority at the expense of the banking community. When the GSA separated deposit taking from investment banking, many large banks had to make a choice. The JP Morgan bank was split into three entities. As we said, Morgan had merged steel companies into US Steel, had financed railroads, and had widespread interests in shipping, mining and other industries. In 1907, he had personally stepped in to shore up the banking system. But the GSA meant that the Morgan financial empire had to make a choice, and it chose commercial banking. JP Morgan became a commercial deposit taker bank in September 1935, leaving a few individuals to form Morgan Stanley, a non-deposit taking US investment bank and Morgan Grenfell a UK merchant, that is, investment bank.

Roosevelt's New Deal brought the banking oligarchy to heel. Unfortunately, it reappeared in the last decades of the 20th century in a less regulated financial sector, and similarly endangered the nation. It became much larger, very profitable, very concentrated and very complicated. Once again, *other people's money* was used to create the Crisis and then to save the financial sector and enable it to maintain its profits. *Other people's money* however was not in sufficient supply to help the individuals who had lost their homes and savings.

But for now, privilege and rampant bank fraud were constrained.

The Next Forty Years

Financial panics and crises in the US were not a recent invention, and were always pernicious. But after the GSA, they stopped.[111] Protection paid for with regulation worked.

The financial reforms of the Great Depression were followed by forty years of financial sector stability. Roosevelt's New Deal had resulted in significant changes to the way the financial system worked and the question on everyone's lips was whether the period of banking stability was a consequence of economic conditions, or a consequence of safer and sounder banking. Bank lending appeared to have been low risk after the Great Depression. The GSA had expanded the federal government's increased role in managing risk and banking supervision, and the New Deal had restructured the US financial sector, thus influencing global financial activity for the next forty years. It was reasonable to claim that the stability was due to the New Deal. It was a Good Deal.

During the period of stability, economic development was strong and income inequality fell. The downward trend of income inequality contrasted with high levels of inequality prior to World War I, and the upwards trend which was to appear in the 1980s. From time to time minor changes in the financial regime were made, but generally, the seas were calm. Commercial banking followed the 3-6-3 rule: borrow at 3%, lend at 6% and tee off on the golf course at 3 o'clock. As a Berlin Wall existed between US commercial and investment banks, commercial banking, investment banking, insurance and mortgage lending were separate industries. There were a few large commercial banks located in the New York and Chicago money centres and thousands of small local and regional banks dotted throughout the country. As banks could not operate across state lines, consolidation was limited.

The downside was that the GSA protected thousands of inefficient small banks. Not a good thing. Consolidation would have enabled a more efficient, less costly and less risk prone financial system. Critics of the GSA had argued that the moral hazard introduced by deposit insurance would lead to uncontrolled, excessive risk taking, and this of course did not happen. Deposit insurance did encourage depositors to ignore the soundness of institutions and place funds in riskier banks and earn higher rates. But deposit insurance did not come alone. It came with enhanced prudential safety and soundness standards that the regulators actively enforced.

A factor that contributed to stability was fiscal policy. The New Deal anticipated Keynes' fiscal policy solutions, and his advocacy of government spending. After World War II, Keynes' ideas became widely accepted and underpinned government financed recovery and investments in the west. The UK followed Roosevelt and the New Deal and expanded the role of government in the economy and industry, but went much further. It took control of health, steel production, air and train travel, petroleum and telephone services. The sentiment was that the experts that had taken the country through the War might organise the economy more effectively. Regulation was effective.

Thomas Piketty has this to say:

> The Great Depression triggered by the Wall Street crash, stuck the wealthy countries with a vengeance ... a quarter of the working population in the United States, Germany, Britain and France found themselves out of work. The traditional doctrine of "laissez faire", or non intervention by the state in the economy, to which all countries adhered in the nineteenth century and to a large extent until the early 1930s, was durably discredited. Many countries opted for a greater degree of interventionism. Naturally enough, governments and the general public questioned the wisdom of financial and economic elites who had enriched themselves while leading the world to disaster. People began to think about ... "mixed" econom[ies], involving varying degrees of public ownership.[112]

In 1951, the FED's independence from the US Treasury was firmly established by the FED Treasury Accord, an agreement between the Department of the Treasury and the FED. During and immediately after World War II the Treasury had pressured the FED to keep interest rates low so that the war debt could be financed cheaply. This debt had risen to $4 trillion by the cessation of hostilities. The Treasury's goal was purely political, but keeping interest rates low, coupled with the high inflation of the late 1940s, risked an overheated economy and further inflation. The FED did not accede and since the Accord, the FED has set interest rates independently and determined monetary policy guided by economic stability, with little influence from politicians facing re-election.

After the war years, the US economy grew and became dominant, globally. Monetary policy in the 1950s and 1960s was a *lean against the wind* policy. The goal was to keep both inflation in check and economic growth and prices stable. It was successful. The FED raised interest rates when it was necessary to cool an overheating economy. It *lent* against inflation. It lowered interest rates to promote growth when the economy slowed. The war on the Korean peninsula and a couple of small recessions did not impact prosperity.

The 1970s, however were trying times. Bretton Woods and fixed exchange rates had failed, the US came off the gold standard in 1971 and the cost of debt refinancing and then the Vietnam War had caused inflation to climb from its 1% level in the early 1960s. In October 1973, the Yom Kippur war broke out and, in retaliation for the US support of Israel, OPEC put an embargo on oil exports. The price of oil shot up from $20 a barrel to $75 a barrel in a few years.[113] Customers had to line up at the gas (petrol) stations in the US, which resulted in odd-even rationing. Nixon's disastrous wage and price controls of the 1970s, which he introduced when inflation hit 5%, further fuelled inflation when they were repealed. In June 1981, inflation peaked at just over 13%, the US prime rate hit 20%, and the three-month Treasuries paid 16%. After Yom Kippur, the war in Vietnam intensified. Then we had Watergate, an Islamic revolution in Iran, and another oil shock, and the Soviet invasion of Afghanistan. The policymaker response to rising inflation was slow. Annual growth had declined from 3% per annum in the 1950s to below 1%, and foreign competition had become significant. Japanese cars were better and cheaper than American cars and inflation remained unchecked.

In the 1970s, European debt problems surfaced and the Herstatt bank failed. They were major reasons behind the formation, in December 1974, of the Basel Committee on Banking Supervision, the BCBS, within the Bank for International Settlements, the BIS. This organization gave us the first Basel Capital Accord in 1988. The BIS[114] focus on cross border capital flows had become a focus for banking risk, and regulation had taken an international dimension.

Until the 1980s, the markets were relatively simple with financial organizations and corporations trading simple assets like stocks, bonds, foreign exchange and simple money market instruments. However, the problems of the 1970s destabilized the markets and participants sought new ways to make money. From the 1980s, changes in the financial sector began to take place, and throughout the 1980s, at an increasing pace. Deregulation, designed to unwind the existing regulations that constrained what financial products and services could be offered and which institutions could offer them, increased in momentum. As we will see, many were concerned that financial services companies, in order to remain competitive needed less regulation. Some thought that without deregulation, the banking system would be a hindrance to growth. Also, advances in technology and the first steps towards globalization, would require changes in the financial services industry.

In 1979 Paul Volker, the new chairman of the FED, instigated a dramatic change in monetary policy in order to confront double-digit inflation. High interest rates were pushed higher, into the high teens and his vice like grip on the money supply slowed the economy and lowered inflation. The policy was successful in lowering inflation, but resulted in a recession from 1981 to 1982, when unemployment resulting from lower economic output peaked at almost 11%. Inflation was down in 1982 at 3%. A politically unpopular policy had been necessary to bring it down.

The 1970s, the Great Stagflation, a period of high inflation and recessions, gave way to the Great Moderation, a period of economic stability, and lower volatilities and growth from the late 1980s. Although the Volker measures resulted in a short-lived recession, they paid off with an extended period of low inflation and stable growth, which in turn promoted economic stability, notwithstanding the many short lived crises across the globe. The 1980 inflation problem had been a global phenomenon and it's taming led to prosperity in Europe and beyond. Other advances like inventory management contributed to stability. Unemployment was under 6% by 1987, and the Great Moderation lasted until the Great Recession.

There had been about ten mild recessions post World War II, when, as a result of deregulation, the S&L industry suffered a major crisis in the1980s. A large number of them failed. It was a harbinger which foretold what was to come. The stock market collapsed in 1987, and there was a string of foreign disasters in the 1990s, in Japan, Scandinavia, South America, Asia and Russia. Finally the US, experienced a problem when the Long Term Credit Management hedge fund collapsed.

Roughly, fifty years after the stock market crash of 1929, the Great Depression and the GSA, deregulation had begun to take hold and the needs of the marketplace had changed.

The First Bangster Awards

It is now time to announce the first Bangster Awards. The judges have voted and Sebastien, the chief judge, has announced the results. Nicholas Biddle and JP Morgan paid bribes, engaged in insider trading, created monopolies and eliminated competition, which they abhorred. They defrauded the public. They had had no shame. They are Bangsters.

Franklin Delano Roosevelt and Louis Brandeis each receive Gold Stars. Roosevelt put outstanding reforms in place and ignited development in the US. Brandeis was prescient, had courage and intellectual strength, and provided a foundation for Roosevelt's actions.

The first award table is:

Bangsters	*Gold Stars*
Nicholas Biddle	Franklin D Roosevelt
JP Morgan	Louis Brandeis

3

Banking the US Way

T here is a mountain of information you might want to know about banking and finance, and what follows is a short summary of how some of the key institutions fit into the picture, focused by what is relevant to the Crisis, the Great Recession and bank malfeasance and fraud.

The banking system in the US is different from the banking systems in the other parts of the Western world. The Glass-Steagall investment bank and deposit taker distinction was a US only risk control innovation. Furthermore, the US has an alphabet soup of regulators, and even its central bank, the FED has many parts that are spread across the country.

A toxin was incubated in and trafficked from the US to the global financial system. Breaking down the barrier between deposit taking and investment banks provided fertile soil for the virus to flourish, then migrate and spread. So for these reasons, much of this section is US centric. However, the US was only where it began, and not where it ended.

The global financial system is centred in the mid-Atlantic. While North America and Europe have 12% of the globe's population, in 2014, they accounted for 48% the globe's GDP,[115] down from 70% in 1962. So even though the infection spread globally, the financial institutions in North America and Europe were the significant carriers.

In the US, many kinds of banks and financial institutions serve the public. There are deposit takers and investment banks, insurance companies, mortgage providers and the GSEs, Fannie Mae and Freddie Mac, hedge funds and many kinds of investment funds. There is also the US central bank, the FED, and federal and state banking regulators and supervisors, and financial utilities like the ratings agencies. US politicians are involved via the US Department of the Treasury. The Treasury is part of the executive branch of the US government and represents the US internationally on economic and finance issues. The US GDP is 22% of global GDP, so the Treasury is influential

We will begin by looking at some of the organizations in the US private sector, and then we will look at the FED and the other public sector regulators and supervisors.

Most of the US banking and financial sector remained static from the Great Depression until the 1980s, when we began to see major changes. We will examine these changes in Chapters 5 and 6, but here we will describe the pieces as they were prior to the changes.

We will begin with the deposit takers and investment banks.

Deposit Takers

Commercial banks, S&Ls, and the various types of credit unions and savings banks are deposit takers. As we entered the Millennium, Citigroup, Bank of America and JP Morgan Chase were commercial banks. Goldman Sachs and Morgan Stanley were investment banks. Washington Mutual was an S&L.

Depositors have accounts at deposit takers, and account features vary from bank to bank, but often include checking facilities and certificates of deposit. Deposits usually earn interest. Deposits are loans to banks, and must eventually be returned to depositors. Demand deposits must be returned when the depositor requests so, and time deposits are returnable only after an agreed period. We say that time deposits are returnable at maturity. When we deposit money into an account at a deposit taker, it has a fiduciary responsibility to safeguard the funds.

The deposit taker's business is to lend its deposits to customers, and make other safe investments. The goal, of course, is to earn higher rates of interest, and returns, on loans and investments than what is paid for deposits. If a bank does this, it can be profitable and prosper.

Because deposit takers have a fiduciary responsibility to safeguard deposits, they must have loss absorbing capital and regulators are responsible for ensuring that a bank's risks are within acceptable limits, so that its deposits are safe. The amount of capital is determined by the bank's lending and investing risks, and there must always be enough capital to absorb *almost all* losses from defaults on loans or investments. We will discuss bank capital later in this chapter and say what *almost all* means in practice.

Deposit takers are funded by shareholder capital, depositor funds and funds that the bank borrows, often by issuing long term bonds or shorter term certificates of deposit. Prior to the Millennium, they were the most significant providers of credit, and remain so today. However, recently non-deposit takers have become prominent lenders too. Deposits are a good source of funds to lend as they are predictable. The deposit retaining behaviour of a bank's customers can be estimated from economic conditions and customer demographics. Furthermore, we need to save and deposit taking serves important social and economic goals. When we are young, we save for homes and investments, when we are older, we use savings for mortgages and school fees, and later on in life, we use savings to provide for retirement. So even though the amount of national deposits varies from time to time, we usually do a good job at predicting the variations, and hence can use a high proportion of deposits to make loans and investments. The deposit taker model has been sound and has passed the test of time.

Commercial deposit taker banks provide the many banking services that facilitate our daily lives, our businesses, trade and the development and safeguarding of the economy. For example, they provide funds transfers, bill payment services, customer check writing, safety deposit boxes, and trade and finance products like letters of credit. Often they have customer-facing tellers and customer service officers! They make loans to individuals for cars and houses and personal expenses, and they lend to businesses. In the jargon, lending to businesses transforms the nation's savings into capital.

S&Ls, savings banks and credit unions are also deposit takers. All accept deposits, but their lending and investment practices differ, and offer fewer banking services than commercial banks. Initially, S&Ls were small community deposit takers that offered savings accounts, time deposits and mortgages. Some provided auto and personal loans. They paid depositors more interest than commercial banks, and charged less for mortgages than other mortgage providers. They served their local communities, encouraged savings and facilitated home ownership. They performed similar roles to building societies in the UK. Until recently, most S&Ls had no shareholders as they were trusts owned by their depositors. Today, however, they have shareholders and some are very large. S&Ls had their roots in the 19th Century, and after World War II, they provided baby boom home financing for the returning US servicemen, and in doing so supported extensive suburban housing development.

In the US, (and in most other countries), depositors benefit from a safety net. US deposit takers pay deposit insurance premiums to the FDIC, and if a bank fails, its deposits, up to certain size limits, are protected. A failed bank is seized by the FDIC, which operates the bank until the failure is resolved. It can be broken up, otherwise restructured or sold to another bank. In the interim, depositors experience little inconvenience, and deposits remain available for withdrawal. Perhaps there is a new name of the door! As the deposits are insured, deposits are relatively easy to attract.

If a sound deposit taker runs short of funds and cannot meet withdrawal demands, in other words, if it has a liquidity problem, it can turn to its central bank, which in the US is the FED, and borrow against collateral. In the US this is known as discount window borrowing. [116] Central banks are thus lenders of last resort.

Deposit takers are licenced by governments. In the US we say they are chartered, and they can be chartered by either a state government or the federal government. Prior to the 1861 – 1865 American Civil War, only states chartered banks and banks could do business in only one state. Some states required banks to be state owned. There were many problems, including conflicting regulatory standards and the money supply was difficult to manage. The services offered to the public varied significantly from state to state, and thousands of banks issued their own bank notes, at times well beyond their redemption capacities.[117] Merchants and banks would only accept a bank note if it was satisfied that the issuing bank was sound, and this constrained trade. Interstate travel and trade usually meant currency exchanges for as many states as visited.

After the civil war, there was a need to develop a national identity and integrated national markets. An urgent need was to meet the costs of the civil war, as the state banks held extensive war debt. As the US grew, these constraints became enormous handicaps. Nationally chartered banks, it was hoped, would solve a number of these problems. So, in 1862, Washington began to charter national banks and a national currency was created.[118]

National banks, like state chartered banks were subject to the laws of the state in which they operated, so could only operate within a single state, but their introduction was the source of considerable discussion as it enhanced the control exercised by the federal government at the expense of the states.

Commercial banks make profits derived from the difference between what is earned on their loans and investments and what they pay for deposits and borrowings, and fees from the myriad of banking services they provide.

S&Ls also make profits from the difference between what is earned on loans and what is paid for deposits and borrowings, but as they do not provide much in the way of banking services there is usually little fee income. The profits of S&Ls are thus more sensitive to the interest rate difference (differential in technical terms) between what they pay for deposits and what they earn on loans and investments, the spread. Apart from fraud or stupidity, not much else mattered. If the differential remained healthy, the S&Ls made a profit. Through the end of the 1960s, the S&Ls thrived and led the housing mortgage market. They could charge less for mortgages because their cost of funds was lower. They paid less tax. In 1981, the size of the S&L mortgage market was $650 billion, which had expanded to $1.2 trillion by 1986. The S&L mortgage market was the largest financial market in the US, but in the early 1980s S&Ls began to fail.

Regulation Q and inflation meant that the interest the S&Ls had to pay to fund their existing low interest long-term loans was much higher than their income. By the early 1990s, almost 900 had failed, the FSLIC, the S&L regulator had failed, and these failures cost the US taxpayer $153 billion. Incompetence and economic conditions were also factors. We will return to this.

Credit unions originated in Europe in the mid-19th century and in the US arose because banks were reluctant to lend to lower income groups. The only options for the less well off were corrupt money lenders and loan sharks. To counter this, credit unions came about, with the first in 1907. The depositors are members of an association, for example, a group of employees, a community, a church, and so on. They are not-for-profit, cooperative, tax exempt organizations that take deposits and make loans to members, but offer few other banking services. There are state and federally chartered credit unions, today there are 9,500 of them, with 90 million members, and total assets of almost $1 trillion. Their deposits are insured. Credit unions pay more interest than commercial banks on deposits and charge less for loans, and the initial deposit requirement is lower.

Investment Banks

Investment banks are not permitted to accept deposits, are free to invest in any way they see fit, and are not closely regulated. Investment banks invest their owners' money, or money lent to them by individuals or entities who understand the risks,[119] or funds raised by selling shares to the public. Their regulator is the SEC. They are an American institution. Banks in Europe and elsewhere that take deposits and offer investment banking products and services are known as *universal* banks.

Initially investment banks emerged in the US to provide capital for projects that required substantial amounts of money:

projects to make railroads, to open mines and develop industry. In the UK, these projects could be met by tapping the resources of the major commercial banks, Barclays, Westminster Bank and Lloyds. Colonialism had created a bond market, which enabled investments in foreign lands, but in the US, the need for capital far outstripped the capital resources of the commercial banking system and investment banking was born. Investment banks were intermediaries. They brought investors with capital together with firms that needed it and they raised capital for companies who issued bonds. Initially investment banks were funded by capital provided by their partners, who were in it for the long haul, borrowings, and until the GSA, by deposits.

When Glass-Steagall split the US banking system into deposit takers and investment banks, by far the largest proportion of banks remained deposit takers. The practice of using *other people's money* for investments required significant resources, and was concentrated in the northeast US, where most of the large banks, those with substantial resources, were located. Deposits were a cheap source of funds. The deposit taking side of commercial banks had become an in-house source of capital for the activities of their investment banking colleagues, and so depositors' funds became exposed to excessive risk while being used to generate significant profits for the bank's partners. When deposits were no longer available, life became harder and most banks elected to be deposit takers only. Some larger northeastern banks did elect to provide only investment banking services, and other investment banks came about as divestitures.

After the GSA, there were four major investment banks in the US: Morgan Stanley, Kuhn, Loeb & Co., Brown Brothers and Kidder Peabody & Co. During its first few years, Morgan Stanley found life difficult, but by the 1940s it had established itself as a first class banking organization. It is the only investment bank to have maintained a dominant position from the GSA until the present. One time powerhouses like Salomon Brothers, Kuhn, Loeb, Drexel Burnham Lambert, Dillon Read, and Brown Brothers Harriman were acquired or went away.

Much later, when investment banks became public companies, and the partnership structures fell by the wayside, they were able to take advantage of substantial shareholder capital and the nature of investment banking changed. In 1972, when John Mack, the CEO of Morgan Stanley during the Crisis joined the company it had one office, 350 employees and $12 million in capital. It became a public company in 1986 and by the beginning of the Great Recession, it had 60,000 employees, 1,200 offices in 36 countries, and several billion dollars in capital. Its balance sheet, $1 trillion before the Crisis, and $650 billion after, was still enormous.[120] In the first five years after becoming a public company, its return on shareholder equity averaged 25%. Goldman Sachs had 2,000 employees in 1980 and 34,000 in 2011. Goldman became a public company in 1999. It had become clear that to compete with the large commercial banks, investment banks needed more capital.

Investment banks rely very heavily on the short-term money markets to fund their day-to-day operating expenses. It's a cheap source of funds, and as long as short term funds remain available and can be rolled over, the practice can enhance profits substantially. But it is a high risk funding strategy as the Crisis showed. All five of the *Big Five* have gone. They had become significant providers of credit notwithstanding that they were less stringently regulated than commercial banks.

Investment banks provide brokerage services for individuals and corporations; they turn private companies into public companies with initial public offerings and sell securities to institutional investors like pension and hedge funds. They trade securities, including stocks, bonds, asset backed securities and derivatives. They trade in the foreign exchange markets. They underwrite stock and bonds issued by a company to the public, provide advice on how to do this and manage the process, which includes applying for permission to do so, preparing a prospectus and distributing it to prospective investors. Besides underwriting a new security, they can trade it, either for an investor or for their own account. They can buy an entire offering and sell it to the public, or simply help in the sales process. They offer merger and acquisition's advice and can manage an acquisition and raise private equity.

The Shadow Banking Sector

Investment banks, hedge funds and similar institutions that do not accept deposits are parts of the *shadow banking* system. Until the repeal of the GSA in 1999, the shadow banking system's influence was minimal, but after 2000 this changed. Paul McCulley introduced the term shadow banking in 2007[121] for non-bank financial intermediaries that provide services similar to commercial banks but which lie outside the regulated deposit taker bank sector. It includes many components that we will meet in subsequent sections, for example securitization vehicles, asset-backed commercial paper conduits and non-bank mortgage companies, and of course hedge funds.[122]

The shadow banking system has grown dramatically in recent years and was a key contributor to the Crisis and the Great Recession. The value of US shadow banking transactions in 2007 was $24 trillion, half the $50 trillion global shadow banking transactions. In 2014, the US transactions topped $100 trillion. In 2007, the combined assets of the five largest US commercial banks were $6 trillion, the assets of the then *Big Five* investment banks were $4 trillion. The combined US hedge fund assets were $1.8 trillion.

It is difficult to estimate the size of the shadow banking system accurately as most transactions are not reflected on traditional balance sheets. Many shadow-banking entities are sponsored by commercial banks, or are subsidiaries, so opacity reigns. The shadow banking system relies heavily on the short-term markets, the repo markets and the commercial paper markets (we will look at these markets shortly). It's well nigh impossible to look at these markets and determine what comes from the shadow banking system and what does not. Today, the shadow banking system provides consumer credit and business loans and by the time of the Crisis, it had overtaken the deposit taker loan volumes.

The risk in the shadow banking system is a major concern. It has historically been highly leveraged with poor disclosure requirements. The system is complex and its interrelationships opaque. The interconnections mean that the failure of one can easily lead to the failure of another. There is no lender of last resort and no FDIC style winding up process.

Sometimes money market mutual funds are deemed to be shadow-banking components. They do not, however, rely on short term funding, rather they provide it, and they are somewhat regulated. The point is somewhat academic.

The Government Sponsored Enterprises

Home ownership in the US is a tradition stretching back centuries, linked to the early development of the country as it expanded west. Since nationhood, home ownership had been a national political and aspirational goal. In fact, when the constitution was first drafted, voting was limited to white male landowners, and immigrants flocked to the US motivated by the lure of land ownership and prosperity.

In the turmoil of the Great Depression, in 1934, Congress created the Federal Housing Administration, the FHA. The FHA was part of President Roosevelt's New Deal housing strategy, and aimed at rejuvenating home ownership and mortgage lending with standardized, guaranteed mortgages. A few years later, in 1938, the Federal National Mortgage Association, Fannie Mae was created to guarantee a healthy supply of mortgages by providing mortgage originators with funds so that they could continue to originate residential property mortgages. Fannie bought mortgages from mortgage originators like the S&Ls, banks, and specialized mortgage companies. This meant that funds for new mortgages were always available to mortgage originators. Consumer reliance on fly by night, hard to refinance, short-term mortgages was soon eliminated. The mortgages had to conform with FHA defined underwriting standards, and so were known as conforming mortgages. Fannie held on to most of the mortgages it purchased, funding them by borrowing, and profiting from the spread between the mortgage income and the funding costs. Occasionally mortgages were sold to investors. After World War II, Fannie added the Department of Veteran's Affairs, VA, home mortgages to its portfolio. Fannie was a central piece of the nation's housing policy.

By 1968 Fannie's debt had risen to $7 billion and was a part of the US national debt. Fannie, a federal government agency was backed by Washington and so borrowed cheaply, but mortgages were long-term thirty-year commitments, so Fannie's balance sheet had grown and grown. US President Lyndon Johnson's social program, the Great Society, had to be financed and when the US became embroiled in the expensive war with Vietnam, Congress wanted to remove the $7 billion from the national debt. So the Johnson administration made changes. It made Fannie into a public corporation, and created a new US government owned corporation, the Government National Mortgage Association, Ginnie Mae with the mission to facilitate affordable housing for the less affluent, the lowest 15% on the family finance ladder. Ginnie took over many of Fannie's guaranteed mortgage portfolios, including the VA financed housing mortgages. Ginnie sold these conforming mortgages to investors to replenish its funds, so its balance sheet did not have to expand. Ginnie guaranteed the timely payment of principal and interest for the mortgages, making it easier to sell them, and earned fees by doing this. As Ginnie was government owned, the guarantees were backed by the full faith and guarantee of the US Government. Borrowing costs were thus low, and resulted in consumers paying less for mortgages. Ginnie enjoyed income on the spread in addition to the guarantee fee income.

Even though Fannie was privatized, with shareholders that earned dividends, it acted like a government agency because of its mandate to support the housing market. Because of its Washington support it was able to continue to borrow cheaply. Pressure from the S&Ls resulted in the creation of the Federal Home Loan Mortgage Corporation, Freddie Mac in 1970, with a mandate to buy

S&L originated mortgages. At first it was owned by the S&L industry, but in 1989 it too became a public company. Freddie competed with Fannie, and as they were public companies, were profit motivated. Both Freddie and Fannie have continued to support the mortgage market to the present day, and although they eschew mortgage origination, they have partnered with mortgage originators, which has resulted in considerable growth.

Ginnie Mae was the first to securitize mortgages and began to do so in 1970. Freddie soon followed suit. Recall that securitization is the process that makes tradable securities from pieces of debt, a more efficient way of selling mortgages than selling them one by one. When Ginnie sold mortgage securitizations to investors, it continued to guarantee the timely payment of principal and interest of the constituent mortgages and so earned fees, as well as replenishing its funds. Freddie did the same. The securitization process meant that Ginnie and Freddie absorbed default risk, leaving the interest rate and prepayment risk with investors. Prepayment risk can arise if interest rates fall. A mortgage holder can then refinance a mortgaged property with a lower cost mortgage and prepay the existing mortgage. The investor then loses the income stream, and at the worst possible time as the repaid funds can only be re-invested at a lower rate.

The Ginnie and Freddie securitizations were called pass through securitizations, with losses, after guarantees, shared by all investors in proportion to their investments. Later we will see how tranches and waterfall style payments greatly increased the marketability of securitizations and resulted in an explosion in the market.

When interest rates spiked in the early 1980s, Fannie, incurred enormous losses as the spreads collapsed, and became negative. So in 1982 Fannie also entered the securitization business. Neither Ginnie nor Freddie suffered from the consequence of the interest rate hikes as the interest rate risk had been passed on to investors in securitizations. Fannie's losses resulted in a negative net worth in the billions, so Washington came to the rescue and tided Fannie over while it transitioned into the securitization business. Its CEO, David Maxwell engineered a turn around, and by the time he retired in 1991, the firm was again very profitable. In 1990, Fannie's profits were its largest ever, over $1 billion.

Investors assumed that if the GSEs failed, Washington would bail them out. And indeed, Washington found a way to keep Fannie alive in the 1980s. This meant that investors were willing to accept a lower rate of interest for GSE loans. The value of this benefit was and is in the order of ½%, or billions[123] for the multi trillion dollar US mortgage market.

Because the GSEs were a key part of the national housing strategy, with Washington support, they enjoyed financial advantages. They were exempt from both state and local taxes, they did not have to file financial statements with the SEC, and each enjoyed a US Treasury $2.25 billion line of credit. They had very low capital requirements, 0.45% for securitizations and guarantees, and 2.5% for mortgages. This compared very favourably with the 4% that commercial banks and S&Ls had to hold. From 1988, Basel permitted banks that lent to the GSEs to hold less capital against the debt, and there was no Basel limit on the amount of GSE debt that a commercial bank or S&L could hold.

As public corporations, with cheap funding and implicit Washington support, the GSEs could hardly do poorly. Investors viewed them as almost as safe as US Treasury securities, and banks and S&Ls that held GSE debt incurred minimal capital charges. When the FED in late 2001 decided to discontinue 30-year Treasury bonds, the 30-year GSE bonds became surrogates.

The US housing market was and is enormous. The volume of GSE securitizations grew from $350 billion in the 1980s to $3.5 trillion in the subsequent twenty years. Sixty million American families lived in mortgaged properties and almost all of them were GSE conforming mortgages. The investors in GSE securitizations were global and included pension and other funds and central banks. All saw value and security in US real estate and recognised the influence of US housing policy and Washington's support.

Money Market Mutual Funds

Money market mutual funds offer investments that mimic deposit accounts. They accept funds as investments, but the *deposit-investments* do not earn interest. They earn a return based on the return on the investments that the funds make.

Money market funds are highly liquid. They are professionally managed, and when individuals and corporations contribute to a fund, the contributions are pooled and invested collectively. The returns enable a yield to be declared and substitutes for the interest that commercial banks pay to depositors. Investors make investments in money market funds in much the same way that individuals deposit funds into accounts at commercial deposit taker banks.

Money market funds developed in the US as a way to attract deposits away from deposit taker banks. As they were not FDIC insured, they were not constrained by the Regulation Q cap on what deposit takers could pay to depositors. The first mutual fund was formed in Europe in the late 18th century and the first in the US about one hundred years later. US mutual funds became popular in the 1920s and the first modern money market fund was formed in 1971. Investors buy units in a fund, and earn a return paid in units. Money market fund units are maintained at $1 each. When a fund declares a return, more units are created and distributed to the current unit holders. Investors can buy and sell units freely and funds are re-valued on a regular basis and the new value expressed in units. For example, suppose you make an initial investment of $100 in a money market fund. This would buy one hundred $1 units. If after a year the fund has made 3%, you would see that you owned 103 units. In effect, your investment has earned $3. It's the same as depositing $100 into a commercial bank savings account and earning 3%. The difference is that money market funds do not guarantee a specific return and commercial deposit taker banks usually do.

The money market fund industry took off when Merrill Lynch began to offer money market accounts. They gave Merrill a way around the prohibition against financial institutions offering both deposit accounts and brokerage services. The money market accounts were investments, not savings! Money market funds have grown from $3 billion in assets in 1976 to $2.7 trillion.[124] In 2011 there were about 650 funds in the US.

Money market funds invest in short-term[125] high quality, low risk and highly liquid debt securities, for example, short-term U.S. Treasuries, certificates of deposit and corporate commercial paper, so they provide investors with a safe haven. As they are highly liquid, they are important providers of liquidity to financial institutions. Returns to investors are usually a little higher than the returns from deposit taker bank savings accounts, and pension funds and other conservative institutional investors invest in money market funds extensively.

Money market funds have no entry and exit fees, which means that investors can use money market funds as bank accounts. Some funds indeed offer limited check-writing facilities and other deposit taker type account features. Some money market funds also provide investors with tax-advantaged gains by investing in tax-exempt municipal securities.

Money market funds are investments, and not deposits, so there is no deposit insurance and they are very lightly regulated. Historically, they have been extremely safe investments.

Problems occur rarely, but when they do, the value of a unit can fall below $1. If this occurs, the fund is said to have *broken the buck*. This has occurred only three times since their widespread adoption in 1971, and the last time it occurred was during the Crisis when the Reserve Primary Fund *broke the buck* as a result of writing off Lehman debt, when Lehman declared bankruptcy.

One reason that there have been so few problems is that many money market funds have sponsors and guarantors, and these have stepped up to infuse cash when needed. Banks sponsor money market funds in order to promote their own business, and reputational issues mean that they often have to step in and cover any losses incurred by their sponsored funds. Money market funds do not hold loss-absorbing capital and while the sponsors typically do, no capital provision is made for money market fund sponsorships, a problem in itself. So, if for example, a deposit taker sponsor bails out a fund, it will have to restore its own capital, at a time perhaps, that is not opportune.

Hedge Funds

Hedge funds are private, professionally managed investment partnerships. Investors are subject to minimums, usually in excess of $1 million. Investors enter into agreements that state they understand the risks and that they have sufficient recourses to absorb heavy losses. The number of investors in a fund is limited. Withdrawals can be made only on a scheduled basis, monthly, quarterly, etc., and are based on the fund's then value. Hedge funds trade for their own account, are highly leveraged, cannot be offered generally to the public and are immune from most US securities laws, and avoid many licensing requirements. Disclosure requirements are minimal. They have become very popular in the Millennium.

Hedge fund managers often invest their own money in the funds they manage, and funds pay managers management and performance fees. Arbitrage trading fuelled the growth of hedge funds and today the funds invest in diverse markets and use a variety of investment strategies. The strategies can be complex and often aim at market neutral strategies, strategies they pay off regardless of whether the markets rise or fall. Most hedge funds do not hedge, they arbitrage. They go short one asset and long in another. They make money if the price of the shorted asset falls or the value of the purchased asset increases, or both. Going short means you borrow an asset (and pay a small rental fee), promising to return it at a later date, and sell it. If the asset decreases in price you benefit because when you buy it back to return it, it's cheaper.

When you go long an asset, you buy it and own it, and you benefit if it increases in value. What hedge funds do is use the money they receive when they sell the short asset to buy the long asset. The returns are thus leveraged as very little invested capital needs to be utilized.

Hedge funds rely on investment banks to execute trades, and the growth in hedge funds has provided additional revenues for the investment bank industry.

Many funds have billions in managed funds. Their combined assets prior to 1990 were less than $30 billion, but they grew to $1.8 trillion in 2007. In 2014, their combined assets were $2.5 trillion. As hedge funds are unregulated, there is a large amount of out of sight risk, and as margins are thin, volumes are high which means large amounts of borrowed money, and leverage. During the Great Recession, hedge funds incurred extensive losses, for example, in the third quarter of 2009 alone, they recorded losses of $180 billion.

Hedge funds can make substantial profits and incur heavy losses. For example, in the late 1990s, Long Term Credit Management, LTCM, collapsed when its $4 billion capital was reduced to almost nothing. Its leverage had been over 100 to 1. We will look at LTCM soon.

As hedge fund exposures have become significant, both the US and the European Union have introduced regulation that requires more extensive reporting and greater transparency. The funds have also been game for fraud.

The Monolines

Insurance companies take in premiums and cover insured losses. For example, you can insure against your house burning down. You pay premiums and in the sad event that you lose your house due to fire, the insurance company pays you for your loss. The insurance industry is thriving, and insurance companies in the US are regulated at the state level.

Monoline insurance companies provide financial product insurance, bond insurance, and it's usually all that they do. Insurance coverage means that the issuer's interest payments and principal repayment are guaranteed in the event the issuer defaults. Like any insurance, the monoline receives premiums in exchange for the guarantees, and the premiums reflect the likelihood of payment defaults by the issuer. AMBAC introduced municipal bond insurance in 1971, and by the mid-1980s, there were four big monoline insurers, including AMBAC. Prior to the Crisis and during the Great Depression, the monolines suffered ratings downgrades as insured bonds were downgraded. Some were bankrupted, so the Crisis questioned the monoline business model.

As the rating of an insured bond is usually much higher than an uninsured bond, bond insurance is a form of credit enhancement.

Immediately prior to the Crisis, in 2006, monolines had insured $3.3 trillion, however, this was backed by only $47 billion in cash reserves, reserves from which claims would have to be paid.[126] The Crisis meant they did have to pay extensive claims, many monolines could not, and for example, AMBAC failed.

Almost Banks

Apart from conventional banks, there are organizations that are banks in all but name. General Motors Acceptance Corporation, GMAC provided automobile related financial services, including auto leasing for customers of General Motors and General Motors dealers. It operated the GMAC Bank, which made substantial profits for General Motors before it encountered extensive financial problems during the Crisis. GMAC was eventually bailed out by Washington and became Ally Financial, a bank holding[127] company. It took until 2010 to return to profitability.

In 2009, Ally Financial had 18,900 employees and 15 million customers globally.

Similarly, Daimler-Chrysler Financial Services offered a comprehensive range of automobile centric financial services, including leasing, dealership financial services, commercial fleet management, car insurance and other banking services. The corporation became heavily involved in the financial markets, and in 2003, more than 50% of its profits came from foreign exchange trading. It too had Crisis problems.

GE Capital was formed during the Great Depression to help GE's customers finance their appliance purchases. In 2002, it was the third largest US bank and its earnings were a significant part of GE's earnings. In 1991, GE capital funded 10% of its medium term notes with structured notes, and by 1993, this had jumped to 50%,[128] a harbinger of the disaster to come. Structured notes enter our discussion soon.

The Short Term Credit Markets

The short-term credit or money markets are markets in which one party lends to another for short periods, often overnight. There are two important markets, the commercial paper market and the repurchase agreement or repo market.

Companies issue commercial paper. It's a loan from an investor to a company, priced according to current interest rates and the credit rating of the company. Commercial paper loans cost less than bank loans, so are attractive to borrowers, and lenders treat commercial paper as relatively safe and attractive as it pays more than short term Treasury debt. Commercial paper is issued for short periods, up to 270 days, but usually for much shorter periods. The 270-day limit comes about because it avoids registering it with the SEC, which lowers its costs. The issuers of commercial paper use the funds to finance their day-to-day operations, payrolls, rent, etc.

Companies issue commercial paper in order to lower their financing costs. Usually the paper is rolled over, that is renewed, at maturity. Commercial paper thus becomes long term funding made up of many consecutive short-term obligations. A benefit is that commercial paper funding can be matched to funding requirements from day-to-day, week-to-week or month-to-month. A risk is that short-term rates may rise, and when the paper is rolled over, it is more expensive, more expensive than longer-term bank debt. Because commercial paper is unsecured, only companies with excellent credit ratings can issue paper at reasonable rates.

Commercial paper has been issued by companies for over a century. In 2009, 1,800 US companies relied on commercial paper. The value of the paper outstanding at year-end 2007 was $1.8 trillion.

The repo market is large, and in 2007, half of all investment bank funding came from the repo markets. Repos are short-term collateralized loans, often overnight. They are sale and repurchase agreements. A security is sold and simultaneously the parties agree that it is to be repurchased. The repurchase price is greater than the sale price, and this difference represents interest, or yield and is known as the repo rate. The buyer of the security is a lender and the amount lent is secured by the security, and the seller is a borrower of collateralized funds. On the agreed repurchase date, the cash is repaid and the security returned.

The borrower always suffers a haircut, so for example, if the borrower offers $100 in collateral, a little less can be borrowed. If credit becomes scarce or the lender loses confidence in the borrower, the haircut increases, the lender may demand better collateral or may refuse to lend to the borrower. If haircuts rise and repo borrowing becomes difficult, borrowers may have to sell assets funded by repos or otherwise manage the cash shortfall. A key advantage of repos is that they are bankruptcy safe and if a borrower fails and goes into bankruptcy, the lender owns the securities that were to be repurchased.

Repos can be arranged directly between two organizations or can be arranged using the tri-party repo system where an intermediary acts as an administrator and custodian for the securities repoed. Two banks in the US, JP Morgan Chase and the Bank of New York Mellon are the principal tri-party repo agents, and in Europe, the main agents are Euroclear, Clearstream and SIX.

The size of the US tri-party repo market peaked in 2008 at $2.8 trillion. By 2010, after the Crisis, it was about $1.6 trillion.

Central Banks

Besides banks, a countries' banking system has a central bank, regulators and supervisors. A central bank, is a government agency and is at the centre of its nation's monetary and financial system. All countries have one. Europe is an exception. All members of the Euro currency union have their own central bank and in addition, the ECB is the central bank for the eighteen countries that comprise the Euro currency union. It was established in 1998. The FED is the US central bank, the Bank of England is the central bank of the United Kingdom, and the Bank of Japan and the Bank of France are Japan's and France's central banks, respectively.

Central banks are central banks for an economy, the economy of the country in which they are located, and they help make economies function. Economies have goods and services that are produced, bought and sold, and central banks facilitate their production and monetary exchange, and they play a key role assisting monetary systems develop over time.

Crucially, central banks help maintain macroeconomic and financial stability, the two main things that central banks do. They are complementary functions. The first means optimizing output and growth for an economy, avoiding big swings and recessions, maintaining high employment and keeping inflation low and prices stable. The second means ensuring that a nation's financial system functions properly and that financial panics and crisis are ameliorated or prevented.[129]

How do central banks achieve their lofty goals? There are two sets of tools. To maintain macroeconomic economic stability the main tool is monetary policy. Central banks can raise or lower short-term interest rates by buying and selling securities in the open market. Lowering interest rates can stimulate an economy and encourage spending, investment, production and employment. Central banks can tackle inflation by raising interest rates. The cost of borrowing is increased and investments, goods, and services cost more. Higher interest rates thus restrain demand. Short-term rates influence long-term rates.

To maintain financial stability and deal with financial panics and crises, central banks can inject liquidity, money, into an economy. Panics can arise because deposit takers accept deposits that finance fixed, long-term maturity assets and if depositors suddenly withdraw funds, a bank can have a liquidity problem. Central banks can lend to a bank against long-term loans or other good assets in order to restore stability. The bank avoids a fire sale of its assets, which could lead to failure and it avoids putting restrictions on withdrawals. Banking panics are bad enough in themselves, and can spread to other parts of the financial sector and other sectors of the economy.

Providing short-term loans to banks can remove uncertainly, calm the markets and restore stability. So central banks lend freely to solvent banks against collateral at slightly discouraging rates to deter abuse. It's important to remember that central bank lending can resolve a liquidity problem and not insolvency. (Bagehot's rule).[130] They are *lenders of last resort.*

Another tool that central banks rely upon is safety and soundness regulation. Regulation assesses risk within a bank's portfolios, and ensures that its processes are sound. If individual banks are healthy, then the likelihood of a panic and a crisis is reduced.

Central banks can be regulators and often are, and there can be many other bank regulators. Different regulators usually focus on different subsectors of the financial sector. In a few cases, no regulation is undertaken by the central bank, and all regulation falls into the hands of one or more regulators.

Central banks usually manage their currency's exchange rate by buying and selling it in the markets and sometimes they try to influence rates by discussing their views with other market participants. Some central banks act to smooth rate changes, others target bands or pegs against other currencies or currency baskets.

Monetary policy takes time to take effect and politicians are elected officials that face the ballot box every few years. Thus, central banks must be independent from their legislative authorities so that their decisions are shielded from short-term political goals. Today, most central banks operate independently, and the few that do not, invariably encounters problems. There is considerable consensus and evidence that independent central banks deliver better results than those constrained by government interference.[131] As we said, the FED Treasury Accord of 1951 established the FED's complete independence from Washington.

The first central bank was Sweden's in 1668, the Bank of England, a private institution until after World War II, dates back to 1694, and the Banque de France opened its doors in 1800.

Regulators and Supervisors

Governments enact financial legislation, regulators formulate the legislation as rules and supervisors police them. Often regulators and supervisors are the same, and the distinction between legislation and regulation is one of detail. A government may legislate consumer protections, but regulators spell the protections out in detail, as, for example, what disclosures must be made when selling complex financial products.[132] Financial institutions, markets, and activities are the things that are regulated.

The perennial question is always: how much regulation? The western economies view finance as a private business driven by profits. But the business of finance is different from other areas of commerce as money, the commodity of banking, is the lifeblood of all business. Money is a public utility, and the flow of money must be safe and sustainable.[133] So the question becomes: to what degree should the business of private finance be permitted to be profit driven? Western governments have answered it by promoting private sector banking *with controls*.

Regulatory failure was a key the problem that lead to the Crisis. Tim Geitner, then US Secretary of the Treasury, remarked:

> Our financial system operated with large gaps in meaningful oversight, and without sufficient constraints to limit risk. Even institutions that were overseen by our complicated, overlapping system of multiple regulators put themselves in a position of extreme vulnerability. These failures helped lay the foundation for the worst economic crisis in generations.[134]

While most countries have only a few regulators, banking regulation in the US is fragmented and performed by an alphabet soup of regulators, some federal and some state. There are separate regulators for deposit taking, investment banking, securities, commodities and insurance companies often at both the federal and state levels, and more than one regulator can regulate an institution. Sometimes institutions have several regulators, and others can choose their regulator and this can lead to regulator shopping and regulatory arbitrage. Outside the US, the scope of each of a fewer number of regulators is usually much broader.

When the Crisis hit there were four major federal deposit taker regulators: the FED, the FDIC, the Office of the Comptroller of the Currency, the OCC, and the Office of Thrift Supervision, the OTS. The OCC regulates and the OTS regulated federally chartered banks, and the FED and FDIC regulate state chartered banks. The OCC regulates the national banks, the largest banks, and the OTS regulated the S&Ls. The OTS was put out of its misery in 2011 and its functions absorbed by the OCC. The FED regulates state banks that are members of the FED, and the FDIC regulates those that are not. The majority of state banks are not members of the FED and number many thousands. State regulators regulate insurance companies and state chartered banks. The SEC regulates the investment banks. Got it?

Dodd-Frank[135] made substantial changes to regulation, including the introduction of the Financial Stability Oversight Council, the FSOC, and dissolved the OTS. The FSOC plays a coordinating role and looks for risks not detectable by the menagerie of other regulators. Systemic risk can arise because of market interconnectedness and rarely seen market situations.

Other regulators include the Commodity Futures Trading Commission, the CFTC, which regulates the futures and options exchanges, and has a small role regulating the OTC markets, the Federal Housing Finance Authority, the FHFA,[136] which regulates the GSEs and the Federal Home Loan Bank System, the National Credit Union Administration which regulates the federal credit unions and the Bureau of Consumer Financial Protection which regulates non-bank mortgage lenders, student, and payday lenders, and all banking consumer business.

The overarching focus of regulation and supervision is the stability of the local and global financial systems. As credit is the lifeblood of market economies, regulation ensures, hopefully, that the credit system is functioning and stable. Other matters are also important: monetary policy, deposit insurance, regulatory compliance, banking customer privacy, disclosure, fraud protection, anti-money laundering, usurious lending, and credit for the poor. Since the 1960s, for example, customer protection has been a Congressional mandate in the US, and truth in lending provisions requires lenders to provide detailed information on credit terms, and the expression of interest rates as annual percentages, or APRs. Europeans have recently been concerned with stability, and more recently with money laundering.

There are four major banking regulation components: safety and soundness, deposit insurance, bank capital and systemic risk. The first leads to a more stable economy, deposit insurance minimizes bank runs, adequate capitalization provides a cushion against losses, and systemic risk looks at the risk of interconnectedness and risks that slip through the cracks. Even though banks pay premiums for deposit insurance, ultimately the buck rests with governments, so they have a stake in making sure banks are sound. In 2012, the major post Dodd-Frank regulators were:

Regulator	Regulates	Regulated Banks	
		Number of Banks	Assets (trillions)
OCC	National banks, federal savings banks and federal branches of foreign banks	2,100	10.0
FED	Bank, financial, securities and S&L holding companies, systematically significant companies, state FED member banks, US branches of foreign banks and foreign branches of US banks, and some payment, clearing and settlement systems	850	2.0
FDIC	Federally insured deposit takers, including state banks that are not members of the FED and state chartered savings banks	Regulated 4,300 Insured 7,000	Regulated 2.5 Insured 14.0
FSOC	The risks in the system as a whole, risks not examined by other regulators	12,250	14.5

SEC	Investment banks, securities exchanges, brokers, dealers, clearing houses, mutual funds, investment dealers, some hedge funds, the credit ratings agencies and securities swaps dealers		The market was £26 trillion

Figure 2: Post Dodd-Frank Major US Banking Regulators[137]

The regulation of securities activities is quite different. It is based on disclosure, fair dealing and fraud detection. It does not concern itself with risk taking other than to ensure that all risks have been clearly disclosed. Investments can result in losses, so securities regulation does not concern itself with limiting risks, only ensuring that investors are provided with sufficient information to assess them.

The Federal Reserve System

The US central bank, the FED consists of two parts, a Federal Reserve Board of Governors in Washington and twelve regional Federal Reserve Banks. This structure reflects the Jeffersonian - Hamilton compromise. Washington had input and some control, and the regions a voice via the regional Federal Reserve Banks. The structure means that the FED is not controlled by powerful banks, but, on the other hand, can do little to control these banks. Despite the exertions of Brandeis, there is no way to rein in high risk lending, and clearly, as a lender of last resort, the FED is a source of moral hazard. Also, there are conflicts. No one at the time of the FED's creation foresaw that the board of the New York regional FED, the NY FED, would become elected by the largest and most influential banks in the country.

As a central bank, the FED is a lender of last resort and controls interest rates. It is also a bank regulator. The Washington FED Reserve Board of Governors is a US government agency, but the twelve regional FED banks, each located in a federal reserve district, are private entities. Centralized power is thus constrained. The Federal Open Market Committee, the FOMC, determines monetary policy and sets interest rates. It is made up of the seven FED Board governors, the president of the New York FED and four positions which rotate amongst the presidents of the eleven other regional banks.

Both the FED Board and the regional FEDs operate independently from the branches of the US government. Decisions are not ratified, nor is there oversight. The only influence is indirect: Congress determines salaries. The FED Board and chairman are appointed by the President, cannot hold an elected office and cannot be part the administration. The Chairman reports to Congress regularly and liaises with the Secretary of the Treasury. The regional FED banks carry out FED policy locally and represent the interests of the regional economies. Their boards have nine members. The FED Board chooses three members, including the chairman and deputy chairman, and the banks in the district elect the other six members. Three must be bankers, so the regulated have a say.

The FED manages interest rates by influence, by buying and selling securities in the open market, in a similar fashion to many other central banks. The FOMC determines a target federal funds rate and the NY FED trading desk buys and sells government securities, trading (mostly) with the primary dealers,[137] and moves the federal funds rate by increasing or decreasing the demand for funds in the accounts held at the FED by its member banks. If the desk buys securities, it creates money and puts it into the financial system and banks have more money to lend. This lowers rates. If the desk sells securities, money goes out of existence, there is less money to lend and rates move higher. The trading desk thus moves the actual federal funds rate towards the target rate. In the past, we spoke of printing money and removing it. Today the central bank alchemists do not make gold, they use desktops to do the equivalent by adding zeros to, or taking zeros from numbers, account balances! The federal funds rate influences other rates like the prime rate, the Treasury note rates, commercial paper rates and other consumer loan and mortgage rates. While the ECB and the BoE focus directly on price stability, as many other central banks do, the FED focuses on both price stability and unemployment.

The FED is a safety and soundness regulator for state banks that are members of the FED system and for bank holding companies, and with the FSOC, it's a systemic risk regulator. It protects consumers, and oversees the truth in lending laws, including watching for abusive mortgage lending practices.[138] It is an umbrella regulator. The FED provides payment services by the US Fedwire payments system, and is a bank for the federal and state governments and various foreign official institutions.

State chartered banks can elect to be members of the FED, in which case their local regional FED bank regulate them. There are benefits to FED membership, but banks pay for it, and must hold stock in their regional FED equivalent to 6% of their capital. The local FED bank also regulates the bank holding companies in their districts, and national banks are always members if the FED.

All FED member banks must maintain a reserve in an account at the FED. The reserve requirement is determined by the bank's assets. It's usually about 10%. Members can borrow from each other, and from the FED. As loans mature and are repaid and new loans are granted a bank's reserve requirement change daily, so banks actively trade reserve balances. If a bank determines that its balance is greater than what it needs to be, the excess can be lent to a bank in need of reserves. The rates for each transaction are negotiated between the borrowing and lending banks and the weighted average of the transactions on any one-day is the effective federal funds rate for the day. When a bank borrows from the FED it does so at the discount window, and at the discount rate, which is usually a little above the federal funds rate.

The FED is funded by the interest it earns on the government securities it holds, and fees, and so there is no need for an appropriation from Congress. The FED declares a profit, and after a set dividend of 6% is paid to the member banks, the balance goes to the US Treasury. In 2010, the FED's profit was $82 billion, so $79 billion went to the US Treasury, $1 billion was withheld as a working balance and a dividend of $2 billion was paid to the member banks.

There are several controversies. The large New York banks effectively elect the president of the NY FED. They are not likely to elect someone not sympathetic to them. So, for example, Jamie Dimon, the CEO of JP Morgan Chase was one of the three banker directors of the NY FED during the Crisis and the Great Recession. Dick Fuld, the CEO of Lehman Brothers was another. Stephen Friedman, a former CEO of Goldman Sachs was chosen by the FED Board to be the chairman of the NY FED, which appointed Timothy Geitner to be its president. This arrangement is incestuous and rings of crony capitalism. And the FED was sympathetic to the large banks in the early 2000s, when capital reductions were on the table, and the sympathy continued in the aftermath of 2008. Finally, the NY FED regulates bank holding companies like JP Morgan Chase and Citigroup, but the OCC regulates the banks owned by them, as they are national banks. Hardly a workable arrangement.

The Federal Deposit Insurance Corporation, FDIC

We noted that the FDIC was created in 1933 as part of the New Deal to provide security for depositors in the US deposit taker banks. Today it has three roles: it provides deposit insurance, it regulates the state chartered commercial and savings banks that are not members of the FED, and it resolves failed banks. It's a safety and soundness regulator and is involved in consumer protection. The FDIC is a government agency and employs 4,500 staff. It is backed by the full faith and credit of the US government.

Banks pay deposit insurance premiums based on the size of their domestic deposits. The insured deposits have a ceiling. Initially this was $2,500 per depositor, and by 2014, it had grown to $250,000 per depositor, and per account for various account types. To qualify for insurance, a bank must show that it is well managed and profitable, and today, about 7,000 banks are FDIC insured. As deposit insurance is a source of moral hazard, and encourages risk taking, insured banks are regulated. The taxpayer is protected.

Deposit insurance has greatly reduced the number of bank runs. The rate of bank failures fell from thousands per year to zero immediately after the FDIC's creation. At the time of writing in 2015, the FDIC has had a perfect record. Not one depositor has lost a single cent from FDIC insured accounts, and the FDIC has resolved thousands of banks.

The FDIC keeps a bank watch list and it suspects that a bank is in danger of failing, it can take action. The bank may be taken over by the FDIC. In practice, when the ratio of the bank's assets to capital falls below 2%, the bank goes on the watch list. If the bank does not raise more capital or sell itself within 90 days, the FDIC can step in and resolve the bank. It seizes it. When this happens, the FDIC puts a new sign on the door and runs the bank as normal. The bank is sold, either whole or in parts, or wound down and the deposits and assets sold to another bank. Deposits are safe and depositors rarely notice any changes other than the sign on the door! Creditors may or may not receive something, but shareholders are wiped out. The process minimizes disruptions to the financial sector and local community. Typically, the FDIC looks for a resolution that is at the least cost to the FDIC.

The FDIC resolution process is necessary as bankruptcy can take months or years, and during bankruptcy proceedings, deposits are frozen. Bankruptcy protects creditors, not the public and depositors.

The FDIC limits Washington's exposure by ensuring lending standards are high and ethical. Clearly, it's better to make sure that a bank is operating smoothly rather than to resolve it, so the FDIC plays a major supervisory role, and is a backup regulator for the FED and the OCC. The life of the FDIC would be easier if it did not have to resolve banks, and so has pushed for higher capital ratios and a lower leverage ratio. The capital and leverage proposals circulating in the early 2000s, prior to the Crisis, recommended lowering capital requirements and was supported by the other regulators, but not the FDIC, and only more recently has there been support for increased capital from the other regulatory bodies.

The FDIC has consistently maintained that banks should not be allowed to determine their capital. It needs to be set independently from bank management, as management is incentivized to keep capital levels low so that the return on capital, hence bonuses, are higher. As deposit insurance means moral hazard, there is little downside in this for senior bank executives.

A problem arises when the FDIC has to resolve a number of large banks at the same time. Large bank resolutions are expensive, premium fee increases may be necessary, and it's the smaller and safer banks that have to meet the increased fees. During the Crisis, the FED assisted the larger banks to a much greater extent than the smaller banks, a dereliction of duty, and the costs were borne by the taxpayer.

The Office of the Comptroller of the Currency, OCC

In 2012, the OCC regulated almost 2,100 banks, including 100 large and medium sized banks and 2,000 community and federal savings banks. It was also responsible for regulating 50 or so branches of foreign banks. The total assets regulated were $10 trillion, representing 70% of all commercial bank assets. In 2012, the OCC had 3,800 employees and a budget of $1.23 billion.

The OCC was established as a US federal agency in 1863 when Congress passed the National Banking Act to create national banks. Today the OCC operates as part of the US Treasury and charters and regulates national banks, federal savings banks and the US branches of foreign banks. The OCC is a safety and soundness regulator, monitors compliance with banking law and the treatment of banking customers. The Comptroller of the Currency heads the agency and it is self-funding as it imposes fees.

The OCC reports annually to Congress on the state of the banking sector. It works with the Basel Committee (see later in this chapter), and besides sitting on the board of the FDIC, the Comptroller of the Currency is a member of the FSOC.

The Financial Stability Oversight Council

Systemic risk arises despite the effective operation of the other regulators. Systemic instability has many causes, including unsuspected correlations and interactions between the different parts of the financial system. The FSOC is responsible for systemic risk, and coordinates the efforts of the other regulators. The FED, however, is the primary regulator for all financial firms, bank and nonbank, that are systemically important.

The FSOC can designate financial institutions, banks and nonbanks, as systemically important. Systematically important institutions attract more stringent capital requirements and must prepare *living wills*, plans for their orderly liquidation. The FED and two-thirds of the FSOC may determine that a firm represents a "severe threat" to financial stability and order it closed, in which case the FDIC administers and resolves it.

Until the Crisis, the FED had overseen systemic risk, and this had been sufficient. A mere FED announcement that it was ready to lend was sufficient to deal with the string of recent crises. These included the stock market crash of 1987, the junk bond collapse, the dotcom crash and the 9/11 attacks. However, in 2007, the FED's provision of liquidity failed to restore stability, and the FSOC was created.

The Securities and Exchange Commission

The SEC protects investors and maintains fair markets. It is not a safety and soundness regulator and it does not focus on risk taking. Its focus is disclosure and fraud in the securities markets. Although banking deposits are afforded deposit insurance, investments in stocks, bonds and other securities can lose value and there are no guarantees that investments will maintain their values. The SEC ensures however, that risks are disclosed, so the challenges for regulation are therefore different.

Investors make their own decisions, and the SEC's job is to ensure that the information provided to them is accurate and that the markets are transparent. The SEC overseas the securities exchanges, brokers and dealers, the investment banks and advisors, mutual funds, and to a lesser extent the ratings agencies. It has the authority to enforce. It guards against insider trading, accounting fraud, and providing false or misleading securities' information. Furthermore, the SEC is a public educator.

The SEC employs 3,500 staff and has five commissioners, each appointed by the President. One is the chairman. Not more than three of the Commissioners can belong to the same political party, ensuring non-partisanship. The chairmen of the SEC, the FED and the CFTC, and the Secretary of the Treasury serve as members of the President's Working Group on Financial Markets.

The SEC was established in 1933 in response to the post-World War I surge in securities activity. Misleading information and fraudulent stock sales were fuelled by easy credit and widespread abuse of margin financing. Half of the $50 billion in new securities offered after World War I, had become worthless by the time of the stock market crashed in October 1929. Investors and banks that had lent to them lost large sums of money, and the public lost faith in the capital markets. Congress created the SEC in 1933, to restore investor confidence by providing investors and the markets with reliable information and clear rules for fair dealing.

Companies offering securities to the public must provide potential investors with true and reliable information about the securities and their risks. Those who sell and trade securities, the brokers, dealers, and exchanges, must treat investors fairly and honestly, and make the interests of investors paramount. Securities markets must be fair, orderly, and efficient. So today, a major function of the SEC is to protect the $26 trillion US securities markets.

The SEC is also a law enforcement agency. It brings civil actions in federal court and prosecutes when necessary. Every year, thousands of actions are pursued.

The Sarbanes-Oxley Act of 2002, mandated reforms to enhance corporate responsibility, financial disclosure and combat corporate and accounting fraud. Then Dodd-Frank added to consumer protections, added trading restrictions, strengthened regulation of financial products, corporate governance, disclosure, and transparency.

Credit rating agencies are registered with the SEC as Nationally Recognised Statistical Rating Agencies, the NRSRAs. Their activities are monitored in order to promote compliance with statutory requirements.

Although the SEC is responsible for regulating the investment banking sector, in 2004 it effectively abrogated its responsibility and outsourced it to the banks themselves. It agreed to let the *Big Five* use a Basel II VaR methodology for calculating the capital for their broker dealer operations. We will talk about VaR shortly, but the result was that by the time of the Crisis, they had become very highly leveraged with leverage ratios over 30:1. Before it failed, Bear's was 33:1. The SEC thought that the financial markets could police themselves! Three of the five failed; the remaining two took refuge as deposit takers.

Regulation Slipping Through the Gaps

The OTS was created in 1989 during the savings and loan crisis. It was the successor regulator to the Federal Savings and Loan Insurance Corporation created in 1934. Its responsibility was to regulate the S&Ls, the federal savings associations and their holding companies, and the federally insured state savings associations. As a federal regulator, it could permit branches of S&Ls to be opened nationwide under a single regulator, avoiding multiple state regulation, which in some cases avoided splitting regulation between the OCC and the FED. This, however, resulted in the OTS regulating a number of financial institutions that were not S&Ls, and about which it had little knowledge nor expertise, for example, AIG. Notwithstanding the alphabet soup of regulators, some financial organizations slipped through the cracks.

The Bank of England and the European Central Bank

The BoE is the central bank of the United Kingdom. It was founded in 1694. Its role is to maintain monetary and financial stability in the UK, the Sterling area. It became a public organization after War II, so unlike most central banks, was a private organization until quite recently. Like the FED and ECB it is independent from its government. In 2012, the BoE was given some regulatory responsibilities and the Prudential Regulation Authority, the PRA, a prudential regulator became a part of it. Its primary role includes systemic risk, and the supervision of banks, building societies and credit unions, insurers and major investment firms, about 1,700 financial organizations.

The Financial Services Authority, FSA, was eliminated in 2012, and the Financial Conduct Authority, the FCA, was made responsible for regulating the financial services industry in the UK. It protects consumers and promotes stability and healthy competition between financial services providers. The FSA and PRA work hand in hand.

The ECB was born on 1 June 1998. It is the central bank for the eighteen European member states[139] that use the euro as a currency. The ECB works with the national central banks of these countries and together they form the Eurosystem. The focusses are price stability and maintaining the value of the euro. Only the ECB can create euros, which was introduced as an electronic means of payment on 1 January 1999. Banknotes and coins followed in 2002.

Europe's economy is the world's second largest, so the ECB, the BoE and the FED work together, often with other central banks to maintain global stability.

Rating Agencies

The rating agencies, the NSRAs, are financial utilities. Initially they earned revenues by rating corporate and government bonds. Investors who wished to learn more about potential investments paid subscriptions and received ratings, and then made investments using them. Rather than spend time investigating thousands of potential investments, investors would be able to make decisions by paying a small fee.

To determine ratings, the NRSRAs use a large number of pieces of information, for example the quarterly filings made by public corporations. They interview senior executives and take into account general market assessments, current news, and market data. What eventually developed was a cartel. Moody's, the oldest and largest began to offer ratings in 19077, and today, Moody's, Standard and Poor's and Fitch are the major members of the cartel.

Ratings of BBB and above are investment grade securities. Those below are high yield bonds, and were first known as junk bonds. All the investments made by some conservative investors like pension funds and mutual funds must have an NRSRA rating, and often can only invest in investment grade bonds. If they are permitted to invest in high yield bonds, then the percentage must be low. At the high end, bonds rated AAA or treble A have the same default risk as Treasury bonds, and corporations inherit the ratings of their bonds.

When Basel II was adopted, it made extensive reference to NRSRA ratings and minimum capital requirements became dependant on them. Their influence became ubiquitous, however, they claimed no liability if the ratings were inaccurate as they sold them as *opinions*. The agencies hid behind the First Amendment of the US Constitution. Today, although the SEC is their regulator, they are subject to little oversight, and lack any meaningful accountability.

From the 1970s, the NRSRAs began to earn revenues from the issuers of securities, including securitizations. An issuer who wanted to sell a security would pay an agency to rate it and at the same time, continue to charge subscriptions for access to its ratings and research. A conflict of interest, but non-one seemed to notice or if they did, they did not care. As the revenues earned from issuers became significant, the agencies became incentivized to accommodate them. The agencies became consultants and worked with issuers, tweaking ratings in order to provide them in accordance with the issuers, their customers, wishes. The paymasters wanted high ratings, and the agencies wanted the business. Issuers shopped for ratings, and the agencies put profits before integrity, which was sacrificed for market share. The issuers needed investment grade bonds and the NRSRAs obliged.

NRSRA rating costs were between $30,000 and $350,000, the latter for exotic products. As thousands of bonds needed ratings, and ratings had to be constantly updated, the ratings business became exceptionally profitable. In 2000, Moody's became one of the most profitable companies in the Fortune 500. Its revenues grew from $564 million in 1997 to $1.6 billion in 2005. Its market capitalization was $15 billion, about the same as Bear Stearns. Bear revenues, however, were $7 billion, and had 15,500 employees compared to Moody's 2,500. Moody's margins were near 50%, and structured finance, which accounted for just over one quarter of its revenues in 1999 grew to one half by 2005. When Moody's went public it boasted that it rated $30 trillion of the world's debt in over 100 countries, and Warren Buffet became its largest single shareholder. He held 15% of its stock. Why? Because the securitization business which depended on ratings had exploded. It became absurd. In 2007 there were only 6 AAA rated companies, but thousands of AAA rated tranches of securitizations.

Models were a major ratings tool, and as the exotic product business increased so did the agencies' reliance on statistical models. We will take a good look at models in a later section, but suffice it to say that the models were generally poor, and remained constantly under development. Different types of debt required very different models, for example, there were fewer problems with corporate debt as its performance had been established over many business cycles, over many booms and busts, but housing debt was much more difficult to model.

The agencies published their models to establish transparency and credibility, but this resulted in them being analysed by securitizers which then tweaked their products and aligned them with the models. Employees of ratings agencies earned far less than their banker colleagues. The securitizers needed staff to game the ratings so credit ratings agency employees were recruited by banks. Any ability for an NRSRA to provide good ratings soon evaporated. Moreover, there was little attention paid to model risk. What would be the consequences of model error? If the boundary conditions failed, if we had an investor panic, would the problem become systemic? With no way to evaluate models, the practice of ratings shopping became a race to the bottom.

Bank Capital

A bank's assets are its investments and include the loans it has made and reserves deposited at its central bank. A bank's liabilities are what it has borrowed and include depositors' funds. Capital began life as an accounting concept. It is the value of all that a bank owns, its assets, less what the bank owes its liabilities. It is the accounting way of measuring the value of a bank. A bank's capital or equity is a fundamental part of its balance sheet.[140] As we will see, capital is loss absorbing.

When a bank is formed, shareholders pay money to buy shares in it. The shares are (common) equity or capital and shareholders then own a part of the bank. While they have no right to return their shares and recover their investment, unlike debt holders, they enjoy the right to receive dividends from profits. Simply, capital is that portion of a bank's liabilities for which there is no contractual repayment commitment. There are many kinds of shares, but the simplest kind are common shares, and these usually form the largest class of shares.

Capital is shown on the liabilities side of a balance sheet.

Bank shares in publicly owned banks are traded on stock exchanges, and shareholders can buy shares from other shareholders or sell them to the public. Banks can usually buy and sell their own shares. Furthermore, a bank can create and sell more shares to the public, increasing its public ownership, and capital. If a bank buys its own shares it can hold them as investments, and they appear on the asset side of its balance sheet, or it can use the purchase to reduce its capital, by extinguishing shares. This option is one way, as shareholders cannot force a bank to buy their shares back. Importantly, as shares cannot be returned, capital serves as a cushion in case the value of the bank's assets fall or the value of its liabilities increase. Capital is loss absorbing, and if banks never made losses, it would not be necessary to hold capital.[141] When profits are made they appear in the balance sheet in the capital section as retained earnings, and the amount of capital increases. When losses occur retained earnings, hence capital decreases. Capital thus absorbs losses, and banks must ensure that there is always enough capital to absorb losses and survive. The fundamental balance sheet relationship is: Assets = Liabilities +Capital (which includes retained earnings).

Why do we need to consider losses? A bank's assets are mostly loans, and a borrower may not repay all or part of a loan or the interest earned on it. A bank is thus exposed to default risk. A bank can also suffer funding risk if it cannot fill the gap between its short term borrowing and long term lending. Banks borrow short-term both for their depositors' convenience and because it costs less than their earnings on longer term customer loans. A bank's profits come from the spread. Short term borrowings have to be renewed until the longer-term loans are repaid. If a bank is unable to renew its short term borrowings it may suffer a liquidity problem, and could be in danger of failing, even if all its assets, its loans are perfectly sound.

Many bankers confuse reserves and capital. They say that capital is set aside (where? one is tempted to ask) and hence is not productively used. For this reason they say capital is expensive. This is incorrect. Capital is used in the same way as borrowings, and is lent or invested in the same way that borrowings are lent or invested. Capital is simply un-borrowed funds available for productive use in the usual way. The argument that capital is costly because it is not productively used, that it is sitting idly waiting to absorb losses, is erroneous. Capital is utilized, and is not costly. In fact, higher levels of capital are beneficial for banks, the financial system and society. The misrepresentation comes from a conflict of interest. The reason that bankers claim that capital is expensive has everything to do with compensation and nothing to do with its cost and reality. The higher the return on capital, the higher the compensation. With less capital, the return on capital is higher than with more capital. So to justify less capital a myth is promoted: capital is expensive.[142]

If a bank has more capital it benefits from a larger loss-absorbing cushion, the bank's stability is enhanced and the fragility of the financial system is reduced. With sufficient loss absorbing capital, the downside risk of a bank is borne by the bank's shareholders and not by its creditors, nor its depositors, nor deposit insurance, nor the taxpayers. Higher capital is therefore a good thing. One hundred years ago banks held far more capital.

Cost of Capital

There are many more non-financial corporations than there are banks, and non-financial corporations have much higher capital levels than financial corporations. If capital was expensive compared to borrowing, one would expect non-financial corporations to borrow extensively too. But they do not. Nonfinancial companies compete with financial corporations for capital, and while Silicon Valley start-ups may exhibit high risk investments offering high returns, and public utilities low risk and lower returns, a bank's solicitation of capital can be no more expensive than a non-bank's solicitation.

How do we determine the cost of capital? Clearly, dividends paid to shareholders are part of the equation. Another factor is that capital is retained and does not need to be repaid. If we paid 5% in interest costs for a returnable loan, we would expect to pay more if the amount was non-returnable. This is why equity holders, holders of capital earn dividends. We must always remember that dividends exhibit optionality. They do not have to be paid. Another factor is the benefit to the bank from holding capital. The more there is, the higher the loss absorbing capacity, and the higher its insurance value. Investors are willing to accept lower returns if investments are safer, and this means that the incremental cost of capital decreases as the absolute amount of capital increases.

A bank has a choice. It can borrow for a known periodic cost, and then eventually pay the loan back. Or it can accept the same amount of money, never pay it back, and only pay for it when the bank has earned a return. Common equity holders are last in line in bankruptcy. Even in a disaster, a bank must pay debt holders what it can. What would you do? Nonfinancial corporations chose to take on capital, and eschew borrowing. Me too. Banks should also.

Why do providers of common equity do so? In reality, they do receive dividends, and as the shares of equity trade on stock exchanges, investors expect the value of their investment to increase. And of course, debt is repaid, and the returns on it cease. If an institution buys back its equity, capital, any benefits for the holder cease, but in this case, the sale price is invariably attractive to the equity holder. Some corporations find they need never pay dividends because the value of the shares continues to appreciate. Finally, what a corporation pays as dividends typically is in lockstep with the price at which the shares of common equity trade, as investors will determine what they are prepared to pay for the shares based on its expected total return.

When investors make equity acquisition decisions, bank stocks stand in line with nonfinancial sector stocks. Investors invest based on their assessment of risk and reward. Nonfinancial corporations do not rely heavily on borrowing, hence, an expectation of a competitive rate of return for nonfinancial corporations does not rely on borrowing. If a nonfinancial corporation found that equity was more expensive to offer than borrowing, they would finance their operations with debt. But they do not. Banks do borrow extensively, but as investors buy bank stocks, they must too offer a competitive rate of return. The question then is why bankers say it costs less to borrow, when nonfinancial corporations think that borrowing is more expensive. As we said this is linked to compensation.

For banks, the debt to equity mix is a significant determinant of risk. Losses for a highly leveraged balance sheet can wipe out the equity holders, so the higher the leverage, the higher the risk and the higher the return an investor wants. A highly leveraged bank may indeed find the cost of putting on more capital is greater than the cost of borrowing. But this is an extreme, and assumes that more borrowing is an option. Leverage which results in equity being higher cost must not be permitted, and in any case, investors can shy away from providing both capital and loans.

Some suggest that capital is expensive because a bank's market capitalization is usually substantially less than its book value. But there is no connection between the two, and any book value is irrelevant as it can be manipulated, for example, by not taking write-downs, maintaining overly optimistic marks, or otherwise disguising losses in order to substantiate enhanced bonuses. Market capitalization is a measure of what the bank is worth to its shareholders.

The cost of capital is not only a direct cost to a bank itself, but also a potential cost to the larger economy and society as a whole. Banks benefit from government subsidies and bailouts. With ample loss absorbing capital there is less likelihood that government subsidies will be needed. So higher capital levels benefit everyone, including deposit insurers, regulators and taxpayers. There is no downside to holding higher levels of capital, and banks are safer. If the financial sector was less fragile then the cost of capital to the larger economy would be significantly less. Today, when the financial sector is so much more interconnected, higher levels of capital are a necessity. Furthermore, if there is a large cost to society and our economies when financial institutions fail, even if we had to pay more for loans, which we do not, this would simply be a necessary cost of doing business, just as paying rent, salaries and utility bills.

To illustrate the fragility of the financial system, consider the contemplated dividend distribution of JP Morgan Chase in 2012. It proposed to pay $19 billion to shareholders. If it had retained these earnings, capital would have increased by 10%. The bank, however, sustained a $5.8 billion loss, but the distribution was approved.[143] Lunacy!

Other attempts have been made to demonstrate that GDP will fall, employment will increase, creditors will not lend and people will be less happy. All nonsense.[144] Increased capital does not limit lending, it enhances lending by lowering the risk of the lender's failing, and enhances stability. Bankers borrow as much as possible, even though it imposes a direct cost on the economy because it is the bankers that benefit. It's all about bonuses.

Leverage

Leverage is the ratio of a bank's assets (or for some, liabilities, it makes little difference) to its capital. A bank's capital is its own skin in the game, and the business of banking is to borrow and lend both capital and borrowings. In a nutshell, the higher the leverage the higher the return on capital, but the easier it is to go out of business.

Suppose that the value of a bank's capital is $20, the value of its loan book, its assets is $100, and the value of its deposits (and any other borrowings), its liabilities is $80. Leverage is thus 5 to 1. If the bank makes a profit of $10, then the return on capital is 50%. If capital is increased to $40 and borrowings lowered to $60 so that the $100 in loans remains the same, leverage is 2.5 to 1 and a profit of $10 means that the return on capital is less. It is 25%. Conversely, increasing leverage, let's say to 10 to 1 means, given the same $100 loan book and $10 capital, and profit, the return on capital of 100%. So higher leverage means a greater return on capital, and this means bigger bonuses.

The problem is the down side. A $10 loss in the first case means that capital is reduced to $10. A problem, but the bank is still in business. And similarly in the second case, the bank remains in business, even more comfortably, but the destruction to capital is far less. It drops from $40 to $30. But in the last case, the higher leverage has meant that the bank is wiped out. The bank has no capital left, and unless it can find new capital quickly, it is not only dead, but also buried.

Leverage	Initial Capital	*Profit of $10*		*Loss of $10*	
		Capital Becomes	Gain	Capital Becomes	Loss
2.5:1	40	50	25%	30	25%
5:1	20	30	50%	10	50%
10:1	10	10	100%	0	100% and dead and buried

Figure 3: Leverage at Work

So, when profitable, expanding lending capacity by increasing leverage means higher returns, higher shareholder dividends, often share price increases, and larger bonuses. Shareholders, including senior management shareholders can realize greater profits by selling their shares. Reaching higher share price levels often means increased bonuses for senior executives too. Clearly senior management is incentivized to increase leverage. But the cost is that losses can wipe out a bank, quickly.

When institutions are *too big to fail* this becomes a danger as senior management benefits from the upside and is not penalized by the downside. Management is incentivized to increase leverage and take higher risks knowing that the bank will be bailed out if substantial losses are made. Regulators thus play an essential role by requiring minimum capital levels and constraints on leverage. For these reasons, the determination of bank capital and leverage must be completely independent of bank management. If a bank's capital falls below the regulator defined threshold, the regulator must have the authority to deal with the problem and, if necessary, to shut the bank down.

Furthermore, in many cases, the interest paid by banks on loans is tax deductible. Not so for dividends. This means profitability is greater when leverage is higher. If you are a senior banker, what would you want? A further reason why the determination of capital and leverage levels must not rest with bankers.

If a bank sustains losses, one way to deal with the reduced capital is to lower leverage by selling assets. If many banks suffer losses at the same time, then fire sales result if they need to sell similar assets. This exacerbates the problem and brings us closer to government bailouts.

Another advantage of lower leverage is that investors pay more for capital when leverage is low. Investor risk is lower. Furthermore, it costs the taxpayer less as the government subsidies, deposit insurance, a lender of last resort facility and bailouts are used less. The fact that there are these subsidies means that senior bank managers and bank boards of directors take less cognizance of risk.

Enter Basel

We said in chapter 2, The Next Forty years, Basel came about because of the economic turmoil in the 1970s. Oil at $75 a barrel, coupled with higher interest rates, inflation and unemployment and lower growth, and the other problems had to be dealt with.

Bank Herstatt, a small private German bank in Cologne failed in 1974 and the German regulator closed its door. A trader, Danny Dattel had lost almost half a billion marks.[145] The bank had purchased Deutsche marks and sold US dollars in the foreign exchange market for delivery on the day that the German regulator had happened to schedule for its closure. For such transactions, currency payments are delivered to a bank located in the currencies' jurisdiction and in business hours, so the marks were delivered to Herstatt in Cologne at the end of the German business day, before the regulator closed its doors. The dollars were to be delivered to the banks' various counterparty's bank accounts in the US on the same day, but by the time the dollar delivery was to take place, at the close of business in New York, Herstatt was dead. New York clocks are set six hours behind the clocks in Germany. So Herstatt received its marks and its US counterparties did not receive their dollars, millions of dollars. The banking system had found new ways to stumble with the onset of international business.

Doing business across regulatory borders highlighted the need for new settlement rules and for a level playing field for banks doing business internationally. To address these issues, Basel was born in 1974 and subsequently the Basel Committee on Banking Supervision at the Bank for International Settlements, the BIS, published its first accord, the Basel I Accord, in 1988.[146] The BIS had come into existence after the First World War and was well positioned to take a role in international regulation.

The aim of Basel I was to provide a framework for bank safety and soundness and enable banks to operate on an equitable basis across jurisdictions. Safe settlement rules must apply universally. Banks should not be able to choose a domicile based on differences in regulation. Risk measurement must be uniform. Common capital requirements must apply, and Basel should facilitate cross border trade and economic development. Regulation is jurisdictional, so a bank is subject to its home country regulation, and what came to be practice was that if a home regulator judged that a bank was Basel I compliant, the bank would be able to do business across international borders, in other Basel jurisdictions. A major focus of Basel I was the determination of how much capital a bank should hold. Prior to Basel I there had been few attempts to formalize capital requirements. An assumption was that if we got capital quantification right, then a number of other safety and soundness issues would be resolved.

Basel I was a European initiative, and notably it was developed in a very consultative fashion, so the European banks had considerable input, and influenced the capital determination requirements significantly. Europe adopted Basel I immediately and the US followed suit in 1992. In 2004 Basel II, developed over many years, and not finalized until 2006, began to be adopted, and then after the Crisis, Basel III was promulgated.

How Much Capital?

To answer the question, how much capital should a bank hold, the Basel Committee introduced the concept of risk based capital and Basel I provided a way to quantify it. The Committee said that if a bank held capital equal to 8% of its risk-weighted assets, then this would be sufficient to absorb losses in almost all circumstances. The Committee also defined risk-weighted assets for credit risks. This became the minimum capital requirement, and was known as the Basel I regulatory capital. Basel capital was a "cushion against sudden financial shocks (such as an unusually high occurrence of loan defaults)"[147] and losses on loans are absorbed by capital, which is accordingly reduced by the amount of losses. If a bank sustained losses greater than its capital, the bank was wiped out, it was bankrupt.

When a bank becomes bankrupt it means that the holders of the bank's common shares are wiped out. The bank's assets are sold and the proceeds distributed amongst the liability holders. The holders of common equity do receive a payout if there is something left after everyone else has been paid, but this happens rarely as the losses absorbed have reduced the value of the common equity to zero. Of course the depositors must be protected, and as we said, the FDIC ensures this in the US.

Besides common shares, preferred shares are capital. There are many forms of preferred shares, but usually they pay fixed dividends and these are paid before common share dividends are paid. Preferred share dividends may be cumulative or non-cumulative. This means that in any one period, if cumulative preferred dividends are not paid, they accrue to the next payment period, so all past cumulative dividends must be paid before any dividends can be paid to common shareholders. If non-cumulative preferred share dividends are not paid they are lost. A bank may have many classes of preferred shares, and different classes can pay different interest rates and be cumulative or non-cumulative. All preferred shares stand in line in bankruptcy before common shares, and after debt. This means that debt is repaid first, then if anything is left, preferred shareholders, then again, if anything is left, common shareholders. To reiterate, it's rarely that case that the holders of capital receive anything from bankruptcy.

As well as common and preferred shares, there are many forms of hybrid capital instruments, instruments which are a cross between debt and equity. Hybrids are treated as debt and receive interest payments until the organization needs more capital, at which time they are converted into equity and used to absorb losses. In bankruptcy, hybrids stand behind debt, but ahead of preferred. Hybrids are a way of making debt loss absorbing, and prior to a hybrid's becoming capital, the return on capital, hence bonuses, appears higher. As interest payments can be tax deductible, hybrids are a way of maintaining artificially high returns and bonuses. Banks are prepared to pay slightly higher interest for hybrid debt in order to be able to declare higher returns, and bonuses.

An important component of capital is tangible common equity, TCE, which is common equity less *intangibles.* TCE arises because some assets do not appear on balance sheets, as they are not physical things like buildings and factories, or financial assets like bank balances and investments. The main ones are goodwill, copyrights, patents and brand names, computer software and designs, and intellectual property. When one bank buys another bank, the price paid is often far more than the value of the assets minus the liabilities, the capital. However, this value is not something that can be relied on in a crisis as it cannot be turned into cash easily, or be loss absorbing. If we assume that intangibles are of little value when a bank is near bankruptcy, and take them out of the equation, we are left with TCE. The *tangible* in TCE is tangible.

We also have loss-reserves, not to be confused with reserve deposits at a bank's central bank. Loss-reserves absorb expected future losses incurred in the normal course of business. For example, a small (hopefully) percentage of credit card holders will default and using historic, demographic data, we can estimate the losses and set a reserve aside to absorb these losses. As loss-reserves absorb losses, they are capital.

It's important to recognise that even well capitalized banks are not fail safe as contagion can cause problems. The unregulated shadow banking system, for example, is a significant source of financial risk, and losses in the shadow banking system can be contagious and cause extensive problems in other parts of the financial sector, even for the strongest of banks.

Finally, before returning to the Basel I minimum capital requirement, it's also important to note that the value of a bank's capital is not static. Its value rises in good times, when profits are made and there are fewer defaults, and falls in poor times, when there are more defaults.

So what is a risk weighted asset, or RWA? Some assets are higher risk than others. US Treasuries or UK gilts are risk free, but loans to corporations have risk, and loans to some corporations have more risk than loans to others. If we determine capital based on risk, then low-risk assets need less capital than high-risk assets and assets with no risk require no capital at all. Basel I defined risk weights for all assets in a balance sheet on a bucketing basis. Assets are assigned to buckets according to these risk weights. The value of the RWAs for each bucket is determined by multiplying the bucket total by the risk weight for the bucket. The total RWAs for the balance sheet is the sum of the RWAs for each bucket, and the minimum Basel I regulatory capital is 8% of this total.

As an example, suppose we have $10 million in commercial loans and that the risk weight for these loans is 8%. The RWA for commercial loans is thus $800,000. Suppose that we also have $10 million in residential mortgages and the risk weight for mortgages is 4%, and $100 million in sovereign debt, with a 0% risk weight. We see from the table below, that the RWA for the balance sheet is $1,200,000. The Basel I regulatory capital is therefore 8% of this, or $96,000. We should note that risk weights are mostly between 0% and 100%, although there are a small number of categories that incur a risk weighting of greater than 100%.

Asset Bucket	Asset Total ($)	Risk Weight	RWA
Commercial Loans	10,000,000	8%	800,000
Mortgages	10,000,000	4%	400,000
Sovereign Debt	100,000,000	0%	0
Total	120,000,000		1,200,000
	Minimum Capital at 8% of total RWA		96,000

Figure 4: Basel I Risk Weighted Assets

This approach makes sense, but determining the risk weightings for each category is difficult. Moreover, why should the capital be 8% of the total RWA? It should certainly vary over time, as economic conditions vary. Furthermore, Basel I did not distinguish between, for example, different categories of commercial loans. Some are higher risk than others. This has led to banks being incentivized to hold higher risk assets within a bucket. Nonetheless, Basel I became widely accepted and established as the minimum capital calculation rule for many jurisdictions globally.

Basel II and III

Basel II greatly expanded on Basel I. It encompassed not only the quantification of capital, but also many safety and soundness issues, and commented on the role of regulators and disclosure. Basel II provided minimum capital specifications for market and operational risks as well as credit risks. The minimum Basel II regulatory capital became the sum of the capital for each of these risk types. In addition, Basel II provided capital calculation options. Capital for each of market, credit and operational risk could be calculated using RWA techniques similar to Basel I. It also provided advanced, probabilistic calculation options that utilized bank specific models with inputs determined by banks themselves. It was assumed that the banking community had become more risk aware, and that the techniques they had developed were sophisticated. Leopards, however, do not change their spots. They were not!

Credit risk has always been the major risk incurred by banks. So, Basel I focussed on credit risk only. Since the 1980s, however, banks had become increasingly engaged in trading in the financial markets, and exposed to market risks. As banks became larger and employed more staff and opened more offices in more countries, operational risks became very significant.

Credit risk models determined the probabilities of loan defaults, and estimated of the losses and amounts that might be recovered. VaR models were used to determine market risks. They came in many forms, but eventually models based on historic data became widely used. Various alternatives for determining operational risk losses became available, all of them new, and none particularly useful nor widely accepted.

As banks themselves developed the models and provided the data, they could influence the amount of capital they held by using advanced model dependant options. It was simple for a bank to develop a model and feed it with data that produced the result it wanted, lower capital. Not surprisingly they did. Models used by one bank provided very different results from models used by other banks, even with the same data. The assumption that the advanced calculation options produced good results was nonsense.

Basel II permitted regulatory capital arbitrage as banks could game calculations. For example, Basel II set the risk weight for securitizations at 5%, so a bank could securitize corporate loans with 8% risk weights and calculate capital based on a 5% risk weight.[148] The risk of the loans, however, had not changed. Basel II was in fact not more sophisticated, but less sophisticated.

Proponents of Basel II argued that Basel I overestimated capital because its risk weights were not sufficiently granular. Some corporations were obviously less sound than others, but they were all assigned the same risk weight. All sovereign debt was not zero risk as the European sovereign debt crisis starkly confirmed much later. Furthermore, when sovereign debt problems arose and write-downs were required, it was not possible to do so as there was no capital to absorb the write-downs! Asset sales, at depressed prices followed with further losses. This was not something new. Latin America in the 1980s and 1990s had shown us that sovereign debt is not risk free. What was missed is that problems with Basel I were not an endorsement of Basel II.

There was considerable "outside" pressure for Basel II. Focussed by the need to ensure that New Yorker's were employed, Mayor Bloomberg and New York Senator Chuck Schumer retained McKinsey the consultant to weigh up the pros and cons of Basel II. Not surprisingly, in 2007 McKinsey came down firmly on its side. As the FDIC's Sheila Bair pointed out,[149] McKinsey's motivation for promoting Basel II had little to do with its merits and everything to do with earning considerable revenues by providing Basel II consulting and models to the New York banking community. Senator Schumer wrote to Sheila Bair: "I believe your determination to keep complex, financial institutions tethered to the outdated Basel I standards actually jeopardizes the safety, soundness and efficiency, and competitiveness of our markets, I do not agree that more capital is always better, particularly where banks create strong capital systems to internalize their risks."[150] Poor Chucky!

The initial comprehensive Basel II calculation options were published in 2004 and the European banks immediately began to implement Basel II. In the US, there was resistance as everyone knew it would lead to a decline in capital levels. Despite its shortcomings, the Basel I methodology was transparent and clear, objective and enforceable and less malleable by bankers. There was work to be done, but it could be implemented easily.

Despite concerns over lower capital levels, the US banks argued for Basel II. They wanted to ensure they could maintain competitiveness with their European competitors who had implemented Basel II. As they held less capital, so must US banks. This does not hold water, of course, and what was really at issue was compensation. The FDIC argued against Basel II and weighed in favour of a risk weighted asset basis: "Instead of regulators setting clear, enforceable parameters for determining the riskiness of bank assets, Basel II essentially allowed bank managers to use their own judgement",[151] it said. Lower capital levels would expose the FDIC as failures would increase.

The FDIC argued persuasively for lower leverage. This would also help many European countries. Switzerland had bank assets six times its GDP. Holland and Luxembourg had low populations and large banks, and their banking assets far exceeded their GDPs. The failure of a large Dutch, Luxembourger or Swiss bank would put an enormous strain on their economies. Unfortunately, the collapse later of the Icelandic banking system illustrated this well. At the time, the assets of the Icelandic banks were 850% of its GDP, $330,000 for every man, woman and Icelandic child![152] The FDIC used leverage ratios for the US banks it insured, and the regulators in Canada and Australia also used them. Furthermore, leverage ratios cannot be gamed. As it turned out the FDIC was prescient!

As we have discussed, the SEC authorized the investment banks to implement Basel II in (August of) 2004. By doing this, the SEC, in effect, outsourced risk management to the industry and abruptly abrogated its regulatory responsibilities by reducing its supervisory head count. Leverage increased dramatically giving the investment banks a competitive advantage over the commercial banks and S&Ls. Each of the Big Five soon had leverage ratios of over 30 to 1. Excessive leverage was a big part of the problems to come.

A major problem with Basel II was that it assumed that banks and regulators had the capability and willingness to manage risks, notwithstanding that history had shown otherwise. The risk management functions of the financial sector had, and still has, little ability to assess and manage risk, and even less motivation to do so. In the years prior to the Crisis, when the larger banks did employ risk managers who understood the issues, they were side-lined. The Great Recession later vindicated the view that the larger banks were clueless and irresponsible when it came to risk management, and simply did not care. Add to this that banks should never be able to influence the amount of capital they hold, and we see that Basel II should never have been seriously entertained.

Because Basel II was expensive to implement only the big banks could determine their own capital levels. The smaller banks were subject to the more prescriptive Basel I. They did not have the resources to implement models and game them, and to see through the mathematical obfuscations. So while regulation was aimed at the larger banks, it was the smaller banks that were penalized.

The problems with the US real estate market exposed the Basel II capital calculations, and demonstrated how they understated capital. Concisely, contrary to what the historic data said, the data on which the Basel II capital calculations relied, mortgage holders defaulted in droves, and in concert. By mid-2007, when the subprime mortgage problems had become widespread, it was clear that the Basel II capital numbers were completely off, and support for Basel II declined globally. By December 2007, the capital base of the western banking systems was completely inadequate. The turmoil of the Great Recession resulted in a rethink, and not a single US commercial bank nor S&L has used Basel II for capital determination.[153] After the Crisis, Dodd-Frank killed it.

The Crisis and Great Recession drove Basel III. It is global and was endorsed by the G20 in 2010[154]. In the US, most of Basel III was incorporated into Dodd-Frank. Today it applies in the US to all FDIC insured institutions, the bank holding companies and some of the systematically important non-bank financial companies. Banks with assets less than $500 billion can chose to use Basel I. Basel III redefined and increased minimum capital requirements, introduced liquidity ratios and a leverage ratio. Here we will only outline a few of the major Basel III pieces. All of the requirements are to be in place by 2019. In the meantime, banks can continue to pay dividends and bonuses even though their capital levels are low. In other words, the banks that were rescued during the Crisis remain free to compensate senior management at absurd levels!

The minimum capital requirement went from 2% to 7% of RWA and was comprised of common equity of 4.5% and a capital buffer of 2.5%. In difficult times, capital can drop to 4.5%, but then no bonuses nor dividends can be paid until the ratio is back at 7%. Regulators can raise the capital requirement to 9% during a boom in order to slow down lending. A surcharge of 2.5% was introduced for the *too big to fail* banks. The definition of capital was narrowed and excludes hybrids.[155] Counterparty limits have been strengthened. Today these requirements are subject to strengthening.

Capital is divided into tiers, Tier 1[156] and Tier 2 where Tier 1 is mostly TCE. The Basel II reliance on credit agency ratings for capital calculations[157] was removed. A bank must be able to demonstrate that it can withstand adverse economic and financial scenarios, and withstand heavy losses, so stress testing has been strengthened.

Basel III addressed liquidity by introducing two ratios, the liquidity coverage ratio and the net stable funding ratio.

Basel III left a number of problems unresolved, especially for derivatives, for example, credit default swaps were used to insure against defaults, but did not take into account that the insurer might fail. Banks continued to game the rules, in fact, JP Morgan Chase declared publicly that it did so and had every intention to continue to do so, aggressively.[158]

There were many Basel III distractors. The IMF suggested that constraining the leverage of bigger banks would increase the cost of loans by up to 1.4%, reduce global GDP by 3.1% and cost 9.7

million jobs globally between 2011 and 2015. The claims were without merit and nonsensical. The Basel Committee showed that boosting capital by 10% would increase the cost of bank capital by less than one third of one percent, and that there was no evidence that higher leverage increases borrowing costs. The BIS predicted that a two percentage point increase in the target ratio for TCE would reduce GDP by no more than 0.3% over four years. Any costs are insignificant compared to the costs of another Great Recession and, further, stronger capital and liquidity requirements result in long-term benefits for global GDP. BIS research had shown in 2010 that banks with a strong risk-based capital ratio, but with high leverage ratios were the banks most likely to have a problem in any subsequent crisis, and that banks with low leverage ratios were the least likely to face a problem, and concluded that risk based ratios alone are a poor indicator of a bank's health.

Much later, in June 2010, Bob Diamond, the then CEO of Barclays, announced that preventing banks from counting preferred and other hybrid securities as Tier 1 capital would cut the credit that banks could extend to customers by $1.5 trillion.[159] There is not one shred of evidence for this claim, and he did not try to give one. It exemplifies the irresponsibility of senior management and was made solely with personal financial goals in mind.

No New Bangsters

We have discovered no new Bangsters in this chapter, so the table remains the same. To remind you, the award table is:

Bangsters	Gold Stars
Nicholas Biddle	Franklin D Roosevelt
JP Morgan	Louis Brandeis

4

Exotic Worlds

From Hedges to Missiles

T he US space programs had faltered by the 1980s and its engineers, mathematicians and astrophysicists found new homes in finance. Banking became more technical, more mathematical, and by the 1990s, a new banking model had taken shape. The space program engineers were building weapons of financial mass destruction, otherwise known as derivatives.[160] They became the black holes of finance and sucked everything into their dark interiors. Deposit taker banks acted like investment banks, and the risk landscape changed from an ocean of calm seas with an occasional squall, to a stormy ocean ploughed with mines.

By the time the stage was set for the Crisis, the new trading activities of the major banks were making significant contributions to their profits. The instruments and products traded had evolved from stocks, bonds and foreign currencies, which many understood, to derivatives and complex structured products, which few understood.

Derivatives

We often invest in things that are a part of the real world such as houses, pension plans, and shares in a company, currencies and metals. Derivatives, however, have only an indirect connection to the real world. A derivative is a contract between two counterparties[161] whose value depends on the value of something else like cotton, oranges or gold and financial things like currencies and interest rates. This "something else" is derivative's underlying.

Derivatives have been around for centuries. The Greeks used them to speculate, and the Amsterdam stock exchange wrote derivative contracts in the 17th century on tulip production. Derivative contracts as futures on agricultural products came of age in the US with the birth of the Chicago Board of Trade in 1849, a commodities exchange. Today the city of Chicago is home to some of the world's largest commodities and derivatives exchanges. The city was born when the taming of the Wild West was well underway, railways had arrived and the rapidly growing US population, which needed feeding, resulted in the expansion of farming and agriculture.

Volatility in the financial markets in the 1970s bought derivatives into the world of finance where they were used to provide insurance, and then speculate on currency exchange rates, interest rates and equity prices. The Chicago Board Options Exchange opened in 1973, and by 1984, currency options were traded on both the Chicago Mercantile Exchange and the Philadelphia Stock Exchange.

Derivatives are always variations of two kinds of transactions, forwards and options. A forward is an agreement to buy or sell something at a future date, the settlement date, for a price agreed today, and an option gives you the option, but not the obligation, to do the same thing. Futures are forwards that are traded on exchanges using standardized contracts. Up until the 1970s the derivatives markets consisted almost entirely of futures and options contracts traded on regulated futures and options exchanges. A farmer that produces a seasonal crop like oranges, or beef might use a futures contract to sell the crop at a future date for a price agreed today. This gives the farmer protection against a fall in price. The farmer's income is guaranteed and shielded against market fluctuations, due perhaps to the weather, overproduction or disease. Futures enable farmers to plan. A risk taker takes the other side of the contract and benefits from the upside if the sale of the commodity realizes more than the pre-agreed price, but takes the risk that it may fall below this price.

An example of a futures transaction is an agreement to buy British pounds three months from now using an exchange rate that we agree today. You agree to buy £50,000, three months from today at $2 to the £, or for $100,000. You might do this if you expect to need pounds in three months, and you thought their cost might increase, or perhaps you simply want to lock in a rate and not take the risk of an increase. Usually, to do a transaction like this, you would have to make it fit into a standardized futures contract. You may indeed find a contract for a purchase £50,000, but the settlement date may not be the date you want. It may be a few days or weeks either side of it.

There is a large market for standardized futures, and there are many futures exchanges and kinds of futures contracts. The underlyings include all sorts of commodities like gold, livestock, fruit, currencies, interest rates, even the weather and sporting events. Futures are easy to buy and trade as you do not need to find a counterparty. You use an exchange and a broker. However, there is a much larger market for customized forward contracts,

contracts that do not fit neatly into standardized futures contracts. They trade on the OTC markets, banks arrange them and charge fees.

We said an option is the right, but not the obligation to buy or sell an underlying in the future. The right to buy is a call option and the right to sell is a put option. When you enter into an option, you pay for the right, by paying a small, non-refundable premium. Rather than entering into a futures contract you might choose to pay a 5-cent premium for an option to buy pounds at $1.95 per £. If the cost of the pounds increases, and you still need the pounds, you exercise the option. If the pound falls below $1.95, you would forget it, and buy the pounds at the market price. Generally, options are traded like futures on exchanges, they have standard contract terms, and you can be a buyer and a seller of both puts and calls. Also, like futures, customized options trade in the OTC markets.

Futures and options are similar but differ in important respects. Options do not commit you to exercising them, but you make a small upfront payment. When you enter into a futures contract, you must either sell it before the settlement date, or take delivery of the underlying. Both futures and options serve an actual need.

Futures and options are traded on exchanges in quantities far in excess of the availability of the underlying. Contracts that are to be settled at some future date are known as open contracts and almost all open contracts are closed prior to their settlement date by offsetting them with equal and opposite contracts for the same delivery date. Futures contracts for sale are offset with contracts for purchase. When equal and opposite contracts are not offset, delivery takes place and the payment is made.

The value of a contract to buy or sell a commodity in the future depends on many things including the price of the underlying. All derivatives are side bets. Rather than buying cotton, you buy something whose price depends on cotton. When you do this you can introduce dependencies, so the risks can be disguised, and may not be obvious. These dependencies include interest rates, the availability of the underlying, its price and volatility, and its delivery cost.

By the 1980s, many foreign exchange controls had been removed and the major currencies floated freely. Their markets were often volatile. With volatility also in the oil markets, and high inflation, consumers and businesses looked for protection from changing foreign exchange and interest rates, and turned to the futures and options markets to lock in prices for their goods and services. Derivatives trading flourished and the financial institutions became major players. Casino banking was born as derivative bets were used to achieve all sorts of ends, including, moving risk around the balance sheet, massaging P&L and lowering tax obligations. The term *financial innovation* was coined, but innovation really meant nothing more than finding new ways to make money, and usually more obscurely.

Today the OTC markets for derivatives dwarfs the exchange traded markets as there are few constraints. OTC deals can be customized to match a customer's needs, for example, a multi-year exposure to a mixture of currencies and interest rates can be hedged with a single OTC transaction. This flexibility resulted in the OTC markets flourishing by the 1980s. Furthermore, exchanges were, are regulated, and prohibited certain kinds of transactions and market manipulation. In the 1970s and 1980s, market manipulation was part and parcel of being a trader. As a boxer might feint in one direction, a dealer might sell a currency hoping to influence the market. If the market assumed the sale resulted from the dealer's view that the currency would lose value, others might also sell the currency resulting in its value falling. The dealer could then profit by buying the currency back at a lower price.

In summary, freely floating currencies resulted in an exponential expansion of currency and interest rate derivatives and the constraints of standardized contracts led to commercial and investment banks expanding the OTC derivatives markets. Fees were earned by constructing derivative deals between two customers with different views or requirements and banks, as brokers, made fees from both sides of a deal, from both the counterparties.

Interest Rate Swaps

Many sorts of derivatives were developed and from the early 1980s, swaps became increasingly popular. It has been the largest derivatives market for many years.

In 1981, the World Bank and IBM entered into the first modern swap. IBM swapped US dollars for Swiss francs with the Bank. The World Bank wanted US dollars, but avoid the high cost of obtaining them by issuing using US dollar bonds. The dollars it wanted came from the swap. The World Bank was happy. IBM had Swiss franc debt, so it used the Swiss francs it received from the World Bank to service this debt. IBM was also happy. Generally, a party with a surplus of one currency, and a need for another can swap the surplus with another party with mirrored needs

Furthermore, two parties can match interest rate based cash flows using an interest rate swap, and a bank that arranges the match can make good fees. A party with a fixed rate income stream can swap the fixed payments with variable, floating payments enjoyed by another party. The vanilla swaps market is the market for swaps that replace one cash flow with another. Salomon Brothers introduced interest rate swaps and traded vanilla swaps, currency swaps and a combination of the two.

Suppose a company issues a bond with a long maturity date, many years into the future. The company's funding cost is then locked in for the life of the bond. Borrowing short-term risks interest rate increases when the funding is renewed and a company often borrows long-term because it prefers to know, and be able to manage, its funding costs rather than risk rate hikes. In doing so, it foregoes any benefit from rate decreases.

However, after the long dated bond is issued, the company may decide to bet on short-term rates remaining low. Short-term borrowing costs are almost always less than long-term borrowing costs because short-term principal repayments permit more frequent rate adjustments, keeping rates in line with the markets, and avoid the risk of not being repaid as there is less time for things to go wrong. One way to bet on short-term rates is to do an interest rate swap. The fixed payment stream is swapped for a variable payment stream. For example, a commitment to pay 5% each year for two years on an amount of $10,000,000 can be swapped for a commitment to pay the variable rate, LIBOR plus 1% for the same period. If LIBOR remains lower than 4%, the company is better off by the difference. The amount on which the payments are based is called the notional amount. In this example, it is $10,000,000.

Why would a company do this? There are many reasons. The companies' funding has been locked in at 5% for the long term, say ten years. It can try to lower this cost from time to time by placing bets on short-term rates. Why would its counterparty want to take on the 5% fixed rate? For exactly the opposite reasons. The counterparty may be exposed to variable rates and prefer to lock in a fixed rate for its funding costs. Or the counterparty may simply be speculating.

Clearly, it does not make sense to swap fixed with fixed, so all vanilla swaps involve floating rates. You swap fixed for floating or floating for floating. Also, payments are netted, so one party pays the other the difference between the payments. Notional amounts are not exchanged, so there is no risk that they will not be repaid. Risk arises only in respect of the payment streams, and these are considerably smaller than the notional amounts.

It's important to note that the risks are not symmetrical. The commitment to pay 5% fixed is, clearly, a fixed commitment. There is no interest rate risk and the exposure is known and contained. But the commitment to pay a variable rate, while known, is not contained. While unlikely, LIBOR could increase dramatically, and the floating rate to be paid may indeed become very large. There is no upper limit.

Almost any kind of financial asset can be swapped, and when interest rate payment streams are swapped, the streams can be based on different currencies. Bonds, equities, foreign exchange and commodities can be built into swaps, with options, that are near impossible for customers to understand. All derivatives are zero sum, so there is a customer winner and a customer loser, but the derivatives dealer never loses. Dealers make two sets of fees, one from each customer, and if the dealer takes one side of the derivative, then there are more fees and profits by breaking a deal into its parts and hedging them. As customers rarely understand the more complex deals, dealers have a field day with fees, and of course, dealers hope to lock in business as the deals they put together are difficult to duplicate.

As time passed swaps became very complex. Inverse floaters are swaps whose interest rates go in the opposite direction to the market. They are usually spiced up with options. So as market rates decrease from 5% to 2%, the interest rate for an inverse floater might go from 5% to 20%! Reverse convertibles pay a fixed interest rate or a share of stock depending on the share price and the price's recent history. There are hundreds of different swaps and derivatives, but few have any practical use.

As swaps can be customized at will, and regulation and accounting rules fell behind in the 1990s, P&L deferral and tax avoidance became a significant use for swaps and other derivatives. Earnings can be smoothed over reporting periods and tax savings accrue. Casino banking took derivatives far from productive hedging of commodity prices. For example, in 2007, Porsche manipulated and increased earnings by using derivatives. Profits were up €3.7 billion, 276%, to €5.8 billion from 2006. However, during this period, Porsche's earnings on its car business fell 30%![162]

The market for swaps is enormous. In mid-2009 the size of the vanilla swaps market, measured by notional amounts was $350 trillion. The market value, the amount that would have to be paid to settle all vanilla swaps, was $14 trillion. The way to look at these numbers is as follows: the sum of the notional amounts is the total amount on which interest, fixed or floating is paid. The market value of a swap is the difference between its interest payments.

When a swap is first agreed the two interest streams mostly cancel each other out, but in time we can expect one interest payment stream to become larger than the other. The market value of the swap is this difference, and the global market value of the vanilla swap market is the sum of these amounts. In 2000, the total notional amount was thus six times the GDPs of all countries on the globe. The differences alone in the interest payments approximated the US GDP.

The bigger banks run enormous swaps and derivatives books. In the early 1990s, the notional value of JP Morgan's derivatives was $1.7 trillion and accounted for half the bank's trading revenue.[163] The market then expanded in the early 1990s to a wider range of customers, including small banks, pension and other funds and midsized companies. Derivatives indeed make good sense for investment banks, the larger commercial banks and dedicated derivatives dealers.

Early on, in 1985, recognizing that their interests would need protection, an industry group of bankers defined standards for swap deals and other derivatives, and the International Swaps and Derivatives Association, the ISDA, was born as the industry body representing the derivatives business.[164]

Arbitrage

There are many trading strategies and an important one is arbitrage. An arbitrage opportunity arises if two investments which should have the same price do not. For example, if you find that you can buy Swiss francs in the Hong Kong market at one price and sell them in London for more, you can profit by doing so. Arbitrage opportunities rarely last for long, as dealers continuously look for them, and exploit them. Buying Swiss francs in Hong Kong will push the price of the franc up and selling them in London will move it down, so differences quickly disappear. As the price differences are small, arbitrage dealing usually means dealing in large amounts.

There are often arbitrage opportunities that can be leveraged only by specialized arbitrage dealers. They are difficult to find, and the volumes required to realize a profit can be enormous. For example, one might find that there is a small price difference between two far dated US government securities, the US Treasury bond maturing in June 2040 and the September 2040 bond. The price difference resulting from the extra month's interest for the latter is negligible in practical term, years prior to settlement, however, market demand for one can temporarily move the prices apart. An investor with a significant position in one might liquidate it and cause its price to fall. A strategy is to buy the cheaper bond and sell the more expensive bond, and wait until the prices converge, when a profit can be locked in.

Arbitragers can profit when other market participants do not price complex products correctly. They can strip complex products apart and sell the pieces separately. The market may happen to price the coupons of a bond differently from their contributions to the bond price when sold separately, and arbitragers can benefit by coupon striping.

Conduits, Structured Investment Vehicles, and Special Purpose Vehicles

Banks can create and use off balance sheet entities to segregate, house and hide investments. When a bank creates an off balance sheet entity, it is the sponsor of the entity. These entities, known as conduits, hold assets and liabilities that are not shown on the sponsoring bank's balance sheet. Conduits hold no loss absorbing capital and they are not transparent, so investors and lenders to them have little idea of their risks. These risks, however, remain risks for their sponsors. They are very lightly regulated.

Banks create conduits to house long-term, illiquid assets which are funded in the short-term markets, often (by asset backed, or collateralized) commercial paper. The longer maturity, less liquid investments have higher yields than short-term funding costs, so conduits enable highly leveraged investments, and can be profitable even when spreads are narrow. Conduits do not isolate risk, as was their intention, they concentrate risk, and are bankruptcy remote, so if a sponsor has problems, investors in the conduit are shielded.

Conduits usually serve as temporary parking facilities for their assets, while they are being built. When complete, the assets are delivered to one of two other types of entities, special purpose vehicles, SPVs, and structured investment vehicles, SIVs. They are close cousins. One difference is that SIVs are more closely tied to their sponsors as they provide some of the funding. Basel I permitted conduits, SPVs and SIVs if the term of any debt to the sponsoring bank was less than one year. This was an easy condition to meet as a sponsor could lend for less than a year and then renew the loan immediately prior to its maturity. For ease, we will use the term conduit to include SPVs and SIVs.

A major problem with conduits is that if the short-term credit markets lose confidence in a conduit, or the conduit does not perform well, the sponsor might have to take its assets onto its balance sheet. When this occurs, there can be a number of adverse consequences. Capital has to be put in place, or the assets sold. Conduits thus introduce a major source of risk, under the noses of regulators and shareholders. In the 2000s, conduits dramatically enlarged the shadow banking system and significantly contributed to the Crisis and Great Recession.

Prior to the Crisis, by early 2007, the outstanding commercial paper funding for conduits was $1.4 trillion, not insignificant! At that time, there were 29 SIVs with assets of $368 billion, and almost $100 billion was sponsored by Citigroup in five SIVs.

Structured Notes and Structured Finance

By the late 1980s, as a result of increased competition and falling margins, OTC options and swaps had evolved into structured notes and structured finance. By the early 1990s, these structured financial products played an increasingly important role and a major source of profits for the larger financial institutions globally. Financial engineering was a part of their armoury. Embedded options were used to lower funding costs and complexity meant that competitors could not easily commoditize them. This meant higher margins and profits. Developers of structured financial products need access to many markets for hedging, so customers and smaller competitors were unable to compete.

Structured notes are bonds with all sorts of weird and wonderful, creative pay outs. They can be based on almost any conceivable combination of financial instruments and indexes and almost always include swaps and embedded options. Structured finance uses securitization type processes to repackage financial assets in order to obtain higher credit ratings.

Dollar Thai Baht Linked Notes

A good example of structured notes were the Thai baht-linked structured notes issue by Credit Suisse First Boston[165] in the 1990s, and extensively described by Frank Partnoy in his book, FIASCO.[166] The notes were one-year bonds issued by a US government agency. The principal and returns were in US dollars and the notes paid 11.25%, double the returns paid by other US government agency bonds at the time. The value of the principal was, however, linked to the value of the Thai baht, so the free lunch had a cost. The Thai baht was linked to a basket of currencies and if the Bank of Thailand, the Thai central bank, kept the value of the currency within the basket, the principal would keep its US dollar value, but if the Thai baht devalued, the principal would lose value, and could be lost in entirety. These notes were bets on the Thai baht disguised as US dollar investments.

At the time, bonds denominated in Thai baht were high risk as the Thai baht could devalue, but the returns were attractive. There were institutions that took a positive view of Thailand, but were prevented from investing in Thailand, or in the Thai baht, by regulations. They could not bet on foreign currencies. These notes enabled them to bet on the Thai baht. The organizations often understood the risks, and they could buy these notes as they were AAA or AA rated and issued by a US government agency.

However, there were far more organizations that had little understanding of the risks. They included state pension funds, mutual funds, school districts, state and local governments and insurance companies, and they naïvely took the word of the First Boston salespeople that the investments were safe and state of the art. As US government agencies issued the notes, what could go wrong? They were unaware that the notes could reduce in value drastically or become valueless. They and their regulators did not recognise the words *Thai* and *baht*. It was casino banking. First Boston made millions. Customers lost billions.

The positioning of a US government agency as issuer was a sham designed to mislead investors and regulators. It provided a way to side step regulation. Furthermore, Credit Suisse First Boston had an AAA rating, so investors, shareholders and regulators were unconcerned.

In early 1997, various large Thai corporations began to buy dollars with baht. They had extensive US$ debt and wanted to ensure they could service it. Much of their debt-fuelled investment was financed by short-term US dollar loans that had to be rolled over continuously. The Bank of Thailand had supported the baht for a number of years and quickly entered the market to support it again, selling US dollars and buying baht. Before long, it had committed its entire US dollar reserves of $26 billion. While the baht had remained in the basket, investors in the Thai baht linked notes did well, however, on 2 July 1997 the Bank of Thailand abandoned the baht. The baht fell 15% immediately, and over the next year, by another 50%. Many investors were wiped out, and many Western banks panicked. They had lent excessive amounts of money to Asian banks and were concerned that they would not be repaid.

Soon after the baht collapsed, Indonesia, the Philippines and Malaysia abandoned their currencies. We must remember that South East Asia was, and remains, a mine of crony capitalism and governments had been supporting their industrialist partners by keeping rates unaligned with reality. The IMF, led by the US, engineered a $17 billion bailout for Thailand, with another $42 billion for Indonesia. So much for the war against moral hazard.

Quantos

Quantos are structured notes that pay an investor in the investor's home currency, but where the risk is a foreign currency exchange or interest rate. For example, US investors use can US dollars to place bets on the pound exchange rate or euro interest rates, and receive returns in US dollars. Why do this? Because many organizations are not permitted to bet on some or all foreign currencies, and some could only bet using their home currencies. So if you held a view on an inaccessible currency, you could place a bet using an accessible currency using a quanto, and who would know? Quantos were another way to circumvent regulation.

Frank Partnoy provides an example where the Federal Home Loan Bank of Topeka, Kansas issued $100 million in notes with coupons that paid 2*US LIBOR – UK Libor + 1.5%. The principal was to be repaid in dollars[167]. Analysing the risks is difficult as foreign currency exchange rates are correlated with home and foreign interest rates and more often than not, these risks cannot be hedged. So even sophisticated customers usually cannot quantify quanto risks.

Quantos found a way around regulation and enabled fund managers to demonstrate good up-front returns, earn attractive bonuses and then move to a new job before the downside losses surfaced, often years later.

MX Missiles

Frank Partnoy explains MX missiles well. Morgan Stanley made enormous profits from these deals. The biggest problem was hiding the details from the regulators. It was more than casino banking, it was fraud, topped off with theft.

Morgan Stanley created the missiles, called American Mortgage Investment Trusts, AMITs from two types of securities, a premium security and a discount security. A premium security is expensive and a discount security is cheap. Each AMIT contained 50% of each. Suppose the premium security is $10 per unit and the discount security $1 per unit. Thus, a product made with 1 million of each is worth $11 million and the average value of each unit is $5.50. The customer buys an AMIT for $11 million, holds it for a few days, and then sells half of it back to Morgan Stanley. However, the 1 million of the 2 million units sold back to Morgan Stanley, are sold not for $5.5, but for $10 million, as all and only the expensive securities, the one million premium securities are sold.

Fraud entered when the profit was declared. The customer stated the cost of the one million units sold back to Morgan Stanley at their average purchase cost of $5.5 per unit, or $5.5 million. The revenue was $10 million, and so the profit was $4.5 million. The customer held on to the balance of the units, worth only $1 million, and when they were sold, the sale would realize an equal and opposite loss of $4.5 million (at today's market prices). But this did not matter because the customer declared a profit today. You, the customer's executive responsible for the deal, earned a great bonus. If the maturity date of the discount part, the part you hold is twenty or thirty years into the future, that's excellent because you have your bonus, have years to find a new employer, and can retire before any losses are seen. Well done. AMITs were blatantly dishonest.

Morgan Stanley sold the first AMIT to a Japanese customer in 1992, and continued to sell AMITs through the 1990s. Profits were 1 to 2% per AMIT, tens of millions. Not bad.

The only thing left for us to do now is to show how the premium and discount securities can be put together. That's even easier than finding customers for AMITs.

Mortgage payments can be divided into interest and principal payments and securities can be created by stripping the payments apart, into IOs, the interest only parts, and POs, the principal only parts. Holders of IOs receive the interest payments and PO holders receive the principal repayments. IOs and POs are called strips. There is nothing new here. But from IOs and POs, a hybrid can be formed, an IOette, which contains a mixture of both parts, mostly IOs and a few POs.

The AMIT premium securities are IOettes. The discount securities are zero coupon bonds, bonds with no coupons and a single principal repayment at maturity.

The principal of an IOette is the sum of its POs. IOette coupons come from its IO components, which vastly outnumber the POs, so compared with the value of the POs their value is very large. For example, if the sum of the POs is $1 million, then the IOette principal is $1 million. If there are 2,000 IOs, each of which pays

5% on say $100,000, then the total of the IO returns is $10,000,000. This is the IOette return, which is ten times the IOette principal, so the price of an IOette is many times its face value. In this example, the face value is $1,000,000, but the returns over the life of typical 30-year mortgages are $300 million. There is the risk is that mortgages may be prepaid, in which case the interest paid by the IO component evaporates and falls to zero and the PO component becomes immediately available. This does not affect their values.

A zero coupon bond with a face value of $1 million is worth, say, $1,000 today. Putting this together, we see that the value of each premium security is $1 million, and each discount security is $1,000. Voila! The only thing missing from the above are fees, so add in, let's say, 4% on top.

The 1992 AMIT was so profitable for Morgan Stanley that it was called the MX missile. It sold for $571 million, the investor realized an immediate gain of $400 million and Morgan Stanley's fee was $75 million.[168] Wow!

At this stage, you may be confused, so you will understand why investors were often confused. You might try a second reading, but then again, AMITs made no sense other to enhance bonuses.

Structured notes were very successful. Their volume rose from $20 billion in 1971 to $50 billion in 1993. By the mid-1990s, structured notes had become a significant part of the medium-term funding strategies of US corporations. The details of these funding strategies were hidden from regulators and shareholders, and often buried in subsidiaries. Avoiding regulation became a driver behind margins, as customers would pay handsomely for a way around regulation, especially if they could not determine the value of the notes in the first place.

Securitizations

Structured finance repackages debt in order to sell it more efficiently. The packages, new securities, are called securitizations and the process is known as securitization. Financial institutions securitize debt by bundling mortgage debt, credit card debt, auto loans, Latin American debt, and personal and commercial loans, etc., into bonds. The securitizations are collateralized by the collateral that secures the individual pieces of debt. The debt building blocks can be anything that gives rise to recurrent repayments, and thousands of loans, typically, are bundled into a securitization. Securitizations are divided into pieces, or tranches, and sold to investors, the payments made by the individual debt holders go to the securitization, and then to the investors.

Investors pay more for securitized debt than for the original pieces of debt. Why would investors do this? Firstly, the original pieces of debt are not easily tradable. Trading loans one by one is inefficient and further, purchasers need to evaluate each loan. If loans are packaged before their sale, the process is more efficient. As investors pay a premium when readily tradable instruments are built from non-tradable instruments, securitizers can profit. Secondly, securitizers structure securitizations so that it appears that risks are lowered. Easy, as the risks are hidden in off balance sheet conduits.

To make a securitization, a conduit is created. The conduit buys the individual pieces of debt, takes the collateral and receives the debt repayments. The conduit then creates collateralized bonds and sells them to investors. The funds raised by the sale of the bonds pay for the pieces of debt, and investors earn a return based on the debt repayments. Conduits need to finance themselves, and usually do this by issuing short-term commercial paper.

The process is initiated when lenders, for example, mortgage originators, sell the loans they have made to securitizers. The sale generates funds, which are then used by lenders to make more loans. This enables lenders to focus on the process of lending. When a loan is sold, its default risk is transferred to the buyer, the conduit. When the conduit's bonds are sold to investors, the investors inherit the default risk. The process opens up investment opportunities to investors that were previously inaccessible, and expands the sources of funds available to lend.

Securitizations are bonds, but with one significant difference from traditional bonds. Traditional bonds have a face value. Interest is paid to the bondholder for the life of the bond according to a payment schedule and determined by the face value and the interest rate, which may be fixed or variable. When a bond matures, the issuer repays the face value of the bond to the bondholder, with the final interest payment. In contrast, each payment made by a securitization has a principal repayment amount and an interest payment amount, as the principal amount is amortized over the life of the securitization. Each time a payment is made, it reduces the outstanding principal. In this way, the payments made by the debt holders repay the individual loans bundled into a securitization, and there is no final repayment of principal.

When mortgage securitizations were introduced, they were pass-through securities. Monthly payments were distributed to the investors with no investor receiving any priority over any other. Ginnie Mae in 1970 was the first to issue pass-through securitizations. Later, when securitizations were divided into tranches, the tranches were sold individually and structured so they could be ordered by risk and return. Tranches are ordered by a payment priority. Investors in the highest tranche are paid in full before investors in the lower tranches receive anything, so this tranche bears the lowest risk. Then the investors in the next highest payment priority tranche are paid, so this tranche has the next lowest risk. And so on down the tranches until we reach the tranche with the lowest payment priority and the highest risk. The payment priorities are waterfall like, beginning with the tranche with the lowest risk. In the diagram the watering cans lower in the waterfall are filled with water only when those higher up are full.

There are three types of tranches: senior, mezzanine and equity (also known as junior). The senior tranches have the least risk and pay the lowest returns. The equity tranches have the highest risk and pay the highest returns. The mezzanine tranches are midway.

If there are no defaults and all scheduled payments are made in full, all tranches receive their full allocations and can fund the payments due to the investors. However, if there are defaults and some payments are not made to the conduit, the lowest tranche is the first to suffer a shortfall. If there are insufficient funds to make any payments to the lowest tranche, then the second lowest tranche suffers a payment shortfall and so on. This means that the senior tranches are protected. If the higher tranches account for say, 70% of the securitization, then there would have to be a massive 30% default rate for payment shortfalls to hit them.

Paying investors according to a payment priority enables the rating agencies to order the tranches by risk. The most senior tranches usually receive AAA ratings, and the returns might be 0.1 or 0.2% above LIBOR. At the lower end, the rating may be BB and the returns significantly more, perhaps 3% or 4% above LIBOR. Dividing a securitization into tranches facilitates its sale because the different needs of different investors can be met by selling a tranche with a risk and return profile that matches the investor's requirements.

The ratings agencies are an essential part of the securitization business. Without ratings, the securitizations would be difficult to sell. The ratings agencies had rated corporate bonds for years and were trusted by investors. Few investors are in a position to understand the risks inherent in the individual pieces of debt, and with ratings, the tranches came with accepted risk assessments and investors invested based on them.

Besides debt-collateralized securitization, there were many other kinds. For example, in 1997, David Bowie securitized his intellectual property rights. Bowie issued $55 million in 7.9% 10-year bonds collateralized by his expected royalties. He took $55 million up front and forgave tens of years of royalties that paid the interest on the bonds.

Mortgage securitizations bootstrapped the securitization business. Freddie Mac and then later, Fannie Mae entered the mortgage-backed securitization, MBS, market shortly after Ginnie Mae pioneered pass-through securitizations, and for many years, these organizations were the only organizations that securitized mortgages. Then Wall Street arrived. The US mortgage market is one of the biggest capital markets in the world and Wall Street wanted in. Wall Street developed what were called private label securitizations and in June 1993, the first private labels were introduced. GSE securitizations came with payment guarantees, but private labels did not. The demand was so high for securitized investments that guarantees did not have to be offered.

It took a while to sort out the issues, and notably Louis Ranieri, the head of the mortgage-trading desk at Salomon, steered legislation through Congress that solved the problems. It was a case of Wall Street guiding Congress towards the best interests of Wall Street, and MBS became one of the most successful Wall Street products, until the Crisis and Great Recession resulted in their markets collapsing.

The post-war baby boom had produced millions of potential homeowners, and funds had to be found for mortgages. In the 1980s, rising interest rates and deregulation had rendered the S&L industry dysfunctional, so it could not service the mortgage market. While the GSEs dominated the market for securitized conforming mortgages, private labels, with no mortgage fodder constraints and no guarantees came into their own, and the demand for private label MBS grew rapidly. Investors bought the tranches and the proceeds provided funds for mortgages.

The benefits of securitizations were many. Originators made up front fees while interest income was subject to capital requirements and was earned over time. Securitization was a volume business. Originators and securitizers could choose to retain securitizations in their own portfolios. Securitizations expanded the source of funds available to lend, and spread the risk to investors. But on the other hand, securitizations were opaque and not easy to evaluate, so investors relied on the rating agencies and their models and although the risk was supposed to be spread between thousands of investors, it became concentrated in the financial sector.

Mortgage Backed Securities

Many years ago, when an individual took out a mortgage, the mortgage repayments were paid to the originator of the mortgage, and mortgage originators paid a good deal of attention to the credit worthiness of mortgage applicants. When mortgages began to be securitized, this changed. The originator was no longer exposed to mortgage default risk for any significant time.

An MBS is a securitization built entirely from mortgages. The mortgages may be residential mortgages or commercial mortgages. The difference between the two is the collateral. Private residences collateralize residential MBSs. Offices, schools, hospitals, blocks of flats, and so on collateralize commercial MBSs. The mortgage borrower receives funds, buys property, and repays both the principal and interest over time.

MBSs have payment default risk as well as prepayment risk. When interest rates fall, a mortgaged property is usually refinanced at a lower cost. The MBS that owns the mortgage loses a payment stream, but receives the outstanding principal.

The major securitizers provided mortgage originators with warehouse lines of credit to facilitate the process. The lines enabled originators to issue mortgages, and were replenished when the mortgages were purchased by the securitizers.

An example MBS is shown in the diagram *The CMLTI 2006-NC2 MBS*.[169] New Century Financial was a large US West Coast mortgage originator focused on feeding high-return subprime mortgages to private label, Wall Street, MBSs that paid a premium.

In 2006, Citigroup purchased 4,499 mortgages from New Century Financial for $972 million. New Century used $12 million of its own funds and warehouse loans to originate the mortgages. The major lenders were Morgan Stanley ($424 million), Barclays Capital ($221 million), Bank of America ($147 million) and Bear Stearns ($64 million). New Century used the financing for two months to originate the mortgages. When Citigroup paid for the mortgages, New Century took a 2.5% commission, or $24 million, doubling its investment in two months. The balance of $948 million paid for the financing costs and repaid the warehouse lines.

The senior and mezzanine tranches paid dividends at spreads above the one-month LIBOR rate. Fannie Mae bought all the A1 tranche, and the balance of the senior tranches were sold to twenty other investors. Securitizers bought the mezzanine tranches, mostly for CDOs (which we will discuss shortly), and Citigroup retained part of the equity tranche and took a 1% commission of $9.7 million.

Tranche		S&P Rating	Spread	Some of the investors
Senior (78%)	A1	AAA	0.04	Fannie Mae
	A2-A	AAA	0.04	20 investors: China, Italy, France, Germany; a home loan bank in Chicago, a hospital, the Kentucky Retirement System and JP Morgan
	A2-B	AAA	0.06	
	A2-C	AAA	0.24	
Mezzanine (21%)	M-1	AA+	0.29	Fund managers, domestic and foreign banks, asset managers, and a CDO
	M-2	AA	0.31	
	M-3	AA-	0.34	2 CDOs; 1 asset manager
	M-4	A+	0.39	CDO, 1 hedge fund
	M-5	A	0.40	2 CDOs
	M-6	A-	0.46	3 CDOs
	M-7	BBB+	0.70	3 CDOs
	M-8	BBB	0.80	2 CDOs; 1 bank
	M-9	BBB-	1.50	5 CDOs; 2 asset managers
	M-10	BB+	2.50	3 CDOs; 1 asset manager
	M-11	BB	2.50	NA
Equity (%)	CE	Not rated		Citigroup, Capmark Finance
	P, R, Rx			Three tranches

Figure 5: The CMLTI 2006-NC2 MBS

The success of the MBS market meant industry-wide changes. New kinds of mortgages and mortgage companies came into existence. The new companies were not banks, so were outside the banking regulatory system and only lightly regulated by the SEC. Some companies promoted high lending standards and sold their mortgages to the GSEs. Others, the "hard money" lenders focused on what became the subprime market. Hard money? Yes, because the borrowers were poor, usually had poor credit histories, and their loans required large down payments. Hard money loan companies soon came to feed Wall Street aggressively with mortgages for private labels. The rates charged to borrowers were higher, so higher yields were offered to investors and Wall Street earned higher fees. Fannie and Freddie could not touch these mortgages, and did not compete. As the new companies were non-banks, they had no deposit bases, and relied on lines of credit, warehouse lines, and the short-term money markets.

Even though the GSEs were eventually permitted to buy non-conforming mortgages, almost overnight, the non-bank mortgage originators began to take significant market share. In 1989, it was just under 20%, but by 1993 it had grown to over 50%. Mortgage brokers became significant. Many non-bank originators could become far more profitable by using low cost freelance agents. Although everyone knew that loan quality would fall, as brokers pushed mortgages on to customers, origination volumes would increase dramatically, as would profits. On top of that, with S&Ls closing in droves, there were many brokers looking for work.

Interest rates in the early 1990s meant that borrowers could refinance their mortgages, and mortgage holders took new lower cost mortgages and repaid their existing, more expensive mortgages. But there was a twist. Refinancing meant that owners could also take equity from their homes. The cheaper mortgages not only repaid the more expensive mortgages, but also provided cash. Homes became piggy banks. Subprime lending became widespread and it not only financed new homeownership, but also refinanced existing homes. Soon, more than half of the subprime loans were refinancing loans, and refinancing resulted in equity being removed from the mortgaged property.

The market share of the hard moneylenders soon led to market dominance, and some were enormously successful. Subprime lending was airborne, and the volume of subprime securitizations grew. A problem was the ethics of lending to subprime borrowers. Washington wanted to make it possible for low income groups to own homes. But to do this the mortgage costs would have to be higher. What practices were legitimate? Cracking down on subprime lenders would reduce their capacity to make subprime loans. By the mid-1990s, interest rates had begun to rise, and this meant even more subprime mortgages as prime lenders withdrew from the market. The subprime business also meant other sources of revenue for the banking sector, as the successful subprime, non-bank lenders, could do IPOs MBS issuances from the 1900s through the Crisis are shown in the diagram.

As you can see, the securitization world exploded from 2001 to 2006. By 2012, as a result of the Crisis and Great Recession, it was dead.

Collateralized Debt Obligations, CDOs

Collateralized debt obligations, or CDOs are similar to MBS, but almost any form of debt serves as their fodder. CDOs are made from student loans, credit card debt, personal loans, mortgage debt and tranches of other securitizations including MBS and other CDOs. CDOs are tranched like MBSs into senior, mezzanine and equity tranches. Often the mezzanine and equity tranches of MBSs filled CDO tranches.

Although structurally similar, there are important differences as the characteristics of the underlying debt can differ in significant ways. Houses are important to us as they provide us and our families with something that we need, shelter, and a place to keep our possessions. They cannot be driven away across state and national boundaries, like cars. Students and credit card holders can move interstate and abroad. They can disappear. Generally the risks in an MBS are lower, so offered higher yields than other securitized debt products.

MBS and CDOs are examples of asset-backed securities. These are bonds that are collateralized by assets of some form, assets which are expected to retain their value and enjoy a steady payment stream.

The equity and lower mezzanine tranches of MBS and CDOs were difficult to sell as they had lower ratings, so the solution was to sell them into other CDOs. The CDO market developed at the Millennium partly as a result of moving MBS equity tranches into other securitized products, where they were retranched and sold. Equity CDO tranches magically became AAA rated as they moved up the tranched payment priority ladder, and retranching became a trillion dollar business. It permitted securitizers who had had to hold on to the lower, unsaleable equity tranches to remove them from their balance sheets. Remember *innovation* is simply a new way to make money more opaquely. It was nothing less than financial alchemy that permitted BBB tranches to become AAA CDO tranches and saleable. A slight of hand created gold from lead. In time, more than 80% of the hard to sell securitization tranches became tranches in CDOs.

When one CDO contains tranches from another CDO, it becomes a CDO-squared, or CDO^2. The CDO^2 *innovations* purchased the highest risk, highest yielding debt from CDOs, retrenched it and fed the demand for higher returns. As a result, securitizers squeezed out more yield, but at much higher risk.

When re-tranching occurs repeatedly, it increases risk across the board. The assets in the higher tranches are protected only by the payment priority ladder and as the lower tranches are high risk, they are prone to payment short falls. Preposterously safe meant in reality preposterously dangerous. This was more than ratings arbitrage, it was ratings fraud. You could start with junk bonds, then securitize, perhaps a few times, and end up with AAA bonds. After CDO²? CDO³ of course! CDOs became known as Chernobyl Death Obligations.

When CDO mangers built a CDO, they did not have to disclose all the details of the collateralizing debt until the CDO was finalized, so the contents often changed during the building and sales process. CDO managers were compensated based on the value of the CDO, regardless of the quality of its contents, so they did not care what went into them. Another source of ratings laundering.

CDOs generated millions in fees for CDO managers and issuers and the volumes rose astronomically. In 1988, $900 million in CDOs were issued, in the following year, $3 billion, and in 200 $60 trillion.[170]

Synthetic Collateralized Debt Obligations

Synthetic CDOs enable securitizers to build securities, even when there are no building blocks to build them from, when there are no raw materials. They came about when the demand for securitized investments far exceeded the supply of their raw materials. They are bets pure and simple, as an investor gambles on the performance of another CDO. Synthetic CDO returns are determined by the behaviour of a reference CDO chosen by the issuer.

Synthetic CDOs have two sides, a short side and a long side. An investor that purchases the long side receives payments from the holder of the short side and the payments mimic the payments made by the reference CDO. The holder of the long side is a seller of insurance. The long side holder receives premiums from the short side holder, and if the reference CDO fails, the long side holder pays the short side holder and covers the failure. The long side owner is like an investor and the short side owner a debt holder. As there is no actual debt, the short side holder could be another investor, a CDO or synthetic CDO or the instrument's securitizer!

Synthetic CDOs are a way of generating something from nothing and they greatly extended the problems of the Great Recession. As there were no limits on what they referenced, they were risk multipliers. When the CDO markets collapsed during the Crisis, the hundreds of billions of dollars in CDO losses translated into trillions of dollars when the synthetic CDO losses were tallied in. One of the reasons that they were popular was that you did not have to go to the trouble of actually making a loan in the first place!

MBSs are comprised of mortgages and mortgages serve a purpose. MBSs enable homeowners to finance their homes. This is not the case for synthetic CDOs. They have no underlying social or economic value.

During the years before the Crisis, synthetic CDOs were spider webs of risk. Wall Street, however, sold them as securities, as safe and secure as Treasury bills. But synthetic CDOs existed solely to make bets. They exponentially increased leverage and when they did touch reality, the pieces of reality they touched were poorly written subprime mortgages given to households that could not afford them.

Credit Derivatives

As new exotic products were developed by one organization, others would mimic the product and margins would collapse. So as competition in the mid-1990s pushed up against profits, many banks wanted to expand and develop the derivatives business. Default risk was the largest risk that commercial lending banks took, so JP Morgan, Bankers Trust and Merrill Lynch developed derivatives that enabled a bank to sell off the default risk associated with bonds and loans, and of course to bet on it.

Traditionally, most banks had managed credit default risk carefully. Credit officers went through extensive training, loans were often syndicated and made to a diverse customer base, and credit limits were strictly enforced. The big question was how could derivatives help manage credit default risk? If default risk could be reduced or eliminated by using derivatives, banks could save capital, free up credit lines, and lend again. Lending with the same capital levels meant higher profits.

The short-term repo and commercial paper markets had developed, and corporations had begun to finance their operations more cheaply by exploiting them. Furthermore, corporations began to rely on lines of credit, loans that could be drawn down in times of need, precisely at the times when banks did not want drawdowns. Some loans were higher risk than others, and rather than fret about the problem, it made sense to sell the risk off.

In 1994, JP Morgan did its first credit default swap. The counterparty was the European Bank for Reconstruction and Development.[171] Exxon, had drawn down on a $5 billion credit line, and JP Morgan removed the default risk by paying premiums to the European Bank, which assumed the risk. In was a win-win. JP Morgan lowered its corporate loan risk, and lent the funds again. The Bank earned premiums.

There were tens of thousands of banks exposed to default risk, and JP Morgan saw an opportunity to earn revenues by providing a way for the banking industry as a whole to transfer default risk from balance sheets to investors, so it developed the BISTRO, the first marketable credit default swap, or CDS. Regulatory capital would be lower, credit limits freed up, and default risk better managed. More loans could be made and profits so increased. BISTROs signalled a fundamental change in the way banks do business.[172]

The market for BISTRO style CDS grew quickly. By December 1997, US banks had booked $100 billion BISTRO deals, by March 1998, the volume had grown to $300 billion globally, and JP Morgan accounted for $50 billion of this total. Eventually CDSs became a way for the market to determine the price of default risk. As we will see, CDSs bootstrapped the MBS and CDO markets. These products securitized a wide range of debt instruments, and CDSs became a way of insuring them.

The buyer of a CDS pays a premium to the seller, who agrees to insure the covered debt and compensate the insurer if the debtor fails to pay. The debt can be any bond or similar fixed income security. Monoline insurance companies had provided insurance against the failure of municipal bonds since 1971, and this enabled municipalities to borrow more cheaply, but with CDSs any organization could obtain or provide insurance on just about any kind of fixed income security. The monolines insured a bond only if you owned it. But using CDSs, you could buy insurance on any financial instrument regardless of whether you owned it or not. You could also insure against the demise of organizations and the markets.

CDS insurance is unlike normal insurance. There are no deductibles, policy limits, and higher premiums if you have a bad claim record, or smoke or are overweight! There is no need to own the insured asset. It's like buying fire insurance on your neighbour's house, and doing so for many times its value. It incentivizes you to be an arsonist. The seller of a CDS does not hold a reserve against a default, so you could buy a CDS on almost anything. CDSs were rabbits. They could multiply as there was no limit on the number of contracts and no limit on the amounts insured. One could insure a $1 million bond one hundred times, and generate an exposure of $100 million. And of course, this happened, as it was a way in which derivatives dealers could make profits. As the CDS market is unregulated and opaque, we can only guess at the total number of CDSs or their aggregate value.

The concept was flawed from the outset. Even the name was a sham. CDSs were called swaps even though they were insurance contracts because swaps qualified for regulatory exemptions! As there were no limits, by the Crisis, AIG Financial Products, AIG FP, the division of AIG that developed AIG's financial derivatives, had outstanding insurance coverage commitments of $500 billion. AIG, the parent, had no understanding of the business and was not capable of ingesting the implications. AIG FP could not price the swaps and had no risk assessment capability. And neither did the rating agencies. There were no controls. It was a free for all, and unconstrained profits alone drove the business.

AIG FP and the monolines sold insurance for all tranches: the senior, mezzanine and equity tranches. The senior tranches[173] bore little risk and the premiums were small. The assumption was that it would take an enormous catastrophe for defaults to eat up all the equity and mezzanine tranches. But eventually, so much senior debt was insured that the exposure became significant. AIG's demise was a consequence of AIG FP not holding any reserves, sufficient or otherwise against these exposures. The problem was exacerbated, as AIG FP's regulator was the OTS, a weak regulator, with no expertise at all in any of the new financial products, including CDSs. Over time, AIG FP itself became concerned with the exposure, and pushed the cost up from 0.02 cents per dollar to 0.11 cents. But it was too late, and a mere drop in the ocean.

CDSs enabled credit wraps. In order to aid sales, a securitizer could *wrap* tranches with a CDS insurance contract. An investor could take on the risks in an MBS or CDO, and insure against default using a CDS. Although this appeared to be a good strategy, it too was flawed. No matter how you looked at equity tranches, they were fundamentally toxic, with a high probability of sustaining losses. Someone was going to lose.

It was clear from the outset that credit derivatives, and CDOs, harboured problems. Without credit derivatives, Enron, WorldCom and Global Crossing, would not have been able to borrow so much, and excessive borrowing was a significant factor in bringing each of these organizations to their knees. WorldCom debt made up 75% of the CDO debt rated by S&P. For Moody's 58% of synthetic CDOs had exposure to WorldCom debt.

Derivatives do not eliminate risk, they spread it about, but as Wall Steet sold derivatives within Wall Street, the risk became concentrated. When WorldCom collapsed, insurance companies were exposed to one third of its debt. The unintended consequence was that credit derivatives moved default risk from where it could be managed to those who were less capable of managing it. Risk moved to the less regulated and increased instability.

Models, Value at Risk and Black-Scholes

Most risk assessments use models, so in the final section of this chapter, we will look at models and examine two of those commonly used, the pernicious VaR market risk model, and the Black Scholes options pricing model. VaR is a good example of how absurd things can become. The use and reliance of VaR became ubiquitous, but provided few benefits, was a source of widespread misunderstanding, and led many organizations and people down the garden path. Black Scholes provided good and useable information in a few circumstances, so stood apart from VaR. However, its limitations were rarely taken into account.

Models are used when we have no direct way of finding the results that we want. For example, when trying to predict the weather we can neither identify, nor measure all the factors, nor have a way of tying them together. So we use a model, something that within limits, approximates weather conditions. Models are things that approximate reality.

There are two issues that arise for all models used in finance. First, there is the effectiveness, or accuracy of the model itself and then there is the data upon which the model relies.

All models make assumptions and are designed to work within limits, boundary conditions. When the assumptions do not hold, or the boundary conditions transgressed, the model cannot be relied upon. Furthermore, there is a widespread belief that even though a model provides poor results, as the model is all we have, we can use it. This is as off the wall as the proposal that as we only have contaminated water to drink, we must then drink it! Many products like CDOs are not understood and as a consequence, CDO valuation models are poor. The CDO debt mix, for example, aircraft leases, student loans and mobile home loans, etc., does not provide diversification, but the ratings agency models all relied upon the fact that they did. Even though the assumptions did not hold, these models were, and are used.

An issue with model data is that it is historic. If historic data is not applicable to today's conditions, then it is of little value. An example of this is using historic mortgage default data to predict mortgage defaults today. Apart from a few blips, since the Great Depression, the US property market has experienced continuous growth. The historic data reflects a seventy five year upward trend. But this is not relevant to current conditions. Mortgage origination standards have dropped through the floor, the value of residential property has fallen substantially, there are new types of mortgages, and failures in the regional housing markets across the US are more correlated than the historic data assumes. The effects of defaults are far more severe than the historic data suggests.

Value at Risk, VaR

JP Morgan developed VaR. Dennis Weatherstone, who had been a trader in London, became CEO in 1990 and was faced with the problem of determining the bank's overall trading, or market risk. He wanted to understand whether the operations of one trading desk offset or added to the risks taken by another. Remember that banks had been lending money to customers for centuries, but market risks were relatively new. They arose when banks trade financial products for short-term gain and trading was barely ten years old. Weatherstone wanted to see a consolidated picture. A trader, Till Guildermann, came up with VaR. The 4:15 Report reported VaR for all trading desks in the JP Morgan empire. It came fifteen minutes after the close of trading operations in New York, well after the trading operations in Europe and Asia had ceased.

VaR was not assumed to be the be all and end all, although it did become a central part of the bank's risk assessment methodology. VaR aggregated market risk into a single number and could be applied to portfolios, departments, trading desks and traders. VaR overcome the disadvantages of the numerous other measures like bond duration, which applied only to bonds. JP Morgan made the details public, and soon VaR became the de facto industry standard for measuring market risk. It was used to persuade bank management and regulators that banks were taking on very little market risk.

VaR is a statistical concept and states probabilistically a portfolio's loss for a period of time. So to say that the 99% one day VaR is $10 million, is to say there is a 1% chance that tomorrow's loss (that is for the one day period) will be at least $10 million.

Right from the outset there were misunderstandings. Very few understood what VaR said, and what it did say was very little. Some thought that VaR stated that the maximum loss for the time period. But it clearly did not. The maximum loss, the loss of the entire capital base means bankruptcy. Moreover, there were issues over how to calculate it. The first calculations assumed that profits and losses followed what we know in statistics as a Normal distribution. But this assumption does not hold. Later calculations assumed that VaR could be calculated using historic data. Again, this assumption does not hold. But even though these assumptions were known to be false, billions of dollars were spent building computer systems assuming one or other, or both. Why? There were no alternatives. VaR was all there was.

Whatever the calculations delivered, it was not VaR, and some even proposed that whatever was being calculated was a good and helpful market risk measure. Not surprisingly, many of the proponents of this view were employees engaged in the ongoing VaR calculation efforts.

What does VaR do or mean? One early response was:

> A number invented by purveyors of panaceas for pecuniary peril intended to mislead senior management and regulators into false confidence that market risk is adequately understood and controlled.[174]

What does it mean to say that a loss of a particular amount has a particular probability? What does it mean to say that there is a 1% chance of a $10 million or more loss tomorrow? Some assumed that it means that there will be a loss of $10 million every one hundred or so (business) days. But this is not what the probability statement says. What it says is that for an infinite sequence of occurrences of the *same event*, a loss of $10 million or more, will come about 1% of the time. We may sustain this loss each day for each of the next two hundred days, or two hundred billion days, or we may sustain no losses at all for a trillion consecutive days. Clearly, a one-day VaR of $10 million is consistent with losses of $100 million, or $1 billion the following day! So even if we had good reason for thinking that the VaR statement was true, this is all we could conclude, and this is not helpful. Twisting this around by saying that this really means something else, perhaps that large losses are not likely, or are improbable, is nonsense. The use of probabilities simply disguises reality. As Lawrence Peter said, "Facts are stubborn things, but statistics are more pliable".[175] And of course, what does *same event* mean?

What about the calculation? Benoit Mandelbrot, the mathematician who explored ways to predict weather patterns and the shifting borders between the sea and a beach, showed that Normal distributions do not exist in nature. So calculating VaR based on Normal distribution assumptions is not even close. Today, calculating VaR based on normality assumptions has largely gone by the wayside. But historic data based calculations remain widely used even though they are more misleading. Using historic data assumes patterns that have occurred in the past reoccur, night follows day so to speak. But this is precisely what we do not want. We want to know our risk, we want to know about surprises!

Let's assume, for the moment, that using historic data can get us somewhere. One of the many problems that surfaces is that historic data is always incomplete. What to do? We make it up! Suppose that we have acquired a share position in an initial public offering of a company. The VaR calculation methodology says that we need a minimum of five hundred days past share price history. We do not have this, so we take the share price on the floatation date and use that price for each of the past five hundred days. This does not ever work, and everyone knows it. When the shares in an IPOs begin to trade, their prices are volatile. To artificially set the price at a constant for an entire five hundred day history grossly misstates the data. Why do we do this? Because we cannot think of anything better, even though we know this procedure cannot provide a sensible result.

Nassim Nicholas Taleb developed Black Swan theory. Black Swans are catastrophic events that are beyond the expectation of what our theories and assumptions can tell us. Black Swans are difficult to predict and sometimes seem to be random. They come as surprises, but they have major impacts. They are the events that we want to know about. John Stuart Mill pointed out that while there may be very many confirming instances of the statement *all swans are white*, as soon as one comes across a single Black Swan, then this observation refutes it. We had to wait until we discovered Australia to see that the claim was false. The message is that we need more than historic data!

Extreme events, Black Swans are far more common than what VaR theory predicts. They occur far more often than we have assumed. Price extremes are more common than any VaR calculation has shown, and are unpredictable. Was the Russian default a Black Swan? The models did not predict it, but it is Russian defaults we want to know about. Black Swans are really white, but beyond out current prediction capabilities as Noriel Roubini states.[176]

If one asks why were Normal distributions or historic data assumed? The answer is simple and revealing. The study of statistics has defined many distributions, but the Normal distribution is one of the easiest to describe, and it's the distribution that we know most about. So it seems that even though we knew that neither calculation methodology could provide a basis for the calculation of a VaR, they were easy to use, so they were embraced. The Crisis gave us an explicit counter example. In October 2008, the DJIA dropped more than 10% in two days. According to Normal distribution theory, and the historic data, the chance of this happening is between one in 73 to 603 trillion! Notably, the 2008 VaRs of Lehman, Merrill and Bear did not raise any alerts and all three failed!

Even the Basel Committee was off track. It incorporated in its acceptability requirements for VaR calculations that an X% VaR was acceptable if the calculated VaR actually occurred one in every 100/X business days, *more or less*![177] A Muppet show in the making.

We will wrap up this discussion after we look at Black-Scholes.

Black-Scholes

Optionality in finance was and is ubiquitous. When the use of options increased with the expansion of the derivatives markets, a way had to be found to value them. Options are more valuable when the price of the underlying is volatile and less valuable when the market in the underlying is flat. But until the early 1980s, there was no accepted way of evaluating options generally, or determining their risks. Even though many of the biggest players wanted to expand the trading of derivatives, what constrained the markets was not knowing how to value them. As portfolios could not be valued, managers were unable to control traders and put limits on what they could and could not do.

Fischer Black and Myron Scholes published a paper in 1973, and Robert Merton and Myron Scholes were awarded the Nobel Prize in Economics in 1997. Merton died a few years before it could be conferred upon him. The Black-Scholes model for evaluating options was born, and by the 1980s, quantitative financial engineering, performed by mathematical proficient geeks had become the rage, and Black-Scholes became widely used to value options. It became the holy grail. Clever Texas Instrument hand calculators, churned out the results of Black-Scholes calculations, and proliferated in dealing rooms. Even though the underlying Black-Scholes assumptions limited its application, no one cared. Everyone used Black-Scholes. If the value of a portfolio was misstated, it was OK as everyone misstated it. The formulas looked good, and you could pull the wool over any manger's eyes. Lots of integral and differential signs.

What Black-Scholes did was to determine the value of a financial contract before it came to term. If prices for contracts could be established, they could be traded. Derivatives could thus be priced before they matured, especially options, the simplest and oldest form of derivative.

The insight behind the Black-Scholes model was the assumption that an option could be perfectly hedged, and hence priced. Its price was the cost of the hedge. In many cases, it has given us a reasonable first approximation.

The problem with Black-Scholes is not that the model cannot be made to work, it is that it is misused. It is misused when its limitations, which are clear, are ignored. When market conditions and the Black-Scholes limitations intersect, the model can be relied upon to lead to a sensible result, a good first guess. We must remember that models are never reality, but approximations, so Black-Scholes was never intended to tell the whole story. When market conditions and the model's limitations do not tightly intersect, very often adjustments can be made, in which case the model can be relied upon.

Black-Scholes does not claim to price all options, only European options. European options, which trade in the OTC markets, can only be exercised at maturity. American style options can be exercised at any time on or prior to their maturity date. They are traded on exchanges. Options on bonds and currencies were also problems.

Black-Scholes ties together four variables: the time to maturity of the option, the price of the underlying, the risk-free interest rate, and the price volatility of the underlying. The first three we know, and we say they are observable. But price volatility, which the model assumes remains constant for the life of the option, can only be estimated. In order to demonstrate that the required assumptions were rarely accommodated, we will set many of them out. Generally, Black-Scholes assumes:

- That there is a risk free rate, the rate of interest we earn on an investment that is without risk

- That it is possible to borrow or lend an unlimited amount of money at the risk free rate. This is unrealistic

- That it is possible to buy or sell an unlimited amount of the underlying. This also is unrealistic. In fact, it's impossible.

- That stock price changes always follow what we call random walks. The stock price goes up or down with determinable probabilities. This does not happen.

- That any underlying stock or other instrument pays no dividend. But most do, and moreover those that do not can be sources of income. For example, although there are costs when selling short, revenue can be generated by stock lending.

- That there are no transaction costs, even though there always are.

- That many variables follow a normal probability distribution, which they do not

- That a perfect hedge, a hedge without arbitrage is possible, but in reality hedges are dynamic

- Black Swans are not accommodated, but their effects are drastic. Although stock market crashes are rare, Black-Scholes assumes they never occur. But they do.

- The markets must be liquid

Although, in each of these cases, it is often possible to make an adjustment and preserve the model's validity, this is not a practice, so Black-Scholes does not deliver sensible results.

Another major failing is the volatility smile. Black-Scholes determines different volatiles for different values of its variables. If volatilities are graphed against the other variables, when the underlying is a currency, the graph looks like a smile. For stocks, the graph is skewed and for commodities, it is something else again. The upshot is that different underlyings are given different volatilities when they should be constant, and the variations depend on the underlying instrument. In technical language, we say that the volatility surface should be flat, but it is not.

Apart from all these issues, Black-Scholes became a fixture. Why? The major reason was that the options and derivatives markets needed a valuation method. Another was that Black-Scholes prices could be calculated easily, by using hand held calculators and desktop computers. Another is that in many circumstances, it was a good first approximation. Another reason was that in 1980s, academic, mathematical finance needed models, and here was one and it did not matter that it was all we had. Another was that bankers did not understand Black-Scholes, but believed that as it had been developed by a few university professors with PH.Ds it must make sense. When Myron and Scholes won the Nobel Prize, the Black-Scholes model became unassailable. The problem was, and is that bankers are not clever.

The model provided an industry-standard that could be used to assess the value of financial derivatives with optionality, and became a pillar for enormous economic growth. It was one of the reasons why *innovation* went virile. By 2007, the derivatives market was $1,000 trillion annually, ten times the value, adjusted for inflation, of all products made by the world's manufacturing industries during the last century.[178]

The fact that static perfect hedges are an illusion is a key to a wider problem, a problem that underscores all the problems listed above. The model assumes that quantities are infinitely divisible, that time flows continuously and that variables change smoothly. This sounds esoteric, but these assumptions are significant, and are the kinds of assumptions made by mathematical physicists. And it's not surprising that they have been made. Part of the academic mathematical finance program was to make economics like physics. However, the assumptions are unfounded. Ian Stewart, for example, tells us that we need financial models to take into account the effects of herd behaviour, where traders copy other traders. This is clearly something that our current models do not do, but herd behaviour plays a significant role in market behaviour, and pushing financial crises, including the Crisis, over the edge. All is OK until the chief lemming jumps, and then everything collapses, together. It's a consequence of the instability of what is modelled. This instability is not ubiquitous. One airplane crash does not lead to a string of others. But this did occur during the Crisis, and Black-Scholes became a loss generator.

There are also other assumptions in need of justification. In practice, money is not infinitely divisible. This matters. Individuals take yes – no decisions, and sometimes equivocate. In these cases, variables do not change smoothly. All models that rely only on the assumptions of mathematical physics cannot represent the unstable reality well. As a consequence, the financial sector has done little more than guessed its way forward.

Prior to Black-Scholes options pricing was heuristic, and the evidence today is that heuristic pricing does a much better job than Black-Scholes. No one cared that the Black-Scholes assumptions were way off base, and in reality it was not only not needed, it was not even widely used.[179] But this does not distract from its impact.

So what can we make of all this? We will see in later sections that much of what bankers say is nonsensical and self-serving. They hide behind the perceived complexity of finance and issue pronouncements substantiated by opaque and often meaningless claims. The two models discussed here have no rationale, and no justification, but enabled bankers to push forward with revenue generation. This practice characterizes our financial world today.

Derivatives and Social Value

In 2002, Warren Buffet described derivatives as financial weapons of mass destruction.[180] Do derivatives have any utility or social value? While it is clear that futures on commodities have a purpose and satisfy a real need, there is no need for synthetic CDOs. Investing in the long side or short side of a synthetic CDO is simply placing a bet. They do not assist mortgage origination, the issuance of student loans or credit cards. No one would be granted a loan because of a synthetic CDO investment. They do not create growth, but have enormous downsides. Similarly, unconstrained CDSs simply magnify the downside. So what are the derivatives that we should be able to use, and rely upon? We will try to answer this in the last chapter of this book.

No New Bangsters Again

Once again, we have found no new Bangsters in this chapter, and the tables remain the same. The current awards remain:

Bangsters	Gold Stars
Nicholas Biddle	Franklin D Roosevelt
JP Morgan	Louis Brandeis

5

Change

European colonialism driven by profits, but justified by Christianity, culture and table manners had followed an expansionist and exploitive political agenda. While the colonized suffered disease and death, subjugation, discrimination and displacement, London rose above the squalor and by World War I had become the centre of the globe. By the 1980s, New York had become the centre of the globe's investment management business, Chicago the centre of exchange-traded futures and options and London had developed from its century's old entrepôt beginnings into an insurance and universal banking hub.

Since the Great Depression, industry had needed three kinds of financing. Short-term loans were provided by commercial banks. Long-term financing, achieved by issuing bonds, and equity financing were provided by investment banks. The US debt was held by the federal and local governments, consumers and corporations and rose significantly in the 1980s. In 1977, it was $323 million, but by 1985, it was $7 trillion.[181]

Prior to the 1980s, commercial banks issued little corporate debt, and were not large organizations. The financial assets held by the US investment banking industry were small by today's standards too, and their assets accounted for less than 2% of US GDP. The US GDP had grown at 4% annually from the end of World War II. This was all to change.

After the trying times of the 1970s, inflation began to take its toll on the commercial banking sector. The markets had remained simple as the age of large trading profits was still to come. Deregulation had become a part of the political agenda of the Reagan administration in the US, and Margaret Thatcher's *nation of shopkeepers* in the UK. Deregulation would remove constraints on what financial products and services could be offered, and which institutions could offer them. Some floated the idea that without change, the current financial system would not be able to evolve and support economic development. World War II had resulted in tumultuous disruptions, but that was in the past, and it was now time to move forward. Technology was taking us towards globalization, and finance needed to be part of it.

The first major issue was Regulation Q. Inflation driven interest rate increases were putting commercial banks and S&Ls out of business. Inflation peaked at 13% in 1981, but the Regulation Q cap remained at 6%, and depositors were moving funds into accounts in the investment banking sector, into accounts not subject to the cap. The commercial banks reacted with new products like money market and NOW accounts, but it was not sufficient to stem the haemorrhaging of funds from the deposit takers into the lightly regulated shadow banking system. So Congress disposed of Regulation Q, deposit insurance was increased from $40,000 to $100,000 and various other measures introduced to shore up the commercial banking system. It was not enough and some failed. As a consequence, many questioned the viability of deposit taking banks. Perhaps it was just not sufficient to rely on cheap depositor funds, and perhaps other sources of income were needed. Bank lending returns were volatile, so they needed to find new ways to profit. Providing investment bank products and services to existing customers seemed to make sense, and from the 1990s, the commercial banks did just this. Furthermore, US commercial banks began to trade on their own accounts. First in London, where the GSA did not apply, and then in New York. Fearing that Wall Street might lose ground to the City,[182] the FED deregulated them and in doing so permitted deposit takers to expand across state lines. The changes substantially increased their risk profiles, risk profiles that were FDIC guaranteed. The deposits became exposed to investment bank risks and trading, and opened up a completely new world of risk.

Automation also played an important role. It enabled the expansion of bank customer bases and transaction banking. Relationship banking, always expensive, was not cost effective and the 1980s saw a transition from relationship banking to transaction banking. Cross border banking needed it, as did trading from multiple banking centres. Mini computers had given departments their own computing facilities and restructured how organizations used computers and data centres. Mini computers enabled cross border and multi-jurisdictional banking. They were a way that local and departmental requirements could be efficiently implemented.

The FDIC legacy, the thousands of small city and state banks were not without problems. In 1984, Continental Illinois, the seventh largest bank in the nation with assets of $40 billion failed. It was not alone and so many banks failed, that by 1988, bank failures were at a post Great Depression high. For the first time in its history, the FDIC sustained a loss, and losses continued until 1991. This reinforced the doubts about how deposit takers did business.

By the Millennium, we had returned to the irresponsible gambling and extreme wealth generation characteristic of the period before the stock market crash of 1929. Ethics were shelved as banks began to deploy the missiles described in the previous chapter. The stability of post-World War II banking was left behind.

Finance's New Academic Face

Behind the scenes, there were significant developments. In the late 1960s, academics had developed theories about how financial markets worked. They said that markets were *efficient* and that the value of financial assets reflected the available *information*. This was the Efficient Market Hypothesis, the EMH, but it's difficult to understand what it actually meant. Indeed a number of interpretations were promulgated.[183] The weak EMH stated that the price at which an asset trades reflects all publicly available information.[184] But what could this mean? What did *information* encompass? Clearly, some investors would buy or sell financial assets based upon the information they possessed. Clearly some did not. But assuming all did what explanatory value does the weak EMH have? It seems to state that the decisions taken by the investment community are informed. But this is clearly not always the case. The EMH was an attempt to say something meaningful, but relied upon the concept of *information*, so only kicked the can down the road.

A stronger statement added that prices at which financial assets trade change *instantly* in order to reflect new publicly available information. This again, apart from the *instantly* qualification, states what is obvious. However, prices do not always change *instantly*, otherwise we would see no arbitrage opportunities. Some prices change over long periods of time. Take the value of your home, for example. Markets are able to digest equity related earnings data quickly, but for assets like land, businesses and some pension funds, the market is slow when it comes to valuing them. However, does this really matter? Prices often do change and change as new information becomes available, and price changes are often driven by the new information. But, we knew this already. The strong EMH was taken by some to mean that there was never sufficient information available for one to predict the markets, and so the price of an asset could only be its market price. A cop out!

What we knew as the Chicago school became dominant and promoted economics as a science like physics, with testable, empirical hypotheses. Markets were *rational* in some sense and *efficient* and a job of economists was to explain this. Economic test tube experiments would validate economic theories, albeit that they could often not be replicated. Hopefully, we could discover economic theories that would enable continual growth by scientific economics, avoid booms and busts, keep populations employed and control inflation. Some Chicago zealots promoted this financial fundamentalism with religious zeal. Economic resources were to be organised by free markets, with minimal government interference. Quantitative monetary theory would resolve the challenges of unemployment, inflation, and growth. The dogma was camouflaged by science, mathematics and integral signs.

By the 1970s, academic finance was being taught in universities and mathematics was used to propose answers to all manner of questions, ranging from financial statement analysis and product pricing, to policy and growth expectations. The door was opened for new products like interest rate swaps and currency options. Mathematically anchored financial consulting changed banking and the non-financial industries. Consultants, including investment bank consultants, addressed questions like how much capital was needed. How much debt? How should we balance increased returns with increased debt and leverage? Technology and quantitative finance joined forces to enable desktop pricing for products that were forever increasing in complexity.

Academic finance resulted in new tools, new sources of revenue, new markets and, importantly, lent credibility to a new ideology. This was a time when it was not difficult to publish academic research papers on mathematical finance. If there was minimal intelligibility, the greater the obscurity of a paper, and the more exotic the subject, the higher the chance that it would be considered seminal. Lots of integral signs made publication a certainty.

The (strong) EMH became a justification for deregulation. A consequence of the EMH was that unencumbered markets determined asset prices, so regulated markets interfered with prices and did not allocate risk in an efficient manner, whatever that meant. This argument lent support for market liberalization and the free flow of capital across borders, including into the developing countries. With no regulation, banks could do as they pleased, itself a refutation of the EMH. The EMH also said that traders could not outperform the markets, contrary to reality. Some traders consistently did so. Some traders used better models than others did, but this only gave them an advantage.

The problem was that the Chicago school legitimized an approach to finance that had quite limited application and benefits. The reason behind the initial success of academic finance had more to do with being blindsided by mathematics than reality. What was missed was that markets can defy any understanding. They can appear to have no logic, to be idiots. Perhaps, like some humans! At the end of the day, mathematical finance and its plethora of models underestimated risks, mis-stated them and missed them. And no consideration was paid to high impact rare events, nor to the human lemming effect, nor the actual markets. It was ungrounded ideology.

The enthusiasm for mathematical finance and its models had its critics, and was soon to be seen for what it as, and limited value in value. Thomas Piketty, discussing the contributions of Kuznets tells us that

> ...optimistic conclusions ... the profession's undue enthusiasm for simplistic mathematical models based on so called representative agents,[185] and

> To put it bluntly, the discipline of economics has yet to get over its childish passion for mathematics and for purely theoretical and often highly ideological speculation, at the expense of historical research and collaboration with the other social sciences.[186]

Pablo Triana[187] says that the financial terrain is untameable and lawless. It is fraught with unexpected and unimaginable monstrous rare events, which actively shape the markets, and historic data cannot help us much with predictions. The financial terrain cannot be tamed by mathematics. One cannot help compare the recent attempts to do so with the past and thankfully forgotten attempts to model the brain with today's mathematical concepts. Many aspects of mathematical finance have the empirical basis of astrology. That is none. Quantitative risk modelling is not only a forlorn exercise, it is dangerous, and theory gone wild. Mark-to market valuations for complex derivatives are of little value and dangerous. The Basel attempts to quantify capital quantification are simply wrong. Consider sovereign debt.

As we have seen banks should simply not be permitted to do what they want:

> ...banks should not be allowed to do as they pleased, financial innovations were [not] necessarily good, and that free financial markets would [not] always produce optimal social outcomes. ... it might have remained only a cry in the academic wilderness or an esoteric Wall Street doctrine ... it had the fortune of

being in the right place at the right time … [And we will consider later that] Reagan made deregulation an ideological crusade[188]

The S&Ls, Ideology and Deregulation

Reagan's program of deregulation was ideologically driven. "Government is not the solution to our problem," he announced in his inaugural address, "government is the problem".[189] Less government in the private sector would enable it to become more productive, and more creative. We would all be better off. He thus spearheaded an attack on financial regulation, cutting budgets and staff, and their leadership, and installed political leaders that would pursue a deregulated free-for-all financial sector. Donald Regan, the CEO of Merrill Lynch, became Treasury Secretary. Regan was an ideological zealot. My top priority is "the deregulation of financial institutions … trying to deregulate as soon as possible in the field of interest rates, mandatory ceilings, things of that nature.[190] The financial services industry had inherited regulation enacted in the 1930s, but rather than modernize it, Reagan wanted to eliminate it. The Chicago School gave his program credibility.

He started with the S&Ls. When inflation took a grip in the 1970s, Regulation Q meant that their deposits moved to money market accounts, as we have discussed. When Congress removed Regulation Q, and many of the differences between the S&Ls the other deposit takers were eliminated, life for the S&Ls was supposed to be easier. Interstate S&L and commercial bank mergers were permitted and they were permitted to offer checking accounts and commercial loans. They could invest in corporate bonds, including junk bonds, and offered adjustable rate mortgages with few restrictions When signing the legislation, President Reagan said:

> This bill is the most important legislation for financial institutions in the last 50 years. It provides a long-term solution for the troubled thrift institutions … it means help for housing, more jobs, and new growth for the economy. Overall, I think we hit the jackpot.
>
> This bill also represents the first step in our administration's comprehensive program of financial deregulation. What this legislation does is expand the powers of thrift institutions by permitting the industry to make commercial loans and increase their consumer lending. It

reduces their exposure to changes in the
housing market and in interest rate levels. This
in turn will make the thrift industry a stronger,
more effective force in financing housing for
millions of Americans in the years to come.[191]

A politically influential industry had used its might to back
Reagan's program. Senator William Proxmire, chairman of the
Senate Banking Committee, called it "sheer bribery" on national
television.[192] Although life was supposed to be easier,
deregulation created a wild west. It became no holds barred, and
life became much harder, and the industry suffered a major crisis.
Fraud surfaced as struggling S&Ls scrambled to survive.

S&Ls made new kinds of speculative investments. They
invested in junk bonds, other high-risk bonds and derivatives. The
S&L management teams and their regulators did not understand
the high-risk products. (Few did). They were out of their depth.
Some simply incompetent, and most ill-informed.

The cost of short-term funding increased while S&L incomes
remained capped. Their mortgages were mostly fixed rate. S&Ls
failed in droves. At one, stage two-thirds of them were insolvent,
but accounting practices disguised the problems. Between 1980
and 1982, 118 S&Ls failed[193] and as we said, by the early 1990s a
further 747 of 3,234 S&Ls had failed. The cost of the failures grew
quickly to $153 billion.[194] As the S&Ls had lent significant funds to
property developers, when S&Ls failed so too did developers.
Washington had to step in.

Commercial banks also failed. Between 1985 and 1992 more
than 1,600 failed as a result of a lethal mix of deregulation, risk
taking, mismanagement and fraud. 534 failed in 1989 alone,[195]
contrasting with the 79 failures in total in the decade, 1970 to
1980. The commercial banking system had become non-
competitive.

The S&L regulator had to make enormous payments to the
depositors in failed S&Ls and despite a $10 billion bailout from
Washington in 1986, it too failed. The FDIC came to the rescue and
a new regulator, the OTS, was created. The S&Ls were required to
hold more capital, and restrictions on investments were put in
place. However, the change of regulator was little more than a
change of name, and the problems continued. The OTS was the
same OTS that regulated AIG, Countrywide and Washington Mutual
in the 2000s!

The S&L crisis was the first real crisis since the Great
Depression. Its catalyst was deregulation. There was little

likelihood that the problems would have occurred absent deregulation. It was a stark condemnation of Regan's deregulatory policy. Reagan and his dogmatic administration had no clue.

The overall cost of the S&L crisis, in inflation adjusted dollars grew to $340 billion, a cost that was met by taxpayers. Millions lost their life savings.

There were other problems too. Rather than admit insolvency, some S&L CEOs resorted to creative accounting schemes to make their businesses appear sound so that they could attract investors, when in fact they were losing money hand over fist. Relaxed regulation made fraud easy, and over 1,000 S&L employees went to jail. Ernst and Young and Arthur Anderson paid large settlements. Charles Keating became a household name. The S&L he ran, Lincoln Savings and Loans Association, failed and left Washington with a $3 billion bill, and 23,000 customers with worthless bonds. He spent four and a half years in jail for fraud. Neil Bush, the son of President George H. W. Bush and brother of President George W Bush cost taxpayers $1.3 billion. He was lucky as he avoided jail, and only paid fines.

Although Reagan was out of office by the 1990s, his administration had facilitated the adoption of mathematical finance into political philosophy and dogma. People such as Alan Greenspan, Robert Rubin and Larry Summers maintained this ideology for more than a decade. The collapse of the Soviet Union in 1989 further underscored the popular view that free market capitalism had the answers.

The S&L crisis and the failure of many commercial banks were not isolated events. They were a sign of problems to come, and in the 1990s, there was an unprecedented succession of problems that stressed the global financial systems and their economies. To expand on what we mentioned before, we saw the Japanese asset price bubble collapse in 1990, the Scandinavian currency crisis in the early 1990s, the tequila currency crisis in Mexico in 1994, crises in Brazil and Argentina, the Asian currency crises in 1997, and the Russian sovereign default problem in 1998. There were individual failures as well, for example, Drexel Burnham Lambert in 1990, and Long Term Capital Management in 1998, a follow on from the Russian default. The Millennium closed with the dotcom bubble.

The First Rollers

A number of factors led to the emergence, the *innovation,* of complex derivatives.

Few dealers had any real understanding of the mechanics of options trading, and the lack of understanding, notwithstanding Black-Scholes, meant that traders differed over how to evaluate them. Different valuation models gave different results, some models were clearly better than others, and some traders were more successful than others. Technology made it easy to use models as then the heavy lifting work was done by hand held and desktop computers. But the models used by one successful trader soon became well known by others, and margins narrowed.

Exchanges were regulated, so dealers were constrained, and could rarely manipulate the markets, while OTC dealers were not so constrained. This meant there were a limited number of techniques that options traders use to could exploit the markets. One technique was based on put-call parity, and relied on the fact that cash market and options dealers were usually in different teams, and rarely knew what each other was doing.

Economically equivalent financial transaction have the same price.[196] A call with a short cash position can be made equivalent to a put that is we can create put-call parity. A call with a short cash position of the same principal amount is the same as buying a put for the principal amount because, ignoring transaction costs, both benefit if the currency depreciates, and there is no downside if the currency appreciates. Normally you buy a call if you think the currency will appreciate, and a put if you think it will depreciate. A competitor who learns that you have bought a call would assume that you are bullish on the currency. But if you have created a put by shorting the currency, you are in fact bearish. The competitor would rarely learn of your short position, so if the competitor took the bait and assumed that you were bullish, and went long the currency, you have an advantage. You can sell the currency to force the price down, and hope that the manipulated competitor will eventually have to do the same, at a loss. You can then profit.[197] But techniques like this soon became common practice.

OTC transactions are privately negotiated, so the details are not public. They were unregulated and traders can manipulate unregulated markets. A trader could front run, for example. For stock brokers, front running means executing an order for one's own account prior to a customer order in the expectation that the customer order will move the market. A company executive may front run a sale or purchase of the company's stock when the executive learns, before it is made public, that the company will be bought or sold. It is illegal in most markets, but not so in the OTC markets. Furthermore, as OTC derivatives are off balance sheet transactions they are hidden from investors and shareholders. OTC derivatives trading teams thus had a large amount of freedom, and this opened up the markets.

Throughout the 1980s and 1990s the major participants in the OTC markets included Bankers Trust, Bear Stearns, Morgan Stanley, JP Morgan, Salomon Brothers, Goldman Sachs, Credit Suisse First Boston and Citibank. Up until the1980s, customers were treated as golden. Investment banks offered first class service to first class customers and were their partners. But this changed. When trading became a significant activity, customers became objects from which to profit. They were fair game. Traders searched for naive customers, derivatives sales became wars and trading floors did not care whether what was sold made any sense whatsoever for customers. Their interests were secondary to profits. Compensation was tied to profits, and return on equity was the benchmark for bonuses. Traders *blew up* customers and *tore their faces off*, Wall Street parlance for *rape*.

Derivatives, including regulation and tax avoiding derivatives, were sold to a wide range of its customers. If the derivatives were complicated, so much the better as they would be difficult to understand and harder to duplicate, competition would be held at bay, and margins maintained. If customers did not understand them, they would not be able to value them. Even better! So we saw the introduction of inverse floaters, and the other nonsense derivatives that we have mentioned.

Wall Street Vegas

In the early 1980s, Bankers Trust, a large New York bank withdrew from the competitive retail banking business in New York City and by the mid-1980s had built a successful currency options and swaps trading business. It was then the second largest vanilla swaps dealer after Citibank. The notional value of its swaps book was $30 billion, a substantial part of the global market for interest rate swaps. But by the 1990s, margins and profits had shrunk, and swaps could be duplicated easily, so their competitive edge had disappeared.

There were other problems. The practice was to announce estimated earnings at year end, and then sometime later announce finalized and audited financial reports. Unfortunately, Bankers Trust mis-stated its profit for 1987 by $80 million, a very big number in those days. Preliminary earnings were announced based on input from the OTC options trading desk. Andy Krieger, an options trader who had made a string of exceptional profits, year on year, marked his positions showing a $300 million profit for the year. When the back office evaluated the outstanding options deals, it estimated that the profit was overstated by $80 million. Krieger's P&L, while still remarkable, was nearer $200 million. The back office determined that the trading desk had overestimated volatilities by 25%. Valuations of positions had become more complicated and neither the back office, nor the trading desk had any clear idea of how to revalue options.

The bank had to restate its earnings. It would be a substantial restatement, and to gloss over it would be fraud. The bank was also concerned that a large part of its $600 million trading profits, somewhere between $200 and $300 million came from a single individual. The previous highest single contribution was $18 million. It did not want to draw attention to this.

If the bank tried to hide its earnings, both the SEC and the Department of Justice would have strong cases against both it and its auditor, Arthur Young. On the other hand, few understood the intricacies and the lawmakers were out of their depth as were the regulators, as were its boards of directors and shareholders. Apart from the issues being complex, the banking industry had become powerful and an election was coming up and both Bankers Trust and Arthur Young were big campaign contributors. The earnings were restated after some months and neither Bankers Trust nor Arthur Young were prosecuted. The issue was whether the actions of Bankers Trust were reasonable. The law enforcers did not know how to answer the question, and the matter was dropped.

As a result of the problems, the bank began to focus on more complex OTC derivatives and under the direction of Charles S. Sanford, the bank's chairman, it had grown a full-service derivatives operation by the mid-1990s. He built a financial technology team to support the development of new customized derivative products and sharpened risk management expertise so that the risks could be captured and managed. The bank entered the business of structured finance, and the financial engineers and quantitative analysts "quants" began to develop OTC derivative products for which customers would pay a premium, products that enabled earnings to be manipulated, by moving P&L from one quarter to another, to minimize tax and circumvented regulation.

Sanford revamped compensation, and the bank began to measure profitability and compensation against risk. A trading book profit of $10 for one book was better than the same profit for another book if it was earned with less risk. How to measure risk? A good question.[198] Bankers Trust introduced RAROC, the risk adjusted return of a banking activity measured against the capital needed to carry out the activity. There were a plethora of interpretations and definitions, but for RAROC, the basic concept was sound. Compensation should be paid according to both profit and risk, and not just according to profit.

Capital is a loss absorber so a higher risk activity attracts more capital than a lower risk activity. If we could determine the capital required for an activity based upon what is needed to ensure survival in a worst-case scenario, we would solve two problems. We could allocate capital and we could assess performance and award bonuses. The problem was determining worst-case survival conditions, and many years later, this problem became the problem of determining economic capital.

Bankers Trust determined the risks for its trading activities using fairly basic techniques, allocated capital accordingly, and thus bonuses took risk into account. In doing so a third problem was solved, the problem of measuring performance across different departments.

While RAROC was a step forward, it was indeed a very small step. Banks, for example, could take positions that are within risk limits, but which were too large to be liquidated easily. However, with derivative products, capital allocation and bonus structures in place, Bankers Trust pushed forward.

Japanese Vegas

Regulation avoiding derivatives were wonderful for Japan's insurance business. Japanese insurers were not permitted by the Japanese Ministry of Finance to invest in the Japanese stock market. However, they wanted to boost their performance and thought that equity investments were the way to do it. Bankers Trust knew that Japanese insurers were willing to pay large fees for products that enabled them to skirt regulations, so the bank developed structured note equity based derivatives.

A Canadian bank would borrow Japanese yen from a Japanese insurance company. Instead of making interest payments, the Canadian bank gave a call option on the Nikkei 225 index to the insurer. The Japanese regulator would not need to know this and the details of the deal would not be obvious from the insurance companies' financial statements. The Nikkei was comprised of Japanese stock market stocks and if the market went up, so would the index, the call would then rise in value, and the insurance company could sell it and make money. So far so good, the Japanese insurance company would benefit from a rising stock market with little downside. If the market fell, the call would expire worthless, a better option than owning Japanese stocks in a falling market.

But as a result, the Canadian bank would have unwanted exposure, to both yen and the Japanese the stock market. So Bankers Trust simultaneously exchanged the yen for Canadian dollars, and gave the bank an option that mirrored the option given to the Japanese insurance company. The Canadian bank's exposures evaporated. The Canadians welcomed these deals as the effective interest rate for Canadian dollar borrowings by this route was lower than in the Canadian dollar market.

To cover its yen and Japanese equity exposures, Bankers Trust made covering bets with European investors who wanted to make long-term option bets against the Japanese stock market, and entered into hedging Canadian dollar and yen swaps. The options and loans had matching tenors, three to four years. Bankers Trust made good fees, and these deals were of course unregulated. And everyone was happy, until the bill for the free lunch had to be paid! When the Japanese stock market fell, the Japanese insurance regulators, the shareholders in the insurance companies and the Japanese pubic were not happy. By circumventing regulation and speculating on Japanese equities, the insurers had incurred large losses and the cost ended up with the Japanese buyers of insurance, the public.

These kinds of deals are called equity derivatives and in 1989, Bankers Trust made $200 million, one third of its profits, from equity derivatives. This success meant that the other major Wall Street investment banks began to place bets using equity options.[199] Bear, Goldman, Salomon and Morgan Stanley sold them to the Japanese financial sector. Similar derivatives enabled Japanese companies to show profits today by pushing offsetting losses out for years.

Morgan Stanley developed a series of products, AMITs, which we have described. Remember the particularly successful MX missiles. Morgan Stanley had begun to offer OTC derivatives in the early 1990s using its derivatives groups in London, New York and Tokyo. They were immensely successful. Seventy people made $1 billion in two years. That's $15 million per individual! Morgan sold interest rate swaps and structured notes, the deals were high risk, and when customers made losses they were hushed up. Many deals avoided regulation, a major derivatives business driver. Like the other investment banks, Morgan Stanley's customers became profit fodder, and the sales teams went on safaris in search of elephants, gullible customers.

Banks were not shy about shouting about how much money they made by selling complicated deals to customers that did not understand them. Derivatives were sold to commercial organizations, local governments, insurance companies, state and federal governments, pension, mutual and other funds, school boards, in fact anyone! Investment managers looked for higher yields and earned bonuses based on returns, so if a derivative could result in profits today, regardless of long-term risks and losses, they would buy it, declare the immediate profit, earn a good bonus and move to another employer before the deal collapsed. When the derivative began to show losses, they already had their bonuses.

The markets and the culture of finance had changed, and by the end of the 1990s were out of control. The closing bell of the NYSE, once relevant in the 1980s, was eclipsed by the much larger unregulated OTC market that traded 24 hours a day. There were almost as many assets off balance sheet as on balance sheet. Derivatives were difficult to understand, and their risks were not reflected in financial statements in any meaningful way. Corporate financials were annotated with opaque and often meaningless footnotes, which if they had been understood would have shocked investors, analysts, journalists and market commentators. Most of them would have run for the hills. The markets had become dysfunctional serving only the profit motives of Wall Street greed of epic proportions. Ultimately, it led to the Crisis. The tax and banking laws of Bermuda once associated with drug traffickers and the Mafia came to the assistance of the major Wall Street banks. Boards of directors could no longer understand, let alone manage corporations and financial institutions.

In the mid-1980s, the notional amount of outstanding swaps was $70 billion. By 1992, the size of the derivatives market had ballooned up to $40 trillion, double the value of the market capitalization of all US stocks and ten times the national debt. By 2010, it was $615 trillion. US banks held $212 trillion, 97% of which was held by five US banks, JP Morgan Chase, Bank of America, Citigroup, Goldman Sachs and Morgan Stanley. The foreign exchange trading volume, $1 trillion per day in the early 1990s, had risen to $4.7 trillion per day. In that year, the global economy was $60 trillion, and 25% of this, the US GDP. The US national debt was $9 trillion or $29,000 per person, its highest ever.

Salomon

Like Bankers Trust, Salomon also changed what it did as an investment bank in the 1980s. It too made bets in the market for its own account and employed financial engineers to design new products. Betting on the market was far more profitable than earning fees by providing advice and commissions, trading for customers. The Arbitrage Group was very successful. In 1981, its profit was $100 million, one third of Salomon's profit. By the late 1980s, the profit had grown to $500 million and in 1991, it was $1 billion, almost 90% of the entire company's profit. In 1992, the

Group made another $1 billion.[200] Salomon paid enormous bonuses. In1989 they ranged from $3 million to $23 million. Notably, John Meriwether, a leader in the Arbitrage Group, earned $10 million, which dwarfed the $2.3 million bonus of the company's chairman John Gutfreund.

Arbitrage opportunities do not last long, so the Group exploited technology and relied on models that were more sophisticated than those of its competitors. It was not the best man, but the best model that won. They developed a global business. In Japan, it was easier to issue convertible bonds than to issue new shares, so the Group bought Japanese convertibles, hedged the interest rate risk, and created options, which they arbitraged. The Group found a way for Germans to buy German stocks and avoid tax. It used Italian sovereign debt to exploit Italian tax subsidies. The Group's customers were easily exploited, as they were unsophisticated, so customer profitability was good.

Although the complex arbitrage business made exceptional profits, there was little understanding of the risks and traders were not closely supervised. By the 1990s, Salomon was out of control. John Gutfreund looked at the P&L only and ignored the risks. Large losses were made, but not discovered because of outdated accounting systems and technology. A task force in 1993 found unrecorded losses of $280 million. As with Bankers Trust, Salomon's derivatives valuations were guesses, at best! Salomon harboured fraud. One trader, Paul Mozer, created sham transactions to hide profits with transactions that had no commercial value. He aggressively manipulated Treasury auctions, firstly by bidding outside bidding limits and then by putting in false bids in the name of other organizations.[201] Mozer was prosecuted, convicted and jailed, and this led to the removal of the top four Salomon executives, including Gutfreund.[202] But the penalties were minimal. Mozer was sent to a low security jail for four months and paid fines and penalties totalling $1.4 million. Given that he had made $12 million in the preceding three years, it was not a big imposition. The senior officers that were forced out paid fines totalling $225,000, tiny when compared to their earnings. The crime for which Mozer was jailed was making false statements to government officials, not fraud or market manipulation, charges which because of their technical nature would have been difficult to understand let alone prove. The lesson is that you can commit fraud, but you cannot lie to the government!

The Dice Roll The Wrong Way

On 4 February 1994, the FED pushed the federal funds rate, up from 3% to 3.25%. Alan Greenspan, the FED chairman, wanted to put the brakes on any inflation. Greenspan did not understand the limited value of managing short term-interest rates when there was an enormous number of (undisclosed) derivatives floating about in the financial system. As a consequence of the rate hike, a Tsunami hit Wall Street. The structured notes that had been engineered by Bankers Trust, Credit Suisse First Boston, Salomon Brothers, Morgan Stanley and others, were mostly bets that interest rates would not rise, and the bets had been lost. Wall Street had hedged its exposures, but when the public became aware of what had happened, it rang alarm bells. Damage to the bond market was $1.5 trillion.[203]

The hedge funds were badly hit and some failed[204]. George Soros called derivatives financial alchemy[205] and told the House Banking Committee on 13th April 1994 that the risks in some derivatives "may not be properly understood even by the most sophisticated investors".

It was the first sign of problems ahead.

Bankers Trust had sold structured notes to unsophisticated organizations that did not understand them. Orange County, in California had 2.6 million residents, 200 schools, and many cities and districts. Robert Citron, the county's financial executive, an elected office, bought short-term high-risk bonds with returns tied to interest rates. If interest fell the bonds would retain their value, however, if interest rates moved higher, the bonds would suffer heavy losses. When short-term rates increased, the county sustained losses of $2 billion, $750 per County resident. Citron had leveraged its $8 billion balance sheet by borrowing in the repo market and invested $24 billion in short-term structured notes. Incredibly stupid. He was able to do this because the County's outdated investment guidelines permitted him to do so: three to five year tenor, and issued by highly rated issuers.

How could anyone gamble so much, for so long and lose so much? The answer lies in the structure of the notes. All had hard to evaluate features. Many of the notes were inverse floaters. A typical floater may pay a fixed rate less a floating rate like LIBOR. So if LIBOR increased, the returns would fall by the increase. Citron's strategy became a disaster when interest rates increased. Citron did not understand the notes and did not shop around. As a consequence, he also paid enormous fees. Although Merrill cautioned Citron on more than one occasion, but he didn't listen. Merrill earned $62.4 million in 1993 and 1994.

The rating agencies were asleep. They kept the rating of Orange County's notes at AAA right up until its bankruptcy in December 1994. They failed to take the market risk of the notes that Citron bought into account, the risk that their value may fall if interest rates increased. This debacle raised eyebrows. Robert Froehlich of Van Kampen Merritt said: "If rating agencies can't keep track of one of the largest counties in the US, what is the value of their ratings on other counties?"[206]

Orange Country did not mark its positions to market. It did not know how. As a consequence, disaster struck quickly. It announced its first losses on 12 April 1994, even so the agencies kept the County's notes at AAA. Alerts were missed. Citron had made some amazingly stupid statements. When asked for the reasons he thought that interest rates would not rise he replied: "I am one of the largest investors in America. I know these things".[207] When the County was bankrupted it had to lay off 3,000 employees, and Citron was brought to trial. He pleaded guilty to securities fraud and faced a long jail term, which in the light of his dementia, was reduced to community service. Matthew Raabe, Citron's Assistant Treasurer was also found guilty of securities fraud, but inexplicably spent only forty-one days in jail. There were, however, winners. The investment banks that had lent to Orange Country sold the collateral, purchased the notes held by the Country at greatly discounted prices, repackaged them and sold them again!

Undisclosed and unregulated investments permitted investment banks to take *other people's money*, this time from a naïve and unknowledgeable Orange County executive, and place it into risky bets. Citron was blinded by the initial returns, and of course, his bonuses. He failed to consider the downside risks. He did not think, and he was reckless, but he was also raped.

Orange County was not the only organization to suffer. There were school boards, public utilities, towns, pension funds, mutual funds, money market funds and many other bodies that had placed bets and lost. There were also conservative mutual funds that lost. Worth Brutjen a mutual fund manager at Piper Jaffray, placed bets using inverse floaters and zero coupon bonds. The same story. He achieved astounding initial returns, only to lose everything and more as interest rates climbed. Brutjen had ignored the risks. How could a conservative mutual fund place these kinds of bets? Because they could do as they pleased, so long as they made a disclosure of the risks. But as the fund managers did not understand the risks, they could not disclose them. Many conservative money market funds failed. Some were lucky and were bailed out by their sponsoring institutions.

There were many other Bankers Trust pigeons. Gibson Greeting Cards in Cincinnati, Ohio, made and sold greeting cards. In 1991, it was paying 9.33% on a $50 million loan and wanted to lower its borrowing costs. In November, Bankers Trust sold swaps to Gibson that were bets on LIBOR. Gibson would pay a fixed rate of 5.91% for two years and then a floating rate for the third, fourth and fifth years. For the first two years the funding costs were lowered by a substantial amount, $1.7 million per year, and so long as interest rates remained low, the funding costs for years three through five would also remain low.

In July of 1992 Bankers Trust offered a close out deal to Gibson that gave the company a profit of $260,000. Gibson, unable to determine whether or not this was a reasonable deal, took it. The value of the Gibson swap was, however, somewhere between $550,000 and $750,000. This told Bankers Trust that Gibson Greetings was clueless and ripe for exploitation. Gibson was a pigeon. So through March 1994, Bankers Trust sold twenty-nine highly profitable derivatives to Gibson, causing it to place huge bets on interest rates. Typical of the swaps was an unfathomable expression for the interest payable. An example: a fixed rate of 5.5% swapped for floating interest payments of LIBOR squared then divided by six. If LIBOR was below 5.5% Gibson's cash flow was positive, but if LIBOR went above 6%, Gibson's outgoing would become substantial, quickly. The squaring function magnified the downside risk. By year end, the loss to Gibson was $975,000, and Gibson was paying $720,000 for every one percent increment in interest rates. What had begun as an effort to minimize funding costs had taken Gibson a long way from the greeting card business. Before it was over, Gibson's losses rose to $425 million. None of the wonderful details were disclosed to investors, shareholders or any regulator, nor were the Bankers Trust's fees of $13 million.

Proctor and Gamble was another Bankers Trust pigeon. Again, P&G wanted to lower its funding costs, but ended with an enormous swap book. Bankers Trust constructed swap payouts using what was called *good optics*. On the surface things looked good, but underneath the optics were complicated and largely unfathomable constructions. LIBOR, Treasury bond prices of different tenors, options and German interest rates were in the mix. Bankers Trust made $8 million in fees on one deal alone, and soon its fees totalled $25 million. The swaps were impossible to evaluate, not only for P&G but for the Bankers Trust sales teams. The Bankers Trust dealers raped the Bankers Trust sales people! Just as the salespeople tore the faces off customers, the dealers tore the faces off the sales people. Bankers Trust profits remained the same, but how it was apportioned between a salesperson and a trader, how bonuses were apportioned, were determined in the traders favour when the trader could get away with it. They usually did.

In 1992, Proctor and Gamble's derivatives' exposure was $1.4 billion and by 1993 it had climbed to $2.4 billion.

Bankers Trust also sold OTC derivative to many other mid and large sized corporations. The bank made substantial fees, but its customers sustained large losses. The customer losses eventually resulted in many lawsuits, which were always settled out of court. Court documents showed that the Bankers Trust sales teams had blatantly lied to the bank's customers. It is notable that Robert Citron of Orange County pleaded guilty to securities fraud, but no one at Bankers Trust (nor Merrill Lynch) was convicted of anything. The quote of the decade, to be repeated often: "Lure people into the calm and then just totally fuck'em".[208]

The behaviour of Bankers Trust was ubiquitous. Orange County went bankrupt, but Bankers Trust made enormous fees. Merrill Lynch made enormous fees also, $100 million in the case of Orange County. From 1990 to 1993, Bankers Trust was the most profitable US Bank with a third of the profits coming from derivatives and another third from proprietary trading. Commercial banks all over the US preyed upon depositors with offers of enhanced returns based on derivatives. The organizations and sales staff earned profits and commissions when performance was good, but the losses were borne by investors, and the public.

By 1995, the game was over for Bankers Trust. The suits and settlements resulted in destroying the bank's reputation. Customers walked away. It had also become clear that its employees had profited at the expense of the bank's customers and shareholders. The bank never recovered and was sold to Deutsche Bank for $10 billion, a fraction of its recent worth.

Neither the Washington policy makers nor the regulators understood derivatives. When interest rates went up in May 1994, again by half a percent, more extensive losses were announced. The *innovations* had resulted in an epidemic of infectious, connected losses. The regulators thought that derivatives were used to manage risk, but they did not understand that the risks could become concentrated.

Bankers Trust and Salomon weren't the only banks that had problems. Many banks suffered large, often hidden derivatives losses. Two more that did not recover were Barings Bank and Long Term Capital Management hedge fund.

Barings Bank Fails

Barings Bank died in 1995 when it was 233 years old. Its death resulted because of inexplicably dysfunctional management and stupid and fraudulent behaviour by an employee, but it could not have happened without derivatives. They were at the heart of the problem.

Nick Leeson began his employment with Barings in the back office and after a few years was transferred to the bank's Singapore branch as a back office supervisor. He was permitted to trade Nikkei 225 index derivatives on the Singapore and Japanese exchanges. A big mistake. You do not mix front and back office functions. Leeson was able to build up huge positions without the bank's comically incompetent management becoming aware.

At first, he traded conservatively and made modest profits, but when an assistant made a small error, executing a sell rather than a buy, a $30,000 loss resulted. Leeson quickly recovered and as no one questioned the trades, he thought correctly that he was not well monitored, and began to speculate. He hid any losses in a manually tracked account, number 8888. The number of outstanding contracts grew to tens of thousands representing billions of dollars, almost half the volume of the Nikkei 225 contracts traded in Singapore. In 1994, he made a loss of $285 million, but the bank's records showed a profit of $30 million, about 20% of Barings profits. The losses were hidden in 8888. His bonus was $680,000 and he became a celebrated employee.

On 17 January 1995, the Kobe earthquake struck and unsettled the markets and Leeson's naked options resulted in enormous losses. The many requests from Barings Singapore to Barings London for funds to cover margin calls resulted in a visit from senior London staff, but it was too late.

Although Leeson clawed a little back, his losses quickly topped $1 billion and wiped out all the bank's capital. The UK government had no appetite for a bailout, and Barings was sold to the Dutch ING for one pound!

The problems: incompetent supervision, no controls, fraud, opacity within derivatives, and a poor accounting system. Incidentally, the VaR calculations were way off.

The ISDA maintained Barings was not a derivatives problem, but a deceit problem. The deceit problem was, however, also ISDA deceit! The problem could not have occurred if the trades were not derivatives trades and had been understood. They would have been detected.

Long Term Capital Management Fails

Long Term Capital Management, a hedge fund, was formed from the remnants of the Salomon Arbitrage Group. It was positioned as a powerful, highly technical arbitrage trading operation that did not make directional bets. That is, it aimed to profit no matter whether the markets went up or down. It started trading on 24 February 1994, the minimum investment was $10 million, which could not be withdrawn for three years and had a rich fee structure: 2% management fees and 25% of profits. It traded complex and converging arbitrages, and embraced the tools of modern finance: derivatives, risk models, quants, debt and leverage. The derivatives, which had minimal capital requirements, were housed in opaque entities. There was little disclosure.

Initially, it did very well. The returns were 28% in 1994, 59% in 1995 and 44% in 1996. At year end 1997 it had $4.7 billion in equity and $125 billion in borrowings. Its leverage was 26.5. The question that had arisen was would arbitrage opportunities ever dry up? There were 5,000 hedge funds with assets of $300 billion and the industry had grown 20% per year since 1988. Could there be that many pricing anomalies?

The concern had merit as arbitrage margins had thinned and LTCM began taking directional bets,[209] including bets on whether proposed corporate takeovers would conclude successfully. Problems had begun to surface. In 1998, the firm calculated its VaR as $45 million, less than 1% of its equity, but when it attempted to lower it to $35 million, it went in the other direction, up to $100 million. Something was wrong. In the late 1990s, Robert Rubin, then at Goldman, was concerned that leverage and unconstrained derivative exposures might be destructive. LTCM had also experienced poor model results. Problems arose when correlations broke down, but few paid attention to what could occur in unexpected or unlikely circumstances.

Then the Russian default occurred, and the rouble devalued. LTCM and many others sustained heavy losses. To cover losses on rouble investments, investors retrenched and sold off positions. Many of the positions were assets held in emerging market funds, and as a result, credit in the emerging markets dried up. When the majority of the emerging markets funds were down by one third, the turmoil became global. LTCM's models were way off. The fund's capital drained and by August, it had fallen to $2 billion and its leverage reached 50:1. In September, LTCM's leverage doubled to 100:1.

In the late 1990s, some South East Asian economies, economies that produced a quarter of the world's output, and housed two-thirds of a billion people experienced a Great Depression like slump. It struck like lightening and was immune to conventional economic remedies.[210] It instilled fear in some, and Wall Street was spooked. The bankers were afraid that contagion might bring the Asian and Russian crises to Wall Street so the New York FED orchestrated a bailout by the larger banks, $3.6 billion for 90% of the equity of the company. Greenspan remarked that it was the worst crisis he had ever seen. He said it was the price of modernity. Faster markets meant more mistakes! He was blinded by ideology. As derivatives were unregulated, the extent of the contagion was unknown. If LTCM failed, the size and nature of its positions could result in a tsunami-like disruption of the markets and the economies of very many countries. LTCM was a systematically important financial institution well before the Crisis singled them out as problem children. Moral hazard appeared!

The tools of modern finance, excessive leverage, probabilistic risk models, interconnected exposures and derivatives amply demonstrated Rubin's prescient concerns. When all became known LTCM's notional derivatives position was an astounding $1.25 trillion.

The crises of the 1990s and these two failures were not the only examples of poor or non-existent risk management. Toshihide Iguchi of Daiwa lost $1 billion and Sumitomo's Yasuo Hamanaka lost $2.6 billion and led the pack.

The US Home Ownership Imperative

The American Dream of owning one's own home became a widely accepted ideology after World War II as a home owning middle class came about. It was also popular public policy, shared by both houses of Congress: it was an aspiration and underscored upward mobility and success. It was no wonder that when President Clinton spoke at the National Association of Realtors annual meeting in 1994, two years into his presidency, his speech was met with thundering applause:

> More Americans should own their own homes,
> for reasons that are economic and tangible, and
> reasons that are emotional and intangible, but
> go to the heart of what it means to harbour, to
> nourish, to expand the American Dream.[211]

He told us that, home ownership encouraged responsibility, strengthened the economy and made better citizens, provided financial security, encouraged community attachment, independence and self-reliance. Home ownership created jobs and built a middle class. Neighbourhoods of homeowners were more stable and better kept.

Since the Great Depression, Washington had supported the home ownership imperative and provided many incentives. The Fannie Mae thirty-year mortgage made monthly mortgage payments affordable for middle class families, especially as the interest was tax deductible. The 1986 tax reforms removed a deduction for interest paid on any debt *other* than mortgage debt and this kept mortgages cheaper. To further encourage home ownership, federal law gave the S&L industry an interest rate advantage over commercial banks. It had a name, the *housing differential*.[212]

Home ownership, a key constituent of Clinton's national housing strategy, was part of his political agenda. When Clinton became president, home ownership was 65% and his target an ambitious 70%. He almost made it. It peaked at 69% in 2006. He asked the private sector to work with the public sector to achieve the goal,[213] and the GSE private-public partnership strengthened in the mid-1990s:

> by making homeownership more affordable,
> expanding creative financing, simplifying the
> home buying process, reducing transaction
> costs, changing conventional methods of
> design and building less expensive houses[214]

In order to achieve his housing goals, Clinton needed the financial markets and the economy to cooperate. But from 1997, the rise in home prices outstripped income growth and from 1999 real median household income fell for five consecutive years. From 1985 to 2000, the average cost of a home in the US was 3 times the median income, but by 2006 it was 5.2 times. In 2005, the value of all housing in the developed world was $70 trillion, up from $30 trillion in 2000. The US contribution was $11 trillion, and the only way to promote home ownership was to expand credit.

Most Americans thought that home ownership was a good thing. It was a *sure* investment. Over time, homes always increased in value, so provided savings for retirement and something to pass on to one's children. Home ownership is a highly leveraged investment because the down payment is small compared to the value of the property. If real estate increases in value, then the leverage pays off, but if real estate decreases in value, massive foreclosures can result. Unfortunately, the Great Recession showed that home ownership was not a *sure thing*. The home ownership drive plunged the nation into a deep recession, which resulted in record levels of joblessness, impoverished a large slice of the

American middle class and left it without homes and savings. The working class, rather than finding itself on the road to the middle class, regressed.

Contrary to popular ideology, there is little evidence that supports the view that home ownership for all is a good thing. Homeowners are more frequent voters and take better care of their homes, but that is about it. We will return to this issue.

The GSEs in the 1990s

The GSEs played a major role in Clinton's private-public partnership. In 1991, James A Johnson became CEO of Fannie Mae. Johnson, a Democrat, was a seasoned campaigner and politician. He used his political skills to promote Fannie at all costs. In particular, he used the cheap-housing-for-all mantle to defend Fannie from congressional efforts to reduce Washington's extensive support for the GSEs. Opponents were met with politically incorrect accusations of being against cheap housing, derision and reminders that the GSEs were essential pieces of the nation's housing policy. By promoting home ownership, Fannie and Freddie took the teeth out of criticism, and the belief that the GSEs were good for America was entrenched by the mid-1990s.

Johnson's strategy was for Fannie to finance so much lower income housing that Washington could not tamper with its benefits. He argued that the benefits resulted in savings, and these were passed on to mortgage borrowers. But in reality, a third of the savings went to Fannie's executives, its shareholders, Congress and the other beneficiaries of Fannie's largesse.[215] When he testified before the House Banking Committee in April 1996, he claimed that Fannie reduced mortgage costs by ¼ to ½% and this resulted in savings for mortgage holders of between $7 and $14 billion, annually, and with no taxpayer cost.

However, the real reason why Johnson was determined to quash any opposition was that the GSEs had become very profitable and their executives earned enormous salaries and bonuses. Any reduction in the GSE benefits would hit their pay packets very hard. And there was no downside. If the GSEs failed, the taxpayer would cover the losses. The GSEs were quasi-public entities with private style executive compensation motives.

During Johnson's reign, Fannie's balance sheet exceeded $5 trillion, its market capitalization soared from $10.5 billion to $70 billion and it became the biggest financial institution on the globe.[216] Fannie's mortgage portfolio grew to just shy of $500 billion. However, capital levels were well below deposit taker levels and their risk of failure was high.

Home ownership, thus enabled Fannie to become a personal wealth making machine for Johnson and his senior executives, a machine that took excessive risks with low capital levels. Politics and banking had found each other again. The common bond was affordable housing and the housing-for-all mantle.

Johnson departed Fannie in 1999. In 2000, Fannie's return on equity was 26% and Freddie's 39%. GSE debt had risen from $759 billion in 1990 to $2.1 trillion in 2000. Shareholder equity was $36 billion and market capitalization much higher, but leverage was a staggering 60 to1, a clear danger sign. Johnson left Fannie a rich man with a pension of $900,000 a year, an inflation-adjusted consulting contract of $390,000 annually, an office and staff, a car and a driver. He went to Goldman Sachs for a director's fee of $50,000 per year, which by the time of the Crisis, had grown to $500,000 per year. He had earned over $100 million during his nine years at Fannie.[217]

The US Mortgage Market

A mortgage is a loan that enables a borrower to buy a home. Houses, a single asset in a single location, are expensive relative to family's earnings and usually its largest investment. Few people are able to put together all the funds necessary to buy a home, most of us need financial assistance, and mortgages provide this assistance.

A mortgage borrower repays a mortgage over time, in equal instalments, usually monthly, for many years. Part of each payment repays the mortgage principal and part is interest on the outstanding amount. The principal declines each time a payment is made. In the initial years, most of each payment is interest, but as time passes the interest part of the payment decreases as the principal is paid down.

Traditionally, mortgage providers would not lend the entire cost of a home, but required the borrower to make a down payment. They wanted to see some skin in the game. Down payments were in the order of 10% to 20%. While there was no down payment upper limit, in practice, most mortgage loans provided most of the funding for the acquisition a home.

For many years after the Great Depression only fixed rate mortgages were given, mortgages where the interest rate remained the same throughout the life of the mortgage. Most mortgages were 30 year fixed rate mortgages. Mortgages were given to borrowers who passed on three counts, the 3Cs: capacity to repay, credit worthiness and collateral offered.

Traditionally, the funds for mortgages came from depositors and borrowings. So long as the interest income earned, after costs, was higher than the interest paid on the borrowed funds, and mortgage defaults low, a mortgage originating business could be profitable. An originator is always exposed to default risk, and so originators were careful. Over time periods measured in years, all sorts of things could happen. The economy could suffer multiple down turns and borrowers could lose their jobs or encounter unpredictable hardships. So originators did expect defaults to occur, but obviously wanted to minimize them. The conforming mortgage standards required by the GSEs provided a credit assurance that the probabilities of default were low.

Mortgage originators can only originate new mortgages if the funds already lent to mortgage holders can be replenished, so with mortgage-sized amounts going out and only mortgage-sized repayments coming in, mortgage lenders run out of money quickly unless there is a source from which funds can be replenished. Selling mortgage is thus part of the game. Mortgage originators are proficient at originating new mortgages, and if they sell the originated mortgages they are then able to repeat what they do well, origination. The GSE's role was to replenish mortgage funds for conforming mortgages.

Non-conforming loans are mortgage loans that do not meet the GSE conforming mortgage standards. There has always been a good market for non-conforming mortgages. They are easier to originate, but as one would expect, the conforming mortgage market, was much larger, and more liquid.

Mortgages are rarely held to term. If interest rates fall, there is a strong incentive for a mortgage holder to remortgage. Mortgage holders can take a new lower cost mortgage and repay the existing mortgage. Similarly, when home prices rise, a mortgaged home can be sold, and the funds used to repay the mortgage and buy another, perhaps larger home. Or the surplus funds can be used to pay off other, more expensive debt, or simply saved or spent. As mortgages are rarely held to term, default risk is lower.

Remortgaging exposes mortgage lenders to a contingent liquidity risk. A mortgage originator who holds a mortgage hedges the mortgage cash flows with offsetting cash flows. If the mortgage cash flows vanish, the mortgage issuer has to readjust the hedge. Thus, mortgages are contracts with optionality, and the originator's problem is that the option to remortgage is usually exercised at the worst time for the originator, when interest rates have fallen. The problem for lenders becomes exacerbated when neighbourhoods refinance. To manage prepayment options, originators sharpen credit assessments and cash flow expectations by using behavioural assumption models.

The major mortgage risk is credit risk, the risk that a mortgage holder defaults. Continued default can lead to repossession of the collateral, the property, its sale and the repayment of the mortgage loan, together with recovery of the costs of the process. Mortgage originators want to avoid this path. Repossession is messy, it has high social costs and a high repossession rate is bad for business. Even if a mortgage company repossesses a property, it will not recover anything like the entire amount outstanding, nor the costs associated with repossession.

The major mortgage types are:

- Prime mortgages, which are conforming mortgages, given to prime borrowers on the basis the 3Cs: full documentation attesting to income and assets, good credit, and good collateral

- Alt-A mortgages, a broad category where the borrowers are usually prime borrowers, but the mortgages are non-conforming, often because of gaps in the documentation, a high loan to value ratio, or the property is investor owned

- Subprime mortgages, where the borrower has a weak credit score, and there is no or limited documentation

- Jumbo mortgages, which are mortgages whose size exceeds the conforming loan size limits

Many mortgage lenders specialized in subprime mortgages. The top twenty-five subprime lenders were responsible for $1 trillion in mortgages originated to 7.2 million subprime borrowers from 2005 and 2007, and accounted for 72% of all subprime mortgages.[218] All subprime lenders eventually had problems. Providing subprime mortgages increased mortgage volumes substantially as it provided mortgages to a new, large, market segment, to borrowers who previously did not qualify for a mortgage.

Just before the Crisis, Alt-A mortgages accounted for forty percent of the nation's home purchases.

In 2008, the outstanding residential mortgages were $11 trillion and the outstanding commercial mortgages $3 trillion, for a total of $14 trillion, just shy of the nation's GDP!

The Exotic Mortgage Market Supermarket

Adjustable Rate Mortgages, ARMS, have been offered in the US from the early 1980s. When the S&Ls were deregulated, banks could offer mortgages with interest rates that could reset from time to time. Fixed rate mortgages had to anticipate future, unknowable changes in the funding cost of mortgages. An ARM enabled the mortgage rate to be tied to a reference rate, like the federal funds rate, LIBOR or the prime rate, so mortgage originators were able to offer mortgages with rates that tracked their funding cost. As the reference rate fluctuated, so did the mortgage rate. The risk of future interest rate changes was born by the mortgage holders, so the initial rates were lower, as the originator knew that an increase in funding costs was matched by an increase in mortgage income.

Sometimes the mortgage cost was stated as a premium on top of a reference rate, for example prime plus 1.5%. Sometimes there was no reference, and rate resets were stated explicitly, for example, a mortgage could begin with a 5% rate that increased to 8% after two years. Typically, there were limits on the number of resets, caps on the size of the resets and an overall cap.

ARMs became very popular in the 2000s, but the basis for most adjustable rates changed. ARMs were structured with a low introductory rate and much higher rates that kicked in after a few years. The introductory rate was intended, clearly, to attract borrowers.

For borrowers, the problem with ARMs tied to a reference rate, is that if interest rates rise steeply, the ARM payments rise accordingly and can become unaffordable. This can lead to disruptions in the financial sector and the economy. In the UK in 1991, after interest rates had risen sharply, the mortgage market suffered defaults of between two and three times the historical norms. The problem with ARMs with introductory rates followed by resets is that borrowers are lured into mortgage commitments that they cannot afford to pay after the reset.

There are many types of ARMs:

- 2/28 and 3/27 mortgages are 30-year mortgages that reset after the second and third years, respectively, to a higher rate for the remainder of the loan. They often came with stiff prepayment penalties. They made up 31% of subprime mortgages in 1999 and 69% in 2006.

- These are interest only ARMs where only interest, but not the principal is repaid

- There are pick and pay ARMs, where borrowers chose the amount to be repaid each month. Options included negative amortization ARMs, where the payments did not cover the interest and so what is owed gets bigger and bigger each month.

- There are long amortizations where the payments extend for longer than the usual 30 years

For most borrowers, ARM financing was part of a financing strategy where a loan would be repaid and replaced by another loan, perhaps by another ARM or a traditional 30-year mortgage. If home prices increased then this could be a good strategy. However, if they did not, refinancing would not be possible, and the higher ARM payments would have to be paid when they are triggered. Refinancing costs could be substantial, for example, 3% of the outstanding mortgage amount. Broker commissions could be, say $20,000, and if you could not afford to pay a rate hike, you certainly could not afford to pay these fees, even if they were added into the new mortgage.

Securitizing Mortgages

Reselling mortgages motivated mortgage securitization. Securitization streamlined the mortgage acquisition process and expanded the funds flowing into the mortgage markets. New investors were able to invest. Securitization resulted in the mortgage business becoming a volume and fee-driven business. Fees are money in the door today, and banks and their senior executives want money in the door today. Bonuses depend on it. Interest income is earned over years, and many investors want a steady income stream. Securitization made sense to all participants. The *originate-and-hold* model became an *originate-and-distribute* model.

The effect on mortgage consumers was negligible. The mortgage payments were made to a mortgage servicing company,[219] which would pass the funds down the securitization chain. Apart from this, the mortgage holder would notice very little.

The GSEs were the early leaders in the securitization business. They purchased conforming mortgages, securitized them and sold the MBSs to investors. If a mortgage holder defaulted, the GSE guarantee could be invoked. By 1981, the volume of MBSs had grown to $350 billion, up from zero in the 1970s. It was in the trillions twenty years later.[220]

Wall Street loved MBSs both as issuers and investors. Until the housing bubble burst the market was hot. Private label securitizations could be built from subprime and other high return mortgages, so investors earned higher returns than similarly rated bonds. They were immensely attractive. On top of this, securitizers' earned higher fees, and as securitizers were subject to default risk only for as long as they held on to the mortgage fodder, there was little risk.

What was good for the goose, the investors, was also good for the gander, securitizers, so trading and inventorying MBSs became another source of profits for securitizers. The GSEs and the shadow banking system were among the investors that gorged on private labels. Others included the S&Ls, mutual funds, hedge funds, and insurance companies. A problem was that the risk in securitizations was supposed to be disseminated, but it was not. It was concentrated in the interconnected financial sector.

For years, conservative investment funds like pension funds had been accustomed to good yields. By 2000, the 30-year Treasury bond returns had dropped by more than 50%. This fuelled a demand for yield, and for MBSs. MBSs needed mortgages, so investor reach for yield also fuelled the growth of mortgage debt. This demand in turn fuelled the growth of the non-confirming, subprime and other non-traditional mortgage markets. The fact that these mortgages were of lower quality than prime mortgages delighted investors, as the returns were higher. The senior tranches were AAA, and most of the other tranches were investment grade. The only risk was that the value of the collateral might fall below the value of a securitization.

Non-conforming mortgages were originated in much larger volumes as they gave rise to higher returns, higher revenues. The mortgages required less time to process as their origination was easier and cheaper. Originators knew they would sell the mortgages quickly so they did not care about credit quality. In any case, it had become easier to share and verify information using the Internet and desktop technology, so originators could bypass *some* conforming mortgage requirements without necessarily lowering credit quality. For example, if an applicant was a schoolteacher employed in the New York school system in the borough of Queens, who declared an annual income of $50,000, there was no need for written documentation. Originators knew what school teachers were paid, and a simple phone call could verify employment. The problem was that these practices could lead to poorer lending standards if checks were not made and pieces of documentation were eliminated from the process. And the standards fell!

Securitization changed the game as it created conflicting and skewed incentives among the investors, originators, mortgage brokers, securitizers and mortgage servicers. The financial sector had little understanding of the products and the risks involved, and by the mid-2000s, this had become lethal. While real estate backed securitizations expanded credit to those who wanted to buy homes, it also enabled originators to profit from individuals who could not afford mortgages because mortgage originators no longer cared about default risk. Up until the 1990s, and prior to the expansion of private label securitizations, the mortgage business was constrained by the fact that originators wanted to be repaid! As private labels had no payment guarantees the only group in the securitization chain for which default risk mattered were the investors at the end of it.

The only constraint was the FDIC. Motivated by the exposure of its insured base, the FDIC promoted warehouse loan guidance. It insured commercial bank deposits from which warehouse funds were drawn, so was concerned that investors in MBSs could *put back* loans that did not meet a securitizes representations and warranties. And they were right to be concerned as eventually large numbers of loans were put back.

Black Wednesday

There were other issues that surfaced in the 1990s. In October 1990, the UK joined the European Exchange Rate Mechanism, the ERM. It was a major shift in policy. Membership in the ERM meant that the UK would have to adopt economic and monetary policies that would prevent the exchange rates between the pound and the other ERM currencies dropping by more than 6%. The pound entered the ERM at £/DM=2.95. So if the exchange rate fell to £/DM=2.773, the BoE would have to intervene and buy pounds, and force it above 2.773.

On 16 September 1992, Black Wednesday, the UK government withdrew the pound from the ERM, as it was unable to keep the pound above the lower limit. Early in the day, the BoE had raised interest rates from 10 to 12%, and then committed to a 15% base rate, but by evening, it had spent billions supporting the pound with little effect. A devalued pound and ERM exit were necessary.

George Soros, a hedge fund manager became known, inappropriately, as the Man Who Broke the Bank of England. On Black Wednesday, his fund, the Quantum Fund, unloaded its short pound position of US$10 billion and made a profit of $1 billion. The Quantum Fund had been building a short position in pounds for months. Soros knew that the rate at which the pound had entered the ERM was too high. He reasoned that the BoE would have to support it as the UK government was reluctant to raise interest rates to levels comparable to those of the other European ERM countries.

Soros was a World War II Hungary émigré. Today, he is one of the richest men in the world, with a net worth of $24 billion. The Quantum Fund is valued at $11 billion. He has financed liberal political and philanthropic causes since 1970s. They have included anti-apartheid activists and dissident movements in Eastern Europe. In 2003, he said that removing President George W. Bush from office was a "central focus of my life" and "a matter of life and death."

When he emigrated to the UK, he studied at the London School of Economics with Sir Karl Popper, and in 1954 was awarded a PhD in philosophy. He became an investment banker, moved from London to New York, and at one point, his goal was to save $500,000 so that he could return to England to study philosophy. He had developed the theory of market reflexivity at the LSE, and used this theory to guide his investments. He gave up investment banking, became a hedge fund manager, and has been immensely successful. His decision to short the pound was a considered strategy based on his market theories. The actual breakers of the BoE were the dysfunctional politicians that took the UK into the ERM at a rate that could not be sustained, and who then failed to manage UK monetary policy.

Black Wednesday questions the efficacy of currency speculation when the target is a central bank. Hedging the value of a crop of oranges is certainly of value. However betting on the poor decisions of governments exposes taxpayers to their weaknesses.

Krugman is critical: "Nobody who has read a business magazine in the last few years can be unaware that these days there really are investors who not only move money in anticipation of a currency crisis, but actually do their best to trigger that crisis for fun and profit.

The cost of Black Wednesday was £3.3 billion, a cost in reserves, not a cost in funds that could have been used for schools and hospitals. Thus, Soros did not benefit at the cost of the UK taxpayer. It may not always be the case.

Bigger Looks Better

From the early 1990s through 2000, the US economy experienced a boom. GDP increased by an average of 3.9% annually, while inflation was 1.8%.[221] But there had been significant changes. Prior to 1990, the ten largest US companies were industrial or natural resource companies. By 2000, six of the largest ten were technology companies, and the two biggest, Cisco and Microsoft, were less than twenty-five years old.

Robert Rubin, a Wall Street insider and a Goldman past co-chairman, joined the Clinton administration in 1992, and became Secretary of the Treasury in 1995. Proprietary trading, quantitative finance, unregulated OTC derivatives and the new world of securitized products were safe. Rubin, and his appointments, which included staff from Goldman Sachs and other Wall Street organizations, and Larry Summers from the academic world, signalled a more financial sector friendly Democratic administration. The Clinton administration shaped financial ideology up to the Crisis. Free markets were fundamental with unemployment and inequality unfortunate appendages.[222]

Alan Greenspan the influential chairman of the FED was a strong supporter of financial *innovation* and deregulation, and endorsed Reagan's free market capitalism and policy of less government. The FED should not be concerned if prices appeared to be off. The market will correct them. Greenspan eschewed regulation and consumer protection. He had little interest in promoting the FED's important role as a regulator. Although the FED had an obligation and the power to police unfair or deceptive lending practices, Greenspan would have no part of it. He thought that the market would not produce loans that made no sense, and if it did, then there would be no takers! This incredulously stupid view initially won some takers, and of course, Wall Street was an energetic buyer of poor loans. He was captivated by technology, models and quantitative finance. Alan Greenspan was delusional and his reasoning took him to some strange places. But we will say more about this later.

However, it was time for change. The deposit takers wanted a bigger piece of the pie. They wanted to offer more products, including stocks and bonds, they wanted to trade, and to underwrite corporate mergers and acquisitions. They wanted more customers. Technology had enabled transaction banking, banking that could reach more customers without significantly increasing costs. Banks wanted to get bigger. So the politicians in Washington agreed that the commercial banks could make inroads into investment banking. Bank failures had been on the increase since the early 1980s and the FDIC had sustained losses. This meant that something was amiss with the deposit taking business model. The Berlin Wall that separated the deposit takers and investment banks should come down.

Survival and profitability were at stake. Transaction banking would enhance profits. Bigger banks that offered more products and more services to more customers would be more profitable and provide better customer service. Some banks could become financial supermarkets. Bigger organizations would mean consolidation and smaller, inefficient banks would be eliminated. Remember the many thousands of small, inefficient and often dysfunctional small banks, dotted across the US that the GSA kept in place.

Commercial and investment banks invaded each other's territories. Commercial banks became investment banks, and investment banks raised money for customers, including funds which had previously been provided by commercial banks. Brokerage and cash management accounts, and combined checking and money market accounts proliferated. Deposits still funded corporations, but there were now two paths. Funds flowing to mortgage borrowers could flow through non-regulated non-bank mortgage originators, bypassing the traditional banking system. JP Morgan Chase and Citibank were on the way to becoming larger and more influential corporations. Merrill Lynch was a household name.

In 1994, the rules prohibiting cross border banking were relaxed and a feeding frenzy took place, as larger organizations swallowed smaller ones. Banks began to look different. The deposit takers took foreign deposits and the investment banks become larger, with extensive global operations. Risks expanded with the global footprints. The GSA had been designed to shield depositors from the risks of what investment banks did, but by the end of the 1990s, this protection was gone.

As banks became larger, bank lobbying became more influential in all the money centres. Political donations to parties representing all quarters of the political spectrum were significant. Lobbying kept OTC derivatives, a significant source of bank profits, unregulated. As derivatives required minimal regulatory capital, returns on equity, hence bonuses were high. Notwithstanding extensive efforts to regulate derivatives, the banks won.

Annual compensation rose dramatically in the financial sector from the 1980s when it began to diverge significantly from non-financial sector compensation. Financial and non-financial sector compensation was about the same in 1980, $50,000 per annum. By

2010, compensation for those involved in finance had risen to just over $100,000 per annum and the compensation for those involved in the non-financial sectors rose to just under $60,000 per annum. For some, the increased incomes were life changing. If it had not been for the Crisis and the Great Recession, the financial services compensation would be even higher today. The difference cannot be explained by differences in educational level, job security, individual ability and other issues. We should remember that Wall Street incomes became significantly higher than non-financial incomes immediately prior to the Great Depression.

The Second Bangster Awards

We have discovered one more Bangster in this chapter, James Johnson. He bribed Congress to get support for the GSEs, and awarded himself outlandish compensation at the expense of homeowners and taxpayers.

Here is the revised table:

Bangsters	*Gold Stars*
Nicholas Biddle	Franklin D Roosevelt
JP Morgan	Louis Brandeis
James Johnson	

6

Millennium

The 1990s was a decade marked by economic crises. While the Scandinavian currency crisis was closer to home, the *others* were a long way away, in South and Latin America (Argentina, Brazil and Mexico), Asia and South East Asia (Japan, Korea, Thailand, Malaysia and Indonesia) and Russia. The *others*, products of crony capitalism, we were told, had economies that did not trust the markets. They were not like us!

However, the US was not exempt and had its own small crisis in the early 1990s. The problems in the S&L industry resulted in a plethora of non-bank mortgage originators. They made loans to households that could not afford them, treated customers as lambs for the slaughter, ripe for exploitation and objects of derision. Predatory lending resulted loans being made to many households that could not afford them. Bankruptcies ensued and the first mini subprime crisis.

Notwithstanding the problems in the 1990s, it was a decade of economic growth with double-digit stock market growth. Record amounts were invested in the US and other stock markets. It was the longest lasting bull market since World War II.

By the Millennium, the biggest banks had become a lot bigger, they were megabanks, and the Berlin Wall that separated commercial, deposit taker banks from investment banks had been dismantled. The largest banks had global footprints. In 2002, the assets of the global banking were $84 trillion. By 2005, they were $195 trillion,[223] up 133%, and 3.5 times global GDP.

The megabanks high jacked the regulators, who had not kept up with the changes in the financial system. OTC derivatives were a major part of their business, and they were not regulated. The non-bank lenders also escaped regulation. Deregulatory efforts were quarterbacked by Alan Greenspan, an obscurantist and gangster. He was highly thought of, but delusional. As FED chairman, he abrogated his regulatory responsibilities.

A three-member vaudeville act came to Wall Street, *The Committee to Save the World*. It was not funny, but signalled the entrenchment of the US megabank oligarchy. Similar oligarchies were in change of finance for most Western governments.

Decisions were facilitated and conflicts resolved by exploiting their financial might.

Bigger is Better

In October 1998, the FED permitted Citibank, one of the largest deposit takers to merge with Travelers Group and form Citigroup. Travelers was a large financial services firm engaged in insurance and securities, and had already acquired Smith Barney, Salomon Brothers and a number of other financial institutions. The value of the deal was $83 billion, the combined entity had 100 million customers and its assets were $700 billion. It became the largest bank in the US and pushed Bank of America with assets of $570 billion, back into second place. Citigroup offered a wide range of corporate, consumer banking, securities and insurance products and services, and financial consulting. It was a megabank and financial supermarket. However, the merger violated the GSA. If nothing changed, Citigroup would have to divest its insurance business within five years. Ultimately, the Gramm-Leach-Bliley Act, the GLB, somewhat catalysed by the merger, changed the rules and the group remained whole.

JP Morgan Chase evolved into another deposit taker giant. It was the result of a string of New York City bank acquisitions. In 1991, Chemical Bank acquired Manufacturers Hanover Trust, in 1996, the combined bank acquired Chase Manhattan Bank and in 2000, this entity acquired JP Morgan. It was known as JP Morgan Chase.

NationsBank became the largest US deposit taker when it acquired Bank of America, displacing it from its number one position. NationsBank and Bank of America used the more widely known Bank of America brand. Along the way, other banks had been acquired, including Continental Illinois. You may recall that Conti–Illinois was rescued by the FDIC in 1984, at the time, the largest ever bank rescue.

Goldman Sachs, like the other investment banks, struggled after the Great Depression. Until the 1980s, its relationship with its customers, typical of major investment banks, was paramount. The firm eschewed ostentatiousness and glitter. Its employees were company men and worked hard. Acting ethically towards customers was a top priority. Their interests come first. The company was risk sensitive, and models were taken for what they were, models. VaR, for example, was understood to be a reasonable indicator in normal market conditions, but not much use in adverse conditions. The company marked its positions to market on a daily basis, and treated the back office, and the risk managers as essential parts of the machine. It kept $40 billion in short-term liquid securities in a vault as a cushion. By the early 1990s, Goldman was the most admired firm on Wall Street.

But by the 2000s, Goldman had become a ruthless and cut throat money machine, and its employees driven only by money, by bonuses. Customers had become pigeons. It had tens of thousands of employees, billions in capital and a global footprint. Revenues rose from $16 billion in 2003 to $38 billion in 2006. By 2004, trading accounted for 75% of Goldman's profits and investment banking a paltry 6%. In 2003, Hank Paulson, its CEO earned $21.4 million, and Lloyd Blankfein, his successor, $20.1 million. Next year the numbers were $29.8 and $29.5, respectively. When Paulson became Treasury Secretary in 2006, his last year at Goldman, he earned $40 million. He cashed in stock options accumulated during his 32 years at the firm, and left with $1 billion in his pocket.

In 2009, the Goldman Code of Business Conduct and Ethics still stated, "Integrity and honesty are at the heart of our business. We expect our people to maintain high ethical standards in everything they do." [224] It was utter nonsense. Goldman published business principals. The first: "Our customers' interests always come first" was sanctimonious rubbish. Customers were pigeons to be exploited.

Morgan Stanley had begun business in New York in 1935, after the GSA split up the Morgan financial empire. As we said before, in 1972, 36 years later, Morgan Stanley still had only a single office and 110 employees. Like Goldman, customers came first. But by the Millennium, it too had become global with tens of thousands of employees and capital of several billion dollars. Their customers had also become pigeons.

The deposit takers wanted to be universal banks like their European counterparts. The European universal banks, they told us, had an advantage as they operated globally, as both investment and commercial banks. They could hedge exposures with few constraints and more easily diversify their risks. London was taking business from New York and the European banks had entered the US banking markets. Credit Suisse acquired First Boston in 1988 and Deutsche Bank acquired Bankers Trust in 1998. Swiss Bank Corporation acquired Dillon Read in 1997, before it swallowed UBS. It took the UBS brand as its name.

The banking industry thought it had addressed risk. Bankers Trust had developed RAROC, and JP Morgan, VaR. Although RAROC was a step in the right direction, VaR was a garden path that lead nowhere. But to bankers, it sounded good and that was good enough for them. With the focus on risk, the financial industry pushed the notion that they could manage it, and that regulation was unnecessary. Reagan's legacy, an ideology of less government, persisted through the 1990s. Alan Greenspan was at the FED helm and influential organizations like Citigroup wanted deregulation to survive intact.

Sanford Weil, the CEO of Travelers Group, needed to cement the merger between Travelers and Citibank, and campaigned strongly for the deregulation of the financial services industry. Outgoing Treasury Secretary, Robert Rubin, and incoming Secretary, Larry Summers, were on-board. Congress formally deregulated the banking industry by passing the GLB in the last months of the 20th century.[225] The Berlin Wall between the commercial and investment banks came down. Rather than reconstruct the GSA, the GLB neutered it, leaving a regulatory vacuum. When the GLB was passed the deposit takers got what they wanted.

To celebrate, Rubin went from the Treasury back to Wall Street, to Citigroup. He was paid $125 million over the next ten years as the bank self-destructed. Wall Street had begun to do what it wanted.

By the Millennium, the US financial sector had been transformed into a few large megabanks and thousands of small banks. There were three mega deposit takers, Citigroup, JP Morgan Chase and Bank of America and five mega investment banks: Goldman, Merrill, Morgan Stanley, Lehman and Bear. The investment banks had started life as partnerships, but by 2000, all were public companies. Not far behind the three largest deposit takers were Wells Fargo, Wachovia, and Washington Mutual, an S&L.

The investment banks employed far fewer staff than the commercial banks. There were just under 200,000 individuals employed by the Top 5 in 2008. Merrill, with an extensive branch system employed 48,000, and Bear, the smallest, 15,000. The commercial banks employed nearly five times as many. The biggest employer was Citigroup just before the Crisis, before it laid off a third of its staff, with 375,000 employees.

The size of the banking sector in the US was and remains modest when compared to the European commercial and investment banking sectors. Around the time of the Crisis, the size of the banking sector, in assets, in Germany was 135% of GDP, in France 275%, in the UK, 550% and in Switzerland 630%. UBS itself was 370% of GDP. The size of the US banking sector was 97% of US GDP. In Iceland and Ireland, the banks were so large compared to GDP that the countries themselves collapsed.

The megabanks were engaged in deposit taking, trading and investment banking. Trading derivatives and creating securitizations were a major source of profits for each of these banks. All provided warehouse loans to mortgage originators, and their own portfolios held securitizations for investment and trading. They were a lot like hedge funds, betting their capital and highly leveraged borrowings on high-risk investments. Those with deposit taker roots used their branches to raise deposits and the investment banks funded themselves in the short-term markets. Both strategies enabled excessive, uncontrolled risk taking. Greater size can mean more diversity and safety, but the megabanks offset any advantage by taking more risk. They thought that they could manage it. The smaller banks carried on taking deposits and making loans to individuals and businesses, with one exception. They sold their loans to the megabanks, which securitized them.

In 2005, the ten largest US commercial banks held 55% of the banking assets of all the commercial banks, twice what it was in 1990. The increases in the US financial sector assets over the pre-Crisis twenty year period are:

	% US GDP ($2.3 trillion)	% US GDP ($14.7 trillion)[226]
Commercial banks	53%	80%
Investment banks	2%	27%
Hedge Funds		17%
Off balance sheet		31%
Total assets	55%	155%
Financial sector debt	12%	248%
Market value of OTC derivatives	zero	107%

Figure 6: The Financial Sector Asset Growth, 1978 to 2007[227]

By the early 2000s, consumers were paying more, contrary to the claims of the supporters of deregulation. The megabanks became monopolies as they captured market share at the expense of smaller organizations. As they captured market share they increased fees. Consolidation meant conglomerates, which meant monopolies, which meant increased prices.

Financial Innovation

Bankers told us that financial *innovation* meant greater economic and risk management efficiency. Risks were spread widely across a diverse set of investors and financial intermediaries. Specific risks could be allocated to specific financial intermediaries, the intermediaries that could best manage the risks. For example, foreign exchange risk, interest rate risk and default risk could be separated and managed separately. The newly innovated products made the financial system more resilient, more stable and better able to handle shocks. Productivity and growth in the US would increase. Even better if the avalanche of product *innovation* resulted in record profits.

A problem was that the risk were not always spread, but remained concentrated in the financial sector as banks chose to keep significant amounts of it on their balance sheets. By year end of 2007 the balance sheets of the megabanks and the shadow banking system were clogged with toxic debt.

Innovation had become mistaken for *next to useless complexity,* and since the 1990s, inverse floaters, reverse convertibles, and other equity derivatives had flooded the markets. Few questioned the wisdom. Nassim Taleb told us that modern financial technology underestimated the likelihood of extreme events, the consequences of which could be catastrophic. The parallel between financial *innovation* and technological innovation did not hold. Debit cards and swapping fixed for floating rates were useful *innovations.* Increased home ownership at any cost was not. Most *innovations* were used solely to maximize profits and personal income, and provided no economic benefit.

Financial products were vastly more complicated than ever before, and investors had lost any understanding of what banks were actually doing. Boards of directors and senior managers similarly had lost any understanding of what their subordinates were doing. As products became more opaque so did balance sheets. The complexity and obscurity created fertile soil for the growth of toxic products.

Questions arose. Where, for example, do we put derivatives on a balance sheet? The Financial Accounting Standards Board, the FASB, asked this question in 1985. Loans are assets and appear as assets on balance sheets, and similarly deposits are liabilities. For swaps, however, there was no obligation to pay or be paid the notional amount, notwithstanding swaps carried the obligation to pay and receive interest amounts. The financial community had excluded swaps from balance sheets, and this was flawed accounting, and mislead investors and shareholders. Although a notional amount was neither to be repaid nor received, the interest streams represented an asset, cash to be received, or a liability, an obligation to pay cash. That swaps often hedged other risks and this was something important for investors and shareholders to understand. Similarly, volatility needed to be understood. To exclude swaps from the balance sheets was absurdly misleading. Derivatives were disclosed in footnotes. But footnotes had no requirements and were simply comments. If they said anything at all, they were difficult to understand and only to disguise the risks.

The derivative *innovations* were not without opposition. Felix Rohatyn, a seasoned Wall Street banker described OTC derivatives as financial hydrogen bombs built on PCs by 26-year-old MBAs.[228] Others described the 20th century financial *innovations* as the modern equivalent of the alchemists of the Middle Ages, promising spectacular wealth from concoctions and spells: derivatives, securitizations, private equity investments and hedge funds. In reality, any higher than normal returns were a result of temporarily robust economies and not *innovations*, and ten years later, Paul Volker remarked that the only *innovation* that had contributed to growth was the humble ATM. The other *innovations* served only to disguise debt, leverage and risk, and generate profits made at the expense of naive investors. But whatever opposition there was, no one took much notice.

Risk and Regulation

In 1999, as Santyajit Das, ex banker, now critic and writer put it, a new vaudeville act was launched on the front page of *Time Magazine*: Alan Greenspan, Robert Rubin and Larry Summers were the Committee to Save the World.[229] It was neither a great act nor very funny. The act sang songs of praise for deregulation, megabanks and unregulated derivatives, the concoctions that ultimately led to the downfall of the entire banking sector as well as AIG, the globes' biggest insurer.

As banks became larger, they became more difficult to manage and regulate, so less oversight and disclosure became the norm. Many in Washington wrongly assumed that large banks understood what they were doing, and many agreed with the banks that regulation was an impediment to business.

The GLB enabled the formation of *too big to fail* banks. Loans made by one organization were packaged into securities issued by others, then hedged with or purchased by more organizations, from a seemingly ever-expanding pool of investors. Derivatives and their hedges added another dimension, and then there were the tens of thousands of foreign exchange transactions arising from global trade. Neural nets of interconnections arose with the result that no one knew what the risks were, nor who bore them. Minor disturbances in a single organization, market or country were transmitted and magnified just like the neurons in our brains fire and energize connected neural networks. If one connected bank failed, it could have a devastating effect on all organizations connected to it. *Too big to fail* meant that it was better for a government to save a bank in trouble rather than face the consequences of its failure. Systemic risk had arrived. All megabanks were *too big to fail*, but there were more.

The GLB meant that financial organizations had to be regulated by many different regulators, along functional lines. The current US regulatory structure was too complex to mess with, and different activities needed different specialist regulators. How could we ensure that all activities of a bank were regulated? Megabanks themselves did not know all that they did. With multiple regulators, how could we ensure that nothing fell through the cracks? The FED's umbrella role was supposed to ensure that this did not happen. It did not. The megabanks, the financial supermarkets, could not be adequately regulated. To make matters worse, the FDIC guaranteed the deposits of deposit takers, which now included deposits that were used for higher risk, investment banking activities. The US taxpayer was on a bigger hook.

As derivatives did not appear on balance sheets, accounting practices were incapable of measuring the soundness of a bank, and its performance. Technological advances had made the world smaller and enabled banks to process vastly more transactions every day. Desktop computers and servers replaced manual processes. We needed more regulation, more risk management, not less, and a major source of risk, the OTC markets remained free of regulation. We needed a strong grip on safety and soundness, but we could not find our answers in balance sheets.

Congress in 2000 had restricted the regulation of derivatives to a tiny fragment of the business, the exchange traded futures and options,[230] leaving the biggest market, OTC derivatives free of regulation. The derivatives frenzy increased as the problems of the 1990s were forgotten as was Bankers Trust, Barings, Salomon and LTCM. Bankers told us that finance had changed, and the rules under which banks operated were outdated. In any case, they said, they knew what they were doing. But the problems of the 1990s clearly demonstrated that they did not! The risks had been grossly underestimated.

Did derivative harbour catastrophic disasters waiting in the wings. Banks, wanted nothing to constrain their profits, so what to do? It was obvious. Hijack the regulators and politicians and ensure nothing interfered with the P&L. Derivatives were immensely profitable, so profitable that the business could afford a large Congressional lobby. The old partners in the now publicly owned investment banks had exchanged their partnership profit shares for bigger short-term bonuses, with one difference; they had more money to play with and bet. They wanted to use it, unencumbered.

Concerned that regulation may be imposed, the ISDA lobby went into action. It conducted a study that concluded that the industry had the tools, like VaR, the processes, like the ISDA deal templates, and the procedures like marking-to-market positions on a daily basis, to manage derivatives. The ISDA derivatives manual: *Derivatives: Practices and Principles* laid out the story. The simplicity was condemning. The real issue was that the ISDA had buckets of money for lobbyists, and not surprisingly, those involved in the study were employed by the banks making the profits.

Then the lunacy and deception. The ISDA said that derivatives were already regulated as banks were regulated. But only the commercial banks were regulated, and OTC transactions were not on the balance sheet, so escaped regulation. The shadow banking system was unregulated. This claim was a fraud.

The organization told us that notional amounts were not important. It was the 2%, to 4% of the derivatives' notional amounts, the market values that were important. But this is true of all investments. The notional amounts are important. They failed to say that the 1995 global market value of the OTC market was $2 trillion, greater than the largest exposure, historically, of the US bond market, and about 25% of the GDP. The ISDA then contradicted itself when it said that derivatives should not be marked-to-market. The story of Andy Krieger demonstrated exactly why derivatives should be marked-to-market. It wanted to hide volatility, even though investors need to understand volatility!

The ISDA supported VaR for market risk, but VaR shed little light on most derivatives, and no light whatsoever on inverse floaters and other pointless *innovations*.

In June 1993, the G30 released a major report on derivatives, which Dennis Weatherstone oversaw.[231] Its scope included the risks that might slip through the cracks, but it concluded that derivative risks were no more problematic than the risks of making loans or trading bonds. Alan Greenspan announced in 1995:

> It would be a serious mistake … to single out derivative instruments for special regulatory treatment. Such a response would create artificial incentives to structure transactions

on the basis of regulatory rules rather than on
the economic characteristic of transactions
themselves[232]

Greenspan, a laissez-fair zealot was a master at disguising
rubbish with opacity. Who knows what he was trying to say? Let's
not have any rules at all, let's have a free-for-all?

The G30 report encountered political opposition. The OTC
market had grown exponentially and many thought that there was
a need for oversight. Some politicians thought that banks should
disclose their positions and set aside funds as a reserve for bad
bets. Representative Henry Gonzales, a Democratic and head of the
House Banking Committee, was convinced that the risks were
misunderstood. Edward Markey, also a Democrat, and head of the
House Subcommittee on Telecommunications and Finance, asked
the General Accounting Office to study derivatives' risks, and in
1994, the Office released its report, identifying "significant gaps
and weaknesses" in the regulatory oversight of derivatives, poor
risk management and outdated accounting standards. "The sudden
failure or abrupt withdrawal from trading of any of the large U.S.
dealers could cause liquidity problems in the market and could also
pose risks to others, including federally insured banks and the
financial system as a whole." Charles Bowsher, head of the Office,
testified before Markey's committee in 1994: "In some cases
intervention has and could result in a financial bailout paid for or
guaranteed by taxpayers."

In response, bankers told us that banking was difficult for
non-bankers to understand. It was mysterious. They told us, absent
any reason, that the regulation of derivatives was not good for the
US and the economy. Most of the regulators and politicians
believed them, and the press reported on the pronouncements of
their senior officials with little regard for veracity or logic.

Congressman Jim Leach introduced legislation in 1994 to
restrict OTC derivatives, but the ISDA's Mark Brickell vehemently
opposed it. He claimed that the bill would impose unique suitability
standards, so should be defeated. The proposed bill did not, and
this resulted in the good Congressman calling Brickell a liar in a
Congressional hearing on 12th July 1994. Brickell clearly thought
that his misrepresentations would go unchallenged. So
misunderstood was the world of derivatives that
misrepresentation was par for the course. One advocate of OTC
derivatives, for example, referenced research that purported to
support the absurd claim that banks were not at risk as derivatives
never made losses! His evidence was a list of derivatives trades
showing only gains. The research had deliberately excluded the
trades that made losses.[233]

These were the stage props when Brooksly Born, the Chairman of the CFTC, made an attempt to regulate derivatives. She was concerned that unfettered, opaque trading could "threaten our regulated markets or, indeed, our economy without any federal agency knowing about it," she said in Congressional testimony. She had been a successful Washington lawyer and on the board of governors of the American Bar Association. As there was little transparency, she thought that large and unknown derivative positions could build up and cause problems. Born was convinced that Orange County, Bankers Trust, the school boards, municipalities and pension funds that had lost large sums of money were not isolated events. Sumitomo had been caught using derivatives to corner the copper market and swaps were being used to move profits from one quarter to another:

> We were trying to police a very rapidly growing part of the market for manipulation and fraud, but we knew nothing about the market… There were no record keeping requirements. No reporting requirements. The market was totally opaque.

Regulating the OTC derivatives markets would mean that the market would become transparent and operate with loss absorbing capital. She said that we needed to ensure that when commitments were made, there was capital to back them up. Fraud could be monitored for organised exchanges but not so for private garage factories.

She wanted to release a concept paper that asked questions. Could OTC derivatives lead to a financial system meltdown? Should there be greater disclosure of trades and capital requirements to cushion losses? Should there be a central clearing facility? In 2008, we saw that she had been on the right track.

Her views incited fierce opposition from Greenspan, Rubin, Summers, Arthur Levitt, the chairmen of the SEC and Jim Leach, the chairman of the House Banking Committee.[234] They thought that merely discussing new rules would threaten the derivatives market. It might move to London. Summers and Greenspan both told Born that she didn't know what she was doing and that any announcement might lead to a financial crisis. Summers in fact cautioned Born: "if you go forward with [the paper] it will cause the worst financial crisis since World War II".[235] He continued: "the market would implode and there would be lawsuits galore". Greenspan thought that even asking the questions Born posed was dangerous. He said that derivatives were already regulated and the regulation was "properly balanced and appropriate". The motivations were not in doubt. Many large banks earned up to 40% of their profits from derivatives trading.

Prior to this issue, Born had already had a confrontation with Greenspan. Greenspan had argued against dealing directly with derivatives market fraud. He reasoned that if a financial services executive committed fraud, customers would figure it out and refrain from doing business with the executive. Born was perplexed to put it mildly, and as a defence lawyer could make no sense of the remark. Few could.

But she went ahead and on 7 May 1998 published the paper. On the very same day Greenspan, Rubin and Levitt publicly expressed "grave concerns". But there was no crisis. We would wait ten more years!

In July 1998, Greenspan testified before the House Banking Committee:

> Professional counterparties to privately negotiated contracts also have demonstrated their ability to protect themselves from losses, from fraud, and counterparty insolvencies ... aside from safety and soundness regulation of derivatives dealers under the banking and securities laws, regulation of derivatives transactions that are [done] privately by professionals is unnecessary. Regulation that serves no useful purpose hinders the efficiency of markets to enlarge standards of living[236]

Notwithstanding the stupidity of these remarks, Greenspan and Rubin won. Every two years is an election year in Washington, 1998 was one and campaign contributions were needed. Banks were making a fortune and needed regulation like a hole in the head. So even though LTCM had collapsed in October, Congress approved a six-month moratorium to allow the other regulators to develop their own recommendations. The deregulatory wheels were in motion, and Brooksly Born resigned and returned to practicing law.

In November 1999, the President's Working Group on Financial Markets spoke. Summers, the new Secretary of the Treasury, Greenspan, Levitt and William Rainer the new CFTC chairman endorsed the *Over-the-Counter Derivatives Markets and the Commodity Exchange Act*:

> to promote innovation, competition, efficiency and transparency in OTC derivatives markets,

to reduce systemic risk, and to allow the United States to maintain leadership in these rapidly developing markets [237]

OTC derivative were to be exempt from regulation and the Act was passed by Congress and signed into law by the lame duck, President Clinton. It was his last action as President and put a wall in place between regulation and the major profit making activity on Wall Street.

Levitt in retrospect regretted his decision to support the non-regulation of derivatives. Rubin, when at Citigroup, said that he had favoured regulating derivatives and increasing loss reserves, but when he was at the Treasury, he could see no way of doing this, as Wall Street didn't want it, and Rubin wanted to return to Wall Street. If Rubin had spoken out things may have been different. Ego and money led Rubin astray and not supporting Brooksly Born was an egregious display of gross irresponsibility.

In the late 1990s, the notional and market values of OTC derivatives were $70 trillion and $2.5 trillion respectively and there had been almost no activity ten years before. [238] By 2010, the notional and market values had become $615 trillion, up 10 times, and over $20 trillion up 8 times. The volume of credit default swaps, which in 1998 was negligible, became $50 trillion notional value and $3 trillion market value in 2008.[239] The power of the banking oligarchy had kept derivatives unregulated for ten years which snowballed into larger profits and more influence until the Crisis and Great Recession.[240]

Non-Bank Risk

Alliance Mortgage, a non-bank, subprime mortgage originator went public in 1996. Two years later, it was in court over abusive practices and by 2000, it was bankrupt.[241] In the meantime, its founder had banked $135 million and become a rich man. Alliance was only one of many non-bank mortgage lenders that went public before collapsing, after making their founders rich.

Historically mortgages had been provided by deposit takers. They were regulated and their deposits insured. Non-bank lenders did not take deposits so relied exclusively on invested capital, other investors' funds, IPO shareholder funds and the short-term money markets. As they were not deposit takers, they were not regulated, and investor funds were not safeguarded, nor were most of the short-term lenders. Non-bank lenders created a hole in the regulatory net, but they were significant providers of credit to the globe's largest capital market, the $14 trillion US real estate market. The risk that the funding they relied upon might disappear was significant.

The move to the *originate-and-distribute* model meant that the non-bank lenders, like the traditional mortgage originators, did not care at all about the credit worthiness of borrowers. They did not make good loans, and rampant predatory lending was par for the course.

When interest rates increased suddenly in the 1990s, non-prime lender revenues suffered, and heavy losses were incurred, resulting in extensive write-downs. Poor accounting principles had permitted the non-bank lenders to record the present value of all expected future mortgage payments as current revenues. Inexplicable, but it meant bloated profits and IPO investments appeared more attractive. When a mortgage holder defaulted, losses resulted in the value of the mortgage being written down. Like other originators, the equity tranches of the MBSs they built were difficult to sell, and so were mostly retained, so in addition to the write-downs, the collapsing equity tranches created losses. Losses meant that banks withdrew their warehouse loans and the short-term lenders, their support. Many non-bank lenders, failed.

Poor management had made three bets, that both interest rates and mortgage defaults remained low and that the short-term markets would continue to provide funds, and they lost all three of them. The demise of many of the non-bank mortgage lenders demonstrated that regulation had not kept pace with the banking industry. Regulators and the policy makers had not appreciated the increasingly important role played by the unregulated shadow banking system. Investors' funds had been channeled through the shadow banking system by securitizations and OTC derivatives to consumers. We were on our way back to the 1920s.

Dotcom and 9/11

In 1998, LTCM was rescued by a bailout organised by the NY FED, which feared that its failure could endanger the US financial system. Contagion might bring the Asian and Russian problems to Wall Street. When Continental Illinois[242] failed in 1984 it was the biggest bank failure of all time. We heard *too big to fail* for the first time, and the FDIC pumped in billions and guaranteed deposits well over the $100,000 limit. The LTCM bailout was on a different scale. It had debts of $125 billion and 7,000 open derivatives positions with a notional value of $1.25 trillion! LTCM was truly *too big to fail*. LTCM was a harbinger for the future, but no lessons were learned. Few asked why a small hedge fund could become *too big to fail.*

The dotcom bubble was in full swing at the turn of the century. On 10 March 2000, the NASDAQ closed at a new all-time high of 5,048. It had risen from 900 in 1995. But the bubble burst and by the end of 2001, dotcom was over, and 99% of all the Internet company IPOs were trading at prices below their first day closing prices and 50% were trading at less than $1.[243] A mild recession followed and by mid-2002, the NASDAQ was back down at 1,100.

Amazon and a few others survived, but most burned their venture capital. Between March 2000 and October 2002, a $5 trillion paper loss resulted from the collapse of technology stocks.[244] The total wealth that evaporated was more than $8 trillion. Conventional wisdom about growth and profits had been shelved. The widely touted Pets.com made no sense. $1 trillion invested in telecommunications companies went up in smoke, along with 500,000 jobs.[245] Some of the biggest individual implosions were Global Crossing, with $12.4 billion in debt and WorldCom with a debt of $32 billion. WorldCom's CEO, Bernie Ebbers was convicted and jailed for accounting fraud. Enron created fictitious transactions that made loans look like revenues, and falsified information. Citigroup ($500 billion in false transactions) simply looked aside as did Merrill Lynch and JP Morgan Chase ($2.2 billion in false transactions), while Enron's auditor, Arthur Anderson assisted the fraud. Arthur Anderson was forced out of business, and many Enron executives were jailed. Enron was bankrupted, but not one bank executive was prosecuted.

The pump-and-dump[246] analysts had blown up dotcoms, exploiting the misunderstood fascination with Internet technology and derivatives. Media coverage of the financial markets had sustained the public frenzy. It was not organised crime, but organised fraud, and Eliot Spitzer, the New York Attorney General negotiated a $1.4 billion settlement with a number of large New York banks for fraudulent research reporting. Penalties were paid by Citigroup, Credit Suisse and Goldman Sachs. We will see these names linked to penalties again and again. Two analysts, Bloget ($4 million) and Grubman ($15 million) paid fines and were banned from the securities industry for life. Stock analysts gave false recommendations, often to secure investment banking business, on which they were compensated, and thousands of IPOs, private placements and mergers were undertaken based on false information.

Then we had 9/11.

As we entered the new Millennium, Wall Street had overcome obstacles and reached new heights. It had survived the implosion of the S&L industry and the election of a Democrat as US President, the crises of the 1990s, LTCM and dotcom. These events quickly passed, life went on, and nothing seemed to phase the markets. The DJIA took 25 years to get back to its 1929 peak, but it recovered after a fall of almost 25% of its value in October 1987, in less than a year.

The FED Acts

After 9/11, the FED was not content to sit on its hands. In response to dotcom and the post 9/11 downturns, it made credit cheap to stimulate growth and to counter inflation. During 2001, the FED lowered the federal funds rate from 6.5% to 1.75%, on the way down to 1% in 2003. Asian surpluses, looking for a safe home after the Asian crises of the 1990s, and surpluses from the oil producing economies flooded into the US. Investors, including foreign governments, and corporations bought US treasuries and US real estate collateralized securitizations. They assumed they were safe and the markets in which they traded would always be liquid. The pool of foreign money in search of safe fixed income investments was enormous, $70 trillion in 2000. By 2007, it had doubled to $140 trillion.

The US economy bounced back. Cheap money, the American dream of owning one's own home and willing lenders led to a housing and housing construction boom and the mortgage markets flourished. By 2003, there were signs of a strong recovery. The mortgage origination business turned to the subprime mortgage business with new vigour, and predatory finance, and a housing bubble developed. Although the bubble burst in 2007 when our real problems began, we felt good from 2001 until 2007.

By 2002, it was clear that the FED's cheap credit was financing retail property mortgages to the exclusion of business investment. The latter was the reason for the cheap credit, so this was not welcome news. Business expansion would stimulate the economy, but investment grew less in the 2000s than in the 1990s. Willing borrowers and cheap credit also meant that consumer spending on credit cards, auto loans, and personal borrowing expanded in parallel with mortgage borrowing. Consumer debt also soared. The consequences of cheap credit were off target for a number of reasons: Wall Street's voracious appetite for MBS and CDOs, Washington's policy towards housing and the new mortgage products that enabled huge amounts of money to flow from investors into housing.

Commercial paper had been a good investment for pension funds and similar conservative investors. A little more yield could be earned, and the risk of US corporations defaulting was minimal. But over time, a third of the paper became asset-backed commercial paper, and issued by SIVs, and this changed its risk profile.[247] The SIV paper funded less liquid long-term, often real estate based investments. By 2007, the asset backed commercial paper market had risen to $1.2 trillion, and the significant issuers were SIVs, banks and the shadow banking system.

The Jobs and Wasniac, and Hewlett Packard inspired culture of technological innovation had been applied to finance, so *innovation*, in any form must be good, bankers thought. The benefits of *just in time* inventories and the lower costs of the production of goods and services were assumed somehow to extend to complex financial *innovation*. The culture did not question whether *innovation* was in fact, like technological innovation or whether it was beneficial. Credit default swaps must be good for society, after all, they were a form of insurance. Moreover, they might have had a social value if the parallels between traditional insurance and credit default swaps, holding reserves and ownership of the insured asset had been put in place. But, they were not.

Alan Greenspan Speaks

The DJIA was just above 2,700 when Greenspan took office in 1987, and had risen to over 11,000 in January 2006, when he retired. During the same period, unemployment fell from 6.2% to 4.6%. GDP grew an average of 3.9% and inflation averaged 1.8%. This contrasted with the time of Clinton's successor, G. W. Bush, when GDP grew an average of 2.2%, and median income fell from $52,500 per annum to $50,300. Greenspan was credited for the boom of the 1990s, the falling unemployment and low inflation. He enjoyed significant stature and his pronouncements were widely accepted, no matter what rubbish he said. His views were so dominant that when Raghuram Rajan, the IMF Chief Economist, had the temerity to question them at the 2005 FED annual conference, the last one for which Greenspan was chairman,[248] he was shouted down. Rajan's remarks were prescient and Greenspan later recanted.[249]

He embraced laissez-faire capitalism, technology and financial *innovation*, OTC derivatives, deregulation and free markets. The markets, he said, would self-regulate. He accepted the strict EMH, and preached the "transcendent, wealth-creating powers of the market", whatever that meant, and with novelist, Ayn Rand believed that "collective power was a destructive force set against the enlightened self-interests of individuals". Regulation was dangerous and free markets would embrace the good and reject the bad. Whatever could that mean too? He had resolute faith that those participating in the financial markets would act responsibly. He relied not on reason, but on prejudice, dogma and faith. He was, after all, the Oracle.

As FED chairmen, Greenspan focused only on the FED's central bank functions and not its regulatory functions. The FED was the safety and soundness regulator for a large banks and bank holding companies and had a Division of Consumer and Community Affairs tasked with looking after the interests of bank customers. He abrogated his regulatory responsibilities.

Greenspan arrived at the FED in an era of economic arrogance. The makers of economic policy had convinced themselves that economies were under control and manageable,[250] that is until the late 1990s when the Asian and Russian crises struck. However, they did not count, we heard. They were crony capitalists, and crises only arose in troubled economies.

Greenspan was first thought to be a very successful central banker, however, he deserves few accolades. He presided over a period that experienced few problems in contrast to the 1970s and 1980s. The two recessions that came and went during his time was short lived. Paul Volker, his predecessor, had done all the hard work. Volker became unpopular when he imposed the conditions necessary for the recovery he orchestrated. Greenspan took the credit.

Furthermore, the US economy benefited from events that had little to do with Greenspan. Technology enhanced productivity. Desktop technology, email and teleconferencing did away with typewriters and face to face meetings. Software enabled better inventory management. Higher productivity meant higher profits and less inflation.

Greenspan in fact did very little. He blobbed along from Washington cocktail party to cocktail party. While he warned about excessive expectations, he did little about it. The FED should not interfere when bubbles developed, he told us. It should only clean the mess up afterwards. A "take your dog to the park" economist. He was lucky. The dotcom bubble recovery was nearer three years than the textbook eight months and dovetailed into the housing bubble. The FED did not have to guide the dotcom recession to recovery as the housing bubble arrived, thoughtfully, just in time to provide the illusion of a recovery.

Greenspan played a leading role in creating the conditions that led to the Crisis. Decades of free market fundamentalism laid the foundations for the Crisis. He has recanted. There are few today that listen. He misunderstood basic concepts like bank capital, which he confused with reserves. It's quite striking as he was chairman of the organization that holds bank reserves and facilitates banks trading them. With higher capital, when there are problems more of the cost is born by the bank's owners, its equity holders, and less of it by depositors, lenders and taxpayers.[251] This in itself is a reason for higher capital levels.

He suggested that technological advances enabled regulation to be bypassed, that free market resources build wealth and growth, and that markets can regulate themselves, (precisely what we do not want) and that fraud is controlled and eliminated by self-regulation.[252] Self-regulation stabilized the markets. In any case, governments cannot keep up with the markets. It was incredulous, and he gave no reason for these views. Of course, if governments fall behind market *innovation*, then an alternative is to limit *innovation* until governments catch up, but that is not, in Greenspan's view, an alternative. Here is a further quotation:

> With technological change clearly accelerating, existing regulatory structures are being bypassed, freeing market forces to enhance wealth creation and economic growth. ... As we move into a new century, the market-stabilizing private regulatory forces should gradually displace many cumbersome, increasingly ineffective government structures. This is a likely outcome since governments, by their very nature, cannot adjust sufficiently quickly to a changing environment.[253]

This quotation is from the final sections of remarks Greenspan made on the history of banking in the US. He claimed, as usual without justification, that financial crises resulted from regulation.

The chairman of the nation's central bank, and regulator of a significant part of the banking sector, had little knowledge of how to do his job, and little interest in doing it. He was ideologically barred from doing so. He held governments in distain. The only authority was no authority, and laissez faire capitalism. In fact, he tells us that he took the job specifically to not do it. He tells us that he wanted to "engage in efforts to advance free market capitalism as an insider."[254]

Vagueness, obscurity and lack of any support for his pronouncements simply disguised fundamental misunderstandings:

> The free market is a pillar of civilization, which presupposes the productive interaction of people engaged in the division of labour, driven by economic comparative advantage. This implies mutual exchange to mutual advantage among free people ... in either event, human nature being what it is, revival will come. It always has in this society [been] governed by that remarkable document we call the Constitution of the United States.[255]

He boasted about his inability to be clear:

> Greenspan was in fact proud of his obscurantism. Greenspan was cryptic, and boasted of his ability to put fewer thoughts into more words than almost anyone.[256]

Warren Buffett assumed that if he looked at a company report, and could not understand it, then the company did not want him to understand it. It appears that Gangster Greenspan had the same intention. Why would you say:

> There is a very fundamental trade off, of what type of economy you wish to have ... You can have huge amounts of regulation and I will guarantee nothing will go wrong, but nothing will go right either[257]

Greenspan on OTC derivatives was alarming. He thought market participants were sophisticated enough to know what they were doing. There were a number of dissenters. George Soros avoids using derivatives "because we don't understand how they work." We said that Felix Rohatyn thought derivatives were potential hydrogen bombs. Warren Buffett observed five years prior, that derivatives were "financial weapons of mass destruction, carrying dangers that, while now latent, are potentially lethal. ... Large amounts of risk, particularly credit risk, have become concentrated in the hands of relatively few derivatives dealers. The troubles of one could quickly infect the others."[258]

In 2003, he testified before the Senate Banking Committee. Notwithstanding LTCM:

What we have found ... is that derivatives have been an extraordinarily useful vehicle to transfer risk from those who shouldn't be taking it to those who are willing to and are capable of doing so ... The vast increase in the size of the over-the-counter derivatives markets is the result of the market finding them a very useful vehicle ... they are obviously regulated to the extent that banks, ... the creators ... are regulated by the banking agencies, but not beyond that. And the reason why we think it would be a mistake to go beyond that degree of regulation is that derivatives transactions are transactions amongst professionals.[259]

What sense is there in this? Derivatives can be used to transfer risk from one party to another, but the recipients rarely understood what they were getting into. The size of the market, yes, it grew, but to claim that derivatives were useful because of growth is absurd. The market grew because derivatives made enormous profits for derivatives dealers at the expense of naïve and unsuspecting customers. Growth and size are reasons for understanding and regulating markets. Non derivatives transactions, which are regulated, are also transactions between professionals. Derivatives are housed in off balance sheet entities, and the effort to regulate derivatives is an effort to regulate what the current regulatory framework cannot regulate without changes.

Derivatives permitted the financial industry to issue more personal and corporate debt, including mortgages. Trading the debt increased the number of participants exposed to risk. Greenspan told us that banks were concerned about their franchise values and their reputations, and that they would never imperil them by lending too aggressively or using excess leverage. But excessive lending is precisely what banks were doing when he made these remarks, with excessive leverage. The problems spread quickly. As we will, see, interconnectivity destroyed Bear Stearns, Lehman Brothers and AIG. Representative Bernard Sanders, an independent from Vermont asked, "Aren't you concerned with such a growing concentration of wealth that if one of these huge institutions fails that it will have a horrendous impact on the national and global economy?" Greenspan replied, "No, I'm not ... I believe that the general growth in large institutions has occurred in the context of an underlying structure of markets in which many of the larger risks [are] fully hedged". You really could not take Greenspan seriously.

On safety and security, he argued:

> Not only have individual financial institutions
> become less vulnerable to shocks from
> underlying risk factors, but also the financial
> system as a whole has become more
> resilient.[260]

Then the 2008 crisis!

On mortgage origination, he tells us that technological advances have made the process of loan application more streamlined. True. And that mortgages can be tailored to the needs of applicants.[261] A bit like buying a suit. But it was not like buying a suit, it was charging more for less credit worthy applicants. The mortgage did not fit any better.

In 2005, on the subprime markets:

> "Where once more marginal applicants would
> simply have been denied credit, lenders are
> now able to quite efficiently judge the risk
> posed by individual applicants and to price that
> risk accordingly"[262]

The comment is inexplicable, and ill informed, and despicable given that Greenspan was well aware of the predatory mortgage lending and the problems it was causing Main Street. Greenspan had abrogated his responsibility for consumer protection on the basis that the markets would suffice, and now he poured salt into the wounds. Ned Gramlich, a FED governor pushed him to address subprime mortgage regulation. Greenspan had no interest.

Concerning securitizations, Greenspan was incomprehensible:

> Another far reaching innovation is the
> technology of securitization – a form of
> derivative - which has encouraged unbundling
> of the production processes for many credit
> services ... These ... have surely improved the
> efficiency of our financial markets.[263] ...
> Improved access to credit for consumers and
> especially these more recent developments has
> had significant benefits. Unquestionably,
> innovation and deregulation has vastly
> expanded credit availability to virtually all
> income classes. Access to credit has enabled
> families to purchase homes, deal with

emergencies, and obtain goods and services. Home ownership is at a record high.[264]

Improved efficiency? What? Unregulated securitizations were part of the problem that brought down the financial system at enormous pain and cost, for the financial benefit of a few. Efficient profits perhaps? MBS securitizations had expanded credit and enabled families to purchase homes. What he did not say is that many of these families could not afford the credit and the homes, and the consequence of this was a disaster for the global economy in 2008.

Greenspan was very confused on many issues. He thought that capital was expensive, he thought that holding liquid reserves resulted from poor capital regulation, and he thought that financial crises were often akin to natural disasters, and that their mitigation would be too expensive for society. He does not acknowledge the link between flawed politics and financial crises. He acknowledged that higher capital levels would have constrained the Crisis, but he maintained that prevention was not worth the expense.[265]

> [Trying to protect citizens against risks from the financial system] may encompass expensive building materials whose earthquake flexibility is needed for only a minute of two every century, or an expensive stock of vaccine for a feared epidemic that may never occur"[266]

Crises are not natural disasters, they occur regularly, but even if it were, it is precisely because catastrophes occur that we need capital as insurance. Could Greenspan explain himself to any survivor of the last influenza epidemic? Or would Greenspan have preferred to be born in the 18th century? Others have said that the Crisis was a fluke, a once in a lifetime catastrophe. They argue that it should be ignored and prevention would only interfere with what banks do to support the economy. Talk of greater financial stability coming at the expense of growth is hollow.

On Capital:

> (capital regulation would) require the building up of a buffer of idle resources that are not otherwise engaged in the production of goods and services" [267]

This remark is rubbish as any Accounting 101 student would confirm, it is naïve and irresponsible.[268]

Why was Greenspan able to make these comments? The answer is because he was a gangster and a politician. From 1993 until 2000, the economy experienced a bull market and Greenspan received the credit. Total wealth increased, and it did not matter that it was concentrated in the richest of the rich, in the top 0.1%. He became so influential that his comments could move the markets. His obfuscation and rambling sentences, which rolled into each other, simply added to his mystique. Washington accepted what he said, or more accurately, what sense could be made of what he said. By the time we took stock of the Crisis, however, his reputation was shattered.

Arthur Levitt, thought that the Greenspan aura was due to the financial naivety of many members of Congress. "I felt that the titans of our legislature didn't want to reveal their own inability to understand some of the concepts that Greenspan was setting forth … I don't recall anyone saying, What do you mean by that, Alan?"[269] It's a pity they did not.

> "Alan was held in very high regard," said Jim Leach, an Iowa Republican who led the House Banking and Financial Services Committee at the time. "You've got an area of judgment in which members of Congress have non-existent expertise."[270]

> "He had a way of speaking that made you think he knew exactly what he was talking about," said Senator Tom Harkin, a Democrat from Iowa. "He was able to say things in a way that made people not want to question him on anything. Who were you to question him?"[271]

Such was his grip on some of the Washington lemmings, that when Raghuram Rajan, then the Chief Economist of the IMF asked whether deregulation and *innovation* had increased rather than decreased risk in the financial system, he was shouted down.[272]

> Mr. Rajan quickly came under attack as an anti-market Luddite, wistful for the old days of regulation. Today, however, few are dismissing his ideas. The financial crisis has savaged the reputation of Mr. Greenspan and others now seen as having turned a blind eye toward excessive risk-taking.

Rajan said he had planned to write about how financial developments during Greenspan's 18-year tenure made the world safer. But the more he looked, the less convinced he became. In the end, with Greenspan watching in the audience, he said that disaster might soon be upon us. He stated that incentives were horribly skewed in the financial sector, with employees reaping rich rewards, with little downside. This lead to investments in complex products with big payoffs, but which could fail spectacularly. The failure of the tranches held by securitizers might endanger the banking system itself. Interconnectedness had created systemic risk.

His remarks were prescient. We had only to wait a couple of years,[273] but at the time he was met with ideological derision. Donald Kohn, a vice chairman of the FED told us that private party self-regulation was effective and that government regulation undermined stability. He did not give any reasons for making these claims. By 2005, it had become clear that industry self-regulation had failed.

Kohn claimed, again without justification, than Greenspan's monetary policy made the world a better place. He was hopelessly off base. He said that Rajan's recommendations would lead to a reduction in public welfare and that they were at odds with the tradition of policy excellence, the subject of the conference. Rajan's recommendations were clearly at odds with what Kohn described as policy excellence, however the Greenspan policy was not policy excellence, it was a prescription for disaster. All Larry Summers, one of his targets, could muster up was that Rajan was a misguided Luddite.[274] Summers provided consultancy to hedge funds, organizations that made money on the upside, but lost nothing, not even clawbacks, when losses were encountered.

In 2008, Greenspan finally acknowledged that the housing market problems, a once in a hundred year phenomenon, might require Washington's involvement. He admitted to Congress that he had been badly wrong.[275] But again, obscurantism prevailed. He admitted that his free market ideology *may* have been flawed and that he *may* have been in error when he did not support the regulation of *some* derivatives. But when asked whether he should have let interest rates remain low for so long, he blamed investors for not "properly factoring in the risk that housing prices might fall." He admitted that the Crisis, the causes of which he said he did not understand, was a once in a century tsunami, and that more regulation *may* have been required. An exchange between the committee chairmen, Democrat Henry Waxman struck at his obscurantism. Greenspan stated that there was a *flaw in the model that he perceived as a critical functioning structure that defines how the world works*. Waxman's response was a question: You got it wrong?[276] His faith in self-correcting free markets was seen for what it was. "Confused ramblings of a misguided, [simpleton] ideologue".[277] Greenspan admitted a few years after he had left the

FED that he had not understood what was going on: "But some of the complexities of some of the instruments that were going into CDOs bewildered me. I didn't understand what they were doing or how they actually got the types of returns out of the mezzanines and the various tranches of the CDOs that they did. And I figured that, with the resources at my disposal, if I didn't understand, how was the rest of the world going to understand".[278]

Oligarchies

In the 1980s, Louis Ranieri of Salomon helped the Reagan administration to draft legislation that enabled the market for MBSs. That Congress had to rely on Wall Street to draft legislation was a bad sign. Ranieri's efforts marked the rebirth of the banking oligarchy in the US, where large banks and their gatekeepers, lawyers, accountants and consultants purchase political power, which they then exploit to further their own ends. The European banks too evolved oligarchies.

Oligarchies have been around for centuries. In modern times, political power becomes concentrated in a small political elite, the political elite supports a business elite, and enables it to generate excess profits. The business elite in return keeps the political elite in power by buying it votes, or whatever else it takes to keep it in power. The support provided by the political elite to the business elite includes lucrative contracts, cheap funding, tax concessions, subsidies and access to cheap natural resources. The business elite buys votes for the political elite by funding election campaigns, paying for advertising and giving money to voters. It provides politicians with financial favours including participation in lucrative business deals, enhanced life styles, and consultancy and other employment. The process results in the business elite gaining political power that it uses to advance its own interests. Oligarchies are a win-win for both elites. The problem is that they violate equal opportunity, fair competition and free markets and result in fat and bloated elites that harbour inefficiency, incompetence and weak management. They eventually die.

In the emerging markets, besides providing monetary incentives and paying more for services, governments raise import taxes and force out foreign competition, so that locally produced products can be sold at exaggerated prices. In some cases, employees of government owned enterprises actively participate in election campaigns. In extreme cases, in Thailand and Indonesia, votes are purchased from voters with cash.

For business elites, oligarchies make a lot of sense. Why advertise, compete, make better products or cheaper production costs when for less money you can buy the controllers of the nation's natural resources, the national accounts, its taxation policies and revenues and the legislative process. Why care about competition when you can eliminate it?

After World War II, oligarchies emerged in Russian, Indonesian, Korea, Singapore, Thailand, The Philippines and Taiwan. Oligarchies come with corruption and authoritarian governments. In Asia, its retarded development made it easy.

Indonesia's President Suharto (*Soeharto*) concerns were law and order, the welfare of Indonesians and the stability of a diverse archipelago of thousands of islands. Suharto permitted the armed forces (he was an army officer) to dominate the legislative bodies. He enriched his inner circle of family, friends and the military, and embraced crony capitalism. The inner circle, the business elite, controlled businesses that became the backbone of the Indonesian economy, and shaped its development. In return, the business elite and the military kept Sukarno in power. The tools included lucrative government contracts, cheap funding from state controlled banks, subsidies and support from family owned automotive, mining and infrastructure conglomerates. The toll road from Suharto Hatta Airport was financed by cheap funds and every cent of every toll goes straight into the coffers of the oligarchy, the inner circle. The Suharto family controlled more than 80% of the firms listed on the Jakarta (now Indonesian) stock exchange. Corruption thrived, but foreign investors knew that the business elite enjoyed political support and assumed that investments would be safe, and while Indonesia developed, foreign money flowed in. But when the economy faltered, it was another story, and the inflow stopped.

The Philippines developed an oligarchy on Marcos largesse. A dozen families controlled half of the corporate sector and 20% of the value of all stocks trading on the Manila stock exchange. Under Marcos, a promising economy became a basket case.

One of the richest men in the world, Carlos Slim, a Mexican, and the son of immigrants from The Lebanon owns companies that account for 7% of Mexico's economic output. He built his wealth by creating monopolies. His Teléfonos de México and its cellular affiliate own 90% of the fixed telephone lines and 75% of the cell phone lines. The UN measures Mexico as 103 of 126 nations in inequality. 20% of the population earns less than $2 per day. Mr Monopoly earns 14 million times this *every* day. He is the largest private employer, and taxpayer, and legislation that threatens his interests is rarely enacted. As his companies circumvent regulators, they charge higher prices. So strong is his influence on Mexican politics that President Calderón appealed directly to him *to permit more competition*. His empire is so vast that doing business in Mexico is difficult for anyone, and anyone includes the Mexican government. Competition and hence innovation in Mexico has been crushed and Mexico's long term growth has suffered. Mr Monopoly is a one-man oligarchy![279]

Simon Johnson[280] tells the story of the Russia oligarchy in the 1990s. The private sector borrowed heavily, almost $500 billion, from a number of megabanks and undertook a number of large energy projects. It assumed that the growth in the energy sector would create a permanent increase in consumption. The investments created jobs, and the economy expanded. The importance of the oligarchs to the Kremlin grew and political support meant contracts, tax concessions and subsidies. Investors assumed that the loans were backed by the Kremlin so they were given easily. The local banks also lent. Over borrowing, however, ended in disaster, the economy spiralled downward and economic paralysis followed. What then happened was par for the course. The Kremlin squeezed low income workers who did not, of course, like the squeeze. The Kremlin then squeezed the oligarchy, who did not like it either. In Indonesia the government toppled, but in Russia some of those who should have paid were simply removed from the Kremlin's spider web of support.

Oligarchies survive in the good times, but as their growth does not come from good management, innovation, competition and talent, bad times usually lead to problems. When times are tough, government funding dries up, contracts become scarce, the inflow of foreign capital slows and the local currency becomes cheaper. Companies fail, workers lose jobs, incomes fall, services are reduced, taxes increase and inflation follows. Difficult decisions have to be made. The political elite begins by imposing austerity measures on the population at large. As there are not enough chairs to go around, some members of the oligarchy survive at the cost of others. It's musical chairs. The bigger chaebols survived in South Korea, as did Gazprom in Russia, and promptly increased market share, as the smaller, less influential competitors did not survive. When corporate governance is lacking, owners of failing companies take what they can, and run. The political elite then suffers, as their support has disappeared. Indonesia's Suharto fell from grace, as did Marcos.

The Global Banking Oligarchy

From the 1980s, there was staggering growth in the financial sector globally, and Wall Street had become wealthy and powerful. It then became a political machine. Banking had become a central component of Western economies and was a career of choice. It was seductive, prestigious and lucrative. Technology, complexity and salaries were magnets. The US banking oligarchy became firmly re-established, and took Washington captive:

> Despite the scandals and crises that marked the 1990s, this was the decade when Wall Street translated its growing economic power into political power and when the ideology of financial innovation and deregulation became conventional wisdom in Washington on both sides of the political aisle. The unprecedented amounts of money flowing through the financial sector, increasingly concentrated in a handful of megabanks, were the foundation of a new financial oligarchy.[281]

Wall Street had exploited the usual crony capitalism trade-offs. It gained political power by buying it, but with money, it already had, and the megabanks used the political power to protect their profit-making engines. Wall Street used an army of lobbyists, campaign and other contributions and the Wall Street - Parkway revolving door. What Wall Street wanted was no constraints on profits and how they were made, so deregulation was the major objective. It was real crony capitalism with the bribes and under the table money better disguised.

Wall Street financed research was fed to the lobbyists so that they could sell the Wall Street agenda to policy makers. The research was rigged of course, and promoted the Wall Steet ideology that unfettered *innovation* and unregulated financial markets were good for America. The army of lobbyists armed with the self-serving research ensured that Wall Street dogma became Parkway financial wisdom. Washington came to accept that a financial sector with large and powerful megabanks was good for the developed world. Lobbyists relied on outrageous, dogmatic and groundless claims. Bankers and lobbyists argued, and argue for their ideas with unsubstantiated and illogical claims because they are rarely challenged. They are not challenged because bankers and lobbyists claim credibility and knowledge. For example, in 1994 the industry argued that executive stock options should be accounted for at no cost when granted, notwithstanding that options must have a value. The interest groups argued, speciously that if options had to be accounted for with an initial value that all sorts of ridiculous consequence would follow. US firms would not be able to raise money, the economy would suffer, and US firms would be less competitive. It took ten years and a scandalous Enron bankruptcy for appropriate accounting rules for executive stock options to be implemented.

In 2009 the financial industry spent $244 million on lobbying, an increase of 14% over 2007. Inflation during this period was 8%. During the Dodd-Frank negotiations 1,537 lobbyists represented financial institutions in Washington, 25 times the number that represented consumer support groups and other proponents of strong reform.[282] Citigroup alone, then 34% owned by the US government, had 46 lobbyists. The "other side", the public, not a united body, lacked funds. Generally, public anger cannot focus opposition to well-funded lobbying.

Wall Street financed election campaigns for Wall Street sympathizers. It purchased seats on the Hill for them. The Wall Street gatekeepers also made significant contributions and helped elect the sympathizers. They would thrive when Wall Street thrived, and policy makers needed funds to be re-elected.

By the 2000s, Wall Street's major financial conglomerates had become a fertile recruiting ground for Washington's administrators and regulators, and in parallel Wall Street recruited Washington policy makers and paid them enormous salaries for influencing policy. The revolving door was well oiled! Wall Streeters seduced by Washington, promoted the Wall Street agenda, and when they returned to Wall Street, were rewarded with lucrative jobs. These Washington recruits were no longer the senior employees of the pre-1980s era. They were the risk takers, the arbitragers and OTC derivatives dealers.

Each time new legislation was passed, a steady stream of Wall Streeters, individuals with the *expertise* needed to understand how Wall Street worked, were ready to take jobs and implement the legislation. Naturally, they supported the view that products that could not be understood were good for the economy, and that unregulated markets and banks that were *too big to fail* were essential. What was needed was not banking knowledge. What was needed was an understanding that nothing should interfere with Wall Street, with its excessive profit making, and its high-risk activities. Traders who had been schooled in the major dealing room casinos fitted the bill. All experts on how much capital to hold (none), how much risk to take (no limit), how to regulate OTC derivatives (we shouldn't) and how to explain how exotic products work (we cannot, as we do not understand them).

Wall Street promoted itself as an oracle, the only oracle that could explain the benefits of banking in the New Millennium. Banking had moved from the 3-6-3 paradigm of decades ago and was more complicated. It was quantitative, and only Wall Street understood it. Wall Street and Washington began to speak with one voice, the voice of financial wisdom. Finance fulfilled our dreams. It meant that you could get rich by hard work. If you made a lot of money, then what you were doing must be good. Just like drug traffickers and Al Capone, but now with a new twist, credibility. Globally, finance had become a large part of each individual economy.

But of course, few in Wall Street did understand the complexities and most in Washington swallowed the story hook, line and sinker. Even when the Crisis and Great Recession had ruined the lives of millions, many in Congress failed to see the obvious. Why? Because bankers needed obscene compensation, and politicians needed the campaign contributions. Look:

		US Government	Private Sector
1990	Employees in securities and commodities	$32,500	$61,000
2010	Employees in securities and commodities	$45,500	$196,000
	US Cabinet Member	$199,700	
	Chairpersons of SEC, FTC, CFTC	$165,300	
	Employees of Goldman Sachs		$433,000 (2007 high, $661,000)

Figure 7 Private and Government Salaries 1990 and 2010

The cost of a seat in the US House of Representatives had risen from $56,500 in 1974 to over $1,250,000 in 2006,[283] and the financial sector has risen to the top of the contributor list. If one adds the contributions of the gatekeepers, from 1998 to 2008, political campaign contributions totaled $1.7 billion. That's 1,360 seats! And the biggest beneficiaries were the biggest contributors, Goldman, Citigroup, Bank of America, UBS, JP Morgan Chase, and Morgan Stanley.[284]

Many recipients of campaign contributions held important finance related offices: Senator Phil Gram was the Chair of the Senate Banking Committee. His predecessor was Senator Alphonse D'Amato and his successor Senator Christopher Dodd. Barney

Frank was Chair of the House Financial Services Committee and Senator Chuck Schumer, a past member of both the House Financial Services Committee and the Senate Banking Committee. Senator Schumer, a New Yorker from Brooklyn had cut his teeth as a New York State Assemblyman and developed close ties to the New York banking community.[285] Senator Gram was a proposer of the GLB, and legislation, which limited the regulation of OTC derivatives. Senator Schumer backed the GLB. According to Senator Richard Durbin, "[the banks] are still the most powerful lobby in Washington. Frankly, they own the place".[286]

Who passed through the revolving door? Senator Phil Gram became a Vice Chairmen of UBS Warburg. Frank Newman, CEO of Bank of America came to the Treasury in 1993 before returning to Bankers Trust in 1995, first as Vice Chairman and then as CEO. He engineered the sale of the failing bank to Deutsche Bank. Robert Rubin, a significant Democratic fundraiser, became President Clinton's first director of the National Economic Council, and then Treasury Secretary. Rubin had headed up a corporate event arbitrage business at Goldman before moving on to relative value arbitrage. After Treasury Secretary, he returned to Wall Street as Citigroup vice chairman. Senator John Corzine came from Goldman, as did William Brady, who became Chairman of the NY FED. Hank Paulson as Treasury Secretary bought with him Bob Steel, Steve Shafran, Neel Kashkari, Dan Jester, William Dudley, Gary Gensler and Ken Wilson, all from Goldman. Bob Steel then went back to Wall Street as the CEO of Wachovia. Michael Basham went from Wertheim Schroder to the Treasury and then to Salomon and William Corrigan from the NY FED to Goldman. Summers, Treasury Secretary after Rubin joined a hedge fund, and then returned to Washington. Rahm Emanuel, Obama's Chief of Staff was an ex investment banker. Herbert Allison had been president of Merrill. Tim Geitner, the head of the NY FED regulated a number of the banks that he later bailed out. He was pro Wall Street. As Johnson and Kwak note, Geitner had far more contact with the CEOs of Goldman, JP Morgan Chase and Citigroup than with the chairmen of the Senate Banking Committee and the House Financial Services Committee.[287]

> Executives and lobbyists had many sympathetic ears in government, and important policy makers were inclined to follow their advice. Finance had become a complex, highly quantitative field that only the Wall Street bankers and their backers in academia (including multiple Nobel Prize winners) had mastered, and people who questioned them could be dismissed as

ignorant Luddites. By 1998, it was part of the worldview of the Washington elite that what was good for Wall Street was good for America. [288]

At the time of the Millennium, the megabanks held so much political power that any concerns over their risks to the economy and society were not voiced. Few looked at the consequences of the failure of any one of them. Before the Crisis, very few understood that a megabank in trouble could hold the economy and the taxpayer to ransom. More risk and greater profits were the only items on the agenda and few recognised that taxpayers assumed the downside. By the 2000s, however, banking had become fragile and very poorly managed. The systemic risk was enormous and few bothered with the implications of interconnectedness.

Financial Fraud

During the 1980s and 1990s, there were increased efforts to prosecute criminal activity in the financial sector. Over 1,000 S&L bankers were sentenced to jail terms. Michael Milken of Drexel Burnham Lambert served 22 months in jail and paid $1.1 billion in fines and settlements. So the question we must ask is, given the problems that surfaced with derivatives in the 1990s, why were there not more prosecutions of banks and bankers. Why were only customers like Robert Citron of Orange County prosecuted?

One reason is that with its resources the Department of Justice found it easier to prosecute drug trafficking. Derivatives were difficult to understand. Cases of financial wrongdoing were complex and defendants often found ways to wriggle around the charges. Throughout the 1990s, there were two significant charges of criminal behaviour that were successful. Both were cases of obvious fraud and were easy to prosecute. James Martignoni at ABM AMRO in New York left a trail of fraudulent behaviour, including recording a sale of $1.8 billion as $18 billion.[289] Paul Mozer from Salomon was sentenced to four months in jail and paid fines totalling $1.4 million.

Despite the dearth of indictments, many injured parties brought civil actions against banks. Bankers Trust was sued by its customers, its pigeons. It told Gibson Greeting Cards, that a $14 million position was $8.1 million.

But the major reason was that the oligarchy had won freedom from prosecution for white collar crime. When the prosecution found it difficult to piece together an intelligible story, and then had to deal with well-funded research, and a team of lobbyists, success was almost impossible.

The Third Bangster Awards

The Third Bangster Awards has given us another gangster. Sebastien, the chief judge has awarded Alan Greenspan a Bangster award for dishonesty, abrogating his regulatory responsibilities, ignoring regulation, making misleading remarks and sheer stupidity. He relied on faith-based economics. He mislead anyone who would listed. His efforts substantially contributed to the Crisis. Raghuram Rajan joins the Gold Stars. He stood up to Greenspan and his aura, and questioned his achievements

Here is the table just after the Millennium:

Bangsters	Gold Stars
Nicholas Biddle	Franklin D Roosevelt
JP Morgan	Louis Brandeis
James Johnson	Raghuram Rajan
Alan Greenspan	

7

A Race to the Bottom

O ligarchies displace healthy and well capitalized, companies, banks, good corporate governance, transparent accounting, a legal system with the means to enforce contracts, and wind down failing organizations. Banking in the first decade of the 21st century was a banking system absent these assets.

Enron, when it imploded, illustrated how sick the financial sector had become. It could not have happened in the 1990s. Enron was a derivatives trader first, and an energy company second. Its trading business was successful and profitable, and the non-derivatives business a failure. Enron committed accounting fraud, manipulated earnings, misstated profits and deceived employees, its board of directors, its auditors, the rating agencies, the regulators and the public. How the company functioned was a mystery. Not even the auditors could understand how it worked. The board of directors and senior management had lost all control, and deregulation enabled financial *innovations* to take Enron deep into unmitigated risk taking, corporate fraud and white collar crime:

> The rules and principles of accounting ... do not always create measures consistent with underlying economics ... risk management strategies are ... directed at accounting rather than economic performance. Enron had problems producing it's an annual reports from time to time.[290]

Enron (and WorldCom, and Global Crossing) demonstrated that free markets do not self-regulate and deter fraud. Enron foretold 2008: we saw pointless financial *innovation*, deceptive off balance sheet accounting, weak credit rating agencies, ineffective regulation, credulous investors, and an ineffective media.

Let's recap and sharpen what we said when the FED pushed interest rates down in 2001. Families took mortgages to buy, refinance and take equity out of homes, to buy second homes and to invest in residential property.[291] Real estate was a good investment as it always went up. Indeed the seventy year historical upward trend continued until 2006. The demand for mortgages and real estate collateralized securitizations, MBSs and CDOs exploded, and investor funds expanded the pool of money available to buy homes. Builders, developers, insurers, appliance and furniture makers, gardeners and housekeepers all saw their businesses expand. A housing construction boom ensued, and residential real estate increased in price. So did the profits of housing construction contractors.

The demand for the securitizations was insatiable. Most of their tranches had AAA ratings and paid higher returns than US Treasuries. No one considered the implications of a dip in the housing markets, and Wall Street was confident that its risk management practices were good. The securitizations depended on a steady stream of mortgage fodder from which to build them, so mortgage originators went into overdrive. The lower the quality of a mortgage, the higher its return, so Wall Street gorged on subprime mortgages.

Investors in MBS and CDO could not evaluate them so relied on the rating agencies. The agencies relied on models and naïve assumptions. They assumed, for example, that if mortgages were geographically diverse, the risks were manageable. The agencies rated up to 80% of MBS and CDO tranches as AAA. The reason for the high ratings had less to do with risk assessment and more to do with conflicts of interest. The agencies needed to please securitizers, and provide high ratings so that the tranches could be sold. When mortgages were securitized, the details were not provided to investors, so low quality loans could be hidden.

Washington promoted *affordable housing for all* as a national housing policy. Wall Street did all it could to ensure that consumers bought houses so that there was a steady supply of mortgages. Wall Street provided warehouse loans to mortgage originators and locked in volume discounts, and the large Wall Street banks bought originators. Merrill Lynch, Wells Fargo, Morgan Stanley, HSBC, Lehman, JP Morgan Chase, Citigroup, Bear Stearns and AIG all owned originators. Such was the frenzy, that the dysfunctional Citigroup purchased Ameriquest in mid-2007, just prior to it's spiralling out of business! Non-bank mortgage lenders proliferated. They specialized in poorer quality mortgages. Their funding sources were volatile and high risk, and Wall Street dictated the kinds of mortgages it wanted, and it wanted the worst.

Historically ARMs were used to match mortgage interest income with funding costs, but were offered as enticements, with low introductory rates. Financially naïve households did not understand the implications of rate resets. They looked attractive to many. Loans with stiff prepayment penalties and pay option

ARMs were attractive to securitizers, so Wall Street rewarded originators accordingly. Washington Mutual found that pay options were five times more profitable than prime loans, and greatly increased securitization returns, as did interest only and negative amortization mortgages.

Between 1995 and 2002, the percentage of nonprime to prime loans was around 10 to 15%. (in the Millennium, it climbed to 19%!), but in 2003 the percentage rose to 25% to 30%, peaking at 38% in 2006. By 2008 however, it had dropped to 3%.

In 2003, 6% of new mortgages were interest only and negative amortization mortgages, but by 2005, they accounted for 29% of all new mortgages. [292] Stated income loans, liar loans and second mortgages were also popular. Information provided by applicants was rarely verified, and applicants knew it. By 2005, 45% of all loans had no documentation, and applications were dressed up by the originator sales teams so that approval was assured. Ameriquest, one of the largest and more egregious of the non-bank subprime lenders, doctored three quarters of its applications and half the applicants' income statements were enhanced. It paid incentives to sales people when prepayment penalties were included. Soon it became subject to consumer abuse charges, including predatory lending charges, and in 2006 paid $325 million to settle them. It was shut down in 2007. Banks like Wells Fargo incentivized its sales people with bonuses when minority borrowers were steered into subprime loans, even when they qualified for prime loans.

Mortgages had become easier to get in the 2000s, and the property boom meant incentives for property investors and speculators alike and this further contributed to the boom.

President Bush's blueprint for the American Dream allocated $1.2 trillion for loans to minorities. This helped Wall Street private labels as they were unconstrained by the quality of the mortgages, so this also translated into more low quality, high return mortgages.

Originator sales teams told customers that when an ARM's higher rate kicked in, it would never be a problem. If a mortgage holder could not afford the higher payments, then the mortgage could be refinanced. Worst case was the mortgaged home could be sold and the proceeds used to repay the mortgage. Refinancing meant replacing the existing mortgage with a new mortgage, a new ARM with a new introductory rate. Equity was lost in the process, and the problem would be postponed for a couple of years, but then the mortgage holder could refinance again. It was Alice in Wonderland. Originators and brokers earned big fees for refinancing, and it was easy business as refinancers were often repeat customers.

By the mid-2000s, one third of all new mortgages were subprime. Being incentivized by volume meant you spent less time on paperwork and credit evaluations and more time on selling. Higher risk meant higher returns, and higher fees. For Wall Street, the profits were good and losses were taken by investors.[293] The GSEs had a monopoly on conforming, prime mortgages, and Wall Street's private labels fed on the mortgages that the GSEs could not touch.

As house prices increased, so did the percentage of borrowers' incomes spent on mortgage payments, but from 1999, real household income fell in each of the five following years. On average, mortgage holders became less and less capable of making mortgage repayments.

From 1998 to 2006, home prices increased by 67%. In 2007, 7.5 million US homeowners had subprime mortgages and the value of subprime private labels reached $1.5 trillion.[294] Private labels had surpassed GSE securitizations in 2005, and the size of the mortgage market had increased from $5.3 trillion in 2001 to $10.5 trillion in 2007.[295] About the same time, the exposure of the FDIC insured banks to residential property loans was $4 trillion.

More and more subprime loans were used to refinance or buy second homes, and by 2007, less than 10% of new subprime loans were financing new homes. It was clear that a significant number of ARM mortgage holders had had to refinance. If the housing market faltered, so would millions of mortgage holders and most would go underwater quickly. Later, at the end of 2006, subprime delinquencies were 13%, and by 2010, 2.4 million subprime borrowers had lost their homes.

Equity extracted from residential property was used for consumer goods, homes that were more expensive, refinancing homes and paying off other more expensive credit card and other consumer debt. Home equity loans reduced equity in a home and consumers spent on home improvements, flat screen TVs, cars, boats and vacations. In 1986, mortgage repayments had become tax-deductible, which incentivized mortgage debt over other forms of personal debt. From 2000 to 2007, cash taken from housing released $4.2 trillion into the US economy.[296] Total household debt increased from $7 trillion in 2000 to $14 trillion in 2007, and housing debt accounted for 80% of this.

Greenspan remarked:

"The surge in cash out mortgage refinancing likely improved rather than worsened the financial condition of the average homeowner"… "Some of the equity extracted through mortgage refinancing was used to pay down more expensive, non-tax deductible consumer debt or to make purchases that would otherwise have been financed by more expensive and less tax favoured credit"[297]

This was certainly true, but ignored the obvious downside. What would happen if residential property values collapsed? In the seventy years since the Great Depression, housing had increased in value, just ahead of inflation. Most of the increases were in the cities and urban areas.[298] But "a home without equity is just rental with debt".[299] The downside was enormous. Greenspan's comments were naïve and irresponsible.

By 2005, it had become clear that MBS securitizations harboured a high percentage of toxic loans, and as a consequence, the junior tranches became even more difficult to sell. The CDO market was rejuvenated and the riskier, junior MBS tranches were placed into CDOs, and CDOs kept the housing market alive. If jet fuel went up and the mortgage market suffered, the impacts would offset. However, the problem was that there was insufficient jet fuel and too many mortgages, so CDOs became housing debt. By 2006, CDOs had ballooned to over half a trillion dollars.

The supply of mortgages necessary to securitize products fell well below the hungry jaws of the securitization monster, and competition had lowered the spreads securitizers could offer investors. They also had to pay more to originators for the mortgage fodder. The rocket scientists came to the rescue and created synthetic CDOs. The lack of fodder no longer mattered. The supply of underlying securities became infinite! Defaults would mean that losses were multiplied, but few cared. To complicate risk assessments, CDSs were used as credit wraps. The issue was whether the insurer could make payouts in a disaster. The value of CDSs peaked in 2007 at $62 trillion.

When securitizers bought mortgages, the sellers were obligated to guarantee mortgage origination standards. The GSEs initially maintained higher standards, but Wall Street became lax, and specialist firms were used to examine packages of mortgages, and their certifications were often negligent. There were cases of fraud. Of course, securitizers had little incentive to police underwriting standards for the same reason as originators. By 2006, 60% of the mortgages purchased by Citigroup from 1,600 mortgage originators were defective because either they were not written in accordance with Citicorp policy or the supporting documentation was missing, or both.[300] But each of the 1,600 originators was contractually obligated to meet Citicorp standards! By 2007, the percentage had climbed to 80%. A time bomb waiting to explode.

Mortgages could be put back to originators if the originator misled the securitizer. But originators never had sufficient capital to buy them. When it became impossible to put a mortgage back to an originator, a securitizer would agree to hold on to it, but for a credit. It was a two edged sword. Many originators had warehouse loans and securitizers did not want these loans to disappear with the originators.

In 2001, the Treasury had detected predatory lending and by 2007, it was mainstream. Immigrants were prime targets as were residents in the sand states, Florida and New York City. In 2004, the FBI issued a press release warning of an "epidemic of mortgage fraud", it said it was pervasive and growing.

The Home Ownership and Equity Protection Act 1994 amended the Truth in Lending Act, an Act enforced by the FED, expressly required a lender to ensure that it would not lend to a borrower without regard to the borrower's ability to repay. Greenspan had abrogated his regulatory responsibilities and he shot down all attempts to rope in predatory lending on the basis that subprime loans were healthy financial *innovations*. The OCC regulated the big lenders who saw regulation getting in the way of profits. Washington eschewed the regulation of subprime lending because it enabled home ownership.

Finally, some states did attempt to deal with predatory lending, but were pre-empted by Federal regulations. If states attempted to regulate a lending practice and the federal regulator did not, the federal regulator won out.

When Barny Frank, the Chair of the House Financial Services Committee tried to introduce stronger standards in 2005, he met a brick wall. Two pieces of regulatory guidance had been developed since 2000, and no one wanted to extend what were basic guidelines.[301] Any restrictions would interfere with profits. Predatory lending was a major mortgage quality factor.

Betting Against the Bubble

In 2005, David Lereah, a former chief economist at the National Association of Realtors wrote:

There is virtually no risk of a national housing price bubble based on the fundamental demand for housing and predictable economic factors … A general slowing in the rate of price growth can be expected, but in many areas inventory shortages will persist and home prices are likely to continue to rise above historic norms.[302]

Later in the year, Ben Bernanke, the Chairman of the President's Council of Economic Advisors said:

House prices have risen nearly 25% over the past two years. Although speculative activity has increased in some areas, at a national level these price increases largely reflect strong economic fundamentals, including robust growth in jobs and incomes, low mortgage rates, steady rates of household formation, and factors that limit the expansion of housing supplies in same areas.[303]

Both were wrong.

For years, many had thought that a housing bubble was growing, and that sooner or later it would burst. This led to many market directed trading strategies. Magnetar, a Chicago hedge fund, for example, exploited correlation trading. It shorted most of a securitization and took a long position in its equity tranches. The long positions generated revenue and funded the short positions and more. Magnetar made money from the long positions, but if the housing market collapsed, although the equity tranches would collapse first, the senior tranches would not be far behind. Correlation trading bore little risk, and required little capital. Magnetar made $30 billion in such deals. It was all possible because MBS indices, like the ABX had been introduced which enabled speculators to go long or short the housing market.

It was simpler for Morgan Stanley, which began to bet against the housing market in 2003. It took short CDO position bets, and, at first, lost money, it was too early, and the short side payments became a burden. But in 2007, it began to make money, and in that year reaped $1 billion.

Morgan Stanley, like the other large banks also sold securitizations to its customers and then bet against them. In March 2007, it sold an $82 million tranche of a synthetic CDO, Libertas, rated AAA-, to the Pension Fund of the Virgin Islands. Libertas referenced very toxic mortgages and Morgan Stanley took the short side. By year end, the tranche was worthless and Morgan pocketed the $82 million investment and its fees.

The Pension Fund sued Morgan Stanley and claimed that it had misrepresented the quality of the mortgages. Most of the mortgage fodder had come from New Century, a Morgan Stanley warehouse borrower, and the bank knew that New Century had often breached its warranties. Although Morgan Stanley said that it had vetted the mortgages, it had not. Moreover, it knew that Libertas contained extremely toxic mortgages. Morgan Stanley also knew that New Century was about to file for chapter 11 bankruptcy protection and knew why. New Century had run out of money in 2006, because of payment defaults, including defaults on the first few payments of mortgages. The early payment defaults triggered investor mortgage put backs, and New Century spent $835 million repurchasing mortgages, but could not bury them in new securities as the markets had collapsed.[304] When all this came out, Morgan Stanley had to settle with the Pension Fund. By April 2007, New Century was dead.

Not all the large banks were unaware of the possible housing market problems. In 2006, JP Morgan Chase noted that mortgage defaults were on the increase, and with no obvious explanation. Interest rates had not increased and we did not have an economic slowdown. There had also been a sudden increase in mortgage refinancing. In 2005, American households had extracted $750 billion in value from their homes, up sharply from $100 billion the year before, and $500 billion of this was spent on personal consumption and debt repayment. New, naïve MBS and CDO investors had emerged. So JP Morgan Chase curtailed its involvement in the securitization business, forced their originators to raise underwriting standards and shortened securitization times. Few others were concerned, and the securitization volumes of the other large players, Bear, Citigroup, Ameriquest and Countrywide grew substantially.

Goldman Pigeons Customers

Goldman exemplified how the other megabanks exploited their customers using the housing market.

Goldman securitized MBSs, CDOs, CDO^{2}s and synthetic CDOs and could go either long or short the housing market. It made no distinction between customer related trading and proprietary trading. It could sell the long side of a synthetic CDO to a customer and take the short side itself, or it could simply act as a market maker, an intermediary. In 2006 and 2007, it was the number four CDO underwriter.

When Goldman securitized debt, customers bought tranches based on the ratings and Goldman's reputation. Neither Goldman, nor the agencies, not anyone else for that matter, understood the products nor the risks. Goldman was careful to tell customers that it was a market maker, that it had no interest in the product's performance, and that its sole interest was in fees and commissions. However, synthetic CDOs enabled Goldman to launder positions.[305] When Goldman sold customers the long side of a CDO, usually an AAA rated tranche, they assumed that Goldman was a market maker, but in reality, almost always, Goldman was laundering its positions.

Goldman began shorting the housing market seriously in 2006, while at the same time it continued to promote the housing market to its customers. During the year, Goldman sold securitizations for $44.5 billion, and bet against them! It placed mortgages originated by the worst of the subprime originators, including Fremont and Long Beach, into the GSAMP Trust 2006-S-3 MBS. It contained only second mortgages, so there could be no foreclosures, the average loan to value ratio was 99.29%, so the mortgage holders held virtually no equity, and 58% of the mortgages were no documentation loans. Nevertheless, 68% of GSAMP was rated AAA, and 93% investment grade. Goldman knew it was junk, and in December of 2006 bet against it. The bets turned profitable in 2007.[306]

Another 2006 deal was the Hudson Mezzanine 2006-1, a $2 billion synthetic CDO that referenced BBB subprime tranches. It wanted to remove exposure to $800 million BBB rated assets in its books and hedge a long position of $1.2 billion in the ABX index. The prospectus advertised:

> ... [Goldman wanted to] develop a long term association ... [which aligned] incentives with those of investors ... [Goldman] screens and evaluates assets for portfolio suitability ... assets sourced from the Street ... not a Balance Sheet CDO

Goldman was lying. Hudson was put together specifically to clean house, and the assets from which it was built were all from Goldman's balance sheet. At no stage was Goldman market neutral. So much for aligning incentives. Hudson Mezzanine was downgraded in October 2007 when it was worth 60 cents in the dollar. Rather than liquidate and distribute the proceeds to the investors, Goldman delayed liquidation until the following January, when the securities were worth16 cents in the dollar. Why? That is easy. Goldman had shorted the security!

In 2004, Goldman had put together the first of its Abacus deals. There were sixteen in all, for a total of $1 billion. They were synthetic CDOs, and referenced the worst mortgages, mortgages originated by Long Beach, Countrywide, Ameriquest and New Century. In 2007, Goldman built Abacus 2007 – AC1 a $2 billion synthetic CDO for the hedge fund manager, John Paulson. Paulson wanted to bet against the housing market and do so by choosing reference securities, and selling a synthetic CDO. Paulson chose Goldman to build and sell the securitization after Bear Stearns had turned him down on ethical grounds. Goldman rented the Abacus structure to Paulson for $15 million, and the Fabulous Fab Tourre designed the deal and wrote the sales materials. He boasted of selling toxic mortgages products to "widows and orphans", and extolled greed. 55 of Paulson's proposed 123 securities were selected and combined with another 35 securities. The deal contained $909 billion in senior MBS tranches. The sales materials did not disclose Paulson's involvement that he intended to take the short side, that he had chosen most of the referenced securities, and that they were chosen because they were poor quality. The materials lied and represented that a third party CD manager, ACA Management, had selected the bonds. The ratings agencies were unaware of Paulson's involvement, and most tranches were given AAA ratings. The tranches were sold to uninformed investors and before year-end Abacus 2007 was worthless and Paulson made a fortune, $4 billion. In 2010 after an SEC civil fraud complaint, Goldman agreed to fines of $550 million, the largest penalty paid by Wall Street at the time, but a drop in the ocean given its 1Q 2010 profit of $3.5 billion. The Fabulous Fab was convicted in 2013.[307] Customers lost the $4 billion that Paulson banked, who walked free. Why was it not clawed back?

Timberwolf, a $1 billion CDO-squared containing MBSs, CDOs and synthetic CDOs was built in the spring of 2007, and Goldman advertised that it owned equity in Timberwolf, but did not state that it had shorted all this equity and more, with the net effect that it had made a large bet against the housing market. Most of it was rated AAA, but became junk in short order. Goldman won, its customers lost.

Goldman did not care who it raped and the havoc it caused. For example, it sold a synthetic CDO to IDK that wanted to bet against its own customers on a selection of MBSs. IDK sold the long side of the synthetic AAA tranches to its unsophisticated customers: US public agencies, pension funds, schools and fire departments. When the MBSs failed and the mess unravelled, French giant Calyon sued IDK and won. Goldman got off Scott free.

By March 2007, Goldman assumed that the mortgage market was "game over". It was aware that Merrill and Lehman were heavily exposed to residential real estate and that Fremont and New Century were shaky. In addition to shorting the housing market, as AIG had insured many of Goldman's positions, it protected its own neck and bought CDS protection against AIG's failure. It won again, when AIG collapsed.

Wall Street, especially Goldman made spectacular returns in the early 2000s. Profits were $350 billion. The market capitalization of the megabanks rose by $900 billion to $5.4 trillion, a peak. While Goldman was profiting by betting against the housing market, Americans were losing jobs and their homes. Not only did Goldman pigeon its customer, it pigeoned Main Street.

Years on, in March of 2014, Greg Smith, a senior Goldman banker resigned. He was Executive Director and head of Goldman's US equity derivatives business in Europe, the Middle East and Africa. He left because he believed that Goldman had lost its way. He had been twelve years at Goldman and saw a transition from a first class customer treatment culture to customer pigeoning culture. Customers were fodder and to be exploited. They were pigeons to be ripped off. "The interests of customers continue to be side-lined in the way the firm operates and thinks about making money." He reflected that teamwork, integrity, a spirit of humility and always doing the right thing by its customers was a vital part of Goldman's success for 143 years. Now the only objective was to make as much money as possible from customers regardless of their interests. This meant selling products to customers that Goldman had inventoried but which had lost their profit potential, and selling to them whatever made the most profit for Goldman, regardless of their usefulness to customers. The decline was a decline in the moral fibre of the firm. The firm had lost credibility because of the Fabulous Fab, Abacus, Blankfein's God's work and the Vampire Squads.[308] CEO Lloyd Blankfein[309] and President Gary D Cohn had lost all control.

The Bubble Bursts

Housing construction peaked in 2006, at a 30-year high. There were too many houses on the market, and prices had begun to fall. Houses had become too expensive, even with zero dollar down payments, and initial teaser mortgage rates. The 2Q 2007 Case-Shiller home price index said that residential property was down 3% from its year earlier peak. Barons announced that house prices were falling, and that the inventory of homes was the largest it had even been, and boldly predicted that housing prices would fall

30%, nationally, in three years. A year later, they were down 15%. The recently experienced steep increase in housing prices was not due to economic fundamentals. We had fed a housing bubble and it was deflating.

Construction companies stopped building homes and reduced their inventories, and in 4Q 2006, there was a sharp increase in the number of construction industry bankruptcies. Notably Kara Homes filed for chapter 11 protection in early October, just after its two most profitable quarters.[310] Vengeance was quick.

Hank Paulson at a National Press Club speech on Thursday, 13 March 2007 stated that the current mortgage market problems resulted from subprime lending, the erosion of lending standards, the ratings agencies, and the OTC markets. He called for a number of recommendations.[311] But he was not concerned, he said. The problems were contained.

Shortly afterwards, in April, he reasoned that of the outstanding 55 million mortgages, 7.5 million were subprime and their aggregate value was $1.5 trillion. The worst case was that 25% of mortgages would suffer losses, and that the losses would be under $37.5 billion. This was not a disaster.[312] At about the same time, Ben Bernanke estimated that subprime losses would be between $50 and $100 billion. "The impact on the broader economy and the financial markets of the problems in the subprime markets seems to likely be contained".[313] And in June: "at this point the troubles in the subprime sector seem unlikely to seriously spill over to the broader economy or the financial system."[314] The problem, he said, was a subprime problem, and although the subprime loans may have climbed to $2 trillion, the mortgage market was $14 trillion. Subprime was a small percentage of the market. The Oracle Greenspan had said earlier that a major decline in the housing markets was "most unlikely". Oracles do not need to give reasons.

Paulson's logic was simplistic. Why 25%? Doubling the percentage of subprime mortgages, which would soon prove to be a conservative guess, increased losses three fold. Paulson was guessing and the guesses were not clever. As for Bernanke, he told us that all he could do was guess. Six months later, in early 2008, the losses were in excess of $250 billion, and without any sign of relief.[315]

When assessing the extent of the housing problems, neither Paulson, nor Bernanke took into account the explosion of exotic derivatives that had enabled the market to grow. Giving MBS and CDO tranches AAA ratings meant that pension funds and other conservative investors could buy them so the pool of funds available for housing had become astronomical. This had enabled the home financing Ponzi scheme to continue.[316] Synthetic CDOs magnified the problems. What about the spill over into the economy?

Greenspan argued that financial innovation, with its plethora of securitizations would minimize any shock effects. He told us that the credit risk in the global financial system was no longer warehoused in the balance sheets of a few megabanks, but had been widely distributed. Wrong, and not nearly the whole story. The *innovations* had concentrated the risk in Wall Street. The Wall Street banks were all in the same boat. The boat, like the Titanic had too few lifeboats. Greenspan also believed that subprime lending opened up housing to a group that had previously been denied the opportunity to own a home. He was right, the market had been opened up to those that could not afford to buy a home. He refused to acknowledge the consequences of widespread defaults for homeowners, lenders and investors.

The BIS in Basel is a central bankers' bank and so was privy to information that was otherwise unshared by the independent central banks. It was also not accountable to an electorate. In 2007, its researchers had noticed that asset volatilities were low with no obvious explanation, and that asset price were rising while the cost of borrowing was falling. If the usual price correlations fell apart, we could have a problem. They had already cautioned that financial *innovation* was not necessarily good. Why should we assume that the *originate and distribute* mortgage lending was such a good idea? The BIS was acutely aware of the leverage levels and that it was a significant problem. Consequently, we may be more vulnerable, not less vulnerable, as Greenspan had oracalized.

By 1 August, Paulson still believed that the housing market problems were "largely contained". The Bush administration had continued to boast the success of his lamentable policies and in July, the DJIA had hit a new high, over 1,400. The European market disruptions had yet to occur, neither had the BNP Paribas problem, a consequence of the disruptions. However, in the US, the housing market had been in a downhill spin from 4Q 2006.

To understand the problems, we must understand that two principles had been ignored. The first was that mortgage holders must be able to afford *all* mortgage payments. The second was that borrowers should provide a reasonable down payment, skin in the game. Both were forgotten and both were at the heart of the problems. It appears that neither Paulson, not Bernanke took these changes into account.

As the number of subprime mortgage delinquencies spiked steeply upwards, the number of foreclosures did too. House prices were falling and refinancing was not an option. Foreclosures meant more property on the market, and pushed prices lower. Some underwater mortgage holders walked away, which added to the number of properties on the market and further depressed prices. Upward rate resets, a problem for all ARM mortgage holders, was especially so for subprime mortgages. The mortgages had been packaged into MBS and CDOs, which now clogged the Wall Street balance sheets.

When a property is foreclosed, what is realized is far less than the value of the property. A rule of thumb says about 50%. There are legal expenses, the property will have fallen into disrepair, and at this time, the market was depressed. So why do lenders foreclose? Well, they do not. The lenders are the investors in the securitizations, and foreclosures are undertaken by mortgage servicers. Servicers were not incentivized to negotiate deals. They did not have the staff, their legal authority was at best unclear, and they made more money out of forecloses. They earned fees, which came from what was realized in a sale, and paid up front, so they earned much more by foreclosing.

When a mortgage defaults its value as collateral in a securitization evaporates. The consequences of a small number of defaults are "built in" to the pricing of the securitization, however, if there are widespread defaults, the value of the collateral is severely damaged. When the housing bubble burst, the lower rated tranches of real estate collateralized securitizations were the first to be hit, and the prices at which they traded plummeted. When there is no market for the lower rated tranches, you cannot build a securitization. A few of the unsold equity tranches had remained on the securitizers' balance sheets, but more often than not, they had been repackaged into CDO^{2}s. But they too have lower tranches. The market for real estate collateralized securitizations froze, including the market for the AAA tranches.

No one understood the extent of the real estate collateralized borrowing problem. IndyMac, Bear, WaMu, Countrywide and Lehman all knew that they had problems with their real estate holdings. A 2006 Goldman securitization contained loans for which no payments had ever been made! More reasons for investors to eschew all mortgage collateralized debt.

When the securitization business dried up so did the money that it had provided for mortgages, and the subprime business died. This meant even lower home prices.

When the values of the MBSs and CDOs in the Wall Street balance sheets collapsed, their value as collateral for overnight funding also collapsed. The shadow banking system, a major market participant, relied heavily on funding long-term, high risk assets via the short-term markets. It was insanity. If there was any doubt about a borrower's capacity to repay, the funding could be withdrawn, literally overnight!

So, lenders to the shadow banking system first demanded bigger haircuts, which made funding more expensive, and then withdrew it. There were then three alternatives. Borrow more expensively, longer term, or attract more capital or sell assets and generate cash. The first two had become impossible, and the third meant fire sales, which resulted in extensive write downs and losses. When many interconnected institutions lost funding, there was nowhere for them to go, so they looked bankruptcy in the eye. There were dramatic stock price declines, and the problems were not constrained by national boundaries.

The net of it all was that the extensive mortgage delinquencies were disastrous for borrowers, lenders and securitizers alike.

At the end of 2007, another guess at the damage was well above what Paulson and Bernanke had estimated earlier in the year. The IMF thought that the subprime paper losses must be over $500 billion.[317] Others thought it was nearer $1 trillion, but no-one really knew, or knew how to unravel the mess and to find out. What we did know was that there was scant capital to absorb losses.

At this time, there were dispossess proceedings on 1.3 million properties in the US, an 80% increase over the previous 12 months. A year later, 9% of all US mortgages were either delinquent or in foreclosure and by the end of 2009, this had risen to 14%. These numbers reflect all mortgages, some of which were written in the 1980s, well before the subprime problems. Allowing for this, the numbers were astonishing and alarmingly large.

In 2001, the equity in the US housing market was $6 trillion. It rose to $13 trillion in 2005, but was back to $6 trillion in 2010. While the 2005, $13 trillion debt remained $13 trillion, what collateralized it was much less. Many mortgages were underwater and 20% of all mortgages were still underwater in 2012.[318] The US trade deficit grew to $4 trillion, five times the deficit in the 1990s.[319]

House prices fell for six years, from 2006 until 2012. At its peak, residential real estate was around 50% overvalued. In the coastal states of Florida and California, it was nearer 100%. This meant that on average the value of housing collateral had dropped by one third and in some cases by one half. These declines left almost all *recent* mortgage holders with negative equity. If you purchased a home for $100 and made a 5% down payment, the initial loan was $95. If the property dropped in value by one third, to $67, you were very much underwater. You would have reduced the loan amount by making monthly payments, but for recently originated mortgages, the reduction would not be significant. By 2010, homeownership had fallen to 66.9%, right where it was in the early 2000s.

Dotcom Becomes the Housing Bubble

When the housing bubble burst, the effects should have been comparable to the downturn after the dotcom bubble burst in 2001, a short, eight-month recession, or so the textbooks say. The National Bureau of Economic Research tells us when recessions start and stop. They look at a number of indicators, like employment, industrial production, consumer spending, GDP, etc. If they all start to degenerate, then we have a recession. When some indicators begin to recover, the recession is over. In late 2001, the GDP and industrial production were up, so the Bureau declared the dotcom recession was over, but it wasn't. Unemployment increased through mid-2003.[320] The dotcom recession lasted more than two and a half years. In the *Introduction,* we said that there was more to it than an overheated property market and a bloated asset bubble! And there was. The dotcom bubble became the housing bubble, which provided a new investment outlet. Krugman refers to The Onion's article "Recession-Plagues Nation Demand New Bubble to Invest In".[321] Just in time had progressed from inventories to bubbles.

Bernanke[322] reasoned that the bursting of the housing bubble was a trigger, significant in itself, but which exposed a number of vulnerabilities in the financial system and economy. Absent these vulnerabilities the effects would have been much less. In the *Introduction* we summarized the financial sector weaknesses: too much debt, much of it hidden of balance sheet, too much leverage, too much short-term funding, too much risk, *too big to fail* megabanks, ludicrous incentives and compensation, insufficient loss absorbing capital, poorly understood *innovations*, ineffective ratings agencies, interconnectivity, toxic products, extensive, unchecked malfeasance, and so on, incompetence, little integrity, an outdated regulatory system and so on, and all licenced by the global banking oligarchy which provided the glue. It let the financial system self-destruct, and those that saw it coming were ignored. Interconnectedness channelled the toxic infection into systemic risk that resulted in the global financial system, a house of cards, collapsing into a financial firestorm that engulfed the globe's economies.

The Crisis was able to occur because banking had changed. Most of the institutions that took on the risk, were part of the shadow banking system, and were institutions that had never been regulated. They grew to a size that rivalled the traditional banking sector. And therein lies the vulnerability. Regulations should have been extended, as should have the financial a safety net. LTCM was a stern warning. But rather than coming to terms with the fragility of the shadow banking system, Alan Greenspan was in his own make believe world:

> Not only have individual financial institutions become less vulnerable to shocks from underlying risk factors ... but also the financial system as a whole has become more resilient.[323]

There were many related contributions to the problems. MBS and CDO had often been sold with credit wraps, CDS. As the sellers did not hold reserves against payouts, the monolines and AIG developed enormous exposures. The sort of catastrophe that would result in a super senior[324] default would also wipe out the insurers, and they would not be there when needed. A disaster waiting to happen.

Funding MBS and CDO long-term investments in the short-term markets reached complete lunacy in 2007, when Citigroup increased its SIV exposure to $25 billion. Out of sight, out of mind. Another disaster in waiting.

The current vintage of senior management had not been involved in the derivatives business when it developed. They understood neither the issues, nor the risks, nor how the numbers, including the exposures were put together. Traders made bonuses determined by the revenues and profits, but most of the time in house models determined what these profits were. There were few liquid markets so prices could not "be observed". If you traded according to the models, you made money because performance was not constrained by reality. The wool had been pulled over the eyes of the senior managers.

The Rumbles

By early 2007, the Europeans had become very anxious. There were many concerns: risks hidden in the shadow banking system, in particular the hedge funds, leverage, the opacity of credit derivatives and their conduits. The European banks had created Basle and took it as the risk management standard, but hedge funds and conduits were outside its domain, and what was undisclosed, and hidden, was unknown. More than 50% of all CDS were traded in London and many shadow banks were located there.

In February 2007, HSBC made a startling announcement. It issued a profit warning and told shareholders that it had reserved $10.6 billion as an offset against subprime losses. It was the tip of an iceberg.[325] The bank owned a subprime lender, Household Finance, and it was in trouble. Household had experienced extensive mortgage defaults, defaults had not been predicted by its models, so the question was: where would it end?

Then Fremont Investment and Loan failed. In 2007, the Massachusetts Courts had ordered Fremont to discontinue foreclosure on any loans that were "presumptively unfair" and to renegotiate loan terms with struggling borrowers. Fremont declared chapter 11 in March.

New Century Financial, the second largest subprime lender announced substantial losses for 4Q 2006. New Century had been founded in 1995, and by the 2000s, its business had been substantial. In 2004, it originated $20.8 billion in mortgages, and this grew to $51.6 billion in 2006. Three quarters of its loans were fed to Morgan Stanley and Credit Suisse, but when the losses were announced their warehouse lines were withdrawn. New Century was dead in April 2007.[326] Its three most senior officers were not, however. They took away $20 million between them.

Then a minor earthquake. Two of Bear Stearns hedge funds collapsed with investors losing everything. The funds had leveraged their investments up, to $20 billion by borrowing in the repo markets and invested in AAA and AA tranches of CDOs, mostly collateralized by residential mortgages. Concerns over the mortgage markets led the repo lenders to cut funding. At the time, the funds' repo loans were $16 billion, and although Bear pledged $3.2 billion, it was not nearly enough, and too late. The funds were dead. Merrill was able to seize its collateral, but JP Morgan Chase, Citigroup and Goldman all lost their investments. At this time, the DJIA dropped dramatically by 400 points, the largest single day drop since 9/11.

The woes of the mortgage lenders continued. On 6 August the mid-sized mortgage lender American Home Investment Corporation filed for chapter 11 bankruptcy.

Countrywide

Countrywide was born in New York in 1969 and its goal was to become a significant nationwide originator of residential mortgages. By 2006, Countrywide was the nation's biggest mortgage lender. It had 35,000 employees and 500 offices spread across the nation. It was in the top 100 in the Fortune 500 list and responsible for 20% of all US mortgages. It originated 200,000 mortgages per month with a value of $460 billion, equal to 3.5% of the nation's GDP. It specialized in low quality ARM subprime loans. It was the number one lender to low-income groups and specifically targeted immigrants with poor English skills. Minorities had few alternatives, and Countrywide charged them excessive fees. The sales teams steered borrowers into more expensive loans even when they qualified for cheaper loans. It was good business as the company's margins were 3% for prime loans, and 15% for subprime loans. In 2006 revenues were $24.4 billion, profits $2.7 billion and its balance sheet $32.7 billion.

When the housing problems hit, Countrywide's revenues and profits declined, and in early 2007, defaults forced Countrywide to set aside funds for expected subprime mortgage defaults. Twenty percent of its subprime loans had become delinquent, and it had to draw down $11.5 billion from its credit lines. Countrywide's stock fell 75%. The market for non-conforming mortgages began to collapse in early August and by the 10th, it was dead. The company was then unable to roll over its repo funding and it announced that "unprecedented market disruptions" were a threat to its financial condition. It followed its announcement by selling 16% of its equity to Bank of America for $2 billion, and declared a loss of $1.2 billion for 3Q 2007, its first loss for 25 years. The credit ratings agencies downgraded its paper, stock analysts advised shareholders to sell, and the CDS cost of insuring it against default skyrocketed by 22%. It cut 12,000 jobs, began to restructure 80,000 mortgages and moved away from the subprime business, but the damage was done. In January 2008, after rumours of bankruptcy, Bank of America acquired it for $4.1 billion in a fire sale, an acquisition that Bank of America would deeply regret.

The company's business practices were unethical, and appalling. CEO Angelo Mozilo had created the *Friends of Angelo Program* through which Countrywide provided sweetheart mortgage deals. Countrywide gave senior Fannie executives

Friend's mortgages in exchange for preferential fee deals. Jim Johnson, Fannies' ex CEO was given cheap loans totalling $10 million.[327] Many congressional representatives and celebrities were *Friends*.

Internal fraud had become rampant, as the sales teams would do anything to achieve their targets, so in September 2007 Countrywide appointed Eileen Foster head of Fraud Risk. She uncovered extensive companywide fraud, closed a few branches and terminated employees. But this was bad for business, so she was fired. The fraud continued, and informers were made to appear as its perpetrators! Eileen filed a whistle blower lawsuit and was awarded $900,000.[328] Much of this came out in 2011 when Steve Kroft interviewed her in a *60 Minutes* production "Prosecuting Wall Street".

Numerous lawsuits alleged unfair and deceptive practices, encouraging borrowers to take risky mortgages that were beyond their means, false advertising, providing misleading information to prospective borrowers and advertising low rate mortgages yet pushing borrowers into higher cost ARMs at the last moment. Employees falsified mortgage documents, and computer systems automatically recorded salaries of $100,000 per annum for applicants who declared job titles as manager.

In 2009, after the Bank of America acquisition, the SEC charged Angelo Mozilo and other past executives with insider trading, concealing information, securities fraud and failure to make discloses of its lax standards. In October, Mozilo agreed to pay a settlement of $67.5 million and accepted a lifetime ban on serving as an officer or director of any public company. By settling, Mozilo avoided criminal charges and a trial. He did not admit wrongdoing and retained most of his real estate bubble compensation of $450 million. His net worth, $600 million, stayed intact as most of the settlement was paid by Bank of America under the terms of his employment agreement.

BNP Paribas Triggers the First Crisis

As we said in the *Introduction,* on Thursday, 9 August 2007, Paribas, France's largest bank, suspended withdrawals from three of its hedge funds. The value of the funds was small, €1.6 billion, and they had invested in US mortgage debt. The market for these assets had become illiquid, and Paribas announced that it could not value "certain assets fairly regardless of their quality or credit rating". In other words, Paribas could not find a buyer for its subprime bonds at any reasonable price. US mortgage debt was toxic. The suspicions of the European bankers were confirmed, that

US mortgage securities were not as safe as once assumed, they were not AAA bonds.

Banks across the globe has used these bonds as collateral for day-to-day repo borrowing. When it became clear that the value of the collateral had fallen, their markets collapsed. If you could not "see" a price in the market, you could not mark a portfolio to market, you needed to rely on a model, and models for pricing real estate collateralized securitizations were in short supply. If BNP Paribas could not figure out how much its relatively insignificant funds were worth, then how could other banks value their funds?

The BNP suspension resulted in turmoil in the European financial markets, and credit froze. Fearing severe problems, European banks drew back from lending to each other, and their customers. Euro-zone overnight borrowing costs soared to 4.75%, up 0.75%. A financial crisis had struck. In order to calm the markets and provide liquidity, the ECB announced that it would lend to any European bank as much money as it wanted at the official rate of 4%.[329] Forty-nine banks borrowed and the ECB pumped €94.8 billion into the European money markets. The cash infusion was larger than its infusion triggered by 9/11.

The FED had already pumped $24 billion into US banks pushing the federal funds rate towards its target, and added another $38 billion to support the ECB. The ECB then lent another €61 billion. Almost $250 billion in two days! In the UK, Mervyn King, assumed that the credit freeze was a consequence of an overdue market correction, a reaction to years of excess, and required no immediate reaction. The Bank of England held back, but soon its vaults would open too.

The market assumed that many issuers of commercial paper were secured by illiquid, toxic real estate investments and so abandoned the paper. Repo haircuts, usually around 2%, became 5%, then 10%, and then repo funds were withdrawn. At the time, the repo market was $2.6 trillion. Substantial, and for it to vanish almost overnight was a disaster. If you needed short-term funds for your day-to-day costs, salaries, inventories, etc., and could only offer US mortgage market collateral, you were out of luck. You exhausted your capital and then what?

No one knew which banks were heavily exposed, and no one wanted to lend to a bank that held toxic assets. The result, global panic. The LIBOR-OIS spread, a measure of the willingness of banks to lend to each other, jumped to 40 basis points, an historic high. It had been around 10 basis points from August 2006.[330] Firms that relied on the short-term markets, which included all the big players, experienced bank runs not seen since the days of the Great

Depression. The lenders in the repo and commercial paper markets turned to governments, to US Treasuries. On 21 August 2007, the Treasury bill four-week auction nearly failed because there was too much demand!

Not to worry announced the FED. The damage would be limited. It was an absurd claim. The FED's response was to permit a wider range of assets to be pledged as collateral for loans, and to lower the discount window rate from 5.25% to 4.75%. By September, payrolls everywhere had begun to contract.

What had the ratings agencies been doing? In July, S&P had put 612 tranches on watch and Moody's another 399 tranches. Why hadn't they downgraded the AAA rated tranches? In fact, why hadn't they downgraded all mortgage risk? The scare was that if there were major downgrades some investment grade securities would become non-investment grade, and the pension funds and money market funds would be forced to sell them. This would push the market for mortgage risk down further. The synthetic CDOs would multiply the effects, perhaps 50 times! However, in October, the downgrades came and the BBB tranches incurred losses of 65%. 91% of AAA subprime mortgage risk issued in 2007 and 93% issued in 2006 were downgraded to junk.[331]

The ratings downgrades resulted in a flood of write-downs. Merrill Lynch announced its biggest quarterly loss ever, $2.3 billion for 3Q 2007. For the full year 2007 Citigroup, took a $29 billion write down, Merrill $25 billion, Lehman $13 billion, Bank of America $12 billion and Morgan Stanley $10 billion. Would further write downs be necessary? Yes. In 2008, Citigroup took another $63 billion write down, Merrill $24 billion, Bank of America $29 billion, Lehman $14 billion, JP Morgan Chase $10 billion and Morgan Stanley $10 billion. More than a quarter of a trillion dollars written down by the megabanks. Clearly, this could not continue, and some were already insolvent.

While everyone knew that the major participants held toxic assets, there was little confidence that they had been marked accurately, so even after the write downs, there could be extensive losses lurking behind the numbers. Then there were the off balance sheet assets. Banks took write downs only when absolutely necessary, so the smart money said that the quarter of a trillion written down was the tip of the iceberg, that most of the losses were hidden from sight.

Given the falling prices of residential prices and the damage this was doing to the portfolios of financial institutions, one could expect the mortgage business itself to be in deep trouble. And it was. By 3Q 2007, over fifty mortgage originators had collapsed. All the subprime lenders had problems. In 2008, the OCC released a document: "Worst Ten in the Worst Ten" which listed the ten worst lenders in the ten metropolitan areas with the highest foreclosure rates. Twenty-one companies were on the lists. Ameriquest made seven of the ten lists. Roland Arnall, its founder had sponsored other companies, including Argent, which made all ten lists and was number one in Cleveland and Detroit. Long Beach was another, and it made nine of the lists and the top spots in Sacramento, Stockton, Memphis and Denver.

Fitch warned that it might lower its ratings of some of the monoline insurers, the insurers that had issued CDS protection against an estimated $2 trillion on MBSs. The problem was bigger than the consequences for the monolines. If they suffered a ratings downgrade, the CDS protection they had written would be worth less, so the insured portfolios would have to be written down.

If you looked at Wall Street's profits, you would not be alarmed. For year-end 2006, the financial sector accounted for 40% of all US corporate profits, and Wall Street's profits for 2007 were the highest ever. The consolidated profits for FDIC insured institutions hit $150 billion, also the highest recorded.

Recall that in 2007 the New York City financial services sector compensation was $53 billion.[332] This was the year that Goldman paid its employees an average of $661,000 *each,* and the firm's CEO $68.4 million (salary $600,000 and year-end bonus $67.8 million). The average for the five top earners at Goldman was $61 million.[333] At Lehman, Dick Fuld its CEO received $40 million, and Joe Gregory, the number two, $34 million.[334] John Mack, Morgan Stanley's CEO was paid $41 million and JP Morgan Chase's Jamie Diamond received $28 million[335]. In his last full year at Merrill Lynch, Stanley O'Neil its CEO received $91 million.[336]

Moreover, the Wall Street financial engineering machine remained in high gear, and Wall Street congratulated itself for carving out risk and disseminating it. Like Monty Python's dead parrot, it was no more. It had gone to its maker and it definitely was not pining for the fjords.

However, Wall Street balance sheets were more highly leveraged than ever before, and with unprecedented levels of debt. Furthermore, interconnectedness had become a major issue. If one megabank was forced to sell toxic assets in a fire sale, the others would be forced to mark down their portfolios and take losses. Failure of one could result in a pile of dominoes on the floor.

The $2 trillion subprime market had imploded and had become globally contagious. Within a few months the devastation had set in and the supposed risk vacuum had turned into a black hole. Although the $2 trillion subprime market was a small part of the $14 trillion US mortgage market, the securities it collateralized were toxic and could be near worthless.

European Contagion

On Tuesday 28 August 2007, the German Sachsen Landesbank collapsed and was rescued by another local bank, Baden-Wuerttemberg Landesbank. A few days later another German bank, IDK announced a $1 billion loss on US subprime business. It was another tip of the iceberg.

Northern Rock

In September of 2007 Northern Rock, a British mortgage lender suffered a run. The Rock was a building society[337] that became a commercial deposit taker bank. It was the fifth largest in the UK with assets, before its demise, of $200 billion. It was the first run on any bank in the UK since the time of Queen Victoria in the 19th century.[338] Quite an achievement given that in between the last bank run and Northern Rock, we had the Great Depression, two world wars, numerous other armed conflicts and many economic depressions. The Rock asked the Bank of England for funding in August 2007, when short term funding became scarce, and the markets for real estate collateralized securities became illiquid. The request was leaked and this sparked the run in September. It resulted in depositors queueing up to withdraw deposits, with lines extending into the streets. The panic was halted when the Bank of England agreed to guarantee depositors' funds. Some months after it was bailed out, it was nationalized and eventually sold in February of 2008. The total cost to the taxpayer was £27 billion. The OIS-LIBOR index had hit 85, more than double the high of a month or so ago. The Rock did not do much apart from mortgage lending. Its deposits were insufficient to fund its loans so it borrowed extensively in the short-term markets. Leverage on shareholder's equity had soared to 50 to 1.[339]

The chairman of the bank was Viscount Matt Ridley, a position he inherited from the previous occupant, his father, Viscount Matthew Ridley. In Victorian times, the family had owned coal mines. The Ridleys made a fortune. The younger Ridley is an English scientist, author, columnist and member of the House of Lords. He has published numerous books and articles, many of which have been well received. He was the Hayek Prize winner in 2001.

Ridley was responsible for the Rock's strategy, which a Treasury Select Committee described as a "high-risk, reckless business strategy" ... "excessively reliant on wholesale funding" and that it was only able to follow its strategy because the UK government agency responsible for its oversight[340] "systematically failed in its regulatory duty".[341] They explained that the directors were the principal authors of the problem and that the Rock was a systemic risk to the financial system. The Committee explicitly held Ridley accountable as "having failed to provide against the risks that [Northern Rock] was taking and to act as an effective restraining force on the strategy of the executive members".[342] A Select Committee member Michael Fallon, a Conservative Member of Parliament, and later Deputy Chairman of the Conservative Party, but then Minister of State for Business and Enterprise, questioned Radley, Why did [Ridley] endorse a "heavily leveraged bet in the movement of interest rates and on capital markets ... [it] seems to me to be a fairly basic banking error, is it not?" Ridley's response, "We were hit by an unexpected and unpredictable concatenation of events".[343] It was utter rubbish. There were many fore warnings. The Rock should not have taken on the leverage and the exposure in the first place.

Such was the egregious nature of the failure that the Select Committee recommended the implementation of new procedures for handling failing banks, revisions to the depository insurance scheme, and that a single authority be given powers for handling failing banks.

The responsibility for Northern Rock's failure rests with Ridley and we need to look closely at the man and his motivations.

Ridley thinks that greed is good, and that the successes of the rich enrich the poor. The benefits trickle down. In his column in the Daily Telegraph he described government as "a self-seeking flea on the backs of the more productive people in the world ... governments do not run countries, they parasitize unwarranted restraint on market freedom".[344] Governments are a "parasitic bureaucracy".[345] However, on 16 August 2007, contrary to his opposition to government bailouts,[346] regulation, and other interventions, he went cap in hand to the UK flea for support.

His most recent publications, public announcements and speeches make scant reference to the failure of Northern Rock, and his failures, and blames his employment agreement with the Rock for his inability to be forthright. His views are selfish, self-serving and irrational. His political and economic views have had disastrous consequences. He has suffered a string of failures[347] for which he neither accepts responsibility nor has learnt lessons.

It is even more damning that the massive gaps in responsibility, oversight and integrity did not arise because the problems with the Rock were difficult to understand or manage. The short-term funding strategy followed by the Rock was crude, foolish, Neanderthal and certainly not necessary. Thousands of banks avoid stupid strategies. The inescapable conclusion is that Ridley was more concerned with what went into his pocket, and the pockets of his colleagues, than with his responsibilities. He has been unconcerned that the taxpayers had to foot the bill.

Ridley took on the responsibility for overseeing a relatively simple set of processes, but abandoned it in favour of personal gain and childlike idealism, all at someone else's expense. Indeed Ridley, rather than accept responsibility and blame, sees that problem at Northern Rock as stemming directly from "government housing and monetary policy". As The Guardian's George Monbiot writes "it's the state wot made him do it".[348] Ridley's view is not a popular view except among the Great Recession enriched CEOs of the megabanks. Ridley should be dealt with in the same way that judges deal with thieves and rapists that muster the same defence. Ridley was grossly incompetent, irresponsible and negligent.

The FED's Year End Gift

The subprime problems meant that the banking sector desperately needed help, so in December 2007 the FED came to the rescue with a temporary program, the Term Auction Facility, the TAF. The spreads on interbank loans had widened, which meant that there was a lack of willingness for banks to lend. As we said a few moments ago, the FED had already lowered the discount window borrowing rate to 4.75%, but there were few takers as discount window borrowing come with a stigma.

So the FED disguised what was essentially *lender of last resort* lending and offered loans by auction to the deposit taker banks. Initially the tenor was 28 days, which was later extended to 84 days. The loans could be collateralized by assets that were accepted by the FED for discount window borrowing. It was disguised discount window borrowing! Immediately, ninety banks borrowed $40 billion. Most of the takers were European banks, for example, WestLB, Dresdner, DZ Bank, Dexia and Baden Wurttemberg Landesbank all borrowed $2 billion each. It was an exercise in crisis laundering. The Europeans had gorged on toxic products and had almost $10 trillion in US exposure, 70% of the US GDP, and the lion's share was in mortgage risk securities. The FED's actions were coordinated with similar auctions by the Bank of Canada and its European counterparts, the BoE, the Swiss National Bank and the

ECB, which lend $10 billion at the FED's auction rate to banks outside the FED's jurisdiction. To enable these central banks to lend dollars, the FED entered into currency swaps with them.

The last TAF loans were given in March 2010, and over 4,200 loans were extended for a value of almost $2 trillion.[349]

Bear Stearns

Bear Stearns was a large investment bank. It operated globally and had 15,500 employees. It was number five, the weakest and the most leveraged, of the Big Five investment banks. Jimmy Cayne was its CEO.

At year-end 2006, Bear Stearns had $67 billion in capital supporting assets of $350 billion. Its leverage was 5.25. In January 2007, its stock price hit an historical high, $172.69. A year later, at year-end 2007, capital had fallen to $11 billion, assets increased to $398 billion, and its leverage had become 36. Bear's debt was $387 billion.[350] The notional value of its outstanding derivatives contracts was a staggering $13.4 trillion. In September 2007, Bear announced that the funds that it had injected into its two failed hedge funds, and a $1.2 billion write down of its MBS and CDO portfolios contributed significantly to its 61% drop in profits. The company declared its first loss in 83, years, which wiped out 10% its capital.

Bear had been in the residential mortgage business for years. Until 2001, the loans were predominantly prime loans. It began its way down the food chain to super toxic loans in 2003. From 2004 to 2006, it securitized a million mortgages with a value of $192 billion. Bear inventoried MBSs, and used them as collateral for its repo borrowings. It traded CDOs and CDO^{2}s.

From 2005 to 2007, Fortune Magazine had given Bear awards recognizing employee talent, quality of risk management and business innovation. Given Bear's financial condition and a number of regulatory red flags, it's difficult to see how Fortune could do this. But it did. Furthermore, Bear had committed a number of frauds.

When AMBAC, the monoline sought chapter 11 bankruptcy protection, it sued Bear for misrepresenting the quality of the mortgages that it had placed into its securities, and that AMBAC had insured. Bear's goal was $2 billion a month in mortgage fodder and the quality of loans had become lower and lower. When loans defaulted, rather than put them back to originators, Bear entered into settlement agreements with them, and had accepted payments of $1.25 billion instead. It did not pass the payments on to the investors, as you would expect, hoping that any problems would only be discovered after the put back expiry date. Realizing that AMBAC may have to pay out large amounts to those it had insured and find itself in difficulties, Bear bet on AMBAC's failure by shorting its stock. The highly toxic loans that Bear had securitized helped Bear make billions as AMBAC fell apart.

Like all the investment banks, Bear relied heavily on the short-term markets. By March 2008, investors and lenders had realized that Bear's balance sheet contained significant illiquid, perhaps worthless assets. Bear's collateral was real estate based and the markets for MBSs, CDOs and CDS, were illiquid, so Bear could not renew its short-term borrowings. Financing its operations became difficult, and investors, customers and lenders emptied their Bear accounts, including the brokerage accounts. As there was no time to raise capital, disaster was near.

Between 3 March and 10 March Bear's stock fell from $77.32 to $62.30, and the ratings agencies downgraded Bear's mortgage risk debt. The CDS insurance against its failure had increased from 3.16% to 6.19%. Months before it was 0.35%. By 10 March, its cash had dropped to $18 billion, and a few days later, it was down to $2 billion. Its stock had fallen further to $30. Bankruptcy was around the corner.

No one wanted a Bear bankruptcy. It was *too big to **let** fail* and *too interconnected to fail.* Bear had open trades with 5,000 counterparties, and was a counterparty party to 75,000 derivatives contracts. Obviously, Bear's counterparties had counterparties. If Bear failed, there would be liquidity problems for its counterparties and the counterparties of these counterparties, and so on. Payments from a bankrupt Bear might take years to receive, so to raise cash for immediate needs, the counterparties would have to sell assets. As the assets would be sold in fire sales, their prices would plummet. Wall Street was so interconnected that the failure of one of its larger players would be a failure of a counterparty to thousands of transactions. Everyone holding collateral would have to sell it in distressed markets, as thousands would be trying to do the same thing. A Bear bankruptcy would result in other failures. While no one should have been taken by surprise, almost everyone was.

Inaction by Bernanke, Paulson and Geitner would mean a Bear bankruptcy. At first, they arranged a short-term loan so that Bear could find a buyer, but it was too late, and over the weekend, they orchestrated an acquisition by JP Morgan Chase. There was significant horse trading. First, the sale was for $2 per share, or $235 million, and the FED would cover $30 billion in losses in the toxic asset portfolios. A third of the shareholders were employees, and as angry Bear shareholders could hold up closure for months, the $2 per share went to $10, or $1.2 billion, and the FED would cover $29 billion in losses.

On Tuesday 18 March 2007, the markets responded. The DJIA was up, and the CDS insurance costs for the investment banks fell.

The question that remained after Bear was whether there would be similar problems for the other megabanks. The big investment banks had stronger balance sheets than Bear, but not by much. Was the investment bank model still viable? After the Great Depression investment banks were small, conservative private partnerships. Now they were large public corporations, and trading machines.

A few days prior to the demise of Bear, the FED had announced the Term Securities Lending Facility, the TSLF. The FED would swap US Treasuries for illiquid mortgage securities with banks for short periods of time. It would give borrowers good collateral. But rather than strengthening the market, it spooked it. The market took the TSLF as a sign that things were indeed very bad. So after Bear's demise, the FED announced the Primary Dealer Credit Facility, the PDCF. This opened the discount window to the investment banks for overnight collateralized lending. It meant that the regulated deposit taker, FDIC safety net was extended to the lightly regulated investment banks. Back to the 1920s. Banking examiners would be put on site at the investment banks and they would be placed partially under the FED umbrella. Hopefully with the Bear rescue, and the PDCF shoring up short-term funding for the investment banks, and tightened supervision, the markets would return to normal. Total borrowings came to $8.95 trillion and extended the FED's balance sheet by $2 trillion.

Congress was concerned with moral hazard and that saving Bear set a precedent. Bernanke, Paulson and Geitner had taken the view that they had a "fat into the fire" decision to make. A bailout to save the financial system was the better of two very bad alternatives. Bailouts expose moral risk and encouraged excessive and irresponsible risk taking. They told Congress that Bear was a once off, an act of desperation, and not the adoption of new policy. The rescue was necessary to save the financial system.

Barney Frank was not happy and he echoed the thoughts of many lawmakers on both sides of the House. "All these years of deregulation by the Republicans and the absence of regulation as these new financial instruments have grown and allowed them to take a large chunk of the economy hostage and we have to pay ransom".[351] He indicted the US President, G W Bush. Everyone seems to have lost. The Bear bailout was not a private sector injection to save jobs on Main Street. Those rescued were very highly paid traders that had taken stupid and needless risks. Bear employees were responsible for the companies' destruction, and those that were shareholders were rewarded! Senator Christopher Dodd questioned whether the bailout was a justified rescue needed to save the financial markets, or a $30 billion taxpayer bailout for rich executives provided at the expense of the Main Street families that struggled to pay their mortgages.[352]

Also, why was the US Treasury taken by surprise? There had been a single weekend to deal with the problem. There were clearly leadership gaps, and neither the Treasury, nor the regulators understood the activities and the businesses of the banks they regulated.

Many other questions arose. Would the failure of Bear be an isolated event? Were the other investment banks any different from Bear? What about Citibank and Bank of America? The prudent assumption was that all the megabanks were in the same boat. In the long run, they would have to deal with the same problems.

All the megabanks needed to strengthen their balance sheets, lower leverage and increase capital. They needed more cash. The two weakest, Merrill Lynch and Lehman Brothers were both heavily exposed to US real estate. Merrill was more diversified, had a large retail brokerage business end enjoyed good branding globally. In a worst-case situation, there was value in Merrill that would attract buyers. Lehman lacked diversification, was highly concentrated in the US and was the weaker of the two. Merrill had reduced its leverage from 32 to 27 but Lehman's was 31. So, with Bear gone, Lehman had to assure the market that it would not fail. Its gains from the boom years had been wiped out, and the company had lost trading partners. Lehman's stock was down 40%, and needed a buyer. Who? A significant issue was how it valued its real estate based portfolios? Was Lehman playing "mark to make believe"?[353]

Signalling more gloom and doom, another giant, UBS declared a $3.2 billion quarterly loss arising from its subprime mortgage business in October of 2007, and had recently sold a nominal $22 billion in mortgage risk to Black Rock taking a $7 billion loss to help alleviate its woes. By 29 March, the world's stock markets had fallen in value by $27 trillion, an average of 47%, from May 2008, just under half the globe's GDP.[354]

IndyMac

IndyMac, a countrywide spinoff, had assets of $32 billion and $18 billion in insured deposits. It was seized by its regulator, the OTS and handed over to the FDIC 11 July of 2008. At the time, it was the third largest bank failure in the US and the fifth for the year. Its downfall resulted from a balance sheet bloated with toxic real estate assets. Its main business was Alt-A mortgage origination, and most mortgages were originated by brokers so there was little documentation. Its downfall showed that the mortgage problem was not confined to subprime risk and that Alt-A loans could be toxic.

IndyMac had a small deposit base, most of its deposits came expensively through brokers specialized in the business of finding large deposits, and the bank had borrowed extensively from the Federal Home Loan Bank system.

The FDIC was aware that IndyMac was shaky from early in 2008, and had downgraded it in 2Q 2008. Senator Chuck Schumer wrote a confidential memo stating various concerns that, inadvertently and unfortunately, was made public. As a consequence, a run on the bank's deposits began on 2 June, with depositors lining up in the street, outside the bank's doors. They withdrew $3 billion, the Federal Home Loan Bank pulled its credit lines, and IndyMac was dead at a cost to the taxpayer of $7 billion. The problem again, a risky funding model.

Why Are We Where We Are?

By April, mortgage activity in the UK had come to a standstill. There were public disturbances in many European cities, so when the G7 met in Washington on 11 April[355] the global capital markets were at centre stage. At a dinner attended by the CEOs of many major financial institutions, the question was: Why were we where we are? The responses included too much leverage, poor governance, poor lending standards, poor transparency, poor market and product understandings, and so on. Mervyn King, the Governor of the Bank of England said: "You are all bright people, but you failed. Risk management is hard … so the lesson is, we can't let you get as big as you were and do the damage that you've done or get as complicated as you were - because you can't manage the risk element". Jean-Claude Trichet, the president of the ECB added that any requirements for capital ratios, leverage and liquidity standards had to be agreed, and implemented across the board, and Mario Draghi, the Governor of Banca d'Italia, later to be Trichet's successor, reiterated that the crisis was global and hence ensuring liquidity for the money market funds was hugely important.

An IMF report stated that write-downs on mortgage-backed securities could total a trillion dollars during the next two years. In order to expand their loss absorbing capacity, the large European and US banks had put on, collectively, $80 billion in capital. Merrill sold a $4.4 billion stake, with an option to increase it, to Temasek Holdings, a Singapore sovereign, Citigroup raised $7.5 from Abu Dhabi and the Chinese. Barclays went to the Arabian Gulf.

Before the Bear problem, Paulson had concluded that an FDIC type resolution facility for investment banks must be put in place. Bernanke agreed. What was needed was a worst-case end game, a way in which shadow-banking institutions could be wound down without taxpayer bailouts and without sending shock waves through the markets. The broker-dealer business model relied on overnight funding. To wind down a failing large bank would not be easy, as the banks were interconnected. But not being able to do so meant the risk of widespread insolvencies and severe damage to the financial system and the economy.

Paulson knew that capital levels were inadequate, and funding in the overnight markets was subject to rumour and perception. With more capital, the big market participants would be further away from the firing line, and have more chance of weathering any storm. He reasoned that lenders would see this and be more willing to lend. And if the worst did come about and a large bank went under, with an FDIC style failure option for the shadow banking system, an orderly shutdown would be possible, and the markets would be less impacted, or so the theory goes. This in itself would help anchor short-term lending.

As Paulson had been unprepared for Bear, he tried to put in place a contingency plan in case there were more Bears. The *Break the Glass: Bank Recapitalization Plan* was drawn up. If mayhem loomed, the Treasury would purchase, by auction, toxic securities to the value of $500 billion, and pay for them with Treasury securities. The purchased toxic assets could be sold over time, when conditions improved, and unwinding them could be managed by the private sector. The $500 billion was a guess. Perhaps it should be $1 trillion. *Break the Glass* could be put to Congress if and when necessary, in the form of a request for an authority to buy the securities. There were details to be worked out and alternatives. It was a source of moral hazard, but it was a plan.

But it was not a plan. It was neither detailed, nor comprehensive and not the sort of plan that could be put together at the last moment. The moral hazard issue had to be dealt with now, in order to prevent the need for *Break the Glass*. And what was the basis for the $500 billion? Surely, given the stakes, the Treasury should not be relying on guesses. What was really needed was a way to wind down very large, interconnected megabanks, and do so quickly.

On the Monday after the 2008 4 July holiday weekend, we saw that the financial markets in the US remained in meltdown. The stocks of the large banks, other financial institutions, and the GSEs were down. Many were saying that Freddie and Fannie would have to raise $75 billion in capital.[356]

The ratings agencies had been wrong about the risks in real estate collateralized securitizations. The MBS and CDO markets were illiquid. The short-term funding markets had retreated. Many MBS and CDO positions had been credit wrapped with CDS insurance. The monoline insurers had problems. Could the sellers afford payouts? The interconnectedness of the megabanks meant that they were stacked like cards. Despite FED denials, most assumed that if another financial institution ran into problems, it would intervene and save it. But Bernanke and Paulson were hoping that Bear had taught the market a lesson, and they knew there was one item in short supply, political capital. What looked likely was class warfare: the Wall Street fat cats versus the soccer moms.

Paulson and Bernanke needed to be prepared for Lehman, perhaps the GSEs and whatever else was on the horizon, and they needed to send a message about moral hazard. If either Lehman or the GSEs collapsed, neither bankruptcy nor a bailout was an option.

The Fourth Bangster Awards

Sebastien, the chief judge has made six more Bangster Awards. Angelo Mozilo, was a greedy thief, and guilty of insider trading, concealing information, securities fraud, failure to make required discloses, and was banned for a lifetime from serving as an officer of a public company. Greed is Good Lord Ridley, was a fraud, dishonest and a hypocrite. Ridley called governments, self-seeking fleas, but it was Ridley that was the flea. The UK government had to bail out Northern Rock because of his stupid recklessness. He is a Bangster. Jimmy Cayne, even though he was AWOL most of the time, plunged Bear into bankruptcy. He squandered billions on worthless bonds. Allegedly, the worst CEO ever. Hedge fund manager John Paulson, with Goldman's help, misled investors with a security designed to fail, and made billions at the expense of Main Street. Two investment banks are Bangsters. Morgan Stanley made fraudulent representations and knowingly sold toxic products. Goldman pigeoned its customers without restraint, and raped them for billions. It was inexcusable and shameless fraud in both cases.

Only one Gold Star. Barney Frank stood up against the rape of Main Street by the megabanks and demanded a return to regulation. He questioned why taxpayers had to bailout rich executives. He fought the oligarchy.

The current table is are:

Bangsters	Gold Stars
Nicholas Biddle	Franklin D Roosevelt
JP Morgan	Louis Brandeis
James Johnson	Raghuram Rajan
Alan Greenspan	Barney Frank
Angelo Mozilo	
Jimmy Cayne	
Mat Ridley	
John Paulson	
Morgan Stanley	
Goldman Sachs	

8

House of Cards

At the end of the 2008 US summer, the problems had escalated. The GSEs were nationalized by the end of the first week of September, but rather than cool the markets, their restructuring simply underscored that all was not well. By the end of September, 25 financial institutions had failed or been rescued. The five large investment banks became two, which took refuge as deposit takers.

We will look at the events of September in a little detail. It is important to understand how the implosions related to each other. Our goal is to understand why, after the second major financial implosion in the past one hundred years, little has changed.

Fannie Mae and Freddie Mac

The GSEs had two goals, a mission goal and a financial goal. The mission goal was all about affordable housing and the financial goal about shareholder returns. To meet the financial goals the GSEs had began to trade derivatives in the 1990s. By the Millennium, profits and bonuses were good.

By the 2000s, private labels, which fed on subprime, Alt-A and other poor quality mortgages had captured a significant part of the residential securitization business and challenged the 15 year old GSE securitization monopoly. Because returns on the senior tranches of the private labels were good, the GSEs gorged on them. It made meeting their financial goals easier, and enhanced profits, making the GSE executives richer. By 2005, the GSEs owned a third of all private label senior MBS tranches, and a quarter of the lower tranches. As their funding costs were less than Wall Street, their spreads made bigger profits and bonuses. By the mid-2000s, the GSEs had captured $5 trillion of the US mortgage market. Their capital levels, however, were low, between 1 and 2%.

The GSEs were the largest US private borrowers. Their debt exceeded the combined debt of the 50 states! By the mid-2000s, it was $4 trillion, almost as much as the $4.7 trillion US Treasury debt. If we viewed the GSE assets as GDPs, they would be in the top five economies!

The GSEs, however, could only do one thing, mortgages. If the mortgage market suffered, so would they. Their portfolios were massively exposed to interest rate risk. These exposures meant that they were disasters waiting to happen.

In 2003, Armando Falcon, the head of the OFHEO, the GSE's regulator, could see the problems and released a damning report. The message to the White House, the Treasury, and the FED was that the GSEs were far too exposed to US real estate risk. Furthermore, Fannie had systematically overstated its revenues for years, so that its senior executives could take larger bonuses. The report concluded that Fannie's results were "intentionally manipulated to trigger management bonuses". Fannies' increased profitability under CEO Franklin Raines was accounting fraud! When they got advance warning of the report, the GSEs went berserk, but Fannie's response was pathetic: accounting for derivatives was difficult.

It was one of the largest accounting scandals in the history of US finance. Fannie had to restate its revenues by $6.3 billion and paid $400 million in penalties. It agreed to hold 30% more capital and constrain its mortgage portfolios. Raines was out. His 1998 to 2003 compensation had been $90 million, $52 million of which was tied to phony accounting. He kept it all. On top of that, he was given a $25 million severance payment. So engage in massive fraud, pay large bonuses, fire the boss, let him keep what he had *not* earned and give him a golden handshake! Wonderful.

When the subprime lenders collapsed in 2007, Wall Street begun to draw back from mortgage risk. Astonishingly, just after Bear Stearns collapsed, the Bush Administration lowered the GSE capital requirement so that Freddie and Fannie could increase their mortgage purchase. The goal, political, was to guarantee $2 trillion more in mortgages. The good times, however, were over and Fannie and Freddie were losing money. In the first months of 2008, Fannie lost $2.1 billion and Freddie $3.1 billion. It was the first loss ever for Freddie. As they were bought 80% of all mortgages, their combined debt reached $5.2 trillion, now larger than the federal debt. The market was wary, and participation in their auctions dwindled. By mid-year, both Freddie and Fannie were in serious trouble. Were they solvent? Their stock was being unloaded. The CDS insurance on their default had shot up, and short term funding had become difficult. Lloyd Blankfein pointed out, the GSEs were Washington's SIVs, [357] and hid Washington's exposure. The disasters-in-waiting were happening.

On 10 July, William Poole, a former president of the Federal Reserve Bank of St Louis remarked that both Freddie and Fannie must be insolvent. If there was a mortgages default avalanche, they were undercapitalized, and they could not pay the guarantees. They were only able to continue in business because of Washington's support. He referred to them as bastions of privilege, financed by the taxpayer.[358]

China was a major holder of GSE debt, and a GSE failure would result in losses to China of hundreds of billions of dollars. Japan and Russia were in the same boat. At home, their failure would devastate family savings, home values, retirement savings, auto loans, and so on. It would be disastrous for employment, and the US government was de facto on the hook for trillions.

It was clear that the GSEs were probably insolvent, so with this haunting them, Paulson and Bernanke decided to wind down both Fannie and Freddie. The first stop was Congress. They needed money, and Paulson requested a blank check. The Treasury had only become aware of Bear at the last moment, and had only a couple of days to find a solution. The GSEs were a repeat, but worse. Paulson could not even guess at the size of the GSE problem. The US Treasury had learned nothing from Bear, and had dropped the ball again. But this time, Paulson, Geitner and Bernanke had known for months that there could be more problems, but had swept them under the carpet.

The Democrats in Congress wanted to know the full extent of the problem and do something for the homeowners that had suffered. They wanted foreclosure relief as part of any GSE solution. The Republicans did not want to give the GSEs a handout and were opposed to foreclosure relief. They branded Paulson a socialist![359] However, on 23 July, Congress gave the US Treasury temporary authority to support Freddie and Fannie. Paulson had explained that with a big club, the Treasury would almost certainly not need to take any action, as the markets would know that he had the financial capacity to deal with their problems. Unfortunately, the markets disagreed. The problems did not go away.

Paulson and the Treasury had not thought of the obvious. After being given the authority and funds to assist the GSEs, the GSEs would find it impossible to raise more capital as investors knew that the Treasury could step in at any time, and dilute any capital investment. If the GSEs were nationalized it would wipe out shareholders. The stock markets took Freddie and Fannie to all-time lows. So much for Paulson's Wall Street education and market insight!

The Treasury now held power never conceded to any Department of the Treasury before, and which could be exercised in the sole discretion of the Secretary of the Treasury, an individual who had argued that he would not need to use the power and who maintained that he did not seek power for its own sake.

In order to get some answers, Morgan Stanley was retained to assess the GSEs, and reported that they had a huge, huge capital hole. They needed $50 billion in cash, just to meet the 2.5% capital requirement. They could not pay on their guarantees and confirmed that they were insolvent. Without an immediate cash injection, they would not survive more than a few days.

There were two choices: bankruptcy or conservatorship. Conservatorship keeps a company functioning, under supervision, and bankruptcy wipes out the shareholders and bondholders. On 7 September, both organizations were put into conservatorship. The GSEs would not default on their debts to bondholders, and they would not be liquidated. The foreign investors, who had invested $1 trillion, were happy. GSE stock would continue to trade. Hopefully this would keep mortgages flowing, cost the taxpayer less and stabilize the markets.

The Treasury took a $1 billion, 79.9% stake in both organizations. It agreed to lend up to $100 billion to each company. Dividends to the existing and diluted stockholders were suspended. The Treasury would pay the bondholders. The GSEs had to fire all their lobbyists so they would no longer be able to lobby Congress. It was one of the biggest financial rescues ever, beyond anything that had been imagined, and Washington was on the hook for $5 trillion in mortgages.

Congress was not happy. Many had taken Paulson's at his word, and had not expected him to cash the check. But Paulson had not done his homework. He had no clue of the extent of the problems. The Chinese, Japanese and Europeans, however, were happy. Hundreds of billions of securities were now safe. Nevertheless, the credit spreads widened. In mid-September 2008, the TED spread between interbank and treasury yields broke its previous record set during the 1987 stock market crash.

By the end of 2010, the GSEs had accrued $147 billion in investment and credit losses. In 2011, the SEC sued the former CEOs and other former employees for securities fraud. The complaint, their investment strategy meant purchasing higher risk loans so that the short-term profit targets could be met, which meant higher bonuses for executives.

As usual, the ratings agencies were missing in action. They had downgraded Enron only four days before its implosion, and waited until 11 August 2008, three weeks before the demise of the GSEs to lower their ratings, to A-!

Lehman

Lehman Brothers was spun off from American Express in 1994, with Richard Fuld at the helm. When the firm declared chapter11 bankruptcy in 2008, Fuld had been at Lehman for 30 years, and was the longest tenured CEO on Wall Street.

Bear's demise focused attention on Lehman, so immediately after its acquisition, Lehman announced interim numbers. They were good and the stock rebounded up 46% to $46.49, the biggest one day gain since it was spun off from American Express. The rebound was, however, short lived. It lost counterparties and lenders and moral was down. The company then announced a 2Q 2008 loss of $2.8 billion, its first quarterly loss since Lehman and American Express parted company. Why? Because Lehman, like Bear, had a balance sheet clogged with mortgage risk.

In May, David Einhorn a hedge fund manager had advised customers to short the Lehman stock and questioned Lehman's accounting standards. He told us that Lehman had overvalued its assets and understated its leverage[360]. Rather than record what was in fact a repo, Lehman recorded across quarterly reporting dates a sale of assets for cash at the end of a quarter, and the re-purchase of the same assets for cash at the beginning of the next. The accounting trick was known as a Repo 105, as Lehman delivered $105 in assets for $100 in cash, and then paid $100 in cash for the return of $105 in assets. A Repo 105 increased revenues, profits and bonuses for the reporting period, and leverage appeared lower. In this way, in 4Q 2007 Lehman moved $38.6 billion off its books over the year end. At the end of 1Q 2008, it moved $49 billion, and for 2Q 2008, it moved $50.4 billion.[361] It was fraud, pure and simple.

No one trusted Lehman's marks. The inability to mark assets accurately had meant that Bear had been handed to JP Morgan Chase on a platter. Lehman's models were mark-to-make-believe. Einhorn asked why a Lehman $6.5 billion toxic CDO portfolio with $1.6 billion below investment grade was marked down by only $200 million.

Fuld and Joe Gregory, the company's number one and two executives, were unable to understand what their traders were doing. They were both years out of the market and did not understand the new products, nor that their risks dwarfed the risks of the products they had grown up with. Both had lost touch, and there was little strategy. Neither recognised that the US housing market was a problem, and Lehman's exposure to it was huge.

Fuld did recognise that Lehman needed a major investor, but not really why. His explanation for the stock's decline was that Lehman was a shorters' target.[362] He spoke to many potential investors, too many, including the Korean Development Bank, AIG, Citigroup, Deutsche, Morgan Stanley, HSBC, GE, BoA and a number of sovereign wealth funds. As he approached so many, without a game plan, the potential investors assumed that he was desperate. By June, Lehman's survival was at stake, and when he did find interest, he played hardball and asked for too much.

The Treasury thought that like Bear, a Lehman bankruptcy had to be avoided at all costs. As Lehman was probably more interconnected than Bear, a Lehman bankruptcy would cause unimaginable damage. Lehman's $600 billion balance sheet was supported by capital of only $25 billion, and we learned later that $50 to 70 billion of its assets were near worthless. Its daily repo funding was a staggering $280 billion, almost half the balance sheet. Anyone who saw value in Lehman assumed that Washington would step in with a bailout and a fire sale of its assets. Why not wait and buy what was wanted more cheaply, and exclude the toxic assets!

When it came to crunch time, there were only three potential acquirers, the Korean Development Bank, BoA and Barclays Capital. The Koreans walked away because Fuld asked for too much. BoA had issues stemming from its recent acquisition of Countrywide, and eventually acquired Merrill. Then Lehman announced its 3Q 2008 earnings, a loss of $3.9 billion, its biggest ever. Lehman's customers continued to walk and overnight funding evaporated.

Paulson and Geitner called a meeting at the NY FED of the CEOs of the major US financial institutions in the evening of Friday 12 September. Everyone lost in a Lehman bankruptcy. Bear's failure had created a major employment problem in New York City, and a Lehman bankruptcy would make it worse. The US was now in recession and unemployment had hit 6.1%. On the day before, Lehman's stock had closed down at $3.71. They proposed an LTCM type solution. The banks would invest in Lehman so that the toxic assets could be segregated and the remainder of Lehman sold. It was in everyone's interests. As Congress would not permit another bailout, a private solution was the only non-bankruptcy option, but no-one knew how to assess the size of the toxic asset black hole. However, if a private solution was to happen, it had to be put in place over the coming weekend.

Barclays Capital agreed to take Lehman after its toxic assets had been siphoned off. Guesses ranged from $40 billion to $70 billion, but the UK regulator, the FSA stopped it. The FSA did not want any impact on the UK financial system, it was bad enough already. For Barclays Capital to acquire the nontoxic assets of Lehman, it would need a shareholder vote, which would take a few months, and there was no time.

The only alternative was chapter 11 bankruptcy. At 1:45 am on Monday 15 September, Lehman Brothers filed for protection from its creditors in the Southern District of New York with assets of $639 billion. The biggest in US history.

The following week, on Friday 19, Barclays acquired the US operations of Lehman for $1.75 billion in bankruptcy proceedings. Barclays got what it wanted for a steal, it would save ten thousand jobs and keep Lehman in New York. Barclays Capital took the New York building, alone worth $1 billion. The foreign divisions were sold to other organizations.

Winding down Lehman was complex. While some of Lehman's counterparties were able to match deals, and offset open trades, there were many issues that had not been thought through.

Bankruptcy in the UK and Japan froze billions of dollars, including the customer accounts, leaving many counterparties short. Some hedge funds with balances held at Lehman had to sell assets at distressed prices to meet their own obligations, and this meant that some hedge funds failed. Lehman in the US transferred cash balances and collateral back to *its* customers, but Lehman in the UK, and other jurisdictions, could not do this. This took Paulson and Bernanke by surprise. Lehman had loaned collateral from some hedge funds to others, and sorting out who owed what to whom was a nightmare. There was so much money caught within Lehman that investors pulled money from Goldman and Morgan Stanley. The bankruptcy spooked the markets badly.

By 2012, $1.5 billion had been spent in bankruptcy legal fees alone. The assets of $639 billion had become $65 billion and the creditors were still waiting to be paid at year end 2011. It was estimated that the senior creditors would get about 21 cents in the dollar. An FDIC resolution would have realized almost $1. Dick Fuld's compensation was mostly in stock and although he had cashed out $260 million, the balance of his stock, which earlier had made his net worth more than $1 billion, was reduced to $65,000. Fuld's wealth was directly tied to Lehman's, but this was not sufficient to constrain his risk taking.

Merrill Lynch

When Stan O'Neil took the job of CEO at Merrill Lynch in December 2002, a major priority was to resuscitate the firm. Merrill's brokerage business, generated from one hundred branches nationally, had suffered because of online brokerage firms. Up until the time he took office, the company had not taken excessive risks, but he wanted to change this. He wanted to be more like Goldman. He cut costs, and, following Goldman, refocused the business into riskier and more lucrative investment strategies. Merrill began to trade aggressively for its own account. Profits of $2.6 billion in 2002 when O'Neal took over became $7.5 billion in 2006. The changes made sense.

In 2006, Merrill entered the CDO business, and wanted to own it. O'Neal pushed the firm to become the largest CDO issuer on Wall Street, and succeeded. In his first year. Between 2002 and 2007, Merrill underwrote 100 CDOs, and became Number One. [363]. The next in line, Citigroup had put together 73 deals. The fees generated were substantial and Merrill developed a front to back business, issuing mortgages, securitizing them and selling the CDOs. The BBB tranches were bundled into CDO^2s. Merrill demanded high ratings from the rating agencies. In order to ensure it always had sufficient mortgage fodder, it bought up more than thirty mortgage and commercial real estate companies. It owned 20% of Ownit, a mortgage originator that went from originating fully documented loans to a no documentation loan company in six months. Merrill wanted the higher yields. Merrill also bought First Franklin for $1.3 billion in late 2006, but almost immediately, Franklin wrote down billions.

When the subprime business weakened in 2006, rather than take heed, Merrill stepped up CDOs production. Fees toppled $700 million from $44 billion in CDOs, and bonuses soared. O'Neal earned $46 million, and his two CDO lieutenants split $57 million between them. By July 2007, Merrill had underwritten a further $30 billion. The 2Q 2007, revenues were $9.7 billion, with profits of $2.1 billion, up 31% year on year. The problem was that Merrill's senior management, like the senior management elsewhere on Wall Street, was clueless and quantitatively illiterate. They took the models as reality, there were risks not contemplated by the models, and the possibility of Black Swans was beyond them. There were warning signs, but O'Neal and his senior collaborators were drunk on bonuses. Those who tried to caution him were fired.

In 3Q 2007, Merrill's CDO portfolio plummeted. Worst-case loss projections for the quarter of $85 million became $5 billion and two weeks later $7.9 billion. The turnabout was staggering. Merrill's toxic asset portfolio had grown to $55 billion, up $40 billion from the previous year. The CDS protection from the monolines was of little use as cashing in would wipe them out.

Merrill was able to sell some of its rubbish, for example, in July, it sold a $30.6 billion CDO portfolio for $6.7 billion. It was a drop in the ocean.

O'Neil did not understand what was going on, but he did recognise, that Merrill had problems, so he approached BoA, and then Wachovia. Both approaches were unauthorized, and he was fired. He left with $33 million in cash and $131 million in stock.

John Thain, formerly Paulson's number two at Goldman, and then CEO of the New York Stock Exchange, took over. He assessed the damage at $90 billion.

Although Merrill raised $12.8 billion from two sovereign wealth funds, Temasek Holdings of Singapore and the Kuwait Investment Authority, it was not enough. Losses immediately wiped out $8.6 billion! If Lehman failed, the pressure would be on Merrill, and if BoA took over Lehman as rumoured, Merrill would be dead. Merrill approached the bank in early September, and a deal was done over the weekend of the Lehman bankruptcy. BoA bought Merrill for $50 billion in stock, or $29 per share, a 70% premium over Merrill's closing price on the prior Friday. The bank also paid $5.8 billion in incentive compensation in order to retain Merrill staff. Merrill's losses continued, however, and in 2008 came to $27.6 billion. Clearly, BoA had paid far too much! But on top of its woes, Thain had pushed through a $43.6 million bonus package for himself just before the BoA acquisition closed.

AIG

AIG had its roots in Asia; by 2008, it was the globe's largest insurer and one of the USA's largest twenty corporations. It had more than 200 subsidiaries, a presence in 130 countries, 116,000 employees and 70 million customers. The company had an AAA credit rating. Hank Greenberg had run the company since the late 1960s. He was combative and AIG was his personal fiefdom. In 2005 AIG agreed to pay a $10 million fine to the SEC, Greenberg was out and Martin Sullivan became CEO.

Under Sullivan, AIG continued to do well. In 2006, the profits were $14 billion on revenues of $100 billion. Its assets were $1 trillion, and its market capitalization $80 billion. The company, however, needed to modernize. It operated in silos, the division heads were careful to tell senior management only what they wanted to hear, and its IT systems were antique. There was little companywide risk assessment. In 2008, the results took a dive, Sullivan took the blame, and its chairman, Bob Willemstad stepped in as CEO. The losses for November and December 2007 were restated up from $1 billion to $5 billion, and the auditors reported a "material weakness in accounting procedures", but there was clearly more to it. Then, in 2008, its credit derivatives portfolio took a $9.1 billion write down and a $7.8 billion loss, the companies' largest loss ever. AIG needed to raise capital, and Willemstad thought that it might be the tip of the iceberg. He was right. AIG had another loss in the following quarter of $5.4 billion. What was going on?

In 1987, Howard Sosin, a quant, moved from Drexel Burnham Lambert to run a new division, AIG Financial Products, AIG FP. Sosin wanted the AAA credit rating and balance sheet in order to gamble on derivatives. AIG wanted the profits. Within a few years, AIG FP was the fastest growing division of AIG. It had only 380 employees, one third of 1% of AIG's employees. By 2005, its revenues were $3.25 billion, with profits of $1 billion a year.[364] Its contribution to AIG's profits was 7.5%. It was remarkable that so few people contributed so much to the AIG's bottom line.

In 1998, the recent crises motivated AIG FP to develop a CDS business. Customers could insure defaults on loans they gave, and AIG FP's quants would use computer models to assess and monitor the risks. The chance of an avalanche of defaults was remote and AIG FP viewed the premium income stream as "money for nothing". Absent another Great Depression, CDS were safe investments and payouts were a very, very low probability. CDS were sold as credit wraps for products exposed to credit defaults, and could be used to bet on whether the debt within an MBS or CDO would default. AIG FP's models determined that the chance of a payout on CDO senior tranches was 0.15%.

Joe Cassano became CEO of AIG FP in 2001 by which time AIG FP was a leading CDS provider. Investors that bought CDS coverage from AIG FP swapped their exposure to customer defaults with credit exposure to the AAA rated AIG, and AIG FP became exposed to the default risk for an enormous amount of corporate and mortgage collateralized debt.

AIG's AAA rating meant that little or no collateral had to be posted with CDS investors. There were, however, collateral triggers. If AIG's rating fell, AIG FP would have to post (more) collateral. Cassano hid this obligation from AIG's management. What, however, was not appreciated, was that AIG's capital supported its insurance business, and was not available to support AIG FP. AIG's AAA rating, in practice, meant little. The clueless Cassano was unaware of this.

In 2005, AIG FP discontinued writing insurance on subprime mortgage CDOs, but continued with CDS contracts for the AAA tranches of MBSs and CDOs. This did not shield AIG FP from subprime risk as the AAA tranches often contained subprime mortgages. AIG FP did not understand this. Cassano stated in August of 2007, after the Bear and BNP Paribas hedge fund problems that "It is hard for us, without being flippant, to even see a scenario within any kind of realm or reason that would see us losing one dollar in any of those transactions"[365]. The statement simply overlooked the reasons why buyers spent money on premiums.

In 2007, when the markets for MBSs and CDOs collapsed, AIG FP started to receive collateral calls. AIG FP had not set aside reserves against CDS claims because they thought that there was no need to do so, but its exposure by 2007 had become astronomical. Until a few months before, collateral calls were deemed only a remote possibility. However, if AIG was downgraded, even to A, AIG would have an enormous problem, with tens of billions more in collateral calls, so when AIG FP posted an additional $450 million in collateral with Goldman, Goldman bought $575 million in CDS insurance against AIG's failure. AIG FP paid out $2.5 billion in collateral calls in December, and another $2.7 billion was due.

Cassano had considered subprime risk as a credit risk only, and had never considered liquidity risk, the risk that collateral calls could drain AIG FP's funds, destroy it, and severely affect AIG.

The 2007 results were announced at the end of February 2008. Write downs were $11.5 billion. That AIG FP had met $2.5 billion in collateral calls without informing AIG surfaced. It became clear that AIG FP, and Cassano, were out of control. Cassano was ousted. He left with $34 million in his pocket and a $1 million per month consulting contract! The mind boggles! We had to wait for Congress to hear about the retainer before it was withdrawn.

AIG's $1 trillion balance sheet was sound, a surplus of $78 billion assets over liabilities. There was negligible debt, and the company was not subject to the fickle short-term credit markets. It had $40 billion in cash on hand. However, it would not be able to withstand unlimited and large collateral calls.

By September, AIG had paid out a total of $55 billion, leaving it without any cash. Willemstad tried to convince Geitner at the NY FED that the health of Wall Street was tied to the health of AIG. The best guess of the value of the CDS exposure was $500 billion. AIG FP had a counterparty exposure greater than $2.7 trillion in notional amounts, in 12,000 contracts. AIG's exposure included $1 trillion to twelve major institutions. It held 81 million life insurance policies with a face value of $1.9 trillion and tens of billions in retirement accounts, including annuities. AIG had also provided surety bonds for construction projects and public works. Many money market and pension funds held AIG paper. AIG would be subject to large payouts if Lehman failed. If AIG was downgraded, there would be many more collateral calls and if AIG could not post collateral, it would have to file for chapter 11 bankruptcy protection. If AIG went down, so would the financial system. Millions of individuals would be destroyed financially, and it would take years to unwind the outstanding transactions.

Inexplicably, Geitner thought that providing support might worsen the situation, so he said no.

On Thursday 11 September, Moody's said it if nothing changed, it would downgrade AIG's rating on the following Monday. This would mean $10.5 billion in collateral calls. If S&P also lowered the rating, the additional collateral would increase by $13.3 billion. So, on Saturday 13, AIG told the Treasury that it had a $50 billion liquidity problem arising from losses in its derivatives business. AIG could raise $10 billion from the sale of unencumbered securities, but needed Washington's support with a $40 billion loan. This became $60 billion, then $85 billion, and then the money was needed the following day. How could this happen? It happened because AIG had poor and antiquated IT systems and incompetent management who were not capable of using them, so accurate information was scarce. They had a poor understanding of the markets and the risks. AIG FP prospectuses were out to lunch; they were absurdly optimistic, misleading and difficult to understand. They were not only irresponsible, they made fraudulent representations. Its regulator was in the same boat. Cassano was at the heart of the problem. No one was permitted to disagree with him. He understood neither the markets, nor the products, nor the risks. AIG had little idea of what was going on at AIG FP. As the markets collapsed, AIG's numbers got worse.

The US Treasury and the FED decided that there was no alternative but to provide AIG with a credit line of $85 billion. In return, the FED took a 79.9% stake in AIG. Like the GSEs, AIG was nationalized. Although AIG had a large liquidity problem, it was probably solvent, and the collateral was real. Subsidiaries could be liquidated and the loan paid off. Moreover, AIG was *too big to fail*. As a Basel, European bank could hold less capital if its debt was insured, European banks used CDS insurance to lower capital requirements. The AIG AAA rating provided the wrap. If AIG failed, Europe's Basel banks would have to raise capital in an already distressed market, thousands of counterparties would suffer and the markets destroyed.

When the 3Q 2008 results were announced, the loss was $24.5 billion, the FED was on the hook again. Eventually the total became $180 billion. Then, during the resolution process, $60 billion was paid to AIG to enable it to make good on its CDS obligations to many Wall Street firms.[366]

For the years 2001 to 2007, AIG FP annual compensation had exceeded $1 million per employee. The total compensation was $3.5 billion, which meant that the employees took between one third and one-half of the profits. Joe Cassano himself made $300 million. AIG FP was thus primarily a tool for making money for its employees, not for AIG, and they did so by using the credit rating of AIG. Should a problem arise, as it did, AIG would bear 100% of the downside. Moral hazard exemplified.

After the bailout, AIG's problems did not go away. AIG FP had to unwind its positions, but how? Its management had to go, but what could replace it? The incredulous view was that many of the people that had caused the problem should be retained to sort out the war scene. A bonus plan was put in place to ensure that the boneheaded team that had produced the problems would remain to unwind the mess! We were told that they were "uniquely qualified". The logic was staggeringly stupid and illustrated the myopic and kindergarten like expertise of AIG and AIG FP. In March 2009, the Treasury authorized a payment of $168 million in retention bonuses to employees in AIG FP. This caused an uproar, especially in Congress. The individuals that created the problems should have been fired, with salary and bonuses clawbacks.

When asked to identify the recipients, AIG refused to do so. As it turned out, many who received the retention bonuses were no longer with AIG. We eventually learned: the top recipient received more than $6.4 million, the top seven received more than $4 million each, and, in aggregate, the top ten bonus recipients received $42 million. 22 individuals received bonuses of $2 million or more, and in aggregate, they received more than $72 million. 73 individuals received bonuses of $1 million or more. Eleven of the individuals who received *retention* bonuses of $1 million or more were no longer working at the company, and this included the employee who received $6.4 million. Finally, all employees received bonuses,[367] a kitchen assistant, $7,700, a file administrator, $700 and a mail room assistant $7,000.

Economic 9/11[368]

The lack of a consistent story from the US Treasury: Save Bear, take over the GSEs, let Lehman go, but save and nationalize AIG, helped destroy the markets. If Bear was *too big to fail* wasn't Lehman? It was twice the size of Bear and similarly entangled with thousands of counterparties? After Lehman, lending froze, and the economy headed south.

Christine Lagarde the French finance minister called the Lehman decision horrendous. Jean-Claude Trichet agreed with her. By November the markets were dead, the Treasury and the FED were in overdrive dealing with the mess, and as for the real economy, 533,000 non-farm jobs had been lost, the worst losses since 1974.

Contrary to the expectations of Paulson, Bernanke and Geitner, the aftermath of Lehman's demise was devastating. It spooked the markets badly. The DJIA dropped 4%, its biggest decline since 9/11, and a week later, it was under 10,000 for the first time in five years. The already fragile credit markets were dysfunctional. Every major sector on the S&P 500 index showed a loss. The LIBOR-OIS, which had peaked at 82 during the Bear problems, was over 300. The estimated decline in global market capitalization was in the order of $2 trillion. It was apparent that the US and European economies were on the verge of collapse. It was an economic Armageddon, an economic 9/11.

Bernanke later realized the idiocy of letting Lehman fail:

> I believed that a failure of a major institution in the midst of a financial crisis would not only create contagion through effects on counterparties, but would likely have a troublesome negative effect on broader market confidence.[369]

The remaining megabanks, Washington Mutual, Wachovia, BoA, Citigroup, Goldman Sachs and Morgan Stanley, were close to failure too, and then there was GE, and the automakers.

On Tuesday 16 September, the FED auctioned $31 billion 4-week Treasury bills and received bids totalling $100 billion. They paid 0.10%, down from 1.15% the week before. The market only wanted Treasuries. Funds flowed from Morgan Stanley and Goldman. The money market funds, which had 30 million customers, account balances of $2.7 trillion in the US, $1.5 trillion in Europe and $400 billion elsewhere suffered heavy withdrawals.[370] Moscow suspended its stock markets on Tuesday 16th and kept them closed for three days.

The nation's oldest money market fund, the Reserve Primary Fund with assets of $62.4 billion, "broke the buck". Redemptions were marked at 0.97 cents. It had invested $785 million in Lehman commercial paper, 1.2% of its assets, and marked it down to zero. The fund was relying on Washington saving Lehman.[371] Reserve Primary suffered withdrawals totalling $40 billion, sought SEC permission to suspend redemptions, and then closed. This led to a run on all money market funds. Withdrawals were $350 billion[372] within the week, followed by $85 billion in the next few weeks. Investors were moving funds from uninsured accounts to insured accounts, and risk free US Treasuries. Money market funds invested heavily in the $1.8 trillion commercial paper market, it was collapsing, which meant that corporate America would not have money for payrolls. The damage had extended well beyond the financial sector and into the real economy.

GE, an AAA rated company, could not sell its commercial paper for any term longer than a day. GE was the largest single issuer of commercial paper. If it had problems, so would hundreds of other companies. The cost was not lives, at least directly, but more company failures, hundreds of thousands of jobs and a further destruction of savings.

To stem withdrawals from the money market funds, the FDIC came to the rescue[373] and guaranteed the $1 net asset value of deposits in all money market fund accounts. Premiums were charged. The money market run was a modern day version of a run on a commercial bank, and what halted the run was a government guarantee. Total guarantees $3.36 trillion. In conjunction, US financial institutions were given non-recourse loans to buy asset backed commercial paper from money market funds to provide the funds with liquidity. These measures were successful.

The Europeans were very critical of the US for letting Lehman go. It simply was *too big to fail*. The bankruptcy had been unexpected, and the on-and-off Treasury strategy had contributed to the destruction. Would there be future bankruptcies or would there be more bailouts. They wanted the US Treasury to get a grip on the problems. They wanted it to ignore criticisms of nationalization and socialism and get on with solving the problems that had, after all, developed in the US. The British and Europeans had their own slew of problem financial institutions. The European stock markets had plummeted and the FTSE fallen to 4,880, below 5,000 for the first time since May 2005. The Asian markets were underwater.

The repo markets had ground to a halt and consequently, investors who needed Treasuries could not obtain them via the repo market. Treasuries are often used to hedge inventories of bonds and other assets, and without a source of Treasuries, the markets trading these inventories seized up. Market participants that had borrowed Treasuries, and lent or sold them to other market participants, could not return them as required. The "failed to deliver" Treasuries volume on Friday 12 September, before the Lehman bankruptcy was $20 billion. On 24 September it was $1.7 trillion and in early October $2.3 trillion. Consequently, the FED accepted anything that qualified as tri-party repo collateral and provided repo style funds.

Could the only two surviving Big Five investment banks, Goldman and Morgan Stanley survive? Their balance sheets were stronger than Bear, Lehman and Merrill, but by how much, and were the marks real? How toxic were their balance sheets? Morgan Stanley's stock dropped 30%, and Goldman's 20%.

On the day of Lehman's demise, Morgan Stanley's cash balance was $180 billion, but at the end of the week it was down to $32 billion, this despite an announcement of $1.43 billion in profits. Goldman was better off. It was less reliant on the short-term markets. Both needed capital. In the press, "Goldman, Morgan Now Stand Alone; Fight or Fold?"

Deposits provide a stable source of funds, so both assessed merger possibilities with a large deposit taker, but nothing was possible. The deposit takers' balance sheets contained tens of billions of toxic assets. So a week after Lehman, both Goldman and Morgan Stanley took refuge as bank holding companies. They would be able to accept deposits, but more importantly, they would have access to the discount window, and be regulated by the FED. The March temporary lending facilities were now permanent. Goldman became the fourth largest US deposit taker, and Morgan Stanley was not far behind. Both survived, and the 2Q 2009 profits for Goldman were its largest ever. Goldman set aside $11.4 billion to pay bonuses, also a record. Later, both American Express and GMAC (now Ally financial) became bank holding companies too. The investment bank model was dead.

Morgan Stanley sold 21% of its equity for $9 billion to Japan's biggest bank, Financial UFJ and Goldman sold preferred shares to Warren Buffet for $5 billion. It was a great deal for Buffet as the preferred shares paid a 10% divided, he could buy more at an in-the-money price, and there were restrictions on when the four top Goldman executives could leave or sell their shares. The Buffet investments lead to another $5 billion the next day.

The Other US Dropouts

WaMu was a giant and a basket case. It was founded in 1889, in Seattle on the west coast, and when it failed, it was the largest S&L,

with assets of $307 billion and the sixth largest bank in the US. It was systematically important. It had grown quickly and was heavily into subprime mortgage lending. It had $190 billion in insured deposits. Its management was dysfunctional and permitted the bank to embrace the riskiest subprime mortgages, neither understanding nor acknowledging the risks. WaMu's management could not deal with the organization into which WaMu had grown.[374]

With impeccable timing, in 2005, it shifted its mortgage business away from traditional fixed rate, conforming mortgages to subprime loans. Non-traditional loans were between six to ten times more profitable than traditional loans, and the sales teams were compensated based on volume, and the type of mortgage sold. Often they overwrote the information provided by the applicant so that the loan would be granted, and the commission paid. Sales executives were subject to a minimum number of loans per day, and option ARM loans with low credit scores and low loan to value ratios were targeted. When WaMu was sold to JP Morgan Chase in 2008, its loan portfolio was 90% home equity, 73% option ARM and 50% subprime.

WaMu's regulator, the OTS funded itself by charging fees to the banks it regulated. A significant part of its revenues came from WaMu. WaMu ignored the OTS mortgage guidelines. If it had followed them, its loan origination volumes would have been reduced by a third, WaMu's profits reduced accordingly and similarly the fees it paid to the OTS. Neither WaMu nor the OTS wanted this.

By 2006, WaMu mortgage portfolio delinquencies were up 140% year on year, foreclosures up 70% year on year and first payment defaults well up.[375] In late 2007, WaMu was put on the FDIC watch list, and by 4Q 2007 had recorded losses of $2 billion. The bank needed more capital or be acquired and JP Morgan Chase offered $8 a share. The management team wanted to keep their jobs, salaries and bonuses, so WaMu opted for a $7 billion capital infusion, against the advice of the FDIC.

When IndyMac failed in July 2008, WaMu suffered depositor withdrawals of $1.2 billion per day for a week or so, which then tapered down to $550 million per day a few weeks later.

In early 2007 its share price had reached a peak of $45, but by 11 September 2008 the share price had dropped to $1.75 and it suffered another run. That day $1.6 billion was withdrawn, and customers withdrew $16.7 billion in the following days, 9% of its deposits. Its credit rating was downgraded, WaMu's CDS exploded to 2,742 and on the 25th doubled to 5,266, so on Friday 26

September it was seized. It was sold, without its unsecured debt, to JP Morgan Chase for $1.9 billion. Its shareholders were largely wiped out, as was most of its debt, which included the recent private equity investment of $7 billion. It was a steal. No depositors lost money and the senior debt holders received 55¢ in the $, about where it had been trading.

JP Morgan Chase gained a depositor base, 2,240 retail branches, 4,930 ATMs and 43,200 employees. It was the third largest mortgage originator, and the ninth largest credit card issuer. However, WaMu's balance sheet was clogged with toxic assets. Non-performing assets were $11.6 billion, and the mark-to-market write-downs had killed WaMu. WaMu, like many others had included in its current profits interest to be received in the future.

"WaMu had been horribly mismanaged and was a major player in the kind of abusive, unaffordable, fraudulent lending that had driven the subprime mortgage crisis."[376] The compensation of its CEO, Kerry Killinger for the six years ending in 2008 was $100 million. The FDIC sued him and a couple of other executives alleging that they had taken excessive risk for personal gain and they settled in December of 2011 for $64 million.[377]

In 1Q 2008, Wachovia was the fourth largest deposit taker, with assets of $700 billion. It was also a systematically important megabank. Wachovia brought Golden West, a mortgage originator at the top of the market, in May 2006, and its balance sheet became a large part of Wachovia's problems. It delivered to the bank a mountain of toxic real estate collateralized debt. After the acquisition, Wachovia continued in the same high-risk mortgage business, and the performances of many of its own loans were even poorer than those of Golden West. Its balance sheet, like WaMu, Countrywide and IndyMac was jammed with toxic assets. In 4Q, 2007 Wachovia suffered a 98% drop in earnings, a $708 million loss and its stock price was down 40%. The bank's subprime exposure was $120 billion.

In the summer of 2008, Wachovia replaced its CEO with Bob Steel from Goldman and the US Treasury, and raised $7 billion in new capital, a dint in the losses of $32 billion for the last three quarters.[378] The 2Q 2008 loss was another $8.9 billion. Given the market, Steel's plan to raise more capital became an impossible task. He then aggressively pursued Goldman, Morgan Stanley, Santander, Wells Fargo and Citigroup, all of which wanted to expand their US domestic depositor bases.

Wachovia suffered a run on Friday, 26 September triggered by WaMu's demise. Its CDS had soared to 1,560 and its stock dropped to $8 from $17 a week before. An intelligent guess said that the toxic mortgage book was a $40 to $50 billion problem, and of course, no one could be certain. The daily markdowns meant that Wachovia could not survive and would need an acquirer. No one wanted a second large bank failure the day after WaMu.

Citigroup thought that it had a deal, and advanced Wachovia $4.9 billion to keep its doors open, Wells Fargo jumped in and made a much better bid. There was an incredibly stupid late attempt to reject the Wells Fargo offer by Tim Geitner at the NY FED who argued that to reject the Citigroup deal would destabilize the markets. The reality was that he was the Citigroup regulator, favoured Citigroup and the upside for the bank's senior management and himself. Geitner had always had staff roles until he became Secretary of the Treasury, and Bob Rubin, knowing that Geitner would continue his pro Citigroup stance boosted him into the Treasury role. Geitner's objection did not stick, and Wachovia was sold to Wells Fargo for $15.4 billion. Unlike WaMu, the debt holders were fully protected.

The others? After its two bailouts, Citigroup's stock dropped to $3 per share, 95% off of its recent peak, and after its two bailouts, Bank of America's stock was also down, by 85%.

European Dropouts

The upheaval continued in Europe. In the UK, three days after Lehman's bankruptcy, Lloyds TSB bought the largest UK mortgage lender, HBOS, after it had received a massive government £20.5 billion bailout. Its share price had collapsed and it had suffered a run of £12.2 billion. The shareholders were wiped out and thousands of jobs were lost. Lloyds then became partially state owned, and seven years later, 39% is still owned by the British public. Bradford & Bingley, another building society, followed HBOS. It was broken up and sold its branches and savings accounts to the Spanish giant Banco Santander.

James Crosby was the chief executive of HBOS until 2006. He was knighted for his services to the financial services industry. In December 2012, he appeared before the British Parliamentary Commission on Banking Standards. This Commission, whose members were members of the Commons, the House of Lords and the Archbishop of Canterbury, was set up to examine the UK's banking system following the 2008 financial crisis. The Commission held HBOS' three top officers, Crosby, Andy Hornby, his successor as CEO and Lord Dennis Stevenson, the bank's chairman as entirely responsible for the failure of the bank, and guilty of a "colossal failure" of management. They were responsible for the reckless lending policies that resulted in losses of £46 billion, job losses for thousands and the £20.5 billion taxpayer bailout. The Commission wanted all three to be banned from the industry. Crosby renounced his knighthood, but retained his pension, reduced by 30% to £406,000 a year. The former head of wholesale banking, Peter Cummings, was fined £500,000 and banned from working in senior roles in the financial sector. Andy Hornby, however, kept his pension of £240,000. He became a seller of pharmaceuticals and a bookmaker.

The Commission criticized the then-defunct Financial Services Authority for not establishing that the three were fit and proper persons to hold the required approved person's status in the UK financial sector. It called HBOS an "accident waiting to happen and estimated that 96% of shareholder value was wiped out. From 2004 to 2007, the FSA was "not so much the dog that did not bark, as a dog barking up the wrong tree".[379]

Ray Perman, the author of *Hubris: How HBOS Wrecked the Best Bank in Britain*, said, "For the first time, blame is squarely pinned on the people who deserve it - the chairman [and] the two chief executives ... they fooled themselves into thinking that their initial success was [because] they were better than everybody [else]." Crosby and his cohorts had said that the bank's success was due to their special skills, skills their competitors lacked. The failure was because they possessed no special skills, and HBOS simply pursued traditional banking badly. They lacked the elementary skills needed to run a basic bank.

The Royal Bank of Scotland had grown its balance sheet to £2.2 trillion and become the largest bank in the world. It wanted to continue to expand, and, in late 2007, it tried to take over the Dutch ABN AMRO Group. It failed and needed a bailout. As we said in the *Introduction* by 2009, the UK taxpayer had invested £40 billion and owned 81% of the bank, after which it announced a loss of £24.1 billion, the largest all time loss for a UK company! After more losses of £9 billion, it refocused its business on regional banking in 2014. This takeover was the largest banking takeover of all time. Fred Goodwin, the CEO, disgraced, lost his knighthood. His pension pool had reached £15 million.

The UK pumped £66 billion into RBS and Lloyds. The UK Government ended up with 80% of RBS and 25% of Lloyds. This bailout was equal to 80% of the UK Cameron coalition government five year spending cuts. If RBS and Lloyds had not had to be bailed out? Perhaps we would not have seen the spending cuts.

On 8 October 2008, the UK government announced a plan to stabilize its banking system and bolster confidence. It put an additional £21 billion into the banking system in return for equity. Unfortunately, the UK banking system remained highly concentrated, exacerbating the interconnection problem between financial institutions.

Across the channel, it was the same mess. On 28 September 2008, the Dutch, Belgian and Luxembourg governments provided an €11.2 billion bailout for Belgium's Fortis bank, one of the largest corporations on the planet, and the following day, BNP Paribas acquired most of it. The remaining pieces were sold or nationalized. On Tuesday 30, the French Belgian Dexia was bailed out. It had run out of money. The cost to the taxpayer, €100 billion. Eventually the bank was nationalized. Hypo Real Estate, and West LB cost another €80 billion. Commerzbank, Hypo Real Estate, and many of the Landesbanken were insolvent. The German government, paid €80 billion, and ended up owning a large part of its financial sector. The disaster had spread across Europe.

In October 2008, Iceland's entire banking system collapsed. The country suspended its stock market and seized its biggest bank. During the previous few years, the Icelandic banking sector had grown and catalysed extraordinary growth. Bank balance sheet assets had grown from $21 billion to $135 billion, eight times the $17 billion GDP of this country with a population of 320,000. The Icelandic stock market had increased by 900%, and house prices tripled. This induced a currency crisis, unemployment tripled and many lost their life savings, as the country itself became insolvent. Bank losses were in excess of $100 billion.

By 2003, Iceland had become rich. The three largest banks had been privatized, the financial markets deregulated, and the local currency, the Icelandic krona, floated. Financial controls were reduced. Before deregulation, these banks had no foreign operations and on the world stage were miniscule. The Icelandic regulator had only 40 employees. Only one fifth of Icelandic bank loans were in kroner, as currencies like the yen and Swiss franc could be borrowed at much lower interest rates. The two largest banks offered Internet deposit accounts in the in the UK, the Netherlands and Germany, and paid attractive rates of interest. Deposits streamed in. However, the accounts were regulated by Reykjavik, deposit insurance was inadequate and the Icelandic central bank did not have sufficient foreign currency reserves to act as a lender of last resort.

The Icelandic banks invested heavily in US real estate collateralized products. When the cracks appeared, depositors withdrew funds. The banks could not meet the withdrawals, so restricted them. The banking problems overwhelmed the local economy, and the Icelandic government took over the banking system. Interest rates skyrocketed. Iceland tried to keep money from flowing out, but retail supplies shrank and then evaporated, and foreign workers left. The country's debts were in dollars and euros, and the Icelandic central bank could only print krona. A crisis.

A few private individuals had done well and acquired apartments, boats and planes by borrowing billions. KPMG had continued to report that all was OK till the end, and the ratings agencies had maintained the country's AAA ratings. Its tiny banks had enormous commitments compared to Iceland's economy. When Islandsbanki failed, Iceland's banks owed $8.2 billion to its European depositors. The UK seized its UK assets and guaranteed the deposits of British savers, which resulted in a debt by Iceland to the Netherlands and the UK of €3.8 billion. The IMF provided a $2.1 billion rescue that eventually became $10.2 billion, with the participation of various EU countries.

Reacting in a way that should be emulated by the US, UK and European courts, the former Prime Minister and the CEOs of two of the three major banks were brought to trial.

The Icelandic debacle was an example of moral hazard.

The Republic of Ireland had a similar problem. By 2008, bank assets had risen to eight times the country's GDP. The financial sector was heavily exposed to US real estate collateralized products, and housing development projects had become viral.

When the problems hit, the Irish government provided a €400 billion debt guarantee for its six largest banks, almost all the bank debt in Ireland. Funds then moved from the UK to Ireland, so the UK increased deposit insurance for accounts held in the UK, and, as we said, pumped in more liquidity. Canada and most EU countries followed suit. Ireland suffered a crippling level of debt, 25 times its annual tax revenues. Allied Irish Bank helped. It had set the standard for the globe's worst managed bank. It had €72 billion in loans, but lost a staggering €30 billion, almost a quarter of the countries' annual revenue. A sterling effort for a single small bank! By 2010, the European Union had loaned €85 billion to Ireland. The Irish Treasury and its pension reserve provided €17.5 billion and the IMF €67.5 billion. No one could hold the line against moral hazard.

A problem for Europe was that European bank assets were three times the combined GDPs of its member countries, whereas in the US, they were more or less the equal. All megabanks suffered large declines in assets, Junes 2007 to January 2009, ranging from more than 90% (RBS, 96% and Citigroup 93%) to almost 50% (JP Morgan 48% and Santander 45%).

TARP, a Dog's Breakfast on the Parkway

The FED, the BoE and the ECB had three things to do. First was to halt the destruction. The collapsing banks had to be rescued, the mortgage markets had to be restored, mortgage borrowers recued, and employment and savings recovered. Second, banks must begin to lend again and the economy kick-started. The problem was that the usual monetary policy tools had lost traction. Third, identify what had led to the Crisis and the Great Recession, and rectify the problems. However, the overriding task was to dismantle the global banking oligarchy, the real problem, and to halt bank fraud. This was not recognised.

A number of rescue facilities had been put in place, each aimed at fixing a particular problem.[380] Paulson and Bernanke now wanted a solution that would fix all the problems in one shot, and any solution would need money from Congress. However, Congressional sympathy was in short supply. Influential Democrat, Barney Frank was incensed by the recent events, and Senator Bunning, the Kentucky Republican, complained that the Treasury and FED had used billions of taxpayer dollars to bailout institutions that put greed before responsibility.

Paulson and Bernanke agreed that the FED should remain a lender of last resort, but include the shadow banking system, and implement monetary policy that resolved credit availability, liquidity, employment and inflation.

The Troubled Assets Relief Program, TARP, was to be the all encompassing solution. It was based on the *Break the Glass* plan. The Treasury would buy toxic assets from the financial sector. However, the Treasury and the FED had been unprepared for Bear, and just about everything since, and TARP would be no exception.

Paulson testified before both Senate and House Congressional committees in late September. He told the lawmakers that the root of the problem rested in poor lending standards, and homeowners taking mortgages that they could not afford. The drop in home prices had resulted in financial institutions holding illiquid mortgage collateralized assets that had lost value, and credit had choked because they could not be used as collateral. Banks did not want to sell their toxic assets, as this would result in significant write-downs, losses and failures. Both financial and non-financial companies were suffering. The economy relied on credit, so credit had to be revitalized. If the toxic assets were removed from the system, Paulson explained, this could be achieved, so TARP was the plan. It would enable banks to lend, and they would find it easier to raise capital, something they desperately needed.

The Treasury had examined alternatives for months, and TARP was the best alternative, and could be implemented immediately. It was less costly than the alternatives. If nothing was done we would have a second Great Depression, and many financial institutions would fail, and the credit markets would remain frozen. At stake was the financial wellbeing of America. TARP would help Main Street, as consumers and businesses would be able to finance spending and investments. Job creation, personal savings and retirement funds would recover. The problems were not confined to the US. The amount needed was $700 billion. TARP satisfied the first two tasks, halt the destruction and get banks to lend.

On Friday 19 September,[381] Paulson sent a brief, three page request to Congress requesting the authority to purchase mortgage collateralized toxic assets, from US financial institutions, up to a limit of $700 billion. He asked for the money the following week.

Congress was not impressed and rejected it. TARP lacked oversight and reporting provisions, and protected the Treasury from legal and administrative review. Apart from everything else it needed detail and justification. TARP needed to do more for Main Street. There was no help for the underwater mortgages that had been foisted on Americans by the megabanks. The request was impertinent, and received an *N*. The Republicans saw TARP as socialism, and a further example of government intervention gone mad, and the Democrats saw it as rescuing rich and irresponsible executives.

Paulson was again well behind the eight ball, and Congress knew it. The $700 billion was a guess. The US mortgage market is $14 trillion of which $11 trillion is residential. Well, let's not worry too much about the details. Let us just take 5% of $14 trillion. Voila! $700 billion. It could have been half this or more likely, double. The Treasury had had six months to determine a number, it had done nothing, and with no preparation, asked Congress for the largest, single one time expenditure in the history of the federal government, and gave Congress one week to deliver the money.

When the Congressional rejection became news, the DJIA fell a further 7%, its largest one-day decline ever, and LIBOR doubled from the previous week. The paper loss was $1.2 trillion. Employment had reached 6.1% and best guesses said it would soon reach double figures soon. It did, in a few weeks. Job losses for September alone were 159,000. The commercial paper markets remained dead. The Democrats said that the Republicans had endorsed an anything goes market, with no regulation, supervision or discipline, and we were suffering the consequences. Main Street saw a Wall Street bail for a few rich individuals while homeowners were evicted.

On Friday 3 October, Congress approved TARP on the second attempt.[382] Given the continued destruction of the markets, it had no alternative. It gave the Treasury $350 billion, specifically to purchase toxic assets from financial institutions, immediately, and a further $350 billion, if needed, upon a petition to Congress. When Nancy Pelosi, the Leader of the House proposed the Bill, she attacked the Republicans: "No regulation, no supervision, no discipline, anything goes, and when you fail you get a golden parachute which the taxpayer has to pay. The floor added, the Republicans gave us no jobs, and chaos.

Although Paulson had claimed that all parties were ready and could implement TARP, he immediately backtracked. He announced that the first major outflow of TARP funds was not earmarked for toxic asset purchases, but for capital injections. A TARP Capital Purchase Program, the CPP, would use $250 billion to buy stock in individual banks. Notwithstanding the supposed months of preparation, Paulson told us that purchasing toxic assets would take too long. Capital injections could be made immediately. Things had changed, he said, without saying what, and furthermore, TARP would still have $100 billion for toxic asset purchases. Of course, nothing had changed. He added that purchasing equity would have a greater effect as capital is leveraged. The Treasury would not be able to buy a large enough quantity of toxic assets, quickly enough, to have any impact. At distressed prices, the acquisitions would not realize much new capital, and at face value, taxpayers would be making non-recoverable gifts to the recipients. Capital injections provided taxpayers with more impact per taxpayer dollar. Capital injections had been supported by Bernanke from the outset, and this should have been the plan in the first place.

Part of the plan were pay restrictions for the executives of the banks that used TARP funds, no golden parachutes, and clawbacks. Incredibly, Paulson fought back. He argued that renegotiation of compensation agreements would take months. No one took much notice, and compensation was restrained. When the TARP funds were repaid, these restrictions would be removed.

Paulson called nine major banks to the Treasury and told them that they would accept a capital injection in exchange for preferred shares and options to buy common stock. The nine banks were the four largest commercial banks, the three then operating investment banks, and the two major clearing and settlement banks.[383] The injections totalled $125 billion. Another $125 billion was available for other, healthy banks, and $100 billion was left to purchase toxic assets. The preferred stock paid a dividend 5% for five years, and 9% thereafter. It was cheap capital. The US banking system had been partially nationalized!

...

The FDIC increased the limit for insured accounts from $100,000 to $250,000, provided a temporary, three year, $1.5 trillion debt guarantee, and insured $500 billion in deposits in noninterest bearing business checking accounts. It ended up guaranteeing most of the nation's bank debt. The debt guarantee enabled banks to raise money by selling bonds, and the deposit guarantee stemmed the flow of funds from business accounts held at the *too small to save* banks to *the too big to fail* banks. The latter attracted bailout guarantees.

The announcement of the redirection of TARP funds caused an outrage. Paulson's actions were blatant fraud, and he had lied to Congress. The TARP/CPP was a bailout, pure and simple, and resulted from a great deal of incompetence. To top it off, the injections did not invigorate the credit markets.[384] Paulson lost any remaining credibility. He had no game plan, was inconsistent, and did not even get a bronze star for effort. It had become clear too, that $700 billion was not enough to buy the toxic assets, even at stressed prices.

Congress had wanted a solution to the housing problems, and saw TARP as a way of delivering the toxic mortgages to the Treasury. The Treasury would then be able to provide foreclosure relief by modifying the loan terms. The housing market would be stabilized. This did not happen. Although Paulson said TARP would enable banks to make loans to individuals and to help "struggling homeowners who can afford their homes avoid foreclosure", there was no requirement that banks should lend, and the megabanks did not lend. Between 2008 and 2010, the loans extended by banks with assets greater than $100 billion, the major beneficiaries of the CPP, declined by 11.44%. For banks with assets of less than $1 billion, loans grew by 3%, while they increased capital from 2% to 4%. And of course, the problem remained how to remove the toxic assets? Furthermore, it became clear that the TARP funds had been used to buy stock at prices significantly above the market. TARP was a source of cheap capital.

The initial allocation of $125 billion in TARP funds to the nine bank was:

Citibank	25	Merrill Lynch	10

JP Morgan Chase	25	Morgan Stanley	10
Wells Fargo	25	Bank of New York Mellon	3
Bank of America	15	State Street	2
Goldman Sachs	10		

Figure 8 Initial TARP Capital Injections.

Wells Fargo said it did not need the money, but Citigroup was insolvent. It had just taken a $19 billion write down for the first six months of 2008, and was projecting an enormous year-end loss. Although Paulson repeated the claim that all recipients were sound again and again, and in particular at the swearing in of SIGTARP Chief Neil Barofsky,[385] in December, he later admitted that he had been fully aware, all along, of the precarious status of both Merrill and Citigroup. Sheila Bair suspected, rightly, that one motivation for the collective bailouts was to disguise the weakness of Citigroup. Ever myopic and self-absorbed, John Thain, the new Merrill CEO, was only concerned with compensation restrictions.

Besides the banks, TARP borrowers included insurance companies, the automakers, GMAC and GE. Notably, both GMAC and American Express became bank holding companies. Congress also allocated funds for the three automakers, Chrysler, $14.9 billion, General Motors, $49.5 billion, and Ford.

TARP was another out of control Treasury intervention, another way for Paulson to help his friends on Wall Street. By shoring up their organizations, the gravy train would continue. However, in January 2009, Barney Frank pointed out that TARP had so far failed in two major respects: TARP did not stem the tidal wave of foreclosures, nor had it spurred the banks into lending. He argued "It would be a grave mistake to say that we're going to buy up a bad debt that resulted from the bad decisions of these people and then allow them to get millions of dollars on the way out".[386]

Furthermore, the Washing bailout of AIG enabled it to make good on its CDS commitments, so Goldman received an extra $12.9 billion, Merrill $6.8 billion, Citigroup $2.3 billion and BoA $5.2 billion of taxpayer money!

Gao Xiqing, the president of China Investment Corporation, which managed $200 billion in Chinese foreign assets said, "Finally, after months and months of struggling with your own ideology, with your own pride, your self-righteousness … finally [Washington applied] one of the great gifts of Americans, which is that you're pragmatic." We have "socialism with American characteristics" which paralleled, at last "socialism with Chinese characteristics".[387] Washington, the champion of free markets, had bought stakes in some of the largest financial institutions in the world.

Stress Tests

TARP failed, so the FED and Geitner wanted to stress test the largest banks. The public had lost confidence, so they thought that if they passed a rigorous stress test regime, confidence might return. The balance sheets still contained the root of the problem, the toxic assets, so simply propping up a bank's balance sheet, they now argued, was never going to be sufficient. They proposed to stress test banks with assets of $100 billion or more. If a bank failed, it must raise capital by issuing new common stock. If it could not do so, it must take TARP funds as capital. The stress testing plan was announced on Tuesday 10 February 2009. As it would force troubled institutions to take on capital, and dilute the current shareholders, the DJIA fell 382 points, down 4.6%.

The hidden agenda was, however, that stress testing would provide cover for the weaker banks like Citigroup. When the results came in, Citigroup, despite the $47.3 billion in TARP funds,[388] would be insolvent under stress. Citigroup needed billions in capital, but there was a problem. If it took what it needed as capital, it would lose a tax benefit of $50 billion. So the FED and the OCC overruled the stress test results and deemed that the capital needed was only $5.5 billion, a fraction of what the stress tests demanded! The calculations were ludicrous,[389] and the lack of confidence, now heightened, remained.

The stress tests said that the capital required for all nineteen banks subjected to them, was $75 billion. Bank of America needed $33.9 billion, and Wells Fargo, $11.5 billion, and this made a mockery of the Citigroup number. All banks except GE and Citigroup had to raise funds from the private sector, a re-affirmation of *too big to fail.*

Before the Crisis hit, under Basel II, capital levels would have been greatly reduced, Citigroup by $5.5 billion, Bank of America by $14.6 billion and Washington Mutual by $2.4 billion! Citigroup and Bank of America received multiple bailouts and Washington Mutual failed. The capital reduction for all larger banks would have been 22% and for all banks, 31%.[390] So much so for Basel. It would have led to an even greater disaster.

No Help for Mortgagers

After TARP, pressure from Congress forced the FED to do something for the individuals and families that were suffering from the housing market collapse. In 2008, 3 million properties had received foreclosure filings, almost 1 million homes had been repossessed, and unemployment was up. The Affordable Mortgage Program, HAMP was put in place February 2009. It was a temporary, five year program. HAMP was a way for mortgages to be modifies and become affordable.

HAMP resulted in fewer than 500,000 modifications, less than half the Treasury's target of 1,200,000. The modifications were processed by mortgages servicers who were incentivized to foreclose, and there was widespread fraud.

Mortgage servicers telephoned applicants. If three months' timely payments were made at renegotiated rates, and if the required documentation was received, then the proposed modification would become a five year modification. The servicers initiated hundreds of modifications, but brought few to completion. They claimed that they had not received the documentation. They *lost* the submissions. ProPublica surveyed the applicants and found that the average number of document resubmissions was six![391] Often upfront fees were demanded, not only a violation of the program terms, but illegal. The servicers were swamped with applications and did not put on personnel to deal with them. They wanted to foreclose, and all they needed was an excuse.

Neil Barofsky was the head of SIGTARP, the TARP oversight agency. Barofsky's first day was 43 days after TARP money had begun to flow, when $330 billion had been disbursed. A year later, in December 2009, Barofsky had learnt from bank press statements that TARP funds were being used for just about everything except what they were intended for, lending. SIGTARP proposed that HAMP conversions be automatic after three months. The Treasury wanted no part of it, even though it knew that servicers could not handle the volume, and were incentivized to foreclose. Barofsky commented:

> hastily rushed out for political purposes:
> [HAMP was] ... incomplete and poorly thought
> out, and the Treasury officials charged with
> implementing them couldn't even explain how
> certain aspects of them work, including
> answering basis questions about the HAMP
> incentive payments[392]

HAMP was designed for the lenders, banks, not for the stressed mortgage borrowers. Barofsky concluded that it simply provided breathing room. It "gave the banks time to absorb the losses, while the other … [programs and bailouts] juiced bank profits that could fill the capital holes created by housing losses". It did not matter that distressed homeowners were worse off after HAMP. HAMP was another failure.

He had more to say about other aspects of the Treasuries proposals:

> we are going to put $200 billion of tax payer money on the line to buy asset backed securities that are similar to those that got us into this mess in the first place, and we are going to rely on the [discredited] credit rating agencies and investor due diligence and nothing else? [393]

In other words, replicate the market that had failed, use lax regulatory standards, place reliance on the discredited rating agencies, use poor and incomplete risk models, and assume an inherent trust by investors.

The Financial Crisis Inquiry Commission

Congress established a commission to investigate the causes of the Crisis, and President Barack Obama signed it in May 2009. A panel was appointed, six Democrat and four Republican Congressional leaders, the budget was constrained to $6 million, enough perhaps to pay for the support staff, and it had limited subpoena powers. It interviewed and solicited input from a wide range of individuals. The Commission's report was published in January of 2011,[394] six months after Dodd-Frank became law.

The Commission was convinced that there were many dimensions. Moreover, the financial sector had developed into a dominant force and was not simply an aid to industry and business. Problems in the financial sector were capable of infecting economies, globally. The Commission noted that the technology that had enabled globalization, desktop and laptop computers, with the Internet, had enabled the global spread of the infection nurtured in the US residential real estate markets. It had left risk assessment behind in its wake.

Furthermore, the trillions of dollars tied up in risky US mortgage collateralized securitizations had been distributed globally. The losses, in the hundreds of billions of dollars, destroyed the markets. Banks and the shadow banking system had used these securitizations as collateral for borrowing, but when they lost value, they became illiquid and lending contracted. Synthetic securitizations acted like high powered magnifying glasses and made the problems exponentially worse.

The opaqueness of Wall Street balance sheets and the tangle of interconnections between them meant that the exposures of individual institutions could not be determined. When the markets became illiquid, trading ceased, the stock markets plummeted and the US economy dropped into recession.

Many senior managers were culpable. They knew that their actions could lead to insolvency, and clearly, the liquidity problems were a direct result of the strategies of the megabanks and the shadow banking system.

The Commission drew a number of conclusions:

- The Crisis was avoidable

- The regulators failed and the FED failed to stem the tide of toxic mortgages

- There were extensive breakdowns in corporate governance; there were systemic breaches in accountability and ethics at all levels

- Financial firms acted recklessly in pursuit of profits and bonuses and took on too much risk

- There was an explosive mix of excessive borrowing and risk taking by households and Wall Street

- Policy makers were ill prepared for the Crisis, lacking any understanding of the financial system

- Many toxic credit products served no purpose whatsoever other than to enhance bonuses

- The financial sector used models that it took as reality, which were faulty and which could get things drastically wrong

- Financial innovation outpaced IT systems and management understanding

- Distrust of the markets developed: how could an AAA CDO security turn out to be worthless?

- CDS were not subject to government regulation, and unlike typical insurance products did not require the seller to hold reserves, or in fact the underlying

Dodd-Frank

Dodd-Frank was motivated the Congressional response to the Great Recession. It was wide-ranging and intended to reform US financial regulation. Bailouts had to end, especially those for the *too big to fail* banks. It also addressed proprietary trading and derivatives. It did not suggest that we replace the financial system, and aimed to arm regulators with new powers. President Obama wanted strong consumer protections, transparency for risk transactions, and controls on compensation. It was passed on 2 July 2010.

During the Dodd-Frank negotiations, 1,540 Washington lobbyists represented the financial institutions operating in the US, 25 times the number that represented consumer support groups and other proponents of strong reform.[395] The *other side*, the public, is not a united body, so representation lacked funds and was difficult to organise. Public interests are diverse, and public outrage provides little opposition to well-funded lobbying. As a consequence, the bill met stiff opposition.

However, it was not plain sailing. Time was tough for the oligarchy. Main Street was angry with Wall Street. Profitability had been restored, as had the obscene bonuses, while the rest of the country dealt with high unemployment, evictions, fewer essential services and a poor recovery. The disgraceful behaviour of the megabanks was still in the news. For example, Goldman's participation in the John Paulson CDO, made him billions, while thousands were evicted from their homes. Goldman's fine of $550 billion, the largest penalty ever paid by Wall Street at the time, was a drop in the ocean compared to its 1Q 2010 profits of $3.5 billion.

Dodd-Frank endorsed much of what the Financial Crisis Inquiry Commission had to say. Its major provisions were:

- The FSOC was created and expanded the responsibilities of all US financial regulators to include systemic risk, with the FSOC as coordinator. The megabanks are to be more tightly regulated, and the same for key financial market utilities like, for example, the stock exchanges. The FSOC has ten voting members and is chaired by the Secretary of the Treasury.

- An orderly liquidation authority for failing *too big to fail* megabanks was mandated, and the FDIC is responsible for resolving all failing financial institutions. Megabanks must prepare living wills. When liquidated, boards and management lose their jobs and those responsible suffer clawbacks. An issue is cross boarder resolution and bankruptcy.
- The function of banks is deposit taking and responsible lending. The Volker Rule prohibits bank involvement in hedge funds, private equity funds and proprietary trading. Volker: there is not one shred of evidence that financial *innovation* has aided the economy. The implementation rules have loopholes and do not prevent proprietary trading with taxpayer deposits.
- Credit ratings were eliminated from regulatory functions
- Annual stress tests are required
- Derivative transactions must be transparent and standardized, and central counterparties must play a clearing role
- Capital requirements to be enhanced
- The Bureau of Consumer Financial Protection was created to protect consumers and eliminate abusive practices, including predatory lending
- Securitizers must absorb losses from failed securitizations
- The Collins Amendment, the death knoll for Basel II, eliminated hybrid instruments from capital. Leverage for large banks must be less than for small banks, an international leverage ratio was agreed, and capital for megabanks must be greater than capital for smaller banks.

What it all Cost

If we begin with the US, and added the financial support provided by Washington to the total guarantees, Washington's exposure was $23.7 billion.[396] We assumed that that actual expenditure would be nowhere near this, but it was a staggering number, one and a half times US GDP.

Better Markets reported on 15 September 2011 that US losses for the period 2008 to 2018[397] would be, in excess of $12.8 trillion. This amount is the sum of the actual GDP loss and the GDP loss avoided due to the emergency FED spending and other FED actions. Better Markets also confirmed the FED's Crisis bailout program exposure was $23.7 trillion.

The $12.8 trillion losses include lost GDP, destroyed household wealth, unemployment and under-employment losses, foreclosure losses, direct government bailout losses and emergency spending losses. It is an estimate of the actual and avoided reduction in the flow of goods and services as a result of the Crisis, and the subsequent collapse of the economy during the Great Recession. The actual GDP loss is $7.6 trillion and the avoided GDP loss is $5.2 trillion, which comes from a model developed by Alan Blinder and Mark Zandi.[398]

In addition to this $12.8 trillion, we have:

- The costs of the increased unemployment benefits, estimated at $13 billion, the cost of food stamps and other similar benefits, the cost of TARP, estimated to be between $32 and $78 billion, the $787 billion tax relief package that increases the federal budget deficit by $831 billion through 2019

- The moving and related costs for those evicted from their homes, the cost of the conversion of Goldman Sachs and Morgan Stanley to deposit taker banks, the direct cost of the FED's nationalization of the financial system, lost tax revenues for cities, counties and states, and $8.3 trillion for the provision of the currency swap lines in 2008

- Losses due to human suffering and anguish, the cost of the destruction of human capital, family breakups, depression and the cost of destroyed neighbourhoods

In 2011, the Congressional Budget Office forecast a TARP loss of $34 billion. Christy Romero, the special inspector for TARP announced in 2012, that $15 billion was owed by 351 small banks, banks with less than $1 billion in assets. If we include the TARP related investments in AIG, GM and Ally Financial, the Treasury is short $118 billion. Then the Wall Street Journal reported on 25 April 2012, that taxpayers were owed $119 billion in TARP funds. Furthermore, Washington has consistently excluded the funds provided to the GSEs, about $151 billion.

As we said, Andrew Haldane of the Bank of England estimated the global economic loss would eventually be between $60 trillion and $200 trillion and for the UK alone, it would lie between £1.8 trillion and £7.4 trillion.[399]

What all this means is that whatever the number is, it is large! The academic exercise of taking the cost estimates to dollars and cents in hardly necessary. The number is in the tens, perhaps hundreds of trillions. Haldane's estimate is between one and four times the globe's GDP and is large enough for us to conclude that is that the Crisis and Great Recession were unacceptable and must never be repeated. If this means stronger regulation and redesigning the financial system by breaking up the megabanks and restricting markets, then that is what we must do.

The Fifth Bangster Awards

Sebastien, the chief judge has determined many more Bangster Awards. Hank Paulson ignored the warning signs of the Crisis, was unprepared when it hit, lied to Congress, his bailouts were a mess, and prior to that, authorised Goldman's fraudulent products and strategy. He is a Bangster, as is Dick Fuld. Dick drove Lehman's fraudulent liar loan program and lied to Congress. Then there were the Repo 105s. Stan O'Neal was incompetent, abrogated his CEO responsibilities and acted without board authority. He is a Bangster. Joe Cassano, misrepresented the risks in CDSs, did not disclose AIG FP's collateral calls, marked up positions without justification and prevented AIG FP's CDS portfolio from being evaluated. He is a Bangster. James Crosby, Andy Hornby, and Lord Dennis Stevenson, were a "colossal failure" of management. They were guilty of very serious misconduct. Fred Goodwin, a megalomaniac, was the world's worst banker. RBS, the largest in the world, at the time, made the largest all time loss for a UK company. Senator Phil Gram was a disgraceful, misguided free market zealot who saw subprime lending as part of the American Dream. He was on another planet, and crossed the line.

Only one Gold Star, Sheila Bair, a shining light during this chapter. She opposed the other regulators and the megabanks.

Here is the table:

Bangsters		Gold Stars
Nicholas Biddle	Goldman Sachs	Franklin D Roosevelt
JP Morgan	Hank Paulson	Louis Brandeis
James Johnson	Dick Fuld	Raghuram Rajan
Alan Greenspan	Stan O'Neil	Barney Frank
Angelo Mozilo	Joe Cassano	Sheila Bair
Jimmy Cayne	James Crosby	
Mat Ridley	Andy Hornby	
John Paulson	Fred Goodwin	
Morgan Stanley	Senator Phil Gram	

9

Market Corrections

Woman Realizes Her Customers Are Drunk And Unemployed

Mary, the proprietor of a bar in Dublin, realized that virtually all of her customers were unemployed alcoholics and, as such, could no longer afford to patronize her bar. To solve this problem, she came up with a plan that allowed her customers to drink now, but pay later. She kept track of the drinks consumed on a ledger, thereby granting her customers' loans.

Word got around about Mary's "drink now, pay later" strategy and, an increasing number of customers flooded into Mary's bar. Soon she had the largest sales volume of any bar in Dublin.

By providing her customers freedom from immediate payment demands, Mary got no resistance when, at regular intervals, she increased her prices for wine and beer, the most consumed beverages. Consequently, Mary's gross sales volume increased enormously. A young and dynamic vice president at the local bank recognised that these customer debts constituted valuable future assets and increased Mary's borrowing limit. He saw no reason for undue concern, since he had the debts of the unemployed alcoholics as collateral.

At the bank's corporate headquarters, expert traders figured out a way to make huge commissions, and transformed these customer loans into Drinkbonds, Alkibonds and Pukebonds. These securities were bundled and traded on the international securities markets. Naive investors didn't really understand that the securities being sold to them as AAA bonds were really the debts of unemployed alcoholics. The bond prices climbed continuously, and the securities soon became the hottest selling items for some of the nation's leading brokerage houses.

One day, even though the bond prices were still climbing, a risk manager at the original local bank decided that the time had come to demand payment on the debt incurred by drinkers at Mary's bar. He so informed Mary.

Mary then demanded payment from her alcoholic patrons, but being unemployed alcoholics, they could not pay back their drinking debts. Since Mary could not fulfil her loan obligations, she was forced into bankruptcy. The bar closed and eleven employees lost their jobs.

Overnight, Drinkbonds, Alkibonds and Pukebonds dropped in price by 90%. The collapsed bond asset value destroyed the bank's liquidity and prevented it from issuing new loans, thus freezing credit and economic activity in the community.

The suppliers of Mary's bar had granted her generous payment extensions and had invested their firms' pension funds in the various bond securities. They found that they were now faced with having to write off her bad debt and with losing over 90% of the value of the bonds. Her wine supplier also claimed bankruptcy, and closed the door of a family business that had endured for three generations, her beer supplier was taken over by a competitor, who immediately closed the local plant and laid off 150 workers.

Fortunately, though, the bank, the brokerage houses, and their respective executives were saved and bailed out by a multi-billion euro no strings attached cash infusion from their cronies in government. The funds required for this bailout were obtained by new taxes levied on employed, middle class non-drinkers who have never been in Mary's bar.

With their newly augmented wealth, the executives opened up bank accounts in Switzerland to take advantage of more lenient taxation, and met a number of other wealthy customers with unique cash management requirements. They were able to expand their bank's business and make substantial profits and bonuses by extending money transfer services to Colombian cut flower farmers, Middle Eastern and Iranian iron ore, and rare metals shippers. They expanded into new business, which included selling insurance with no payouts to bank account holders, and, as an exercise in trickledown economics permitted traders to make adjustments to market indices, so that they too could enjoy the champagne. They also provided consultancy services, which promised wealthy customers lower taxes if they opened up bank accounts in Switzerland. In return for commissions earned from the Swiss bank account providers, they gave shares to these wealthy clients in their newly invigorated money transfer businesses.

As you can see, economics in 2015 remains similar to economics in the 1980s and 1990s.[400]

What To Do?

The Great Recession caused policy makers and regulators to rethink the assumptions about financial crises. In 2005, the globe's central bankers thought that they knew how to manage economies. Charlie Bean from the Bank of England spoke at the 2005 Jackson Hole conference about the Jackson Hole Consensus. Monetary policy is the best path to economic stability. It borrows growth from the future. Fiscal policy, taxation and spending means politicians, and that is a waste of time. We must insulate central banks from lawmakers and the whims of their constituencies. Markets work and we can achieve price stability. Financial crises are history, he told us, however, it took but three years for the Crisis to hit.

From the outset of the Great Recession, monetary policy failed. From December 2008, the FED followed a zero interest rate policy, ZIRP, and kept the federal funds rate near zero, but with little effect. Interest rates cannot go lower than zero. The actual lending rate was a lot higher as lenders hoarded cash, and this contributed to lower spending, which was insufficient to keep factories open and workers employed.

Quantitative easing, QE, means buying long term bonds in order to lower interest rates further out on the yield curve. Money is created as the prices of the longer dated the bonds are pushed up, and their returns lowered. As ZIRP was ineffective, a QE strategy was followed from March 2009. When banks lend, the money supply is increased and spending and employment should increase. They did not. The FED expected growth of between 3.4% and 4.5% in 2011 and between 3.5% and 4.5% in 2012. Actual growth was, however, 1.8% and 2.8%.

Ransom, Criminal Activity

After the Crisis, Wall Street held Washington to ransom, the rescue terms were favourable to Wall Street, and the profits of the megabanks were restored. The reason was that Washington was run and managed by Wall Street, and the senior bankers were rich. Why did bankers, policy makers, regulators and the ratings agencies collaborate to build a system that was doomed to self-destruct? Because it made money for them.

That only Iceland,[401] with a limited financial oligarchy, has used the courts to bring the perpetrators to justice, underscores the power of the US and European oligarchies. Finance has returned to the times that lead to the 1930s Pecora hearings, which uncovered extremely reckless behaviour by the financial sector, including, fraud and unconscionable treatment of customers, in order to generate personal wealth and control. We will return to this when we discuss bank fraud and the lack of prosecutions.

What is different today is the nature of the criminal activity. With globalization, desktop technology and the Internet, it has become a whole lot easier to break the law. To reiterate, we continue to see: predatory lending, securities fraud and violations of customer protections, accounting fraud, insider trading, money laundering for some of the most despicable organizations, including the drug cartels, and the military arms of organizations like ISIS, tax evasion, hiding the assets of corrupt dictators, market manipulation and collusion in price fixing. Until the past year or two, these activities have been rarely prosecuted, and they have, and when convictions are obtained, the fines and penalties are paid by shareholders, the innocent parties.

The IMF told us that for crony capitalist governments in the emerging markets, recovery would fail unless the financial oligarchy that was blocking reform was eliminated. This is what we must do.[402] Financially powerful elites, driven by self-interest, have established control of policy and run the country like a profit centre.

Let's look briefly at the particular failures in a little more detail.

President Obama

When President Obama stood for the US presidency, campaign financing had become very significant and as a result, politics had changed. The Democrats and the Republicans had significant differences, but they did not differ over campaign contributions, which has been a major factor in elections. US politics in 2008 was shaped by the 0.01% of the US population, the 30,000 individuals and corporations, that provided 25% of the contributions. Election costs had gone up 20 fold since the 1970s, and these costs were funded by contributions.

	1974 (millions)	2006 (millions)
Senate	28.4	568
House	56.5	1,250
President	69.9	1,325

Figure 9 Per Seat Campaign Expenditures 1974 and 2010

President Obama ushered in a Democratic program that addressed inequality and poverty. He wanted to reign in the rich. Since 1988, the real incomes of the bottom half of American society has fallen or stagnated, while the incomes of the top 1% has soared by more than 60%, and the incomes of the top 0.1%, even more so.[403] Globally in 2014, the wealth of the richest 67 individuals matched the poorest 3.5 billion, half the world's population. The best indicator of an American child's future was the wealth of its parents. The American Dream was long over, and it was back to the 1920s. Inequality is on the rise again.

The first item on the agenda for the Obama administration was the Crisis. In early 2009, Wall Street was in his hands. It needed Washington. The public was angry and the level of bankers' compensation reinforced taxpayer anger. However, Obama put the Clinton and Bush old guard into influential positions. Tim Geitner became Secretary of the Treasury and Larry Summers, who with Alan Greenspan, supported almost all of the bad financial decisions during the last decade, became Director of the National Economic Council.

Washington had two choices, either save the distressed banks, or take them over. Saving distressed banks meant injecting capital, or buying the toxic assets. The bank would retain its current form, with the same directors and management. They and the stockholders would be beneficiaries and the taxpayers would pay the bill. The losses would be socialized and the gains privatized. If Washington took the banks over, an FDIC style resolution would take place. The directors and management would go, stockholders would be wiped out, creditors would suffer a haircut and the bank's assets sold. The taxpayers would benefit. However, the oligarchy won, and Washington injected capital.

Selling toxic assets meant fire sales, which meant write-downs, and losses, which meant more capital to absorb them. Capital was in short supply, so some banks would become insolvent. Although the toxic assets would regain their value over time, banks did not have this. Washington did. So, the banks received taxpayer funded capital and the risk was transferred from the banking system to Washington. A staggering moral hazard.[404]

Congress was incensed. Taxpayers were paying the bills, and those responsible for the problems had simply passed *GO* and received more money. By November, many in Congress were vociferous and critical of Hank Paulson. He had been unprepared again and again, wrong on many issues, ignored Congressional authority, and protected Wall Street at the expense of Main Street. He was flying blind with no strategy and impulsive, and was in over his head. The Democrats wanted foreclosure relief and a plan to address the mortgage problems. The Republicans did not want bailouts. Neither got what they wanted.

Greenspan's charge against deregulation was a large part of the problem. He had tethered the health of the nation's economy to a faith belief. As we said, three years after he left the FED, he was forced to confront the extraordinary trail of destruction he had left. On 23 October 2008, he testified before the House Oversight and Reform Committee. A chastened Greenspan appeared repentant and certainly no longer the defender of untrammelled laissez-faire capitalism. In his prepared testimony, Greenspan told the committee that he had made mistakes, and his judgements had been poor. Obscurantism, however, prevailed. "Those that thought the self-interest of lending institutions to protect shareholder's equity are in a state of shocked disbelief … And what I'm saying is that I have found a flaw in the model that I used to deal with the world.[405] He also blamed investors, and admitted he had not understood what had happed.

Joseph Stiglitz noted that Greenspan was always the lowest common denominator. In 1998, he quashed Brooksley Born's *let's look at regulating derivatives* initiative, he was behind the GLB, he supported the Bush tax cuts in 2001 and 2003, he failed to take on the regulation of derivatives and he supported the SEC's decision in 2004 to allow investment banks to increase their debt-to-capital ratio from 12:1 to almost anything, and he was instrumental in permitting these banks to use Basel.

At the time of President Obama's March 2009 meeting with the CEOs of the largest US banks, he told them that his administration was the only thing between them and the pitchforks.[406] He demanded an overhaul of bank executive compensation and banking regulation, he wanted to tackle *too big to fail* and moral hazard, and he wanted consumer protections. The bankers agreed, however they did nothing for Obama. They resisted tighter regulation, and paid themselves bigger bonuses. They repaid the TARP loans and sacrificed long-term benefits in order to do so.

In September[407] Obama told Wall Street to "embrace serious financial reform, not fight it … Hear my words: We will not go back to the days of reckless behaviour and unchecked excess at the heart of this [C]risis, where too many were motivated only by the appetite for quick kills and bloated bonuses". Bonuses for 2009 should be put to a shareholder vote, and employees "rewarded for long- term performance instead of short-term gains". He wanted lenders to modify more mortgages and extend more small business loans saying, "many of the firms that are now returning to prosperity owe a debt to the American people".[408] "You guys are drawing down ten-, twenty- million dollar bonuses after America went through the worst economic year that it's gone through in decades, and you guys caused the problem. And we've got ten percent unemployment."[409]

Obama's words continued to have little effect. Lending remained constrained, the mortgage problems remained, the mega banks got more mega, more profitable and less controllable. Wall Street remained an insidious oligarchy. Profits reinforced its ideology. Echoes of the last century and some of the names were the same, J P Morgan, Goldman and Sachs.

Although the Crisis could have marked an end to excessive risk taking and profits, Wall Street did not change, and the oligarchy was stronger, with more influence. Prominent economists like Joseph Stieglitz and Paul Krugman, were ignored. Krugman noted that the FED and the Treasury were propping up 'zombie" financial institutions. An opportunity to update the banking reforms of the 1930s was lost and Wall Street continued to hold the economy hostage.

In 2009 Nicholas Brady, the US Treasury Secretary under George H W Bush, stated that President Obama had "wasted" the Crisis.[410] It was outrageous that reform had not followed and implemented more stringent standards for the *too big to fail* banks, consumer protections and central derivatives clearing. The Treasury had failed to consider some proposals and rejected others that would have prevented another Crisis. The alphabet soup of regulatory and related Washington agencies had not been streamlined, the accounting rules had not been reformulated and updated, the divorce of risk from reward, the ludicrous compensation schemes and amounts were still in place.[411]

The US Treasury

Charles Ferguson said, "Their ... response was also marked by a stunning obliviousness to the causes, severity and consequences of the [Crisis] on the parts of Paulson and Bernanke"[412]. The Bush administration did nothing for Main Street and everything for Wall Street. Paulson was incapable of looking in any other direction than Wall Street. Paulson denied the existence of the bubble until it burst, he eschewed derivatives regulation, and ignored the warnings of Nouriel Roubini, the IMF, Christine Lagarde, Jean-Claude Trichet, Mervyn King and numerous journalists, and ignored the fact that the largest financial players were shorting the bubble. He was steadfastly against what would later become the Volker and Collins amendments. His preparations for Bear, the

GSEs, Lehman, Merrill, AIG, WaMu, Wachovia, Citibank and Bank of America, the collapse of the money market funds and the commercial paper markets, were measured in days. Paulson was unprepared at every turn, and the Treasury was often taken by surprise. Paulson's last minute decisions were inconsistent and faulty. He made it up as he went along.[413]. Letting Lehman go was the wrong decision, and caused havoc. When Lehman failed, he had not contemplated the consequences of foreign bankruptcies. TARP, the largest one time expenditure in the history of the US federal government was a result of guesswork, the recipients accrued bonuses until the funds were repaid, and the capital injections did little for the banking system, less for the shadow banking system.

Paulson's style was abrupt and combative, he eschewed blame. He was a bully. He admitted so when he threatened John McCain.[414] In front of Congress, he stammered and reeked od insincerity. His self-absorbed, self-serving and pompous account of the Crisis, presumably, written to camouflage his failures, tells all.[415] He focuses on his work ethic as an end in itself, disguising the material events. Can we really rely on a Secretary of the Treasury who depends on Timothy, verse 1:7 for support? Paulson in his address to the Senate Banking Committee, 23 September 2008 said the following:

> What we are seeking to address with this, is we are seeking to address – first of all, we're dealing with complicated securities, mortgage and mortgage related, and we've got various asset classes here, and we need different approaches for different asset classes. But when we use the market mechanisms, we want – we're looking at thousands, you know, of institutions, because to make this run properly, we need to deal with big banks, small banks, S&Ls, credit unions, because what we're trying to do here, and what I think we'll be successful, is to develop mechanisms where we – where we get values out there, where there's some value that the market can look at.[416]

What more can be said of this unintelligible railing? He was well and truly over his head.

The Fed

When Ben Bernanke was appointed FED chairman, he was more than prepared to deal with crises. He had spent a good deal of his life in academia, and a good deal of that time looking at the Great Depression. When the Crisis struck, he was well aware of the mistakes the FED of the 1930s had made. What made his job more difficult was the mess that Alan Greenspan had left.

Bernanke wanted to expand credit, but the traditional monetary policy tools had little traction. The FED QE program began early 2009, and the only significant consequence was that its balance sheet grew from $900 billion to $2.4 trillion by the summer of that year. It was a scary reminder of how the world of economics has more mines than we care to consider, and what little power the FED in fact had.

Bernanke's decision to lend outside the financial sector and to support the commercial paper and bond markets was necessary and laudable. The FED lent trillions to banks, the shadow banking system and to the auto manufacturers. However, transparency was lacking. The FED lent with little explanation, and was only forced into making disclosures when Bloomberg took court action.[417]

The FED failed to stem the flow of toxic mortgages, and neglected homeowners until early 2009, far too late. The FED had the obligation to promulgate lending standards across the board, to both banks and non-banks, but Greenspan ignored it's responsibly. This was part of the mess he left Bernanke to deal with.

The Regulators

Financial sector regulation had changed little since the Great Depression, but the financial sector had changed radically. Regulation had not kept pace and was archaic. The 3-6-3 banking paradigm was over and casino banking was making the profits. By the Millennium, banking had evolved with new players, products and businesses, but the regulators had not kept up. Moreover, not only were they unknowledgeable, they were often incompetent.

The GLB opened the door to a new dimension of regulatory failure, notably the non-regulation of derivatives, a fundamental cause of the Crisis. After 2000, functional regulation added to the regulatory failures.

> The magnitude of the current financial crisis reflects the failure of an economic regulatory philosophy that proved increasingly influential in policy circles during the past three decades. This philosophy ... held that private financial institutions not insured by the government could be largely trusted to manage their own

risks – to regulate themselves. The crisis has suggested otherwise, particularly since several of the least regulated parts of the system (including non-bank mortgage originators and the major broker-dealer Bear Stearns) were among the first to run into trouble.[418]

Events show that strong regulation is necessary:

> ... the catastrophic failure of financial deregulation, high levels of inequality, and the sorry state of the economy argue for greater government intervention ... The calamity convinced many people across the political spectrum that our financial system was broken – but the subsequent campaign for reform ran aground on the rocks of a monumental lobbying campaign launched by the banks and their allies.[419]

Personal compensation got in the way of regulatory modernization and reform. Lobbying had quashed attempts to regulate derivatives. Jamie Dimon went as far as to claim that regulation was anti-American,[420] an absurd enough claim in itself, but what is significant is that he kept his job.

The banking casino halls must go, and banking must support the credit needs of the real economy. Profit seeking banks have goals that conflict with the goals of society, and banks can cause significant harm when we do not limit the risks take. Self-absorbed bankers with little moral compass defraud their employers, customers and colleagues in order to enhance their own bonuses. "While it often seems that financial stability has no natural constituency, that constituency is actually all of us who want to avoid another autumn of 2008 and its aftermath."[421] Politicians, regulators and central banks have a fiduciary responsibility for *other people's money*. This costs.

Here are some of the things we need to do:

- Ensure that all financial institutions are regulated, including hedge funds, money market funds, credit card banks, non-bank lenders, payday lenders, according to the damage that may result if they were to collapse during a crisis.[422] Regulate the financial markets, including the OTC and derivatives markets; ban products that serve no economic purpose, like synthetic CDOs. Regulate the financial utilities such as the ratings agencies and

monoline insurers, and define insurance criteria for financial products
- Simplify the alphabet soup of regulators in the US, eliminate regulatory arbitrage end ensure that banks cannot choose their regulators, and eliminate the Wall Street and Parkway revolving door
- Empower the CFPA

Too Big To Fail

To recap, if a bank with thousands of outstanding deals with thousands of counterparties fails, all the counterparties expecting to be paid will not be paid. They then may not be able to pay their counterparties, and a chain of failed payment can lead to market turmoil. Declaring bankruptcy does not help as making payments under bankruptcy takes months, sometimes years. In order to limit market destruction, governments step in and bailout failing megabanks, and taxpayers get the bill. It's not only the current taxpayers, it's the generations to come that pay too. This is what we need to stop.

Because they know they will be bailed out, excessive risk taking by megabanks is incentivized. They take bigger risks hoping to make bigger profits, which mean bigger bonuses. Key personal benefit from the upside while taxpayers pay for the downside. Moral hazard. Furthermore, megabanks are incentivized to get bigger, and lenders to megabanks lend at lower rates as the loans are lower risk. Megabanks thus have a competitive advantage over their smaller competitors.

Some small organizations can be *too big to fail*, as the problem is not size, but interconnectedness. LTCM was small, but had thousands of counterparties. Unwinding the mess created by its failure would have cost billions, endangered LTCM's counterparties, and the markets. Interconnectedness needs to be limited too. Besides the megabanks, now bigger after the Crisis, there are municipalities and financial utilities, including the Chicago Mercantile Exchange, that are *too big to fail* too!

There are three ways to deal with this problem:

- Ensure that there is only a small risk of failure by requiring a megabank to hold a high level of capital. Moral hazard remains

- Put in place an FDIC type resolution process for all failing banks. Hopefully, no moral hazard

- Do not permit banks to become megabanks, and *too big to fail.* No moral hazard and it's what we want

Ensuring that megabanks hold more loss absorbing capital is the Basel approach, and the Financial Stability Board, a global regulator, determines the amount for each megabank. It's called the Total Loss Absorbing Capital. The megabanks become systematically important banks, or G-Sibs. In 2015, there were thirty of them.[423] All other banks share a simpler, common calculation for capital.[424]

The problem and the reason for this proposal's rejection is that it does not solve the problem. It provides no guarantee against failure. To have certainty would mean that banks have to hold so much capital that they could not function.

This solution also has a number of problems: how much loss absorbing capital? The answer is guess work. The amount of capital can change suddenly, as economic, market, political and other conditions change, and as a result of epidemics, natural disasters, fraud and terrorism. The amount of capital should reflect the changing scenarios and itself change over time. Sometimes the amount of capital does not help. Lehman at the time of its failure, held 11%. Capital. Market fears about its viability destroyed it. This solution does not accommodate Black Swans, which play a significant part in many bank failures. We cannot predict infrequent, high-impact events, and being prepared for these events is crucial.

Putting in place an FDIC resolution procedure does not help. We can separate the utility functions from the high risk casino functions, and resolve the utility functions with an FDIC procedure. This is not possible for the casino functions. If the problem is that short-term funding has evaporated, we are up against a brick wall. Replacing these funds is a bailout, and that is what we want to avoid. Selling the open deals would take months and inform the market that the megabank is in wind down mode. Any value in the non-utility functions would evaporate, and any remaining short-term funding would be withdrawn. The megabank would die. Finally, we have to deal with the cross border issues. How do we resolve, across jurisdictions, who owns the cash balances, the IT and communications systems, and the shared real estate, and the numerous other shared assets?

Living wills do not help as megabanks resist making them, they are costly to produce and costly for regulators to evaluate. They are not a practical option.

No one wants megabanks, except their senior managers, casino croupiers and directors, those that are paid obscene compensation, and megabanks serve no purpose. Banks greater than $100 billion in assets do not have any advantage over smaller banks. They are not more efficient, there are no economies of scale, and the cost structure of a small bank is no more burdensome than the cost structure of a megabank. Economies of scale vanish at some number less than $10 billion in assets.[425] Without the *too big to fail* subsidy, megabanks are less efficient than smaller banks. There is no evidence whatsoever that large banks are needed because they can achieve things that smaller banks cannot achieve. Megabanks are complicated and what is required to regulate them is substantially different from the skills required to regulate non-megabanks.

For good reason, US regulation prohibits any bank from holding more than 10% of the nation's savings, but after the Crisis, three US banks violated this regulation. They were JP Morgan Chase, BoA and Wells Fargo. As a result of acquisitions, these same banks violated provision that prohibit banks from holding more than 75% of the deposits in some metropolitan areas. The size of megabanks puts them too near the borderlines of many needed restrictions.

Jamie Dimon said that to ensure America's long-term success we need large banks. He did not, however, accompany this remark with his reasons. He thinks that bringing back the GSA would be bad for the US economy and its long term success, and that the US needs large companies to make large global investments, in multiple countries, in order to assure US long term success. He tells us, again without providing any reasons, that only large banks can provide services for the multinationals. He says that breaking up banks would undermine the goals of economic stability, job creation and consumer service.[426] It's all rubbish. The real issue is bonuses and compensation.

A problem that Jamie Dimon must face in 2015 is that the parts of JP Morgan Chase are worth more to its shareholders than the bank as a whole, an issue that becomes even more salient when capital levels are factored in. The parts will be required to hold proportionally less capital.

There are no banks that can provide all the financial services that individuals and corporations need, and if there were, you would never lock yourself into one provider.

Nobel Prize winner, Joseph Stiglitz wants to break the megabanks apart.[427] He says that trying to control megabanks is a losing gambit. The only alternative is to break them up, and that not only loses nothing, it's a benefit. In the US, many parts of the financial system have done well, including the community banks, credit unions and local banks, but the megabanks have reaped havoc. Megabanks are predatory banks.

Stiglitz argues that the "only justification for allowing these huge institutions to continue is that there are significant economies of scope or scale that otherwise would be lost". He adds that there is no evidence for this, whatsoever. He says that the megabanks are "not responsible for whatever dynamism there is in the American economy", then "In short, we have little to lose, and much to gain, by breaking up these behemoths, which are not just *too big to fail* but also *too big to save* and *too big to manage*". The recent bailouts have transferred large amounts of money to the banks with the poorest risk management records. When megabanks pollute the economy, unlike oil companies, they do not pay for the clean-up.

It is in our collective interest to reduce the dependence of households and businesses on a few megabanks. Paul Volcker suggests that we revert to a modern day GSA,[428] and exclude from commercial banks all non-utility functions. Hedge funds, private equity funds and proprietary trading must be housed in separate entities. Mervyn King agrees, and adds that no amount of regulation could limit excessive risk taking, and proprietary trading must be segregated.[429] The UK wants to ring fence, that is, segregate retail High Street, banking from investment banking.[430] The EU agrees.[431] So how do we proceed? We strip off the non-utility functions from the casino, shadow banking functions, and limit the assets to a percentage of GDP. In the mid-1990s, BoA, Chase Manhattan Bank and the NationsBank each had assets of about 3 to 4% of US GDP, and a cap of 4% in 2009 dollars would mean that that domestic and foreign assets together could not exceed $570 billion. Given this limit, in the US, only a few banks would need to downsize. They include BoA, JP Morgan Chase, Citigroup, and Wells Fargo. Globally, there are many more.

What about the shadow banking system? In 1997, the assets of Goldman and Morgan Stanley only exceeded the 2% level in 1997 and 1998 respectively. So let's limit the size of these banks to 2% of GDP. The 4% and 2% of GDP size limitations are supported by Simon Johnson and James Kwak,[432] but a problem, of course, is that we do not want to do this by trial and error!

The UK banking sector is highly concentrated. There are four large banking groups. The assets of these four are each a multiple of the assets of the next largest bank. In countries like Holland and Switzerland, there are incentives for the *too big to fail* to move to centres where they could be bailed out. Size limits these incentives. Today it is inconceivable that Switzerland could bailout UBS, a bank that was insolvent at the time of the Crisis. These problems would be solved.

Citigroup has indeed downsized since the Crisis. Sixty businesses have been sold, It has cut the number of countries and US cities it operates in by 50%, and its pre-Crisis head count of 375,000 has dropped 35%.

When market capitalization is less that book value, a bank is a target for a break up, and the latest developments are that some of the megabanks, for example JP Morgan Chase, may be forced to do so by their shareholders! Megabanks are difficult to manage, competition from regional banks has increased, and the post-Crisis regulatory and compliance costs have soared. Also, a major issue is the IT infrastructure. Consolidation of IT systems had been grossly underestimated and the consolidated systems are inadequate.

Obscene Compensation

The UK distinguished itself in 2012 by boasting 2,714 bankers that earned more than €1 million (£835,000, $1.4 million), up 11% from the prior year.[433] That's almost $4 billion. Germany in second place had a tenth as many €1 million earners. The average compensation, including bonuses and pension plan contributions for the top UK bankers was €1.95 million (£1.6 million, $2.7 million) up 35% from the prior year. Looking only at investment bankers, there were 2,188 in the UK, 117 in France, 100 in Germany and 37 in Spain that earned more than €1 million.

We have already listed the compensation of the CEOs for many of the US megabanks. For the plebs, in 2008, JP Morgan Chase paid 1,626 employees bonuses of $1 million or more. Goldman, with 30,000 employees, paid 953 employees bonuses of $1 million, and 212 others, $3 million or more.[434] In 2009, five of the megabanks, Citigroup, BoA, Goldman, JP Morgan Chase and Morgan Stanley set aside a total of $90 billion for compensation. Goldman had just cleaned up after the Crisis, so paid an average of $595,000 per employee, and JP Morgan Chase an average of $463,000.[435] During this period, three dozen smaller institutions failed. To celebrate, Lloyd Blankfein was Time Magazine's Person of the Year.

These incomes are absurd and put bankers into to the grossly overpaid and under achieving top 1%.

Let's look at how the investment banks justified their compensation schemes. When the investment banks became public companies, new profit sharing agreements were put in place between the ex-partners, now the senior employees, to replace the existing partnership arrangements. Partners had been in it for the long haul, but this focus on long-term success was lost. A *take the money and run* mentality arose with banker money-whores moving to whatever bank paid the largest bonuses. As the new senior employees were the past partners, and sole shareholders, it became the norm that they took the lion's share of the profits, after all they took it *all* before, and they did the work.

The percentage of revenues going to employees of the US megabanks since 2000 has been in the range 35% to 50%. The UK banks have not been so outrageous. Their range was 15% to 30%. In 2013, Barclays paid £1.8 billion in bonuses to employees and £800 million to shareholders. It was not a once off. Clearly, this is wrong.[436] The idea is that profits go to the shareholders, but senior Wall Street bankers use their organizations as risk free ATMs.

For example, Goldman in 2007 had revenues of $46 billion, expenses of $34 billion, which included employee compensation of $20 billion, and so declared a profit of $12 billion. This went to the shareholders, including those that were employees. The employees took $20 billion, directly and about $4 billion as shareholders, and the remaining non-shareholders, $8 billion. Goldman exists for its employees, not its shareholders!

How does Wall Street justify employee compensation? It uses a number of calculations, and it boasts that bankers are smart people, a meritocracy, that deserves its rewards. Both are bizarre, and we will see why. We will look at the return on equity calculation now, and the meritocracy claims in the section on *Brainless Bankers.*

Return on equity is the ratio of profits to equity, or capital. Because bankers view equity as the investment in the revenue generating entity, the bank, they say it is reasonable, they say, to earn a return on it. This does not make any sense. It incentivizes banks to reduce capital, so that the return will be higher, and it takes no account of risk. One dollar made with very little risk is better than one dollar made by taking lots of risk. It takes no account of revenues generated today with built-in future losses. There is no reward for creating value, and management has no skin in the game. If shareholders, bondholders and taxpayers take losses, so should management. The result is excessive, unbridled speculation. Capital is a cushion against losses, protects shareholders and the public, and should not enter be part of profit calculations.

Executive pay consultants are paid to please their customers. They are used to justify ratcheted up executive compensation. They compare what one organization pays its senior employees to others. They are compensated based on salary increments. It's no wonder they always find ways to increase compensation. The claim is that their findings establish objectivity. That's utter rubbish. All they establish is a self-serving snowball. It's keeping up with the Joneses, a stepladder that increments compensation on a yearly basis. They are whores.

Thomas Piketty calls bank compensation meritocratic extremism:

> Another explanation... more plausible... more consistent with the evidence... is that top managers by and large have the power to set their own remuneration, in some cases without limit and in many case without any clear relationship to their individual productivity, which in any case is very difficult to estimate in a large organization.[437]

Warren Buffet despises the trader ethic. They earn far too much, they are not particularly clever, nor intelligent. The trading side of investment banks is run for the benefit of its employees, not shareholders, nor customers. He noted that Salomon's CEO, John Gutfreund, when he was fired, wanted $35 million to walk away. Michael Lewis, an ex-Wall Street trader thinks that trading rooms should be destroyed on ethical grounds:

> More different types of people succeeded on the trading floor that I initially supposed. Some of the men who spoke to us were truly awful human beings. They sacked others to promote themselves. They harassed women. They humiliated trainees. They did not have customers. They had victims.[438] ... The place was governed by the simple understanding that the unbridled pursuit of perceived self-interest was healthy.[439] ... as a Salomon Brothers trainee, of course, you didn't worry too much about ethics. You were just trying to stay alive[440].

Remember that the trading staff and senior management were major culprits. They built the toxic products and sold them to their pigeon customers.

I'll repeat Jessie Norman's quotation from chapter 1: "no reputable study has found a significant correlation between senior executive pay and long-term corporate performance".

Nothing changed after the Crisis which drew the following comment from John Reed, a past Chairman and CEO of Citigroup: "There is nothing I've seen that gives me the slightest feeling that these people have learned anything from the [C]risis, ... They just don't get it. They are off in a different world".[441] Just like Greenspan.

Why should we limit banker's incomes? Many reasons. Not doing so is immoral. Those that caused the problems that we are suffering from today have become very rich at our expense. They are not suffering. The compensation schemes incentivize bad behaviour and the current level of bankers' compensation is not necessary. The Swedish bank Handelsbanken has not paid bonuses for donkey's years, but pays into a profit sharing foundation that distributes the proceeds when individuals turn sixty.[442] Then of course, we know that senior bank executives determine their own salaries, and there is no correlation with performance, either short or long term.

The first move after the Crisis to limit bankers' compensation was made by the European Union. Bonuses have been restricted to 100% of salaries, or 200%, if a proposed bonus gets shareholder assent. It's become part of Basel III.[443]. It leads, of course, to increased salaries, and a lowering of bonus clawback amounts, but the latter can be tackled directly by clawing back salaries as well as bonuses. The UK objects, and since the Crisis, bonuses have had much lower cash elements and much higher stock awards than before. Special allowances, or role based pay, were introduced as fixed pay in an attempt to thwart the rules. As they are clearly discretionary, and hence bonus pay, the megabanks are dropping them in favour of larger salaries. Mark Carney, the governor of the BoE, wants to see performance bonds where senior employees are awarded these bonds in lieu of salary and bonuses. If all goes well the bonds can be cashed after a given number of years. If not, they are subject to clawbacks. The proposal is similar to what Handelsbanken does. It has the additional benefit that disputes over clawbacks become judicial adjudications. As it takes time for inappropriate behaviour to be discovered, the performance bonuses will need to remain non-cashable for many years, perhaps ten.

The argument that bankers will leave the money centres like London or New York and go elsewhere is not credible. They have not and will not. And if they did, it would be a benefit. They are in the underachieving top 1%, the problem. All major banks have branches in the major money centres, and their operation in any one centre can be made subject to the restrictions in the money centres that implement compensation restrictions. Rogue centres would not survive.

The megabanks define a class of employees as *material risk takers* or *code staff*. In 2013, Goldman paid an average of $4.7 million to its 121 material risk takers, JP Morgan Chase paid $2.9 on average to its 209 code staff and Citigroup $2.1 million to its 182. For Goldman, variable bonus pay was 5.5 times fixed pay, for JP Morgan it was 4.1, and for Citigroup 1.6.[444] The recent 100% restriction means that these ratios will change. Some progress!

The Problem of Inequality

Robert Shiller, Nobel Laureate, in 2013,[445] "The most important problem we are facing now, today ... is rising inequality". We need to understand the deep structure of inequality.

Across the globe, equality has not improved in the past few decades. Inequality is a product of political and not merely macroeconomic forces. The US GDP has doubled in the last 25 years, but the benefits have gone to the top earners. In 2012, the top 1% of Americans took home 22% of the nation's income, the top 0.1%, 11%. A similar story in Europe.[446] However, while economic forces contribute, politics provides the path. The recent rise in inequality has not come about because of automation or globalization, as some of our bankers and politicians say. It's a consequence of meritocracy gone insane, it truly is meritocratic extremism.

The recent astonishing levels of income and wealth that we now see has re-energized a debate. The top 1% earn more, and has more, than the rich had at the beginning of the 20th C, not an exemplary period. We all understand that poverty is bad because people suffer, and that it's difficult for the impoverished to escape poverty. But there is much more to it. Billionaires in any one economy slow down development. Those that become billionaires because they are publicly connected have a strong negative effect. Those that do not have an indistinguishable effect.

Stiglitz tells us "Inequality leads to lower growth and less efficiency. Lack of opportunity means that's its [our] most valuable asset – its– people [the globe's population] is not being used". He says that the success of the 1% is correlated with the stagnation of the living standards of the majority.[447] In fact, living standards of the majority have declined in the US and the UK. If we took from the pockets of the top 1%, the money would not disappear. It would go into the pockets of the lower 99%. Those at the top are plundering the poor.[448]

Stiglitz remarks that market democracy is incompatible with extreme poverty. Inequality leads to a replacement of democracy with plutocracy. The top are rent seekers who redistribute wealth in their own favour. They do not earn money, they take it "by rewriting the rules, or by rewarding and being rewarded by their cronies in business and in government".[449] At risk, the free markets. In the years that culminated in the Crisis, bankers sold mortgages to those who could not afford them, entrapped them, lobbied against their attempts to escape from the mess, and further enhanced their wealth. They sold high-risk products to naïve investors who lost enormous sums of money and lobbied against restitution, and further enhanced their wealth.

The top 1% concept was developed by the Occupy Movement, and as Krugman, points out the top 0.1% have benefited far more than the 1% in the last 30 to 40 years[450]. In the same way that poverty is not a character fault, the 1% or 0.1% did not earn their wealth by providing value.

We do not need our wealth being funnelled into the pockets of senior bankers, and moving our society towards a plutocracy. In the developed world, the US and the UK are number one and two. If we look at the undeveloped world, the already establish plutocracy in Singapore surpasses the US in inequality by a comfortable margin.

Brainless Bankers

We asked before how Wall Street justifies employee compensation. We have discussed the calculation side, so now we'll turn to the boasts of meritocracy.

Professional and skilled individuals, doctors, lawyers, builders and bricklayers have extensive training, and are licenced and certified as competent to perform their services. This does not apply to bankers.

Few bankers have more than an elementary knowledge of economics, finance or mathematics. Specialists like software engineers, IT communications personal, lawyers and economists have training in their specialties, and if employed by banks, they are employed as specialists. It is fashionable for large banks to recruit from the pool of recent university graduates. Little weight is put on academic qualifications unless that bank is recruiting for specialist roles. Specific degrees in banking are never required. Graduates have been through an extended period of study, no matter how basic, and hopefully can read and write. It's a benefit, but it's not banking. Its not banking, because banking requires few skills. Individuals become CEOs of banks for a number of reasons. They are good presenters, they have learned to use PowerPoint (a meaningless but necessary cultural artefact), they play the political game well, and occasionally they have generated profits. On the way, they have sometimes run divisions of banks, and they have certainly fired any competitors. They are not promoted because they have a good knowledge of how to run a bank. They are simply good at talking, and deception.

Financial concepts are not difficult to understand, and those that are challenging are certainly not understood by bankers. The language of derivatives is anything but transparent for a reason. Derivatives dealers do not understand derivatives and want it that way. It reduces scrutiny and delivers power. Wall Street hides simple issues and concepts, and says that they are difficult to understand.

Understanding banking does not require any expertise, but bankers present themselves as experts who know about finance and the economy. Governments and policy makers consult them, but what they say is not subject to scrutiny. Anyone who questions them is incompetent. Bankers argue that the issues are so hopelessly complex that it is not possible for mere mortals to understand them. In addition, for bankers, the issues are complex. What is astonishing is that bankers make incredulously stupid statements, repeatedly with an abundance of prejudice but a paucity of fact. When someone said that Jamie Dimon was the smartest banker in the room, they did not mean that he was smart. The remark was meant to remind us that it does not take a lot of neural matter to become a bank CEO. Senior bankers appear to be real life versions of the Tin Man. Neither heart, and certainly no brain. "It is difficult to get a man to understand something, when his salary depends upon his not understanding it!"[451]

Jamie Dimon loves to argue from authority, especially when he cannot marshal any reasons at all for his views. He says he is an "outspoken defender of the truth."[452] As such, he stated in the 2010 JP Morgan Chase Annual Report that large banks like JP Morgan Chase did not benefit from megabank guarantees and did not have lower borrowing costs. He pointed to a few graphs. The rating agencies, however, had stated explicitly that its ratings were based on government guarantees. The bank's borrowing costs were less. They were less because it was rated AAA, and it was rated AAA because of the *too big to fail* guarantees.

He told us that he did not want the Volker Rule because he wanted to be able to hedge by portfolio, something the Volker rule outlaws. "… we think [it] could have huge negative unintended consequences for the American competitiveness and economic growth".[453] What negative effects? There is not one shred of evidence for these remarks. He is motivated because the Volker Rule means less gambling and lower profits and bonuses. The issue here is whether Jamie is simply incapable of understanding the issues, or whether he wishes to be intentionally deceptive. I believe both.

The Many Faces of Dysfunctional Banking

The Unstable Funding Model

The consolidations of the 1980s and 1990s created megabanks, but still left thousands of small banks dotted across the country. Mega banks meant more interconnectivity, and extensive reliance on short-term funding.[454] This reliance remains after the Crisis. Short-term debt is cheaper. Cheaper funding meant greater profits and bigger bonuses. As short-term funding is fickle, it's unstable. Then add to this increased leverage, which made profits and bonuses easier. This meant that the banking industry became undercapitalized, with less loss absorbing capacity. This was aggravated by hiding exposures in off-balance-sheet vehicles. There is no free lunch, however, and the bill comes when it's not possible to roll over the debt.

Financial Innovation

Financial *innovation* meant inventing new ways to make money regardless of other considerations. The *innovations* usually involved derivatives. Most of the products served no purpose whatsoever other than to make profits, but their promoters celebrated them. The multi-trillion OTC derivatives market operated with few rules, like the US Wild West.

Rather than spread risk, securitizations concentrated it in the financial sector, and increased interconnectedness. When banks sold tranches of securitizations to each other, both their balance sheets could contain assets from the other. Tranches could be retranched and end up in CDO²s. How could a B rated tranche become of an AAA security?

Innovations were promoted as a great leap forward, and good for society, but they were used to skirt the rules, and avoid regulation and taxes, and generate profits. They were often hidden from sight, off balance sheet. No one understood the products and their markets, and a few mathematical symbols legitimized them. Sheila Bair wondered in 2007 why the FED and OCC had permitted off-balance sheet entities. She thought it was idiotic. When they were transferred back onto their sponsors' balance sheets, $1 trillion came back, with no capital to support losses.

MBS often served a purpose as did some CDOs, but synthetic CDOs did not. MBS took mortgage debt from the balance sheets of financial institutions and CDOs took a mixture of debt and in both cases, it was handed to investors. Banks have been evaluating risk for eons, but the risk of these constructions was new to banks, the regulators and policy makers, and investors. They relied on the rating agencies, and the agencies got it very wrong. The pure casino products like synthetic CDOs had no value other than to place bets. They were roulette wheels, and exponentially magnified the property bubble losses. The Wall Street Journal gave us an example: $38 million in subprime mortgages was referenced by 38 pools of debt. When the referenced mortgages defaulted, losses exceeded $280 billion.

When the megabanks sold a synthetic CDO to a customer, they were never made aware whether the megabank had bet for or against the product, or whether it had been built to fail.

CDS were dysfunctional insurance policies. There were no reserves and the balance sheets of the insurers during the Crisis were weak. You did not need to own what you insured, so you could insure the same asset, many times. As you could insure against a company, a product or a market, you were incentivized to cause them to fail. You could design a product to fail, insure against its failure, and profit when it failed.

Larry Summers testified before Congress:

> "... the parties to these kinds of contracts are largely sophisticated financial institutions that would appear to be eminently capable of protecting themselves from fraud and counterparty insolvencies"[455]

How wrong could one be? What could Larry have meant by *sophisticated*?

Wall Street's supposed skill, financial engineering, had done little more than generate profits and excessive executive compensation. *Innovation* was a story of incompetence and grossly misunderstood and excessive risk-taking fuelled by personal gain, and unconstrained by regulators and governments.

Risk Management

Banks today are so bad at managing risk that their risk management departments are segregated from the business units and serve little purpose other than to provide boards of directors with meaningless reports with numerous levels of granularity. There is little thought given to risk, and how best to measure and manage it. Risk departments are career graveyards. They have little or no power. This, even though large banks have the financial resources to manage risk.

Risk departments in the 2000s were incapable of understanding the risks in CDOSs, yet their use was permitted by Basel II to lower capital. What few took into account was the ability of the insurer to make payouts, until of course they could not. They did not maintain reserves.

Few considered whether the default risk of the assets packaged into a CDO were independent of each other. It was obvious that mortgage defaults were dependent on the economy, the FED's interest rate policy, home prices and numerous other factors, and that any problem in the housing market could easily migrate into other debt markets. Similarly, with airplane leases, credit cards and student loans. Moreover, when defaults weakened returns for one tranche, the returns from other tranches would be similarly weakened.

Stress Testing

Stress tests are no panacea. Andrew Haldane, executive director for financial stability at the Bank of England asked private sector bankers why they did not conduct rigorous stress tests. A common response was that in the event of a severe shock the authorities would have to step in![456] No need to say anymore.

What stress tests tell us is limited. One reason is that models are used to determine the expected outcomes, and these need to be validated, and that's not possible. How can you test a model for outcomes that represent extremes, and that are never realized! Stress testing is a lose-lose strategy. But it sounds good to say you conduct them. In 2010, the Irish banks that had survived stress tests did not survive reality, and in 2011, it was Dexia's turn. When products are complicated, stress tests cannot say anything before the components of the test are stressed.

The central issue is that risk management departments do the testing and have little understanding of stress tests, less understanding of their limitations, no knowledge of how to conduct them, nor what is being stressed.

Accounting

Accountants and auditors, who were supposed to have the expertise to understand the products and markets, did not. They had little knowledge of derivatives and did not acquire it.

In 2010, PricewaterhouseCoopers claimed that increasing capital would take money away from lending.[457] As a consequence, two percentage points would be sliced off UK economic growth. They did not say why they had come to this startling, yet absurd conclusion. It's an example how the banking oligarchy and their lackeys take licence to make statements, and, in this case a statement that demonstrates an absence of even the basics of banking and economics.

They did not apply basic and sound accounting principles, they did nothing about the off balance sheet conduits. They produced no new ways of looking at a bank's assets and liabilities, and no new risk management concepts.[458] They kept their eyes in the rear view mirror. For example, derivatives did not fit neatly in balance sheets, so derivative exposures were hidden in notes to the accounting statements. Trillions of dollars were parked out of sight, off balance sheet, and out of mind. Balance sheets were opaque.

Auditors, who were in a position to alert boards and investors about questionable practices, did not do so because of conflicts of interest. They wanted repeat business. They did not challenge models because they did not understand them and they did not question securitizations and other products. They did not test models, nor the revaluation marks. They did not question the ratings. They did not investigate obvious predatory lending. Except for presenting invoices, they were faceless non-entities.

Derivatives should appear as an asset for one of the counterparties and a liability for the other. Derivatives are P&L multipliers and can do so in a non-linear fashion. That means that gains and losses can be dramatic. Not only are investors in the dark, so are managers and shareholders. Dramatic swings are what investors, managers and shareholders want to understand. Derivatives are deliberately hidden.

The assets in an off balance sheet conduit are not supported by loss absorbing capital, and do not figure in debt to capital ratio calculations. When the four largest US deposit takers moved off balance sheet assets back into their balance sheets in 2009, the damage was already done! Their sponsors were the loss absorbers, loss absorbers without the capacity. What is astounding is that this practice had brought down Enron in 2001, and resulted in criminal prosecutions for both Enron management and its accounting firm.

There are many differences between GAAP (US) and IFRS (European) accounting. A major difference is that derivatives are included under IFRS. Jamie Dimon often referred to JP Morgan Chase's fortress balance sheet. Under GAAP, capital was 8% of assets, but under IFRS, it was 4.5%. The book capital was $184 billion. Fortress? Which side of the mirror are you looking at?

Technology

Banking technology has been inadequate for years. Traders have no interest in devoting profits to technology, so back office processing was, and is, poor. It took three to four weeks to confirm certain deals and when deals were novated, that is assigned to other counterparties, it took weeks to inform the counterparties. If problems arose, there were further problems sorting out who owed what to whom.

A bigger problem is that without IT resources, opacity is reinforced. The IT staff lacks business skills (as do their business partners), so the development of software and communications for the toxic products fell years behind. We saw that when the exposures of Bear, Lehman and AIG were needed to substantiate acquisitions or bailouts, only guesses could be made.

Technology and risk management are costs, managed by departments and groups that are cost centres. Their budgets distract from profits and bonuses. They are thus starved.

Consumer Protections

Roosevelt's New Deal established consumer protections. Full disclosure was required, so that consumers could understand financial products, and the circumstances in which they could be harmful. In the events that led up to the Crisis, full disclosure was not made and what disclosures were made did not enable consumers to understand the potential problems. Subprime mortgages with teaser rates were damaging for consumers, but they were described as beneficial. Consumer protections failed.

The Greenspan FED abrogated its responsibilities and failed. With the exception of the FDIC, the other regulators failed. Predatory financing ruled as mortgage origination standards dropped through the floor. Lax enforcement and product complexity enabled financial fraud. Auditors stood on the side-lines, as they did not want to harm non-audit revenues, and did not raise alerts.

The worst offenders were the non-bank mortgage lenders, the payday lenders and money remitters. There were abusive prepayment penalties, and other fees. Lenders did not ensure that borrowers had the capacity to repay loans. Yield spread premiums paid higher commissions when a broker channelled an individual that qualified for a prime mortgage into a more costly subprime mortgage. Brokers stripped equity and refinanced at higher cost, taking their fees and other costs from the equity.

In response to the abusive lending practices, Georgia responded with the Fair Lending Act in March 2002, and prohibited loans being made without regard for a borrower's ability to repay. It provided for assignee liability, so originators and investors could be sued for violations. All participants in the securitization chain became accountable for predatory lending.

Immediately the OTS and OCC pre-empted the Fair Lending Act. This meant that state and local law became subject to federal law, which neutered it. Ameriquest threatened to withdraw from, and Countrywide stopped lending in Georgia. S&P, Moody's and Fitch said that they would not allow loans originated in Georgia to be placed into securities they rated. Eventually, Georgia lost out, but twenty five states, eleven localities and Washington, DC enacted similar laws, and the FBI stated that mortgage fraud was rampant, pervasive and growing.

Financial fraud and criminal behaviour had often resulted in civil settlements in which the perpetrating institution admitted nothing, paid a fine and promised not to offend again, but then immediately did so. Schwab sued twelve securitizers based on representations contained in the offering documents for thirty-six securitized MBSs. The defendants were BNP Paribas, Countrywide, BoA, Citigroup, Credit Suisse, Deutsche Bank, Goldman, Greenwich Capital, HSBC, Wells Fargo, Morgan Stanley and UBS. The MBSs were purchased between 2005 and 2007. Schwab applied tests, including, loan to value tests, and found that a very significant percentage of loans, 40% to 50%, failed the tests. The defendants claimed that they had been scammed, just as Schwab had. But the defendants had represented that they had carefully analysed the loans. Unlike Schwab, they had full access to the detailed backup, and furthermore, they had used independent specialist firms to review loan quality. These reviews had revealed extensive quality problems. The loans failed the securitizers' own guidelines.

Securitizers were prepared to push anything out the door, assuming that investors would not discover problems before the expiration of the time limit for putting loans back to them. Securitizers were in bed with loan originators, providing warehouse lines and other assistance. The warehouse loans that provided the funds for predatory loans came from all the megabanks, and they dictated the terms.[459]

> "It is impossible to buy a toaster that has a one-in-five chance of bursting into flames and burning down your house. But it is possible to refinance an existing home with a mortgage that has the same one-in-five chance of putting the family out on the street – and the mortgage won't even carry a disclosure of that fact to the homeowner."[460]

The Consumer Financial Products Agency Act, which encompassed safety reviews of financial products as well as disclosure, was passed by Congress in December 2009. It was limited to consumers, and while it had gaps, it moved us forward in the right direction.

Ratings Agencies

Based on weak assumptions and little understanding, the ratings agencies gave securitization tranches high ratings. Why? They wanted to please their paymasters and protect future revenues. If bonds were given good ratings, they could be sold, and their paymaster would be happy. The agencies forgot about the purpose of ratings and focused entirely on enhancing revenues. They colluded with the securitizers, and provided ratings as they directed, in order to lock in future business. Some analysts, regulators and academics recognised what was happening and warned all who would listen. Few did. When the agencies were questioned about their blatantly unprofessional and fraudulent behaviour, they maintained that they had no legal liability for what they said and that ratings were opinions, and hid behind the First Amendment. Very good business, you give an opinion that means nothing, and you are paid for it. Securitizers wanted to sell securitizations and investors did not want, and did not expect to receive meaningless opinions. They relied on the agencies to provide ratings upon which they could make investment decisions.

Basel made capital determination dependant on credit ratings well before the ratings agencies began to derive most of their revenues from fees. By the 2000s, bank risk was in the hands of a small number of organizations that lived on fees from the banking sector. This was clearly inappropriate, and Dodd-Frank eliminated it.

How could AAA rated securities be created from high-risk collateral? How could financial engineering create no or low risk assets out of high-risk, subprime collateral? In the mid-2000s, there were twelve companies rated AAA and 64,000 tranches of asset backed securities rated AAA. This was completely absurd, and the twelve to 64, 000 ratio should have served as an alert.

Securitization ratings were not all that were amiss. Bear Stearns was rated A2, a high and solid rating, a month before it failed. Lehman remained A2 and AIG, AA until days before they failed and the GSEs were still AAA when they were rescued.

When the housing market problems began to surface, Moody's forced out executives who would not give high ratings. But when the bubble burst, 75% of asset-backed securitizations rated AAA were downgraded. By 2009, 90% of the 2006 and 2007 AAA subprime collateralized securitizations were junk.

The ratings agencies failed, lacked integrity and had little understanding of the products they rated, and their markets. They committed extensive fraud on an ongoing basis. They bear a large part of the responsibility for the Crisis as investors relied upon the ratings, and since the problems, the US Justice Department has taken actions against them. Their senior management should be held accountable for billions of dollars in losses.

Models

Well prior to the Crisis, Wall Street had embraced quantitative finance. The techniques were easy to apply, they did not need to be understood, and they made mangers feel comfortable. They were assumed to produce accurate and useful results. Few people understood the mathematics, and this enhanced their acceptance. If PhDs said they were good, and the details were not accessible to mortals, they must be good. Few questioned them, and quantitative finance promoted false confidence. We saw the Peltzman[461] effect. You thought that they provided safety, so you took more risks. Market participants used CDS assuming that they lowered risks, and then took on more risk. Few considered whether the transfer of risk to AIG had been accomplished, or whether it mattered, or whether AIG could ever make a payout.

Models were often taken as reality. Few realized that models had boundary conditions, and in many cases, they were ignored.

Nicholas Brady, a past US Secretary of the Treasury sums up the problems well:

> "This computer modelling is impressive stuff. However, while these models create the appearance of mathematical certainty about the relationships between markets and the way world events will affect prices it is essential to recognise that, at their root, these models rely upon man made assumptions about human behaviour –not iron bound laws of nature. In addition, the behaviour of derivatives markets can be episodic and illiquid at precisely the times we most need greater liquidity and confidence No matter how sophisticated the maths or how large the database supporting a model, no one can predict behaviour – human or market – with certainty. Inevitably, this means the formulas break down at the most critical times."[462]

In chapter 4, *Exotic Worlds*, we said that VaR told us little of value. Even if it did, we do not know how to calculate it, so attempts to do so are a waste of time. However, billions of dollars have been spent on VaR computer systems and consulting services. Not surprisingly, VaR supporters include the employees engaged in the ongoing VaR calculation efforts, the software providers and consultants. Black-Scholes does have a limited value, however, when used, almost always the results are off because its boundary conditions are violated.

In October 2008, the DJIA dropped more than 10% during each of two consecutive days. VaR theory says that the next time this will occur is between 73 trillion and 603 trillion years from now! Useful. Notably, the 2008 VaRs of Lehman, Merrill and Bear did not raise any alerts and all three failed!

Detractors like Nassim Taleb questioned the applicability of many models used in finance, and the reliability of the results. In particular, extreme events, Black Swans are far more common than what our models assume. However, it's the extreme events we want to know about. For bankers, however, Black Swans were assumed to be colour coded inhabitants of another planet, and tail risk was dismissed.[463]

The consequence of this is that our banks have been using metrics, blindly, that few understood, that purported to tell them when we could expect a problem, but did not. Yet, banks expect us to trust them!

By 2007, model risk had mushroomed and many quantitative methods collapsed. We had learned that many of the models were unsound.

The Oligarchy

We often overlook politics when examining crises. However, politics is precisely where we should begin. A country's political institutions define its banking sector and its functions. What Treasury departments do, and how central banks and regulators work is determined by politics, in every country on the globe. Crises are not random events. There are reasons why they occur, and political environments, its institutions, the elected and the electors are always part of the equation.

Banking and politics have been intertwined for centuries. The C15th Medici Bank, the largest in the world at the time, financed the Medici family's interests, possibly the richest family in Europe. It also managed the fortunes of many of the European royals and others not so royal. Cosimo d' Medici became the Gran Maestro of Florence in 1434, its (effective) head of state. Since independence, US banking and politics have been married, and there were similar marriages in the UK and Europe, Canada, Mexico and Brazil.[464] In fact, there were marriages in most of the Western world. Governments need money, and when they run out of it, banks provide it in exchange for monopoly rights and privileges.

Calomiris and Haber [465] report that in 117 countries with populations greater than 250,000, that 34 had no banking crises in the 21 years between 1990 and 2010, but that 93 did have one or more crises. That is 71% of these countries experienced banking crises. They observed that banks are regulated and asked why they performed so poorly. It is because of political decisions.

What regulators do is determined by politics, and what is inherited from history. They are props on political stages. In the US, for example, there are thousands of small banks. Banks evolved as small organizations, often with just a single branch. The farmers and business interests in the south and west were wary of the moneyed north east and did not want to extend control outside their communities. It took two hundred years to change this, and it was only in the 1990s that banks were allowed to operate across state borders.[466] Single branch banks led to local monopolies, as they had no competitors, and fragility, as banks could not diversify their activities across multiple communities, and thus could not weather local downturns. Calomiris and Haber contrast the development of banking in the US with that in Canada. Canada has had only had two banking crises, and both were insignificant. The US has had fourteen, and the long history of crises was a contributing factor to the FED opening its doors as the nation's central bank after two previously failed attempts.

This story enables us to understand why hundreds of banks failed in the US at the onset of the Crisis and its aftermath, and why there were no failures in Canada. The latter's national banks, with thousands of branches across the country served diverse interests and benefitted from economies of scale. Stability was ensured as downturns in one part of the country or economy were shored up by other parts. Generations of Canadian politicians had learned history's lessons and restrained monopolies.

The US policy makers have allowed an unstable banking model. The Canadians have not. Brazil, Argentina and Mexico have unstable banking systems, and have also been poor providers of credit to their nations. The European banking systems have been stable since the Great Depression, in part because of the willingness of their governments to fight fires with buckets of money. The Australians and New Zealanders have overcome the limitations of their small economies, and occasional problems, with money buckets too.

Governments rely on banks. Protecting them secures funds for government projects, helps them pay for defence and wars, and helps the private sector fund large projects like railroads, airports and dams.[467] Banks facilitate retirement savings and provide commerce with payment systems. Governments protect the interests of depositors who vote for politicians and banks bear the cost of protection by paying for deposit insurance and lender of last resort facilities.[468] Banks elect governments by buying votes for them. Governments pass laws, which protect banks and enable them to profit, so governments are willing accomplices of banks in search of profits. In the US and Europe governments socialized the costs of the Crisis and privatized the profits.

Governments are responsible for ensuring that economies grow. They also determine who and what can be a bank, and what they can do. Governments determine how much banks can lend, and to whom. They determine who gets credit and they determine how losses are allocated. They determine who is regulated and who is not, and the boundaries of regulation. Calomiris and Haber describe the relationship as a partnership, but it's not. It's an oligarchy.

From the 1980s, bank profits have purchased political power in Washington, London and the other European capitals. Banks make campaign contributions, pay for lobbyists and pursue politically salient targets like housing. They influence who is elected and what policies are supported. School ties play a supporting role. Profits purchase research and support from Academia. Good ratings for bad products were purchased from the credit rating agencies by changing the rules and paying them fees. The gatekeepers, the auditors, accountants and lawyers acceded. Their campaign contributions were also significant, and they manipulated financial statements and ignored danger signs. They found they did not need to understand banking. They were gifted the business. All they had to provide was a signature. In any case, better not understand what you are signing.

In the US, the revolving door between the Parkway and Wall Street enables bankers to take time off to play politics and peddle influence. They return to Wall Street with a network of politically influential friends. Politicians land lucrative consulting contracts. Europe is in step. Hundreds of individuals float between Wall Street and Washington. Robert Rubin, ex-Goldman Sachs (26 years) and ex-Treasury Secretary moved back home to Wall Street, to Citigroup, where, as we said, he was paid $125 million. For the bank, its cheap influence. For Rubin, well, thank you! Fraud is ubiquitous. Stephen Friedman, also an ex Goldman CEO, was Chairman of the NY FED at the same time he was on Goldman's board of directors, and at the time Goldman became a bank holding company. While the FED was propping up Goldman, he bought more shares in the bank. The NY Fed's lawyers agreed to this, but he resigned in May 2009 when the Wall Street Journal announced the conflict of interest. Friedman's insider trading and that the NY FED's lawyers agreed to it, is a disgrace. It's time to close down the revolving door.

As a result of political interests, regulation in the 1990s and 2000s promoted instability in the name of profits. Derivatives and other products were not regulated, and the shadow banking system exploded. In 1977, Congress passed the Community Reinvestment Act that required banks to be responsive to the needs of their communities. The act empowered advocates of low income and urban minorities to bargain with banks that were seeking to expand by acquiring local banks. They could deny, delay or promote an acquisition. The payoff was in loans to the local communities. Politically popular programs like mortgage lending were supported in exchange for deregulation and megabanks.

Between 1992 and 2007, almost $1 billion poor quality, high-risk mortgage loans were originated as a result of housing activism. Then, when the activists lobbied Congress, the loans were made part of the GSE targets. The GSEs bought the mortgages so banks could originate more of them. This lowered mortgage origination standards. Minimum down payments went from 20% to 5% to nothing, and by the mid-2000s, the GSEs were buying the full gamut of exotic mortgages. Everyone followed suit, and the weaker standards were adopted across the board. Even prime mortgage holders upgraded their properties, and extracted equity from their homes. Then the Crisis. Political interests delivered systemic instability.

There is a disproportionate share of wealth and power in the hands of the megabanks. The financial sector and its political influence are a serious risk to our economic wellbeing. Washington bailed out companies whose bets had gone wrong, bets that served no other purpose than to line the pockets of the gamblers. The fodder for the bets was taxpayers' homes, yet taxpayers paid for the bailouts. A consistent pattern of unchecked expansionist policies followed by an epidemic meltdown (these are euphemistically called market corrections) took a large toll on the lives of ordinary citizens. The FED and Treasury rigged the game in favour of the megabanks. The politician bankers decided who received bailouts and who did not, and the spoils went to the bankers. Washington behaved like an emerging market government. There were disastrous consequences, and when things got tough, the oligarchy followed history and penalized those on the lowest rung, in this case, the taxpayers. They began with the poorest of them.

By 2010 the *too big to fail* were more powerful, more interconnected and with more political influence than *ever before*, and they had increased market share. Today's banking system is no better than what it was before the reforms of the Pecora commission in 1932. It is more fragile because of globalization and nanosecond technology, but more importantly because the megabanks want it that way. It enables the ludicrous bonuses. *Too big to fail* became *far too big to fail*. The bonuses remained *too big to lose* and the bigger banks *too powerful to confront*.

We hear that the banking system has to be vulnerable in order to be effective. In other words, we need derivatives and fickle short term funding. There is not one shred of evidence for this claim, and there is every reason to avoid short term funding. Fragility, vulnerability and opacity only works for bankers on high salaries. It does not work for Main Street who enjoy no benefit and pay for the losses. Banks can and need to operate safely. Main Street loses nothing and has everything to gain.

When challenged, the megabanks mislead the public and legislators by making outrageous claims, justifying what they say with unsubstantiated self-serving rubbish. They tell us that banking is complex. It is too difficult for mere mortals to understand. Josef Ackermann would have us believe, "(that tighter restrictions on borrowing) would restrict (a bank's) ability to provide loans to the rest of the economy. This reduces growth and has negative effects for all".[469] These claims are self-serving, groundless rubbish. There is no shame.

During the past 30 years, the financial sector in the US and Europe has become a rogue industry. It has subverted political parties, political institutions, and academic institutions. Predatory banking has become a profit making tool. Banks have become casinos that operate with loaded dice. Public resources are used to protect a handful of large banks with extensive political influence. Are big, private and lightly regulated financial institutions good for us? Do we need this kind of financial system? No, we do not.

We need deposit takers, venture capital, ATMs, credit cards, micro lending, Internet banking, checking accounts and bill payments, etc. We need the Volker rule. We need to ring fence retail High Street from investment banking as the UK Chancellor of the Exchequer calls it. But we do not need megabanks and we do not need the oligarchy. We do not need *this* Wall Street. It is a burden on society. There are good reasons for returning to a form of the GSA. The oligarchy must be dismantled, and free markets must replace free-for-all markets.

Thatcherism and Reagan sowed the seeds of elitism with the message, put yourself first and move up the ladder without acknowledging that the top 10% can only be 10%. The decline of the USSR has contributed to the decline of the middle and working classes and the advance of the top 1%. There is less reason to distribute wealth, as there are no competing ideologies. Trickledown economics has become trickle up economics. Democracy has turned into plutocracy.

It is now time to reform the financial system that made the Crisis, not only possible, but happen. It is a serious risk to our wellbeing. Telling bankers to change does not work. Obama's exhortations in 2009 were ineffective. We need an exorcism. The Crisis resulted in the megabanks getting bigger, establishing more political power and paying their executives even more. They were able to do this with money that they used to purchase even more power and influence. In the first nine months of 2009, they spent $344 million on the previously mentioned 1,537 lobbyists. Then add direct and indirect political contributions, funded research, the revolving door and academia. Banks need to be intermediaries and not money extraction machines that endanger societies.

It took six years for a central bank, the FED, to reappear after the 1907 crisis because of an oligarchy's opposition, and decades to recover after the Great Depression. In much the same way, governments today, in the Western World, are informed and controlled by a banking oligarchy. Combined political, economic and financial forces have done and will continue to have a devastating effect on society. We also need strong consumer protections for both individuals and companies that guards against the abusive behaviour of banks even when there are no longer megabanks.

Regulation alone cannot control the megabanks and they must be broken up. The utility functions need to be segregated and deposits insured. The other functions of today's megabanks can remain, as independent smaller organizations that stand on their own feet, and that can never attract a rescue. Breaking up today's megabanks will not solve the problem in itself as any bank absent strict controls and regulation can take on investments with stockholder funds that are beyond acceptable risk limits. The management of banks is incentivized to do this, and even though the taxpayer may be exempt from bailouts, the destruction in the market can be extensive. The 4% and 2% of GDP size limitations supported by Simon Johnson and James Kwak are a step in the right direction.[470]

The introduction of size limitations is a big step forward, but raises the question of why we need to set limits. We should look at the problem from the other side. We should not only attempt to justify limits by looking at the size of banks today. We should be asking ourselves what is the smallest a bank can be? Why do banks need to become large? The only beneficiaries are the rich individuals that comprise the banking oligarchy.

We need to take a stand against $1-one vote and return to one-person one vote. Small banks do not need lobbyists and campaign contributions can come from other sectors of society, and the obscene compensation schemes need to be dealt with by eliminating them.

Two Risk Management Departments

Here we will look at a couple of examples of dysfunctional risk departments. The first bank is a small, South East Asian bank, DBS, headquartered in Singapore. The second is the world's least favourite megabank, HSBC. I have personal experience of both.

The Development Bank of Singapore, DBS is small, so you would expect that it would have a small risk department, however, this department numbered over one hundred and twenty people. Not because the department did anything. Its size was used in public statements to underscore that the bank was able to manage its tiny risk. The department was managed by a chief risk officer, a career DBS banker, an accountant by training, who in her own words did not understand risk. She did not need to. She was a banker. As for VaR, her opinion was that it was important to calculate so that it could be reported in the financial statements. It provided investor confidence in the bank. But she continued, it was only an indication of market risk. She was not able to say what VaR did measure. And of course, this account was at odds with what the bank stated in its financials, which deified VaR and heralded the bank's ability to manage risk by using it. In other words, the bank was using VaR to mislead its customers, lenders, investors, employees and auditors. Two lieutenants, I will call them Ryan and Dill, managed the market risk department. They were even more clueless than she was, and the department was a sham.

Ryan, a mathematician, seemed to believe in VaR because it was the result of a probability calculation. Dill did not know. When I asked why traders must keep within VaR limits, which had never constrained losses, Ryan explained that it was good discipline. All three, the department head, Ryan and Dill thought VaR was a good basis for capital determination as it lowered capital. All three confused capital with reserves.

Ryan was in charge of a team of quants and had a PhD in mathematics. When he interviewed applicants for jobs, he gave them maths tests. He neither understood, nor wanted to understand risk, nor how to measure it, nor the VaR calculation, nor stress testing. Nor could he. He spent his time trying to determine how DBS could avoid using the full range of 500 days of data required for the VaR calculation because it would save money. In other words, even if VaR provided DBS with something meaningful, he chose to undermine its integrity, to save money. Why did he do this? Part of the reason was that cost savings gave Ryan a bonus, and part of the reason was that he had nothing else to do. Charitably, Ryan had an IQ in high double figures.

If Ryan lacked neural matter, Dill was a benchmark for underachievement. One wondered what held his ears apart. Dill began his post-secondary school education by failing a degree at a prestigious university in the UK. He was eventually awarded a runner's up diploma. He had been told he was a mathematician but he was not. He was an insecure individual that understood neither finance, nor risk, nor mathematics, nor treasury. He recruited only those that would not challenge him, nor outshine him, which rather limited the pool. He maintained that the risk system that I put in place must be good because it cost millions of dollars. The reason for the system was not because it enhanced the bank's capacity for risk management, but that it was expensive. The bank could then boast about its risk management capability by advertising that it had purchased an expensive IT system. Dill's dream was to become a manager, something that had eluded him for his entire career. What stopped him in his tracks was PowerPoint. He wasn't very good at it, PowerPoint skills are essential for management, and he spent a good deal of time designing colourful PowerPoint slides. Why not? Must look busy. The rest of his daily routine was spent finding what his bosses said, so he could repeat their thoughts as his own, and somehow get them into a PowerPoint slide. Round peg and square holes.

He also wrote tons of emails that he set for delivery way into the early hours of the morning in order to misrepresent to his bosses that he worked late. He purchased an air conditioner for his office so that visitors would assume he needed it for afterhours work. Dill had many problems. He had worked at the branch of a German bank in London and been fired because he could not manage himself out of a paper bag. His project management skills did not make the lowest rung on the ladder. His people management skills were worse. And needless to say, he played no role in the department's timid role of assessing and managing risk. So why is this important to say? Because even for banks at the lower end of the food chain, where risk management is easy, the bank is incapable of managing risk, so it is ignored. The DBS risk department is a career graveyard, and it exists only because the bank is required to have one. It's also a good place to hide the hordes of the bank's underachievers.

HSBC was a different kettle of fish, a large kettle, with lots of very small fish.

HSBC is matrix managed. This means that employees reported to a number of mangers, which meant that employees did not have bosses. The bank could not manage its staff, and it could not manage itself. Its large and an agglomeration of acquisitions. I reported to four individuals and none of them had any idea of what I was doing, nor what I was supposed to be doing. Staff did what they wanted. It had different dining rooms for different levels, and this was the only source of order.

Risk was managed by who knows whom, or what? The Hong Kong senior risk managers acted like they managed risk for the entire bank as did the UK risk management group. And they did not interfere with each other, or talk, in case duplicity of effort surfaced. Needless to say, their efforts would have collided if they were compared. Ninety percent of the risk teams were IT personnel and had no understanding of risk. One of the bank's policies was to transfer employees in and out of functions that resulted in no specific expertise ever being developed. The managers of the risk software development teams, none of whom had even a basic understanding of risk, worked and lived in London, and the soldiers in Hong Kong and Guangzhou. Supervision? No need

I want to tell you about two very notable individuals. One I will call Larry and the other Will. Larry was in charge of risk architecture and Will, of credit risk systems development. Neither had any clue. You could not understand Larry. I first thought it was a speech impediment, but no, his utterances were simply unintelligible drivel, so much so that some thought that Larry was clever. He had developed a wonderful picturesque PowerPoint slide that purported to show the banks' risk systems. It resembled a multi-coloured Mohican patchwork poncho. It had no rhyme, rhythm, reason or content. When he was asked a question, he would display the slide and grunt something that no one understood. I suggested that he might want to donate it to a modern art museum. Understandably, the bank had neither an IT risk capacity, nor a development strategy nor the ability to implement one.

When Northern Rock faltered, the HSBC chief risk officer situated in Hong Kong, an individual uncharacteristically capable of performing his job, asked for a report showing the bank's exposure to Northern Rock. There wasn't one. After four days, he managed to piece together a picture from phone calls to other banks and the press. This megabank was unable to determine its exposure to a failing sister organization, nor develop a plan to minimize its losses.

Will was also special. He had been with the bank for twenty-two years and achieved nothing. Because of this, he supervised thirty-five people, mostly located where he wasn't. He worked in Hong Kong, and his team was in Guangzhou. One incident of many that stands out: when the Mumbai office wanted to deal in overnight indexed swaps, he was asked whether the credit systems could process them. Will said *yes*, Mumbai went ahead and within a week, HSBC found its globally deployed credit systems had collapsed, and remained so for days. The consequence? The dealers were out of action for days. The cost tens of millions of dollars. Dill's response? He was not provided with sufficient clarity when he had said *yes*. He did not want to say either *yes* or *no*, but the latter may have meant work for him. He was unaware of what the systems did, so what could he say?

The point of these two examples it that at both ends of the food chain there is no capacity to manage risk, no understanding of this, at any level, within the bank, up to the board of directors, and no intention to rectify the problem.

For years, I taught risk management for some of the major banks in South East Asia. I would explain what controls were needed, and what ratios were to be monitored. In just about every case, I would receive telephone calls: "Could we not do this, and could we not do that, can we avoid holding a liquidity buffer? To do so would be expensive. I want to save the bank money. It's better for me if I can save some money." In other words, by not implementing necessary risk management controls the staff earned larger bonuses and weakened whatever risk management capability there was.

What we need to do

The goal: is a "Healthy Banking System, Not Profitable Banks".[471] Although some of this is repeated, here is a summary of what we need to do to restore our banking system. We need to:

- Break apart the oligarchy
- Break up the megabanks
- Shut down the revolving door between Washington and Wall Street[472]
- Constrain lobbying
- Eliminate casino banking
- Adopt the Volker Rule, adopt the proposed UK and EU ring fences around retail banking
- Eliminate zombie banks
- In the US, consolidate the undiversified local banks
- Eliminate off balance sheet entities
- Constrain exposures to the short term-debt market
- Make capital TCE based
- Remove contingent capital
- Reform tax laws that incentivize debt as opposed to capital
- Ensure a minimum capital of between 20% and Eugene Fama's 40 to 50%. [473]
- Constrain compensation
- Restore corporate governance, accountability and ethics
- Ensure CEO and board of director independence
- Eliminate predatory banking
- Regulate all consumer products a from a safety, soundness and perspective
- Eliminate products that serve no purpose

- Require IT systems to function, penalize financial institutions that lack adequate technology
- Implement severe penalties for bankers who use models that do not function.
- Require that a bank's risk management capacity is audited
- Empower risk management departments
- Ban toxic products
- Eliminate VaR and other useless metrics, remove dysfunctional innovation
- Reform the Financial Utilities: the ratings agencies, the monolines, the auditors

The Sixth Bangster Awards

We have more Bangsters again. Sebastien, the chief judge has approved the following awards: Jamie Dimon earns a Bangster Award because he is defender of deception and not a defender of the truth, as he maintains. He heads a crime ring at JP Morgan Chase. Kathleen Corbet said that the S&P ratings for structured products were pointless. Under here watch, S&P gave AAA ratings to toxic securities. Larry Summers was irresponsible, mislead Congress, and told it that banks could protect themselves.

On the Gold Star side, Joseph Stiglitz warned of the consequences of the increasing income 1% and showed why there was no need for the megabanks. Robert Shiller warned about inequality, and Paul Volker wanted a return to the GSA and proposed that speculative derivatives dealing should be separated from the utility functions of banking. They get Gold Stars, as does Paul Krugman who spoke out against inequality and the treasury's disposition to support Zombie banks like Citigroup.

Here is the table:

Bangsters		Gold Stars
Nicholas Biddle	Goldman Sachs	Franklin D Roosevelt
JP Morgan	Hank Paulson	Louis Brandeis
James Johnson	Dick Fuld	Raghuram Rajan
Alan Greenspan	Stan O'Neil	Barney Frank
Angelo Mozilo	Joe Cassano	Sheila Bair
Jimmy Cayne	James Crosby	Joseph Stiglitz
Mat Ridley	Andy Hornby	Robert Shiller
John Paulson	Fred Goodwin	Paul Volker
Morgan Stanley	Senator Phil Gram	Paul Krugman
Jamie Diamond	Larry Summers	
Hank Paulson	Kathleen Corbett	

10

The Band Keeps Playing

T his final chapter looks at some examples of bank malfeasance and fraud,[474] and groups them by perpetrator. We look at products that enabled fraud and related illegal activities by banks and their customers, we describe the recent cases of system wide fraud, and then individual megabank fraud, and then we describe the extensive fraudulent behaviour of many bank executives. Finally, we will draw some conclusions.

No Prosecutions

The Obama administration eschewed prosecution of white-collar crime. The president explained that while much of the behaviour of the financial sector was unethical, immoral and reckless, it was not necessarily illegal. He continued, "If there are loopholes and rules that can be bent and arbitrage to be had, they will take advantage of it".[475]

This is unreasonable. If his administration wanted to pursue the perpetrators, it would have found a way. Furthermore, there were many clear cases of criminal behaviour, including cases of predatory lending and securities fraud, when originators and securitizers misrepresented the characteristics of loans and securitizations. Accounting fraud was rampant. The ratings agencies committed fraud. Insider trading was par for the course. Consumer protections were violated and the product misrepresentations were fraud. Notwithstanding the prosecutions in the 1980s, the occurrences of financial fraud and malfeasance began to surge steeply upwards in the late 1990s. We should have acted then.

Fraud and greed were major ingredients of the Crisis. If the behaviour of the financial sector was unethical and immoral, as the president said, it should not have been swept under the carpet. Indeed, unethical and immoral behaviour is what should be punished! There was no excuse to not prosecute those responsible. Why did this not happen? Because of the banking oligarchy.

All the megabanks committed serious fraud, and continue to do so today. However, all that has resulted is a few whitewashed settlements resulting with megabanks paying insignificant fines, which with the exception of a few cases have been paid by the shareholders. Similarly, there have been few admissions of guilt and few other consequences.

When banks, that is shareholders, pay the penalties and fines, there are two consequences, there is a decrease in profits and dividends, and it creates a need for additional capital. This is true even when the offences include defrauding shareholders! The perpetrators go Scott free, Scott free to commit more fraud, as they know that while they benefit from the upside, they suffer no consequences if caught.

Charles Ferguson[476] asked the question why were Bernie Madoff, Raj Rajaratnam and Martha Stewart prosecuted for financial crimes, and the senior executives of AIG FP, BoA, BNP Paribas, Barclays[477], Bear, Citigroup, Crédit Suisse, Deutsche, Goldman, HSBC, JP Morgan Chase, Lehman, Lloyds, Morgan Stanley, Merrill, Northern Rock, RBS,[478] Santander, Société Générale, Standard Chartered and UBS, and were not? Everyone got away with it, including executives of the ratings agencies, Greenspan and Poulson. They are today, very rich individuals. Not only did the senior executives exploit the public, in many cases, they sacrificed their own firms, and all for their own benefit. On top of this, there was the $1 billion reimbursable, tax-exempt, but off limits entertainment allowances that funded junket travel, lavish meals, cocaine habits, and prostitution, among other vices.

We need to sharpen our teeth. Until the Fabulous Feb was convicted, Bernie Madoff, Raj Rajaratnam and Martha Stewart were the only significant offenders during the Crisis era to be convicted, and Madoff was sent to jail for a long time. It is clearly wrong that only these three were singled out. The prosecution of the Fabulous Feb in 2013 announced a change, and in 2015 the UBS trader Tom Hayes, was sentenced to 14 years in jail for his role in the LIBOR scandal.

Greenspan made the absurd remark that enforcement should be up to the market. While this realigns stupidity with insanity, the remark cannot be dismissed. It was irresponsible and severely damaging as it deflected law enforcement. Banks use other people's money, which must be safeguarded.[479] Greenspan had no regard for other people's money.

Madoff claimed to be tracking the S&P 500 stock index and using options cleverly. No one could understand his strategy, and the numbers did not add up. His bankers and other partners must have known something was amiss. He managed a $65 billion Ponzi scheme, the SEC had received numerous tips, but chose not to act.

Where were Greenspan's *fraud detection and correction markets*? Where were the *responsible* bankers and other market participants who were to act? Lack of action meant that many individuals lost their life savings, billions. Thank you Alan.

The Department of Justice is responsible for prosecuting cases bought to it by the regulators, often the SEC. Because of the complexity of the cases, the Department relies heavily on the SEC, its Wall Street regulatory partners and the Treasury. However, Wall Street has been immune from prosecution. Why? One reason is that the cases are complex, and take a large amount of time, effort and money to prosecute. Prosecuting white-collar crime is much harder than finding a terrorist cell or getting a conviction against crack cocaine traffickers. Another reason was that the Enron debacle resulted in 85,000 individuals losing their jobs, while almost all of them had nothing to do with the problem. Fearing similar consequences, the Justice Department has eschewed indicting financial firms.[480] This is inexplicable. The alternative is obvious, indict the guilty, the senior management. The banking oligarchy gets in the way. It oils the revolving door between Wall Street and the Parkway. Lawmakers, prosecutors, lawyers and regulators became bankers and bankers became lawmakers and regulators, and those on the Parkway, waiting their turn to make large amounts of money, do not want to prosecute their future paymasters. Today's megabanks remain all powerful parts of the oligarchy.

Finally, in 2009, the Justice Department appeared as if it was prepared to prosecute those responsible for the Crisis. It declared that it would "hold accountable those who helped bring about the last financial crisis" and "to prosecute significant financial crimes, ensure just and effective punishment for those who perpetrate financial crimes, [and] recover proceeds for victims". In 2010, it claimed that it had identified 1,500 criminal defendants and ordered $200 million in recoveries. But the 1,500 did not include any significant perpetrators. They were the brokers and minor functionaries who followed orders. They were guilty, but they were the street runners, the mules, not the king pins. They were individuals who lied on written loan applications. Shockingly, the recipients of the $200 million were the perpetrators, the mortgage originating banks.

Between 2009 and 2013, the banking industry paid fines and settlements totalling $ 278 billion. In 2014 alone, it paid another $57 billion.[481] Total, $335 billion. JP Morgan Chase hit the jackpot with fines of $62 billion. Jamie Dimon has run the largest crime spree in the history of finance. William Black explains[482] why Dimon still has a job: fraud generates fictional income that generates profits and bonuses. All senior executives and the boards of directors share in the bonuses. Just as taxpayers picked up the tab for the excesses of the *too big to fail*, the shareholders paid the fines. It was the shareholders of JP Morgan Chase that paid $62 billion. The details are in www.risktraffickers.com.

Products That Enabled Fraud

Many derivative products were promulgated which enabled fraud, theft, money laundering, tax evasion and so on. The products were of two kinds: customized derivatives and standardized equity derivatives. There are thousands of customized derivatives, and here are a few from the 1990s. They have been more fully described in prior sections. There are a dozen or more standardized equity derivatives, including quantos, inverse floaters, reverse convertibles and target redemption notes. Few of these have any legitimate business application, and we describe quantos. When fraud surfaced, what is notable is that no banker was prosecuted. Prosecution was limited to a few customer executives, executives who had been the target of fraud.

German Shares, Tax Free

Salomon sold German shares to German customers in a way that enabled them to avoid German tax. The fraud used specially designed Italian tax subsidiaries, was creative, ingenious and illegal.

Dollar Thai Baht Linked Notes

These notes were issued by (First Boston) Credit Suisse in the 1990s. They were bets on the Thai baht disguised as AAA or AA US dollar bonds issued by US government agencies. The principal and returns were in US dollars and the notes paid a healthy return, double the returns paid by other US government agency bonds. The value of the principal was linked to the value of the Thai baht, and if the Thai baht devalued, the principal lost value. They enabled organizations that were not permitted to bet on foreign currencies to do so. They enabled fraud. The sales people committed fraud by not disclosing the nature of the notes, the positioning of a US government agency as issuer was a sham designed to mislead investors and regulators, and regulation was sidestepped. The end game was that the IMF engineered bailouts of $17 billion for Thailand, and $42 billion for Indonesia. The crony capitalists won.

Morgan Stanley's AMITs and MX Missiles

MX missiles were AMITs developed by Morgan Stanley. The 1992 AMIT was so profitable that it was renamed the MX Missile. These products were fraudulent. They were bets that enabled theft. Fraud entered when the profit was declared. The declared upfront profit hid an equal and opposite loss years into the future. They were hidden from regulators and shareholders. Why? Because customers paid a premium to avoid regulation, they paid for fraud.

Bankers Trust Canadian Dollar, Yen Swaps

Another regulation avoiding derivative was exploited by Japan's insurance industry. Bankers Trust developed Canadian dollar, Nikkei call option, yen swaps. They enabled bets on the Japanese stock market. They were fraudulent, and when the Japanese stock market fell, the Japanese insurance regulators, the shareholders in the insurance companies and the Japanese pubic were not happy. As usual, other banks jumped on the bandwagon, including Bear, Goldman, Salomon and Morgan Stanley. Bankers Trust (and Merrill) also caused the bankruptcy of Orange Country and swindled Gibson Greeting Cards, Proctor and Gamble and many more.

Quantos

Quantos enabled organizations that were not permitted to bet on some or all foreign currencies to do so, by betting in US$, and receiving returns determined by an inaccessible currency. Quantos circumvented regulation. Quantos enabled fund managers to demonstrate good up-front returns, earn attractive bonuses and then move to a new job before the downside losses surfaced. Quantos meant fraud.

System Wide Fraud

Manipulating appearances and PPI were activities that the megabanks undertook as corporate entities. LIBOR manipulation, FOREX manipulation and precious metals market manipulation were frauds perpetrated by individual employees. However, in each case, their activities were undertaken with the knowledge and permission of senior bank executives.

Borrow for Less by Paying More Bonuses

During the Great Recession, some banks, including the megabanks paid dividends and bonuses for appearances only. They wanted to appear stronger than they were, so they could borrow at lower costs. These banks argued that paying bonuses was needed in order to retain staff at the time they were most needed. Nonsense. These individuals caused the problems! They weakened their organizations when they needed strengthening.

Payment Protection Insurance, PPI

PPI is insurance that reimburses a policyholder if circumstances prevent loan repayments from being made, for example, if the holder falls ill, has an accident or loses employment. Of the 53 million policies sold in the 2000s, banks sold 45 five million, and a great number of these sales resulted from miss selling. Sales practices were misleading, fraudulent misrepresentations were made and there was little disclosure. For example, policies were sold to self-employed people (who were ineligible to claim), to borrowers who were wrongly told that taking PPI was a condition of being granted a loan, and consumers who did not realize they were taking out a policy. Hundreds of thousands of policy claims were rejected, and complaints mishandled on an industrial scale. Consumers, individually and via consumer organizations took action.

The culpability of the UK banks was recognised and as a result, by early 2014, the banking industry had set aside £26.0 billion ($40.0 billion) to pay settlements and claims. Lloyds (£12.0 billion), Barclays (£4.1), RBS (£3.1), and HSBC (£2.8) alone set aside £22.0 billion, but as more than twenty thousand claims were being filed per month at the time of writing, this will rise. Sean Farrell has pointed out that total costs today are more than twice the costs of the 2012 Olympic Games.[483] The PPI fines and penalties are detailed in www.risktraffickers.com.

PPI severely diminished the UK banking industry's reputation, and became an embarrassment for its High Street banks. It's a further example of the oligarchy's free for all. PPI was fraud and theft and it's astounding that no individual has been held accountable.

LIBOR Manipulation

LIBOR affects the cost of borrowing for most of us. It is used to set rates for mortgages, credit card borrowing, student loans, derivatives, consumer and business lines of credit, in fact for most loans. The credit market is $800 trillion. The pricing of $350 trillion of this market is directly based on LIBOR and pricing for the balance is strongly influenced by LIBOR. LIBOR is the largest financial cartel in the history of finance by four orders of magnitude.[484] Each business day in London, a few megabanks contribute rates, a few calculations are made and massaged, and average prices for ten currencies and fifteen time periods are announced. The rates are supposed to be an accurate and objective assessment of the rates at which banks will lend on that day to each other on an unsecured basis. They are not.

For ten or more years, traders from fifteen megabanks, and some others too, systematically colluded by agreeing and contributing rates that either helped their bets in the markets or evidenced their bank's perceived financial strength. If LIBOR is increased by 1%, then $3.5 trillion more is charged in interest each year. Consumers then pay more for mortgages and other loans. The lenders earn more, and their traders – and their bosses - make bigger bonuses. A trader does not need to manipulate LIBOR by much to make money. Billions of dollars in bonuses were paid, at our expense.

Barclay's was the first to be fined, and paid $450 million in criminal settlements. The investigations that lead to this revealed significant fraud and collusion by the LIBOR setting member banks. On 3 July 2012, Bob Diamond the CEO of Barclays went before a House of Commons Select Committee in order to explain the debacle, and the next day was fired. Marcus Agius, the chairman had already resigned. Diamond stated that manipulation was not in Barclay's culture. He personally was not in the business for the money. He already had a $24 million home in New York (concealed by a corporate name) and a similar home in London. Perhaps he did not need any more money.

Tim Geitner at the NY FED learned of possible manipulation in April 2008, but did nothing other than to tell the UK regulators. The FED had been aware of LIBOR manipulation from 2007, and one may ask, why the FED did not take action then? The BoE was aware since 2007, and Governor Mervyn King went on record as saying that LIBOR "… is in many ways the rate at which banks do not lend to each other".[485] LIBOR manipulation is egregious, criminal conduct. When the miscreants were caught (red handed, on tape recordings and emails), and the manipulation came to light, it was clear that it was no less than a long running confidence trick played on the public for personal and institutional advantage. It exposed widespread fraud, a lack of integrity and trust, a lack of management checks, and a culture of deceit. Traders who participated in the collusion rewarded each other with nights out, bottles of champagne and expensive meals, no doubt paid for by their employers, that is, the shareholders. A 2008 conversation between RBS trader Tan Chi Min and Deutsche trader Mark Wong illustrated the collusion and reasons:

> **Tan**: It's just amazing how LIBOR fixing can make you that much money, or lose it if [you are] opposite. It's a cartel now in London.

> **Wong**: Must be damn difficult to trade man, especially if you are not in the loop[486]

George Osborn, the Chancellor of the Exchequer said: "It is clear that what happened in Barclays and potentially other banks was completely unacceptable, was symptomatic of a financial system that elevated greed above all other concerns and brought our economy to its knees", "Punish wrongdoing. Right the wrong of the age of irresponsibility." "Fraud is a crime in ordinary business — why shouldn't it be so in banking?"

In December 2012, UBS agreed to fines of $1.5 billion, in fines. As well as manipulating the market, UBS offered financial rewards to dealers if they spread false information. LIBOR scandal fines and penalties, added up to $6 billion in 2015, and are detailed in www.risktraffickers.com.

Recently, UBS trader Tom Hayes was jailed for 14 years for manipulating LIBOR and conspiracy to defraud. He is expected to be the first of many. We will return to Tom in a later section.

FOREX Manipulation

Groups of dealers using chat rooms named *The Players, One Team, One Dream, The Mafia (*or *The Cartel), The Three Musketeers, The Bandit's Club* and *A Cooperative* rigged key benchmark currency exchange rates for their own benefit for at least a decade. The foreign exchange market is $5.3 trillion per day.

In June 2013, Bloomberg News reported that spot foreign exchange dealers had been front-running their customer orders, on a daily basis, by colluding with colleagues and pushing through trades before and during the 60 second window during which benchmark rates are set.

Senior currency traders were caught on chat room transcripts. They agreed trading strategies with competitors and the kinds of trades and amounts that they would make. It was blatant benchmark rate manipulation. The chat rooms were exclusive and membership by invitation only. Globally, hundreds of traders have been implicated.

Regulators in Asia, Switzerland, the United Kingdom, and the United States all acted. Barclays, Citigroup, Deutsche Bank, Goldman Sachs, HSBC, JPMorgan, Lloyds, RBS, Standard Chartered and UBS have been fined. Barclays, Citigroup, JP Morgan Chase, and RBS have been held criminally liable by the US Department of Justice. Some have suspended or fired senior foreign exchange staff. The BoE, by June 2014, had suspended, placed on leave, or fired some 40 of its own foreign exchange employees. In addition to fraud, rate rigging, collusion, manipulation, and aiding and abetting the above, these banks breached customer confidentiality. Conflicts of interest were permitted and illegal profits were made at the expense of customers by exploiting stop loss orders. The first arrest was made in late 2014, Paul Nash, an RBS trader. Each week the equivalent of a year's global trade in physical goods is traded on the foreign exchange markets.

Total fines and penalties in 2015 came to $10.0 billion. Barclays (2.4 billion), Citigroup, JP Morgan Chase and RBS pleaded guilty to criminal charges. Notably, the profits of the banks that suffered the fines made profits in 2013 of $132 billion.

The Swiss Financial Market Supervisory Authority has placed a two-year bonus limitation on UBS of 200% of base salaries for foreign exchange and precious metals employees, globally, and demanded that UBS automate at least 95% of its global foreign exchange trading operations and ensure that customer and proprietary trading are firewalled. The FCA has required banks to renovate their antique legacy IT systems. Currently they can be compromised and hide manipulation from compliance monitoring.

Precious Metals Market Manipulation

Ten megabanks are under investigation in the US for rigging the precious metals market. They include HSBC, Bank of Nova Scotia, Barclays, Credit Suisse, Deutsche, Goldman, JP Morgan Chase, Société Générale, Standard Bank Group, and UBS.

Barclays, Deutsche, HSBC, Bank of Nova Scotia, Goldman, Standard Bank and Société Générale have been subject to civil suits over gold price manipulation in gold derivatives, and eight year conspiracy. Trillions of dollars are involved.

What is at issue is the price setting process for gold, silver, platinum and palladium. Benchmark prices for these metals have been set during conference calls, once or twice a day between a few megabanks, which determine a *fixing*. As of 30 September, $120 billion in contracts were outstanding

Barclays, in 2014, was fined £26 million because it manipulated a gold fixing price at the expense of a customer. The Swiss regulator found *serious misconduct* by UBS precious metals traders, which included front running.

	Total (billions)	Notable offenders (billions)
PPI	$40.0 (£26.0)	Lloyds $18.5; Barclays $6.3; RBS $4.8; HSBC $4.3
LIBOR	$6.0	Deutsche $2.5; UBS $1.5
FOREX	$10.0[487]	Barclays $2.4; Citibank $1.3; UBS $1.1
Metals	$170 million	Barclays $26 million

Figure 10 PPI, LIBOR, FOREX and Precious Metals Penalties

By 2015, the approximate fines, penalties and settlements for the PPI, LIBOR, FOREX and Metals scandals were:

Clearly, these fines do not cover the institutional profits derived from the scandals. Something is wrong.

Individual Megabank Fraud (and some others too)

In the 2000s, there was an explosion of fraudulent activity. All megabanks were involved in most of the common forms, and in this section, we describe some of the more egregious activities of some of the megabanks, and some others.

Allied Irish Bank

We remarked before that by 2008, Irish bank assets had risen to eight times the country's GDP, and that Ireland's debt reached 25 times its annual tax revenues. At this time, the world's worst bank, Allied Irish Bank had extended €72 billion in loans, but had lost €30 billion, a quarter of Ireland's annual revenue.

Two executives, John Bowe, head of capital markets and Peter Fitzgerald, head of its retail bank, met with the Irish regulator, the Irish Financial Services Regulatory Authority, the IFSRA to negotiate a €7 billion loan. Bowe and Fitzgerald were caught on tape discussing the loan and knew that it was not nearly enough, and that it would never be repaid. However, they told the IFSRA that it was sufficient. Bowe and Fitzgerald did not want to frighten the regulator, and endanger the bailout. Bowe admitted that it if the bank failed, it would become obvious that someone at the bank had borrowed too much. The bank's CEO, David Drummer, was caught on tape laughing about the bank's abuse of the Irish government's guarantees, and that employees of the bank should take steps to avoid being caught.

The Allied Irish Bank fraud resulted in an Irish government investigation, and the bank was nationalized. The Irish government provided a €30 billion bailout for the bank, and the IMF and EU, €85 billion for Ireland.

Bank of America

BoA reached a settlement with the US regulators in 2014 of $9.5 billion to settle claims that it miss-sold toxic US mortgage bonds between 2005 and 2007. The bank had fraudulently represented that its mortgage products met regulatory guidelines.

BNP Paribas

BNP Paribas agreed that it committed criminal acts and agreed to fines and penalties of $9 billion for breaking sanctions and money laundering between 2004 and 2012. The transitions were on behalf of South Sudan, Iran and Cuba. The first fine of $8.9 billion was agreed in 2012. This penalty was the largest ever imposed in a criminal case against a financial institution. The US authorities also imposed restrictions on the bank making money transfer and clearing transactions. Thirteen employees were terminated, but the FED has said that the game is not over for employees. Sudan was a key part of BNP Paribas' business strategy, so it concealed and falsified the names of the sanctioned countries. Wire fraud. Apart from breaking the law, the bank provided services to countries with appalling human rights abuses, and, in the case of Sudan, assisted its lawless government to harbour and support terrorists and persecute Sudanese citizens. [488] After, 9/11 financial authorities began to crack down heavily on money-laundering. What previously had been merely a criminal matter became an issue of national security since it could disguise the financing of terrorism. This was clearly true in the case of Sudan, and another reason why the penalty was high. It however has had little effect. Although earnings were almost wiped out in 2012, that was it, and shareholder dividends remained unaffected.

Barclays

Barclays has a long history of fraud, of all kinds. Ex-CEO Bob Diamond and ex-Chairman Marcus Agius are discussed in the next section. They resigned as a result of Barclay's involvement in the LIBOR scandal. Barclays also miss-sold interest rate hedging products to small businesses, and has set aside £1.34 billion for compensation claims. Its PPI bill is £4.1 billion and for the forex scandal, it is $2.5 billion.

Citigroup

Recently it has emerged that Citigroup has been systematically underpaying UK Pension Service payments by manipulating the foreign exchange rates for wire transfers to pensioners who live outside the UK.

The UK Pension Service makes pension payments to UK pensioners on a weekly or four weekly basis. Payments made to UK residents are made in £, and payments made to those not resident in the UK are made in the legal tender of the country of residence. Citibank performs payment services for the Pension Service and Citibank Europe is the branch that makes foreign currency remittances. There are approximately 500,000 individuals that receive either weekly or four weekly payments, and the yearly value of these payments is £1.5 billion.

The agreement between the Pension Service and Citibank is that all payments made in foreign currencies are to be determined using the interbank foreign exchange rate on the day the foreign exchange is made, and that there is no offset. Furthermore, payments are to be received within 3 to 5 days. When making payments in foreign currencies, Citibank fraudulently discounts the interbank rate by 5 to 14% in order to profit. This is not in accordance with the agreement between the Pension Service and Citibank. Furthermore, payments are delayed a week or more. The benefit to Citibank is $100 million per year, plus the benefit derived from withholding funds. Who is paying? Pensioners.

When requested, Citibank refused to disclose the payment information. They commented:

> We confirm the mentioned payments have been processed in accordance with DWP's contract with Citi. Please note that the dates mentioned by the recipient do not correspond to the dates in which FX was performed for these payments. As the dates that the

beneficiaries are referencing differ to the actual FX purchase dates, there will always be a variance due to market volatility.

This is rubbish. Firstly, if this were accurate, we would expect swings both ways, with an approximate net effect of zero. Secondly, and saliently, at all times during each of the 11-day periods taken to make the payments, the interbank rate has been significantly higher than the rate used by Citibank.

Subsequent Citibank communications revealed that the bank had little knowledge of what rates to use, how to use them and that they have consistently used rates strongly in their favour. They eventually agreed that they had made a number of egregious errors. They, however, have not been able to provide the details, and have maintained that the problems relate only to Brazil. There has been no justification for this claim, and payments continue to be made late. Ongoing requests for further information elicit responses that do not provide it. It is clear that Citibank have deliberately manipulated rates in order to profit at the expense of pensioners. An action by the UK Financial Services Ombudsman is under consideration.

Crédit Suisse

Crédit Suisse opened Swiss bank accounts for US citizens so that they could evade US taxes. In 2006, 22,000 accounts were held in the name of American customers with balances totalling $12 billion. The Department of Justice forced Crédit Suisse to plead guilty to a crime. Eric Holder, the US Attorney General said, "This case shows that no financial institution, no matter its size or global reach, is above the law." However, unfortunately it was above the law. Crédit Suisse paid a nominal $2.6 billion in penalties, but no-one in the organization's top management was indicted or resigned. Only seven mid-level executives were implicated. The bank refused to name the American customers. There were few other consequences for Crédit Suisse as the SEC waived a rule that forbade a firm convicted of a felony from serving as an investment adviser. In testimony before the Senate Judiciary Committee, Holder said "the size of some of these institutions becomes so large that it does become difficult for us to prosecute them" without endangering the economy. They are too big to jail.

Crédit Suisse was not the only Swiss bank to have helped US citizens evade tax. By mid-2015, fifteen banks have voluntarily agreed to cooperate, and Banque Pasche and Arvest Privatbank have agreed to pay fines in order to avoid criminal charges.

Goldman Sachs

Goldman made a business out of stretching and breaching the fraud envelope. Its business model depended on pigeoning Main Street.

Goldman shorted the housing market at the expense of Main Street by promoting it to its customers. In 2006, it issued GSAMP Trust 2006-S-3, an MBS. GSAMP contained only second mortgages, the average loan to value ratio was 99%, and more than half of the mortgages were no documentation loans. Nevertheless, 68% of GSAMP was rated AAA, and 93%, investment grade. Goldman knew it was junk, bet against it and made a fortune.

Hudson Mezzanine 2006-1 was a $2 billion synthetic CDO that referenced BBB subprime tranches. Goldman used it to remove exposure in its balance sheet, but the prospectus said that the assets were sourced from the Street. It was misrepresentation and fraud. Goldman lied. When Hudson Mezzanine was downgraded, Goldman delayed liquidation until the securities lost more, so that Goldman could make more.

There were sixteen Abacus deals for a total of $1 billion. They were synthetic CDOs, and referenced the worst mortgages available. Abacus 2007 – AC1 was a $2 billion synthetic CDO built for hedge fund manager, John Paulson specifically to pigeon and defraud Main Street. Paulson used it to bet against the housing market and made $4 billion. The Fabulous Fab Tourre designed the deal and wrote the sales materials. The sales materials did not disclose Paulson's involvement, nor that he intended to take the short side, that he had chosen most of the referenced securities, chosen because they were poor quality. The materials lied. The ratings agencies were unaware of Paulson's involvement, and most tranches were given AAA ratings. Before year-end Abacus 2007 was worthless. Goldman agreed to pay $550 million in penalties, and in 2013, the Fabulous Fab was convicted and fined. More on the Fabulous Fab later. Customers lost the $4 billion that Paulson banked, who walked free.

Timberwolf was a simple bet against the housing market, and junk. It was a $1 billion CDO^2. Goldman advertised that it owned equity in Timberwolf, but did not state that it had shorted all the equity and more, with the net effect that it made a large bet against the housing market. Most of it was rated AAA, but became junk in short order. Goldman won, its customers lost.

Goldman did not care who it raped and the havoc it caused. Customers included US public agencies, pension funds, schools and fire departments. While Goldman was profiting by betting against the housing market, Americans were losing jobs and their homes. Not only did Goldman pigeon its customer, it pigeoned Main Street.

HSBC

Whistle blower Hervé Falciani revealed in 2007 that the Swiss branch of HSBC in Geneva had 30,000 accounts in the name of foreigners with assets of $118 billion. This was not the full extent of the problems, and the bank did not disclose this information. It took someone with inside information.

HSBC acted illegally and knew it. They were aware that the accounts were for tax evasion purposes. HSBC aggressively marketed tax-evasion schemes for UK and EU citizens, and advised customers how to evade tax, and circumvent the tax collection authorities. The bank wrote to its customers and advised them of ways to get around the European Savings Directive.[489] The Swiss branch disbursed millions in depositor withdrawals in non Swiss currencies. Why would a depositor who lived in the UK want to withdraw £200,000 in cash, or a French resident €200,000? The money cannot be spent in Switzerland. The deception, fraud and illegal behaviour were extensive and ongoing.

HSBC explained the fraud by claiming that its Swiss branch had not been fully integrated into HSBC after its acquisition in 1999, permitting "significantly lower" standards of compliance and due diligence. This explanation was utter rubbish. It does not take 6 years to get a new acquisition in order, especially in the light of HSBC's policy that it actively seeks out and takes action against internal fraud, and ensures that there is no money laundering nor tax evasion. It was the Geneva branch that facilitated money laundering by HSBC's Mexican City branch in the mid-2000s. In 2005, the bank was fined $1.9 billion dollars for violating sanctions and money laundering, so HSBC senior management were well aware of the problems with the branch. It was on top of the list for "assimilation".

The activities of the Geneva branch were common knowledge among HSBC staff. When the regional head of human resources in Hong Kong was transferred to Geneva, we knew that her job description had changed. Her job was to recruit high net worth customer facilitators.

The UK response to Falciani's revelations have been lax.[490] HM Revenue & Customs received the leaked data in 2010, has prosecuted only one individual and recovered only £135 million of the £20 billion in the 6,800 accounts with UK addresses.[491] France has recovered £188 million (3,000 customers), Spain, £220 million

(2,700 customers, $2.3 billion), and Australia, £15 million. France, the US and Argentina have begun criminal actions, and the Belgians will issue international arrest warrants for the directors of HSBC. In the UK, The Commons Public Accounts Committee announced that it will hold an inquiry, and the former director of public prosecutions, Lord Ken Macdonald QC has stated that there was sufficient evidence for the bank to be investigated for conspiracy to defraud the UK tax authorities.

Why has the UK recovered so little and not acted more aggressively? HM Revenue failed to warn that there was significant evidence of misconduct at HSBC's Swiss branch when asked to vet Steven Green's suitability for his ministerial appointment, which should have never been made. HM Revenue received the leaked documents eight months prior to his appointment. But then again HM Revenue's head of tax took a consulting job at HSBC after he retired from the Revenue. Cannot let the law and morals interfere with one's income can we? The Conservatives wanted Green on board for a trade development role and soliciting donations. In with $1 one vote and out with one person one vote. During Green's tenure, HSBC had also been involved in money laundering for drug cartels, and the provision of services for Saudi and Bangladeshi banks linked to financing terrorists.

On 2nd September 2015, HSBC's problem became more severe. The Argentinian central bank ordered that HSBC's local chief executive must be removed within 24 hours, and accused the bank of tax evasion, money laundering and financing terrorist activities. In late 2014, HSBC Argentina was accused of helping 400 clients evade Argentinian taxes and hiding money in Switzerland. In March 2015, Argentina ordered HSBC to return $3.5 billion held in offshore accounts. HSBC has denied the charges and says in complies with Argentinian law.

It appears that HSBC provides a full service, global tax avoidance and evasion service to its customers, including the provisions of debit and credit cards that enable customers to draw down balances held in foreign domiciled accounts.

HSBC has admitted accountability for its past transgressions, issued numerous apologies, and promised to make changes. However, another whistle blower, Sue Shelley, the head of compliance at HSBC Luxembourg has denied that changes have been made. In 2013, she was dismissed when she drew this to the attention of her senior managers. Her comments were vindicated by an employment tribunal where she won an action against the bank for unfair dismissal.

In 2014, HSBC paid $550 million to the US regulators to settle claims that it miss sold toxic US mortgage bonds to the GSEs in the lead up to the Crisis. HSBC had fraudulently represented $6.2 billion in MBS as meeting the regulatory guidelines. This bought the total recouped by the GSEs to $17.9 billion of the toxic mortgages $30 billion loss that lead to the GSE bailout.[492] This on top of the 2012 UK $1.9 billion fine for money laundering.

Instituto per le Opere di Religione, IOR

The IOR is the Vatican bank. In June 2013, Monsignor Nunzio Scarano, Monsignor Cinuecento,[493] the head of accounting at the organization that managed the Vatican's property holdings was arrested. The charge, money laundering. Although his annual stipend was €36,000, he had €2.3 million in his bank accounts, and owned a spectacular art collection that he kept in his 17 room apartment located in one of Rome's most prodigious areas.

Nefarious activity at the IOR was well known. There was little transparency nor accountability. Large amounts of cash, from collection plates, (25% of the IOR's business was in cash) were deposited daily, and the IOR covertly makes transfers to churches and voluntary groups in poor countries and failed states without functioning banking systems. In 2013, the religious orders had on deposit $3.1billion. However, a system designed to get money secretly to difficult places has a downside. It invites criminal activity.

An arrest warrant for the bank's chairman in the 1970s and 1980s, Archbishop Paul Marcinkus for complicity in fraudulent activity could not be executed, as the good archbishop went into hiding in the sovereign Vatican state. His colleague Roberto Calvi, president of the Banco Ambrosiano of Milan fled Italy on a false passport, and in 1982 was found dead under Blackfriars Bridge in London. Calvi had mafia connections, and in 1982, the Banco Ambrosiano had collapsed. Its main shareholder was the Vatican bank, and one its directors was Marcinkus.

The Vatican bank is an obvious target for criminal activity, the European Union persuaded the Bank of Italy to investigate, and all banks in Italy were forced to close their IOR accounts. Deutsche Bank managed the Vatican State's 80 cash machines and credit card terminals, and closed them on 1 January 2013, and the council of Europe's anti-money-laundering body announced the Vatican bank was non-compliant. Finally, the office of president was given to a partner in the regulatory compliance firm, Promontory Financial Group. An examination of the Vatican bank's 19,000 accounts resulted in the closure of 3,300 and found 200 serious irregularities.

JP Morgan Chase

Jamie Dimon has presided over the largest ever crime spree. Total fines and penalties, $62 billion, three times the amount required to by Dell computer. The bank was penalized $18.1 billion ($9 billion in fines, $4 to homeowners and $5.1 to the GSEs) in 2013 to settle claims arising from the bank's misrepresentation of toxic mortgage products. The possibility of criminal charges for these claims remains. Another $2.5 billion was paid to avoid unrelated criminal charges, and another $1.0 billion in fines resulted from the London whale incident. Another $4.5 billion went to institutional investors, and provisions for legal costs by 2015 were $23 billion. The bank truly played on. More later when we discuss Jamie.

Lehman

Lehman's Repo 105 was fraud and used to increase profits and bonuses. Lehman's liar loans were fraud. Lehman and Fuld knowingly bankrolled lenders who made toxic loans. We have more to say when we discuss Dick in the next section.

Morgan Stanley

In March 2007, Morgan Stanley sold a toxic tranche of a synthetic CDO, Libertas, rated AAA-, to the Pension Fund of the Virgin Islands. Morgan Stanley knew the tranche was worthless, used it to bet against the market, and pocketed $82 million from the sale of the investment and fees. The Pension Fund sued Morgan Stanley and claimed that it had misrepresented the quality of the mortgages, knew that the tranche was toxic and very likely to fail, and that Morgan Stanley had bet against the market. Morgan Stanley settled with the Pension Fund.

Libertas set a new standard for fraud, and was similar to many securitizations that the other megabanks sold to customers.

RBS

In July 2015, the UK Chancellor of the Exchequer, George Osborne, confirmed the UK government's decision to sell more RBS shares. This tranche of shares was sold at a £1bn loss. The loss would have been £15bn if all shares were sold. The shares were at a low for the year, and the sale actually created a new low. Osborne's justification of the loss was rubbish: "it will promote financial stability, lead to a more competitive banking sector, and support the interests of the wider economy. Now is the time for RBS to rebuild itself as a commercial bank, no longer reliant on the state, but serving the working people of Britain." However, Osborne's efforts to sell off both RBS and Lloyds Banking Group were motivated by his bid for leadership of the Tory party. It is a further example of how the UK taxpayers are defrauded on an ongoing basis.

When RBS was fined £390 million for its involvement in the LIBOR scandal, John Hourigan, the head of its investment bank resigned, and he waived £7.5 million in stock and cash bonuses. Not a big problem for John as he kept £5 million in past bonuses. Both RBS and John denied that he had any knowledge of the scandal. Strange. If he really had no knowledge, why would he leave and forgo the bonuses? Or perhaps he had no knowledge and simply could not do his job.

Standard Chartered Bank

Standard Chartered Bank laundered money on behalf of terrorist organizations, drug cartels and Iran. The bank laundered $250 billion. The bank paid a settlement of $340 million. There are ongoing investigations, and the bank has since been fined $300 million for further money laundering offences for customers in Hong Kong and the UAE.

UBS

UBS's Kweko Adoboli was a 32 year old London trader at UBS. Between October 2008 and September 2011, he exercised unhedged, reckless trades, and accrued losses of £1.4 billion. His maximum exposure to losses was £7.5 billion. He was accused of being a gambler who thought he had the Midas touch. Adoboli said he lost control during the Crisis, and had been pressured by his superiors to change his positions and strategy. He testified that they were aware at all times of his activities, and that he was a fall guy. The prosecution claimed he intentionally violated the bank's trading rules, that he lied, and that he was dishonest. As the loss was large, it was not a victimless crime. Clearly is it inconceivable that his actions were unknown to his superiors. He was convicted and jailed for seven years.

In 2015, the Commercial Court in the UK found UBS and UBS personnel guilty of serious misconduct. UBS had sold derivatives to a German water utility, Kommunate Wasserwerke Leipzig, KWL. The products made KWL a provider of credit protection to UBS. It received premiums for the privilege. The products sustained losses, and UBS sued KWL and two intermediaries for $340 million for loss recoveries. KWL had abrogated any obligation of the products.

UBS, however, had made numerous misrepresentations that included that the products were 'virtually risk free', that the risk of default was indicated by the credit ratings, and that the transactions reduced risk. KWL should not have invested in complex derivatives, and UBS was help responsible for bribery and dishonesty that led to KWL to doing so, and entirely accountable, and their claims dismissed.

In 2015, Tom Hayes was jailed for 14 years for manipulating LIBOR, the bank was fined $1.5 billion for its participation in the LIBOR scandal and paid a $500 million settlement for helping US citizens evade US taxes. Tom has claimed that he did not act alone and that his managers were well aware of his activities.

Clearly, UBS senior management were aware of these activities. Why were they not prosecuted?

Individual Fraudsters

Many individuals stole, laundered money, manipulated rates and the market, assisted tax evasion, and so on. It is clear that many politicians, including Bill Clinton, Gordon Brown, George Bush and other senior leaders pursued policies that pushed the globe towards the Crisis, however, their actions, if misguided, were hardly criminal, so they are not singled out. Some of the very large cast of characters have been prosecuted, but most have not. We will begin the list with some of those that have been prosecuted. We will list only one or two of the most egregious offences.

Individuals that have been prosecuted

- Ralph Cioffi and Matthew Tannin managed the Bear Stearns hedge funds that collapsed in mid-2007. They mislead investors and agreed to a settlement of $1 million to settle SEC charges.
- The CEOs at the GSEs are being prosecuted for fraud. They benefited from misstated revenues, which they used to pay themselves higher bonuses, and mislead investors.

- Geir Haarde, once Prime Minister of Iceland, is the only politician to be prosecuted and convicted. He ignored the warnings that announced the Crisis. Iceland collapsed.
- As we noted, UBS trader Tom Hayes, the first of perhaps 11 others, was convicted and jailed for 14 years for manipulating LIBOR. Tom claimed that his seniors were aware of his activities, and that he was following orders.
- Nick Leeson, even though Bearings dysfunctional management was part of the problem, fraudulently gambled and hid his losses. The bank failed. He was jailed.
- James Martigione re-stated $18 billion as $1.8 billion in order to enhance his bonus. He was jailed.
- Salomon's Paul Mozer created sham transactions in order to hide profits, and manipulated Treasury auctions. Mozer was jailed, Salomon removed its top four executives, and the company was acquired before failure.
- It would appear that Angelo Mozilo, Countrywide's CEO, was a compulsive liar, whose flashy, tasteless attire distracted attention from his vacuity. He was charged with insider trading, concealing information, securities fraud and failure to make discloses of Countrywide's lax standards. He paid $67.5 million to settle SEC claims, most of which was paid by BoA, Countrywide's acquirer.
- Goldman's Fabulous Fab, Tourre wrote the sales materials for John Paulson's bet against the housing market. The materials lied. Uninformed investors lost billions. Goldman paid a fine, of $550 million, and the Fabulous Fab was convicted of providing miss-leading information and penalized $850,000 ($650,000 in civil fines, the balance in clawed back bonuses and interest). Goldman paid his legal fees, but was prohibited from paying the penalties.

> a big fine cannot hide the government's "indefensible" failure to have brought criminal charges against senior Wall Street executives over the financial crisis … Wall Street recklessness, fraud and criminality were at the core of the crash and crisis … History will judge prosecutors and regulators harshly for abdicating their duty to enforce the law without fear or favour on Wall Street as they do on Main Street[494]

Individuals that were not prosecuted

Very many more individuals were involved in criminal activities and fraud, but have not been prosecuted. We list only some of choice examples:

- Lloyd Blankfein was Goldman's CEO after Hank Paulson. Blankfein's tenor at Goldman confirms that stupidity and lack of neural matter are not necessarily impediments to becoming rich. He is accountable for the fraudulent products that Goldman developed and sold, and for making Jamie Dimon style ludicrous, self-serving and unjustified claims. He echoed Alan Greenspan's remark about the Crisis being a once is a 100 year event. He was the lead pigeoner.

- Joe Cassano was AIG FP's CEO and a basket case liar who had no understanding of credit derivatives. He misrepresented the risks in CDSs, did not disclose AIG FP's collateral calls, marked up positions without justification and prevented AIG FP's CDS portfolio from being evaluated. CDS were bets that resulted in AIG's downfall. He walked away will a small fortune, which should be clawed back. He should be behind bars.

- Jimmy Cayne, the pre-Crisis CEO of Bear Stearns, was absent most of the time, a benefit, playing bridge and allegedly indulging in white powder habits, a charge which he denies. When in the office, he was asleep. CNBC named him the worst CEO ever. Cayne bought $40 billion in mortgage bonds that were worthless. Who knows what to do with him? He was certainly a large part of Bear's failure and the losses incurred by investors and customers. They should be clawed back.

- Kathleen Corbet was the pre-Crisis CEO of S&P. She resigned in 2007. She was a driver behind S&P's policies. She admitted that the S&P ratings for structured products were pointless, but an essential piece of S&P's strategy. Money first, ratings second. The agencies gave AAA ratings to toxic securities. She exploited the conflicts of interest. She and her co-executives were irresponsible, acted fraudulently, and should not be free.

- James Crosby, the chief executive of HBOS, appeared before a British Parliamentary Commission on Banking Standards, which found that HBOS' three top officers, Crosby, Andy Hornby, and Lord Dennis Stevenson, were entirely responsible for the failure of the bank, and guilty of a "colossal failure" of management. Although the HBOS regulator found them guilty of *very serious misconduct,* they remain free. HBOS received a £20.5 billion bailout before being taken over by Lloyds TSB and its shareholders were wiped out. Crosby is still creating havoc. Why is he free?

- Bob Diamond, when CEO of Barclays ignored the bank's role in LIBOR manipulation. He appeared before a House of Commons Select Committee in order to explain the debacle and his only defence, apart from denying that he knew what was going on, was that manipulation was not in Barclay's culture. Barclay's has suffered enormous fines.
- Jamie Dimon heads a crime ring at JP Morgan Chase. He is not a defender of the truth as he claims, but a defender of deception. When at first he denied there was a problem, he later admitted, "We made a terrible egregious mistake" in respect of the London Whale event, and that it was not a *tempest in a teapot*. The bank's shareholders paid JP Morgan Chase's fines and penalties of $62 billion. Dimon's compensation during the period when the problems occurred was about $150 million. He thinks regulation is anti-American. Why is he a free man?
- Stephen Friedman, a past CEO of Goldman, while chairman of the NY FED and a Goldman board member at the time that the FED was propping it up, leveraged his insider knowledge and bought shares in Goldman. Insider trading. He resigned in May 2009 when the Wall Street Journal announced the conflict of interest. The incident was a disgrace. He should be prosecuted.
- Dick Fuld drove Lehman into the subprime business and bankruptcy. He bankrolled lenders who made poor loans and underwrote 90% of the fraudulent liar loans. Lehman's fraudulent Repo 105s were used to increase profits and bonuses. Fuld lied to Congress about $500 million paid to him as compensation. He claimed it was $300 million. He remains rich and lives in a Florida palace. His ill-gotten gains should be clawed back. He should not be free.
- Fred Goodwin (Fred the Shred, he cut costs) the megalomaniac and greedy CEO of RBS made the bank the largest in the world, by acquisition, after which RBS made the largest all time loss for a UK company. The attempted acquisition of ABN AMRO, exhausted RBS's capital. When the UK government took the bank over (£30 billion), it was the largest banking takeover of all time. Fred Goodwin was the *world's worst banker*. His pension pool should be clawed back. Where to put him? He would probably find a way to bankrupt his jail.
- Senator Phil Gram was a disgraceful, misguided free market zealot who saw subprime lending as part of the American Dream. He remains unrepentant. "I don't see any evidence that allowing them [the banks] to affiliate

through holding companies had anything to do with the financial crisis nor has anyone presented any evidence to suggest that it did". After Washington, he joined the board of UBS. He was on another planet, and crossed the line. He should be banned from politics and the financial industry for life.

- Steven Green, the CEO of HSBC was fully aware of the bank's Geneva branches' tax evasion schemes. As CEO, he would have had to sign off on them. Part of his job was to coordinate HSBC's fraud detection programs, and all significant activities of the Geneva branch were reported to him. Furthermore, large cash disbursements initiated at any branch, and for any purpose, are reported to the chairman. Why was Steven made a government minister (from 2010 to 2013) and a Lord of the Realm? He refuses to talk. Why was he not prosecuted? Why is he free?

- Greenspan became Washington's financial wizard, the Oracle as a result of the rapid US recovery from the 1987 stock market crash, and the economic and market boom of the 1990s. He was in the right place at the right time. Alan Greenspan abrogated his responsibilities and relied upon faith-based economics. He ignored regulation and assumed it was not needed. He abrogated his responsibilities, and mislead anyone who would listed. His efforts substantially contributed to the Crisis. Why is he a free man? The question is jail or an asylum.

- Stuart Gulliver became CEO of HSBC after Steven Green and was part of most of the bank's problems. He had his bonuses paid into a bank account at the Geneva subsidiary of HSBC, and then disguised this by resorting to a Panamanian company. He told us that he wished to hide his compensation from his HSBC Hong Kong colleagues. This is sanctimonious rubbish. Employees at HSBC Hong Kong often choose to share their compensation with each other. They want to ensure that salaries and bonuses are aligned with responsibilities and performance, and are fair. This is especially so at board level where compensation is discussed and agreed. Consequently, it's an easy matter to hide one's compensation. Non-staff accounts are commonly used. Accounts at other Hong Kong banks are used. I know. My colleagues and I did just this. In any case, if Gulliver wanted to hide his compensation, and did not want to use these options, why not use an HSBC UK or US account? Why would you have a bank account in Switzerland if you do not live there? Because you want to hide money. There is the issue of Swiss bank secrecy laws. If you reveal customer account information, you are out the revolving front door quicker than lightening. So why Panama? Gulliver earned £7.6 million in 2014 and £8 million in 2013. These numbers are outrageous, as are the other HSBC 2014 bonuses. In 2014, 330 HSBC staff were paid a minimum bonus of €1 million, £750,000 each. In response to questions about his responsibility and accountability for the bank's continued malfeasance, he says that he could not know what 257,000 employees were doing. If he cannot do his job, why does he remain CEO and accept absurd compensation? Despite a commitment for enhanced vigilance after the HSBC's Swiss subsidiary debacle, HSBC Argentina, in 2015, came under fire for tax evasion and money laundering. Apparently, Gulliver did not know about the activities of one of his senior appointments. Or did he? HSBC is a UK bank. How can its CEO escape UK residency? Does he manage by helicopter, by remote control?

- James Johnson was a gangster who bribed members of Congress to support the GSEs. Another Nicolas Biddle. As a result, he became a rich man. The GSE taxpayer costs were greater than $80 billion. His compensation should be clawed back. Why is he free? See below the entry for Franklin Raines.

- John Mack learned during a job interview with Credit Suisse in Zurich that Heller Financial, a client of Credit Suisse, was about to be acquired by General Electric. Mack told Art Samberg, a hedge fund manager and Samberg bought all the shares in Heller that he could get his hands on. Samberg made $18 million.[495] In return, Samberg put Mack into the Lucent deal that he was managing, and Mack made $10 million. Obvious insider trading. Because Mack had "powerful political connections", the SEC wanted to turn a blind eye. The SEC investigator, Gary Aguirre was fired when he pursued Mack and Samberg, but subsequently, he was awarded $755,000 for wrongful dismissal.

- Stan O'Neal was incompetent and abrogated his responsibilities. During his term as CEO, Merrill amassed $41 billion as a result of his actions. He was irresponsible and acted without board authority. He is accountable for the losses that Main Street paid for. Thankfully, he played golf most of the time, and the losses were not greater. His compensation should be clawed back.

- When George Bush left the White House, his economic record was dismal (deregulation, poor regulation of mortgage brokers, the GSEs, Enron). Hank Paulson's appointment as Secretary of the Treasury was one of the worst decisions Bush made. He was late to the party in battling the financial crisis, he let Lehman fail and the bailouts were a mess. He lied to Congress, failed to do his job, and made fraudulent representations. He went on a recruiting spree when he found that he could not do his job, and recruited many Goldman executives to do it for him. Moreover, he is accountable for the fraudulent products that Goldman sold. He was a major part of the Crisis. He is still rich and free. His net worth should be clawed back.

- John Paulson constructed a securitization that was designed to fail. It was incredulous that Goldman supported him. He made $4 billion and Main Street paid for it. This should be clawed back and he should be in jail.

- Chuck Prince, CEO of Citigroup authorized products that avoided capital requirements. His actions resulted in $45 billion in losses to Citigroup. Sandy Weill said that his choice of Prince as Citigroup CEO was one of his worst decisions ever. Prince is accountable for the losses. Vikram Pandit continued the practice and aggressively pushed Citigroup towards bankruptcy.

- Franklin Raines was the CEO of Fannie during the years when the company "intentionally manipulated [revenues] to trigger management bonuses". Raines was guilty of accounting fraud, and revenues were restated by $6.3 billion. Raines' compensation from 1998 to 2003 was $90 million, $52 million of which was tied to phony accounting. He kept it all. When he was fired, he was given a $25 million severance payment. The payments should be clawed back, and Raines held accountable.

- Nicholas Ridley was responsible for Northern Rock's strategy, and failure. A Treasury Select Committee described the strategy as high-risk and reckless, and explicitly held Ridley accountable as "having failed to provide against the risks that [Northern Rock] was taking and to act as an effective restraining force on the strategy of the executive members". Ridley thinks that greed is good, and that the successes of the rich enrich the poor. He is not remorseful and a hypocrite. While describing governments as "self-seeking flea[s] on the backs of the more productive people in the world … [they] are a "parasitic bureaucracy", he asked for a huge bailout from the UK flea Government. He should be in jail and his earnings clawed back.

- Robert Rubin failed to deal with derivatives deregulation because, it would appear, he wanted to return to Wall Street. He did not want to upset his future paymasters and he wanted to safeguard the revenues of his future employer, Citigroup. He enhanced his personal wealth at the expense of the taxpayer. When he returned to Wall

Street, he sold influence for Citigroup and made a fortune, $100 million.

Summary of Fines, Penalties and Settlements

The fines, penalties and settlements paid from 2009 through 2014 came to $335 billion! There is more to come. For the UK alone, the projection for 2016 is $30 billion. The major offenders, 2009 to 2014, were: JP Morgan Chase, $62 billion, Lloyds, $30 billion, RBS, $14 billion, Barclays and Citigroup $13 billion each and HSBC, $12 billion.

Conclusions

Since the 1980s, the banking industry has been home to egregiously fraudulent activity. To put it bluntly, "fleecing the public is not an aberration, it's the business model"[496].

We listed above three customized derivatives sold in the 1990s. US investors that were not permitted to invest in foreign currencies invested in the Thai baht. AMITs hid losses from regulators and shareholders and Canadian dollar swaps enabled Japanese insurance companies to invest, fraudulently, in the Japanese stock market. Standardized derivatives like quantos simply made fraud easier. There are thousands of other examples where banks capable of building customized derivatives, or hedging the parts of standardized derivatives, the megabanks, acted fraudulently, and enabled their customers to do so as well. Anyone prosecuted? Only Robert Citron, of Orange County, and his assistant, who were targets of fraud themselves. Derivatives activity has since been minimally constrained, but continues to be a significant profit generator for megabanks, and others.

PPI was institutionalised fraud, and while its victims have been (perhaps only partially) compensated, no senior executives have been held to task. While LIBOR, FOREX and precious metals rates' manipulation was undertaken by junior employees, their employers and senior management were culpable. Their senior executives knew of the abuse, condoned it, and their organizations, the shareholders, paid the penalties. Given the recent spate of fines and penalties imposed on the megabanks, and the changes to the rates fixing procedures, we may have closed the book on the current LIBOR, FOREX and precious metals scandals, however, rates based institutional fraud can arise in many circumstances ranging from ATM transactions, bulk foreign exchange transactions and loan origination.

There are thousands of cases of institutional and individual fraud. Many megabanks, including Barclays, Citigroup, Crédit Suisse JP Morgan Chase, RBS and UBS have admitted criminal fraud. However, very few executives have been punished. The few that have are listed in *Individuals that have been Prosecuted* above. Penalizing shareholder dividends and reducing capital simply weakens an institution, and does not penalize the perpetrators of fraud. This is moral hazard, pure and simple, and the perpetrators are incentivised to commit more fraud. There is upside, but little downside. Individual fraud continues unabated. Why? The banking oligarchy is all powerful.

When penalties are imposed on institutions, the shareholders pay, however, the recent fines are dwarfed by profits. For this reason, the fines have little direct impact, as shareholders barely notice them. Fines reduce capital, the banking industry as a whole is short of capital, and all the megabanks need to put on substantial capital, in the near term. Again, this has little impact. Investors look forward not back. Disclosure is in the hands of the megabanks.

Angelo Mozilo had an agreement with Countrywide that made penalties imposed on him an obligation of Countrywide. When BoA acquired Countrywide, this obligation fell to BoA and it paid his settlement. It had little effect on Mozilo. He remains rich and out of jail. When the Fabulous Fab was punished, the Department of Justice ensured that he had to pay the penalties himself. It is unacceptable that an employer should pay the penalties assessed on an employee. When an employee is found guilty of an offence by a court, it is also an offence in the eyes of the employer. Mozilo was accused of insider trading, concealing information, securities fraud and failure to make disclosures. These offences were both SEC and Countrywide offences. Mozilo should have also paid a settlement to Countywide! Arrangements where employers pay fines and penalties for employees, or otherwise indemnify them, must be banished.

If we are to eliminate fraud executed by employees, we need to hold accountable the senior executives and boards of directors. If these officers are held monetarily liable for the full extent of the fraud, including consequential damages, and are subject to jail sentences, they would be highly incentivised to ensure that employees do not engage in fraud. There are precedents, CFOs and CEOs are fully responsible for financial statements. Partners in partnerships that are not limited are fully liable for the actions of the partnerships.

Senior executives of the megabanks are charged with ensuring their organisations act with integrity. In cases of fraud, rather than accept the word of senior people that they were not involved nor aware, it makes sense, if persecutors require it, for them to have to demonstrate this in a court, according to court evidential rigour. The expectation that this would be an outcome of fraud executed by juniors would incentivize all senior officers to put in place procedures that would reveal fraud.

We listed in the final section of chapter 9 what needs to be done. Some of these things are technical in nature, for example, eliminating casino banking and off balance sheet entities, adopting the Volker and similar rules which split retail from investment banking, constraining exposures to the short term-debt markets and assessing the amount of capital, and what counts as capital. We must eliminate predatory banking. Banks must be made to invest in technology. The insane reliance on models must change, including the reliance on pointless metrics like VaR. Risk management functions must do their job. Products that serve no purpose must be eliminated. The environment in which banks operate must change. We must reform how the ratings agencies, consultants and auditors perform.

There are also issues of acceptable practices like corporate governance, accountability and ethical standards, and the need to ensure that CEOs and senior executives function independently from the board of directors. To these we must add making illegal any agreements where employers indemnify employees and holding senior executives of megabanks responsible for fraud committed under their watch.

However, the above reforms will only help to eliminate fraud if we tackle the underlying, fundamental problems, and to do this we need political change. We need to constrain compensation. We need to ensure that investing and risk taking do not prejudice our entitlement to human rights like food, shelter, freedom of speech and healthcare. We need to halt the encroachment of plutocracy and return to democracy. We need to dismantle the oligarchy, including its servants, the megabanks, and shut down the revolving door between government policy makers and Wall Street, and we need to limit lobbying.

For eighty years housing, a human right, was subject to minimal speculation, speculation that benefitted home owners. Housing appreciated, and kept pace with inflation. Since the 1990s, speculation has spread to investors and risk takers, and become egregious, and homeowners have paid an enormous price. We cannot permit the post 1990s speculation in housing to continue which means that we must find a way to finance it without inviting speculation. There are many ways to do this, including regulation and taxation.[497] In our opening remarks, we quoted Danny Dorling on hoarding food. It is not acceptable and violates humanitarian sensibilities. Human rights overrule national legislation, [498] and national legislation governs how we can participate in the financial markets, accumulate capital and invest.

Banker's compensation needs to be revamped and substantially reduced. Senior bankers neither earn nor deserve their incomes, which they determine themselves. There is no correlation between megabank performance and senior executive compensation. Megabank senior executives are part of the underachieving, non-earning, rent seeking top 1% of income takers who plunder the remaining 99%. Limiting the variable part of bankers' compensation helps but does not eliminate the problem. The fixed element can be increased. Furthermore, fixed components can be manipulated. An example: an employee accepts fixed compensation of $1,200,000 per annum with a discretionary bonus of 100%. The fixed component is not paid, as one would expect, by twelve $100,000 monthly payments, but by twelve $50,000 monthly payments, plus a single additional payment in the twelfth month of $600,000. There is a condition. If the employee's targets are not made, then the final $600,000 can be clawed back, and no bonus paid. Total compensation is $600,000. If the targets are made, then the final $600,000 is not clawed back, and the bonus of $1,200,000 is paid. Total compensation is $2,400,000. Structuring compensation in this way appears to limit the variable compensation element to the EU's 100% limit, however, it's in fact an agreement to pay a fixed element of $600,000 with a variable component of 3 times the fixed component.

The solution to the compensation problem means ensuring that senior bankers cannot determine their own compensation. Ensuring that bankers do not determine their own compensation requires that the notion of fixed compensation is defined, so that games like the one described above cannot be played, and limiting bonuses to a percentage of fixed compensation. How do we limit the fixed element? Senior bankers, by being bankers must not be members of the rent seeking top 1%. Absent eliminating the banking oligarchy, this remains a problem.

Most of the individuals prosecuted, those currently under investigation, did not hold senior positions, and most of those that have not been prosecuted were at the top of their organizations. Dismantling the oligarchy will ensure that the financial sector will no longer be able to buy political influence, and will enable the prosecution of these individuals.

We can reduce the impact of the banking oligarchy by removing lobbyists, limiting political contributions, including re-election contributions, removing crony capitalism trade-offs like power and influence for money, and removing the Wall Street –

Parkway/City of London revolving door. Breaking up the megabanks and strengthening the regulation of the financial markets will reduce the influence of the oligarchy. Eliminating pointless innovation will take one of its tools away. Just under 32,000 Americans, 0.1% of the population, gave an astounding $1.18 billion in disclosed political contributions in the 2014 midterm elections. This is more than 25% raised by the fundraising organizations, the political action committees, etc., from just 31,976 people. The trend is growing.

Eric Holder was wrong when, referring to Crédit Suisse, he said, "the size of some of these institutions becomes so large that it does become difficult for us to prosecute them without endangering the economy". He was referring to the $2.8 billion penalty and the bank's felony guilty plea for helping US residents evade tax on balances of $12 billion. The bank's shareholders paid the penalty, and the senior executives went free. Holding the executives accountable would not have endangered the economy. Removing the senior executives would mean removing some of the dangers to the economy. Waiving the SEC rule that forbids a firm convicted of a felony from serving as an investment adviser, and allowing Crédit Suisse to continue unabated, kept the fraud-perpetrating machine in business.

Although the Crisis invigorated financial fraud, and some individuals are being prosecuted today, fraud continues. Before we close, let us finalize the Bangster Awards.

The Final Bangster Awards

Sebastien, the chief judge has approved the following Bangster Awards. They are:

Bangsters		Gold Stars
Nicholas Biddle	Goldman Sachs	Franklin D Roosevelt
JP Morgan	Hank Paulson	Louis Brandeis
James Johnson	Dick Fuld	Raghuram Rajan
Alan Greenspan	Stan O'Neil	Barney Frank
Angelo Mozilo	Joe Cassano	Sheila Bair
Jimmy Cayne	James Crosby	Joseph Stiglitz
Mat Ridley	Andy Hornby	Robert Shiller
John Paulson	Fred Goodwin	Paul Volker
Morgan Stanley	Senator Phil Gram	Paul Krugman
Jamie Diamond	Larry Summers	
Hank Paulson	Kathleen Corbett	
Robert Rubin	Steven Green	

John Mack   Andy Hornby

Lloyd Blankfein   Stuart Gulliver

Robert Rubin failed to deal with derivatives deregulation. It appears because he preferred to enhance his personal wealth at the expense of the taxpayer. John Mack was guilty of insider trading. He avoided prosecution because had had "powerful political connections". Lloyd Blankfein authorized fraudulent products. He was Goldman's, Chief pigeoner. He said he was doing god's work! Steven Green was aware of the bank's tax evasion schemes, and ignored large cash disbursements. Corruption. He was made a government minister, and with the help of HM Revenue, a Lord of the Realm. Stuart Gulliver hid money in Switzerland, and despite his compensation package and position, told us that he did not know what his staff were doing. There are many more, of course.

Recent history has shown that we can expect banking fraud for as long as dollars vote, for as long as we allow the banking oligarchy to remain intact, determine the rules, and permit fraud related moral hazard. If we can achieve the political goal of eliminating the oligarchy then we will be on our way to eliminating individual and institutional fraud. Breaking apart the banking oligarchy will remove senior bankers from the rent seeking top 1%. Piketty has shown that if we do not, we will be closer to a return to the age of hereditary wealth.[499]

Taxation will help us do this. We do not have to incentive the rent seeking 1% by making it easier for them to accumulate capital.

Our short story must now come to an end, with a call for action. If we do not act, we can expect the plutocracy to encroach on democracy, and the rent seeking 1% to take an ever increasing share of income from the 99%. The 0.1% will take even more.

Glossary

Name	Who or What?
AIG	American International Group
Alan Greenspan	Chairman of the Federal Reserve Bank, 1987 to 2006
Alexander Hamilton	President Washington's Secretary of the Treasury
Alt-A mortgage	A mortgage that fell between a prime mortgage and subprime mortgage
Andrew Jackson	Seventh President of the United States, 1829 to 1837
ARMS	Adjustable rate mortgage, where the interest rate to be paid varies over time
Barack Obama	Forty-fourth President of the United States, 2009 to 2016, and President at the time of writing
Barings Bank	The oldest British merchant bank that failed
Bear	Bear Sterns
Ben Bernanke	Chairman of the Federal Reserve Bank, 2006 to 2014
BIS	Bank for International Settlements, the organization that houses the Basel machinery
Black-Scholes (model)	A way to evaluate options
BoA	Bank of America
BoE	Bank of England, the UK central bank
Brian Moynihan	Chairman of Bank of America, 2010 to present
CDO	A collateralised debt obligation is a securitization, where pieces of debt are packaged together, divided into tranches and sold to investors
CDS	Credit default swap
Conduit	An entity used by a bank to hold OBS items, they may be permanent or temporary. Temporary conduits pass their assets to SIVs and SPVs
Conforming mortgage	A mortgage that could be sold to the GSEs

Countrywide	For a time, the largest US mortgage lender that was acquired by Bank of America as it collapsed during the Crisis
Deutsche	Deutsche Bank
ECB	European Central Bank, the central bank of the Eurozone states, the states that use the Euro as a currency
EU	European Union, which is comprised of 28 member states (at the time of writing), and which are mostly in Europe
Eurozone	The 19 European states (at the time of writing) that use the Euro as a currency
Exotic mortgage	A mortgage, typically subprime with a range of payment alternatives
FCIC	Financial Crisis Inquiry Commission
FDIC	Federal Deposit Insurance Company
FED	Federal Reserve Bank, the US central bank
FHFA	Federal Housing Finance Authority
Fitch	A ratings agency (NRSRA)
FSOC	Financial Stability Oversight Council
Goldman	Goldman Sachs, the investment bank
GSA	Glass Steagall Act
GSEs	The Government Sponsored Entities, Fannie Mae and Freddy Mac
GW Bush	President of the United States, 2000 to 2008
Hank Paulson	Secretary of the US Department of the Treasury, 2006 to 2009 Chairman of Goldman Sachs, 1998 to 2006
HBOS	From Halifax + Bank of Scotland, but generally known as HBOS, and one of the poorly managed Crisis casualties in the UK
Herstatt	A German bank that went bankrupt in 1973 that was a Basel trigger
IMF	The International Monetary Fund
J Pierpont Morgan	The most influential individual in the US financial sector prior to World War I
James A Johnson	CEO of Fannie Mae, 1991to 1999
Jamie Dimon	Chairman of JP Morgan Chase
John Mack	Chairman of Morgan Stanley, 2005 to 2010
Lehman	Lehman Brothers, the investment bank
Lloyd Blankfein	Chairman of Goldman Sachs from 2006 to present
Lloyds	Lloyds Banking Group or Lloyds TSB
Louis Brandeis	US Supreme Court

LTCM	Long Term Credit Management, a hedge fund that failed
Main Street	Many small American towns have a Main street, the town's *main* street. We use the term to mean *average American.*
MBS	Mortgage backed security is a securitization, where pieces of mortgage debt are packaged together, divided into tranches and sold to investors
Merrill	Merrill Lynch
Moody's	A ratings agency (NRSRA)
Nicholas Biddle	Head of the Second Bank of the United States
Northern Rock	A building society which became a deposit taker bank and one of the poorly managed Crisis casualties in the UK
NRSRA	Nationally recognized Statistical ratings Agency
OCC	Office of the Comptroller of the Currency
Off Balance Sheet, or OBS	A bank asset or liability which is not shown on a bank's balance sheet
Options, call option	The right, but not the obligation to buy the options underlying asset
Options, put option	The right, but not the obligation to sell the options underlying asset
OTC	The market where customized derivatives deals are done directly between financial institutions and other participants.
OTS	Office of Thrift Supervision
Paul Volker	Chairman of the Federal Reserve Bank, 1979 to 1987
Prime mortgage	A mortgage extended to borrowers with good credit ratings
Quanto	A structured note that enabled an investor to invest in a home currency and bet of foreign currencies or interest rates
RBS	Royal Bank of Scotland, one of the poorly managed Crisis casualties in the UK
Regulation Q	The 6% interest limit placed on loans that deposit takers could make in order to lower their operating risks
Roosevelt, Franklin Delano	Thirty-second President of the United States, 1933 - 1945
Roosevelt, Theodore	Twenty-sixth President of the United States, 1901 - 1909

S&L	Savings and Loan Association, also known as Thrifts
S&P	A ratings agency (NRSRA)
Sandy Weill	Chairman of Citibank then Citigroup (= Citibank and Travellers)
SEC	Securities and Exchange Commission
Securitization	Packages of debt that are divided into tranches and sold to investors. Examples are MBS and CDO
Shadow Banking System	Paul McCulley called it the "the whole alphabet soup of levered up non-bank investment conduits, vehicles, and structures" which includes the non-bank financial intermediaries like investment banks, hedge and other funds, and off balance sheet entities.
SIV	Structured investment vehicle, similar to an SPV and used to hold OBS assets
Salomon	Salomon Brothers, an investment bank
SPV	Special purpose vehicle, similar to an SIV and used to hold OBS assets
Structured notes	Investments like bonds, but which have many forms of creative payouts, or returns
Subprime mortgage	A mortgage extended to borrowers with poor credit ratings
Synthetic CDO	A collateralised debt obligation without packaged pieces of debt, but which references pieces of debt it does not own, and whose performance mimics the referenced debt
Thomas Jefferson	Author of the Declaration of Independence and third President of the United States, 1801 - 1809
Thrift	Savings and Loan Association, also known as S&Ls
UBS	Union Bank of Switzerland
VaR	Value at Risk, a measure of market risk
Volker Rule	A rule introduced by Paul Volker that is intended to divide deposit taker utility functions of banks from the much riskier investment bank derivative functions
Wall Street	Includes the larger European banks and larger US banks not necessarily located in Wall Street but engaged in extensive banking services, including investment banking.
WaMu	Washington Mutual, an S&L

Resources

Additional Resources are available at www.RiskTraffickers.com:

- A Bibliography
- A Glossary
- The Timeline from the time of the first central bank in Sweden
- Recent fines and settlements
- Megabanks (Too Big To Fail, G-Sibs)

[1] Chairman of the Federal Reserve Board in Washington, 1987 to 2006

[2] Moral hazard arises when for example you insure your car and take less care driving it because it is insured. The downside risk, the cost of repairing damage is covered. For this reason, insurance companies write

[3] Thomas Piketty, *Capital in the Twenty-First Century*, Belknap Press of the Harvard University, March 2014, loc 516

[4] Joseph Stiglitz, "Inequality Is a Choice" *International New York Times,* 13 October 2013

[5] Kasia Moreno, "The 67 People s Wealthy As the World's Poorest 3.5 Billion" *Forbes* March 2014

[6] Buttonwood's notebook, *The Economist,* 6 November 2014 at http://www.economist.com/node/21631059

[7] World Health Organization at http://www.who.int/nutgrowthdb/estimates2013/en/. I have aggregated their estimates for stunted growth, wasted and severely wasted, overweight and underweight individuals as a result of malnutrition

[8] Danny Dorling, *All That is Solid: The Great Housing Disaster,* Penguin, February 2014, P 1

[9] United Nations, The Universal Declaration of Human Rights, United Nations, December 1948, in particular Article 25 at http://www.un.org/en/documents/udhr/index.shtml

[10] Stuart Forbes Macintyre, personal communication, 29 January 2014, Benjamin Todd, personal communication, 11 February 2014

[11] I will use GDP as opposed to purchasing power parity GDP (PPP GDP) because most statements of GDP do not use PPP GDP, and I wish only to provide an approximate size benchmark. PPP GDP eschews a reliance on volatile foreign exchange rates and makes comparisons between economic regions easier. For example to compare the GDPs of the countries in the African continent to European or North American GDPs, one should double them. Moving, however, from GDP to PPP GDP is straightforward.

[12] Neil Irwin, The Alchemists: Three Central Bankers, Penguin, New York, NY, 2013 P 101. GDP was $2.86 trillion in 1980 and $13.1 in 2005

[13] Benjamin Todd, op cit, the contribution of US household spending to the evolution of the problem

[14] Santyajit Das, Extreme Money: Masters of the Universe and the Cult of Risk, Pearson 2011, P 45, and Terry Boehm, personal communication, 26 January 2015, this percentage includes contributions to charities that were tax avoidance foundations

[15] The Over the Counter or OTC market is comprised of private, customized derivatives deals done directly between financial institutions and other participants. Securitizations are tradable securities build from debt. We will discuss both the OTC markets and securitizations throughout and in particular in chapter 4.

[16] Doug McClymont, personal communication, 21 January 2015

[17] I use the term Wall Street to include the larger European banks and larger US banks not located in Wall Street but engaged in extensive banking services, including investment banking. While the lion's share of investment banking activity was centred in New York City and indeed physically on Wall Street, London and other European cities were also major investment banking centres.

[18] Mario Cerrato, "The securitization market in the UK" *Adam Smith Business School, University of Glasgow"* Autumn/Winter 2011 at http://www.gla.ac.uk/schools/business/newsandevents/aspire/issue1 0autumnwinter2011/thesecuritisationmarketintheuk/

[19] This is the risk that mortgage borrowers would not, or could not pay the regular monthly mortgage repayments

[20] Subprime mortgages are mortgages given to individuals and families with a lower credit quality rating than prime mortgage holders, and so were sold to those that did not meet the more stringent, traditional mortgage borrower standards. We will have a lot to say about subprime mortgages. Adjustable rate mortgages are also the subject of a discussion that follows. They are mortgages where the rate increases over time. They are time bombs for mortgage holders who cannot afford the increased payments. The backstop, to sell the mortgaged property, or refinance it would evaporate if the housing market stumbled, as it did.

[21] The domestic residential housing market was $11 trillion, the commercial real estate market $3 million, and the total real estate market was $14 trillion

[22] Larry Elliot, "Credit crisis – how it all began", *The Guardian* 5th August 2008

[23] The first guarantee was for $30 billion, however by the time the deal was completed, JP Morgan Chase agreed to take the first $1 billion in losses, leaving the FED on the hook for $29 billion

[24] Also knows as Thrifts

[25] Fannie was the largest financial company globally with assets of more than $5 trillion

[26] The US Congress set up the Financial Crisis Inquiry Commission in 2010 to "examine the causes of current and financial and economic crisis in the US". The *Report* submitted in 2011 presents to the President, Congress and the American people the results of the Commission's examination and conclusions. Notably one of the conclusions was that the Crisis was avoidable.

[27] Financial Crisis Inquiry Commission, *Report*, 2011, Private Interview P 354

[28] Paul Krugman, The Return of Depression Economics and the Crisis of 2008, W. W. Norton & Company, New York, 2009 P 165

[29] John Hellmann, "Obama is from Mars, Wall Street Is From Venus", New York Magazine, 22 May 2010

[30] The European Union, or EU, is comprised of 28, mostly European,

[31] European Commission "New Crisis Management Measures to Avoid Future Bank Bailouts" Press Release 6 June 2012 at http://europa.eu/rapid/press-release_IP-12-570_en.htm

[32] European Commission *ibid*

[33] Nouriel Roubini and Stephen Mihm, *Disaster Capitalism: A Crash Course in the Future of Finance,* Penguin, London, 2011 describe crises as white swans as supposed to black swans. Black swans are very much the exception and we will look at these shortly.

[34] Paul McCulley, in "Teton Reflections" Federal Reserve Bank of Kansas Economic Symposium, Jackson Hole in 2007 introduced the expression *shadow banking system* as "the whole alphabet soup of levered up non-bank investment conduits, vehicles, and structures" to refer to the non-bank financial intermediaries like investment banks, hedge and other funds, and off balance sheet entities

[35] Andrew Ross Sorkin, *Too Big To Fail*, Penguin, London, 2010 P 4

[36] Alan Greenspan, *The Map and the Territory*, Penguin, 2013

[37] Gretchen Morgenson and Joshua Rosner, *Reckless Endangerment*, Times Books Henry Holt and Co. P 7

[38] Anat Admati and Martin Hellwig, *op cit,* P 5

[39] Bureau of Economic Analysis, *National Income and Product Accounts* Table 1.1.6 at http://bea.gov/national/nipaweb/SelectTable.asp

[40] United Nations, *UNDESA,* 2011

[41] Better Markets is a non-profit organization based in Washington DC that promotes the public interest in financial reform in the domestic and global capital and commodities markets. It in independent and nonpartisan and was formed in 2010. It's at http://www.bettermarkets.com. The report is *The Cost of the Wall-Street Caused Financial Collapse and Ongoing Economic Crisis is $12.7 Trillion*, 15 September 2012

[42] Andrew G. Haldane, "Regulation or Prohibition: The $100 Billion Question" Journal of Regulation and Risk North Asia 2 (2-3), PP 101 to 122, 2010

[43] David Kansas, *The Wall Street Journal Guide to the End of Wall Street* Mobipocket Reader, December 2009 loc 86

[44] Barack Obama, "Remarks By The President On Financial Reform" *White House* Federal Hall, New York, NY, 14 September 2009 at www.whitehouse.gov/the_press_office/Remarks_by_the_President_on_Financial_Rescue_and_Reform_at_Federal_Hall

[45] Neil Barofsky, *Bailout*, Free Press NY, 2012, quoting the US Treasury reports $16 trillion by 2010 and Better Markets, probably closer to the truth, $19 trillion in 2009.

[46] Simon Johnson and James Kwak, *op cit,* loc 2946

[47] U2 measures the un-employment, the marginally attached workers, and those employed part time because they cannot find full-time employment and U3 measures fully unemployed

[48] Bureau of Labour Statists at www.bls.gov; The U3 measure is the commonly published official unemployment rate and U6, a wider measure, better reflects actual unemployment as it reflects the partially employed who would become fully employed if a full time job became available

[49] Neil Irwin, *op cit,* P 378

[50] Better Markets, *op cit*

[51] Charles Ferguson, *ibid,* P 7

[52] Paul Mason " The graduates of 2012 will survive only in the cracks of our economy" *The Guardian* ,1 July

[53] Peggotty Graham, personal communication, March 2014, the significance of the younger unemployment numbers

[54] Nicolas Sarkozy, President of the French Republic, Davos, Switzerland 27 January 2011

[55] Gretchen Morgenson and Joshua Rosner, *Reckless Endangerment*, Henry Holt and Company, 2011, Introduction

[56] Danny Dorling, *All That is Solid*, P 180

[57] International Monetary Fund, *Global financial stability report*, Washington DC, IMF, October 2009

[58] Cap Gemini Consultants, *Global Trade Flow Index*, January 2011

[59] New York State Office of the State Comptroller, *New York City Securities Industry Bonus Pool* February 23, 2010, at http://osc.state.ny.us/press/releases/feb10/022310.htm. In 2008, $30 billion, with $99,000 per employee, and in 2009, $37 billion with $124,000 per employee.

[60] US Census Bureau "Income, Poverty and Health Insurance Coverage in the United States: 2010", September 2011

[61] Many small American towns have a Main street, the town's *main* street. Today we use the term to mean *average American*, or *person*. In the UK, the equivalent is High Street. We will use Main Street to include High Street, and use High Street only when we are talking explicitly about the UK

[62] Jessie Norman, *Telegraph,* 4 December 2013

[63] Thomas Piketty, *op cit* loc 5792

[64] New York Times, "Executive Pay: The Bottom Line for Those at the Top", 5 April 2008, http://www.nytimes.com/interactive/2008/04/05/business/2008040 5_EXECCOMP_GRAPHIC.html

[65] Reuters, JPMorgan CEO Dimon's 2008 compensation falls, http://www.reuters.com/article/2009/03/18/us-jpmorgan-proxy-idUSTRE52H7ZL20090318

[66] Danny Dorking, *Inequality and the 1%,* loc 2403

[67] The CEOs were: Ken Chanault, American Express; Ken Lewis, Bank of America; Robert Kelly, Bank of New York Mellon; Vikram Pandit, Citigroup; John Koskinen, Freddie Mac; Lloyd Blankfein, Goldman Sachs; Jamie Dimon, JP Morgan Chase; John Mack, Morgan Stanley; Rick Waddell, Northern Trust; James Rohr, PNC; Ronald Logue, State Street;

Richard Davis, US Bank and John Stumpf, Wells Fargo. Also present from the industry were Cam Fine, from Independent Community Bankers Association (23,000 banks, $1 trillion in assets) and Edward Yingling, from the ABA.

[68] TARP will figure in our discussion later

[69] President Barack Obama, "Remarks by the President on Financial Rescue and Reform at Federal Hall", 27 March 2009

[70] Andrew Ross Sorkin, *op cit,* P 532

[71] President Barack Obama, *op cit*

[72] We will discuss these to egregious fraud schemes a bit later. Each had a history from prior to the Millennium.

[73] John Mack, "Written Submission of Morgan Stanley to the Financial Crisis Inquiry Commission", *Report op cit* 13 January 2010

[74] John Mack, *op cit* "The Role of Government in Stabilizing and Improving the Financial System"

[75] John Mack, *op cit* P 6, then P 11

[76] Brian T Moynihan, "Lessons Learned" in *Testimony to the Financial Crisis Inquiry Commission Report,* 13 January 2010

[77] Brian T Moynihan, "Introduction", *op cit*

[78] Brian T Moynihan, *op cit* ,Introduction

[79] Brian T Moynihan, *op cit,* Lessons learned

[80] Jamie Dimon, Lines of Business in *Testimony to the Financial Crisis Inquiry Commission,* 13 January 2010

[81] Jamie Dimon, *op cit,* Causes of the Financial Crises

[82] Testimony of Lloyd C. Blankfein, *op cit,* Collateralized Debt Obligations, CDOs and CDO tranches will enter out discussion a little later

[83] Lloyd Blankfein, "Goldman's Non-Apology", *New York Times,* 21 November 2009

[84] Terry Boehm, *op cit*

[85] Simon Johnson and James Kwak, *White House Burning*, Pantheon Books, 2012 loc 277

[86] John Arlidge, "The Debt Collector" *Sunday Times Magazine,* 7 October 2012

[87] Frank Partnoy, *FIASCO,* 1997 P 22-23

[88] Louis Brandeis, "Our Financial Oligarchy", *Harper's Weekly,* November 1913. More on Brandeis later. He became a Supreme Justice

[89] Simon Johnson and James Kwak, op cit

[90] Anat Admati and Martin Hellwig, op cit

[91] William J Black, Bangsters
www.youtube.com/watch?v=oUHS7TVVgww

[92] Simon Johnson and James Kwak, *op cit,* loc 293 quotes from a 1816 letter Jefferson wrote to John Taylor which is printed in Bergh, Albert Ellery, ed., *The Writing of Thomas Jefferson* volume XV (Washington: Thomas Jefferson Memorial Association, 1907) p23

[93] Simon Johnson and James Kwak, *ibid,* loc 332

[94] It *began* in Europe in about 1760. Machines replaced hands, the production of chemicals and iron became more efficient, water and steam power was harnessed, textile production was enhanced and living standards began to improve. The transition was *done* between 1820 and 1850

[95] Simon Johnson and James Kwak, *op cit,* loc 428

[96] Adapted from Ben Bernanke, *The Federal Reserve and the Financial Crisis,* Princeton University Press, 2013, P 10. Bernanke's sources were, for 1873 Elmus Wicker, *Banking Practices of the Gilded Age* (New York: Cambridge University Press, 2006) table 1.3 and for 1914, Federal Reserve Board, Banking and Monetary Statistics, 1914-1941

[97] Charles R Morris, *The Tycoons: How Andrew Carnegie, John D. Rockefeller, Joy Gould and J.P. Morgan Invented the American Supereconomy*, Henry Holy, New York 2005 P 235

[98] Simon Johnson and James Kwak, *op cit,* loc 502

[99] Louis Brandeis, *op cit*

[100] Simon Johnson and James Kwak op cit quoted on loc 571, from Brandeis, Louis, Other People's Money, and How the Bankers Use It (F. A. Stokes, New York 1914). "Other People's Money" originally appeared in Harper's Weekly

[101] Louis Brandeis, *op cit*

[102] The Federal Reserve Act of Congress of 1913

[103] Derek Kelly, *op cit,* the importance and relevance of these observations

[104] Quoted in Johnson and Kwak, *op cit,* footnote 80 loc 4786, from Jerry M Markham, *A Financial History of the United States, Volume II: From J.P. Morgan to the Institutional Investor (1900 -1970)*, M.E. Sharpe, Armonk NY, 2002

[105] Stuart Forbes Macintyre, *op cit*

[106] Stuart Forbes Macintyre, *op cit* especially when the US entered the War after Pearl Harbor was bombed in 1941

[107] Ben Bernanke, *op cit*

[108] Johnson and Kwak, *op cit,* loc 675

[109] Simon Johnson and James Kwak, *ibid,* loc 696

[110] A liquidity problem arises when you do not have sufficient cash to cover outgoings. This is quite different from being solvent. A bank is solvent if it its assets are larger than its liabilities. A liquidity problem can arise for a solvent bank when depositors ask for deposits back, but needed cash cannot be realized from the outstanding loan assets because their maturities are way into the future.

[111] David A, Moss *op cit*

[112] Thomas Piketty, *op cit* loc 2347 to 2356

[113] There were two oil shocks, 1973 and 1979, the latter triggered by the Iranian Revolution

[114] I use the abbreviations BIS, BCBS and Basel Committee more or less interchangeably

[115] World Bank, *op cit.*

[116] The discount rate, one of the tools used to manage the US economy is usually set slightly above the lowest borrowing rates in order to discourage discount window borrowing to fund normal activities

[117] Redemption capacity meant a bank's ability to exchange its bank notes for another bank's note, gold or other assets, and perception played a role

[118] Congress passed the National Banking Act creating national banks, in 1863

[119] Hopefully! This is the basis of an investment bank accepting a loan

[120] John Mack, *op cit*

[121] Paul McCulley, "Tuton Reflections" presented at Federal Reserve Bank of Kansas Economic Symposium Jackson Hole in 2007 *Pimco Global Central Banking Focus.* He called it the "whole alphabet soup of levered up non-bank investment conduit, vehicles and structures"

[122] Vehicles, conduits, yes, bankers tend to employ language which is more complicated than needed. For both, read home or entity

[123] GSE mortgage portfolios peaked at about $5 trillion, so the benefit was in the order of 25 billion, *each year.*

[124] Retail $0.95 trillion and institutional $1.75 trillion

[125] The maturities must be less that 13 months, the weighted average less than 60 days and the limit on any one issue, apart from government securities (and repos) is 5%.

[126] "A Monoline Melt Down" *The Economist'* 26th July 2007

[127] Bank holding companies are companies that own banks. They came about as a consequence of banks being permitted to operate cross boarder and have interests in non-banks. I will often use the terms *bank* and *bank holding company* interchangeably unless it is appropriate to make the distinction.

[128] Frank Partnoy, *op cit* P 69

[129] Ben Bernanke, *op cit* loc 445

[130] Walter Bagehot was an English economist, businessman and journalist. He promulgated the idea in his *Lombard Street* 1873

[131] Independence is found in Europe, North America, South America, Australia and some but not all Asian countries. Notably, not one country that has eschewed independence of its central bank and legislative processes has a significant or well-oiled monetary system. Singapore is an example

[132] A good survey is mark Jickling and Edward V. Murphy "Who Regulates Who? An Overview of US Financial Supervision *Congressional Research Service* 7-5700, 8 December 2010. The view of capital as funds not lendable is however erroneous and the treatment of capital reflects views current in the early part of the first decade of this century. The discussion of Basel III is comprehensive.

[133] Gillian Tett, *Fools Gold,* Free Press Simon & Schuster, 2009 P 24

[134] Timothy Geithner, "Introducing the Financial Stability Plan" *Remarks by Treasury Secretary* 10th February 2009, at http://www.ustreas.gov/press/releases/tg18.htm

[135] The Wall Street Reform and Consumer Protection Act of 2010. Many acts of Congress are known by the their sponsors which in this case were Senator Christopher Dodd, Chairman of the Senate Banking Committee and Congressman Barny Frank, Chairman of the House Financial Services Committee. We will have a lot to say about this act later and the Collins amendment. It was intended to address the problems of the Crisis.

[136] The FHFA is quite different from the FHA, which mostly provides mortgage insurance

[137] They are dealers that trade with governments, and in the US they trade with the FED. They are market makers as they act as intermediaries and sell government securities to other banks.

[138] The Home Ownership and Equity Protection Act (HOEPA) provided for this

[139] There were eighteen at year end 2014

[140] When we are referring to banks, we will use capital and equity almost interchangeably. When we are talking more generally, we'll use equity more often

[141] And we cannot assume that a bank's balance sheets is always accurate. Another reason to hold capital

[142] Anat Admanti and many others in "Greenspan's reasoning on 'excessive equity is misleading" *Financial Times* 30th December 2013 discuss two perverse fallacies held by Greenspan, that capital is a burden and is not available for productive investment and that he confuse the relationship between liquid asset reserves and capital regulation. Greenspan erroneously believes that capital is expensive, that financial crises are often akin to natural disasters and their prevention or mitigation means high social costs.

[143] Dan Fitzpatrick and Matthias Rieker, "Whale's Tail Hits Bank on Buyback" *Wall Street Journal* 9 August 2012.

[144] Anat Admati and Martin Hellwig, *op cit* Footnote 52 p310

[145] Anat Admati and Martin Hellwig, *op cit* P 252 footnote 36

[146] First known as the Basel Accord, it became known as Basel I to distinguish it from Basel II, a later development

[147] Darryl E. Getter, "US Implementation of the Basel Capital Regulatory Framework", *Congressional Report Service*, 14 November 2012

[148] This was, as you might conclude was a controversial if not inexplicable issue.

[149] Sheila Bair *op cit* P 37

[150] Sheila Bair, *op cit* P 37

[151] Sheila Bair, *Bull By The Horns,* Free Press, Simon & Schuster 2012 P 30

[152] John Arlidge, "The Debt Collector" *The Sunday Times Magazine* 7 October 2012

[153] Sheila Bair, *ibid* p 37

[154] The G20 is a group of finance ministers and central bank governors from 19 major countries whose economies which account for 85% of

global GDP, 80% of trade and two thirds of the world's population. The member countries are Argentina, Australia, Brazil, Canada, China, France, Germany, India, Indonesia, Italy, Japan, Republic of Korea, Mexico, Russian Federation, Saudi Arabia, South Africa, Turkey, the UK and the US. The twentieth member is the EU which represents its interests and the interests of the other European countries not directly represented. Spain participates as a permanent guest, and other guests are name from time to time. The G20 now meets annually.

[155] The Collins Amendment eliminated trust-preferred securities and other hybrids from being loss absorbing

[156] For the enthusiasts, Tier 1 is shareholder's common equity plus retained earnings, disclosed reserves and perpetual non-cumulative preferred stock, in effect a high percentage of TCE. Tier 1 capital is TCE plus mortgage servicing and other rights that are liquid. Tier 2 is allowances for loans, and lease losses (ALLL) that increase as loan default risks increase and decrease as actual losses are charged off.

[157] We will have more to say on this later. In effect, the ratings agencies influenced the amount of capital required.

[158] Tom Braithwaite, "Banks Turn to Financial Alchemy in Search for Capital" *Financial Times* 24th October 2011 quotes Jamie Dimon: "we will manage the hell out of RWA"

[159] Announcement by Barclays Bank 23 June 2010

[160] Warren Buffett, "Annual Report", *Berkshire Hathaway 2002* described them as such in 2002

[161] Financial transactions, or deals between two individuals or financial institutions are transactions between two counterparties. Transactions made on financial exchanges however are not transactions between counterparties.

[162] Santyajit Das, *op cit* P 55

[163] Gillian Tett, *op cit* P 29

[164] The ten founding members were Bankers Trust, First Boston, Merrill Lynch, JP Morgan, Morgan Stanley, Citicorp, Salomon Brothers, Goldman Sachs, Kleinwort Benson, Morgan Guarantee Trust and Shearson Lehman.

[165] By 1988, Credit Suisse owned 44% of First Boston, which had resulted from the divestiture of the investment banking business of First National Bank of Boston after Glass Steagall. It became Credit Suisse First Boston in 1990

[166] Frank Partnoy, *op cit* P 60

[167] Frank Partnoy, *ibid* P 71

[168] Frank Partnoy, *op cit,* Pp 214 to 231

[169] This securitization is described in *The Financial Crisis Inquiry Commission Report op cit* Pp 115 to 117

[170] Nouriel Roubini and Stephan Mihm, *op cit*

[171] For details see Bethany McLean and Joe Nocera, *All The Devils Are Here,* Portfolio Penguin 2010 beginning loc1319

[172] Gillian Tett, *op cit* P 21, Pp 51-56

[173] Sometimes called super senior tranches

[174] Barry Schachter, "An irreverent guide to value at risk" *Financial Engineering News* August 1997

[175] Lawrence J Peter, *The Peter Principle* p?

[176] Nouriel Roubini and Stephan Mihm Roubini, *op cit*

[177] This assumes that the X is between zero and one hundred per cent, so that a 10% VaR would occur, more or less one in every ten days. The *more or less* was measured in green, yellow and red lights, with an acceptability score based on the number of times the X percent was met.

[178] Ian Stewart, "The mathematical equation the caused the banks to collapse" *The Guardian* 12 February 2012

[179] Pablo Triana, *Lecturing Birds on Flying* Wiley 2009

[180] Warren Buffett, *op cit*

[181] Michael Lewis, *Liar's Poker* W.W. Norton, New York, 1989 P 44

[182] The City is a popular synonym for the UK financial services sector in London. The old city of London, occupying one square mile (actually 1.1 square miles) was where most of London's banks were headquartered.

[183] Eugene Fama promoted a form of laissez-faire economics where markets are rational, it provides pricing, etc.

[184] Statements of the weak EMH often stress *past* information, however this is superfluous

[185] Thomas Piketty, *op cit* loc 368

[186] Thomas Piketty, *ibid* loc 655

[187] Pablo Triana, *ibid*

[188] Simon Johnson and James Kwak, *op cit* loc 1381 and 1392

[189] Ronald Reagan, *Inaugural Address* 20th January 1981
http://www.reaganfoundation.org/pdf/Inaugural_Address_012081.pdf

[190] Edward Cowan, "How Regan Sees the Budget" *The New York Time*"18th October, 1981 quoted in Simon Johnson and James Kwak, *op cit* loc 1400

[191] Reagan, Ronald, Remarks on Signing the Garn-St Germain Depository Institutions Act of 1982, 15th October 1982, http://www.reagan.utexas.edu/archives/speeches/1982/101582b.htm

[192] Lawrence White, *The S&L Debacle:* OUP, NY 1990

[193] Kay Bonnick, *Why To Big To Fail?* Author House, Bloomington 2010 P 27, footnote

[194] Timothy Curry and Shibut, Lynn, "The Cost of the Savings and Loans Crisis: Truth and Consequences" *FDIC Banking Review* December 2000 Pp 26 to 35, available at www.fdic.gov/bank/analytical/banking/2000dec/brv13n2_2.pdf

[195] FDIC "Bank Failures and Assistance Transactions" *Historical Statistics on Banking* at http://www2.fdic.gov/hsob/

[196] Law of One Price

[197] An example of put-call parity in given in Frank Partnoy *Infectious Greed: How Deceit and Risk Corrupted the Financial Markets* (Henry Holt, 2004, New *York*) P 20 where he describes a strategy of a Bankers Trust options trader, Andy Krieger in the mid-1980s

[198] Risk quantification is of course a key issues and Basel provides a number of ways to determine regulatory capital from risk assessments. Economic capital also requires a holistic analysis of risk

[199] Frank Partnoy, *ibid* P 39

[200] Frank Partnoy, *op cit* P 84

[201] There was firstly a gentleman's agreement to not bid for more than 35% of the securities on offer. When he refused to abide by this agreement it was made into a rule, however Mozer continued to flout the rule, and then when caught again, continued to manipulate the market by putting in bids for other organizations.

[202] They were Gutfreund, Strauss, Meriwether and Feuerstein

[203] Frank Partnoy, *op cit* P 111

[204] Askin Capital Management, a $600 million fund was dead by April

[205] George Soros, *The Alchemy of Finance,* John Wiley & Sons 1987

[206] Katherine Burton, John Pickering and Dave Liedtka, "Credit Agencies Dropped the Ball, Investors Say" *Bloomberg News*, 5 December 1994 p1

[207] Frank Partnoy, *op cit* P 117

[208] Frank Partnoy, *op* cit P 163

[209] Directional bets are bets on the market moving up or dawn. LTCM initially eschewed directional bets and made only market neutral bets

[210] Paul Krugman, *op cit* P 3

[211] National Association of Realtors, 1994

[212] Bethany McLean and Joe Nocera, *op cit* loc 295

[213] Gretchen Morgenson and Joshua Rosner, *ibid* P 1

[214] Gretchen Morgenson and Joshua Rosner *ibid* P 2

[215] Gretchen Morgenson and Joshua Rosner, *op cit* from P 81 tells the story of Marvin Phaup at the Congressional Budget Office in 1995. Phaup determined that the benefits accruing to Fannie and Fannie were $7 billion in 1995 and that Fannie and Freddie retained ½ of that for themselves.

[216] Gretchen Morgenson and Joshua Rosner, *ibid* p5

[217] Gretchen Morgenson and Joshua Rosner, *op cit* P

[218] The Centre of Public Integrity *The Subprime 25* 6th May 2009 at http://www.publicintegrity.org/2009/subprime-25

[219] The first few payments may go to the originator, while it scheduled the sale of the mortgages

[220] Bethany McLean and Joe Nocera, *op cit* loc 332

[221] Bureau of Economic Analysis *National Income and Product Accounts* at http://www.bea.gov/itable/error_NIPA.cfm

[222] Paul Krugman, *op cit* loc 212

[223] Anat Admati and Martin Hellwig, *op cit* P 60

[224] Goldman Sachs *Code of Business Conduct and Ethics* May 2009

[225] It was known as the Financial Modernization Act of 1999

[226] World Bank, *World DataBank* at http://databank.worldbank.org/data/home.aspx

[227] [227] World Bank, *World DataBank* at http://databank.worldbank.org/data/home.aspx

[228] Gillian Tett, *op cit* P 31

[229] Santyajit Das, *op cit* p129

[230] Commodity Futures Modernization Act of 2000

[231] Set up in 1973 and funded by the Rockefeller Foundation, the G30 was comprised of a group of bankers and academics. Its chief was Paul Volker

[232] Alan Greenspan, "What?" Congressional Testimony 1995

[233] Warren Heller, Director of Research of Veribanc Inc.

[234] The bond Buyer newspaper compared her to a salmon "swimming against raging currents" quoted in Manuel Roig-Franzia, *op cit*

[235] Manuel Roig-Franzia, *op cit*

[236] House Committee on Banking and Financial Services, *Hearings* 17 and 24 July 1998 at http://commdocs.house.gov/committees/bank/hba50076.000/hba500 76_0f.htm

[237] Report of the President's Working Group on Financial Markets, "Over-the-Counter Derivatives Markets and the Commodity Exchange Act" in www.ustreas.gov

[238] Simon Johnson and James Kwak, *op cit,* loc 213

[239] BIS *Semi-Annual OTC Derivatives Statistics 2012* at http://www.bis.org/statistics/derstats.htm

[240] Gillian Tett, *op cit*

[241] Bethany McLean and Joe Nocera, *ibid* loc1793

[242] The seventh largest bank with $40 billion in assets

[243] "That was Then", *The Economist*, 26th January 2002

[244] Gillian Tett, *op cit* P 85

[245] Frank Partnoy, *IG op cit* p267

[246] Analysts pump up the stock after an IPO for 180 days after which the restricted insider stock can be sold

[247] Asset backed commercial paper is paper collateralized by assets. The collateral can vary from mortgages to student loans and credit card loans, and so on.

[248] Raghuram Rajan, "Has Financial Development Made the Work Riskier?" *Proceedings, Federal Reserve Bank of Kansas City*, August 2005 p 313 -69, and delivered at the FED's annual conference for central bankers and economists. Larry Summers denounced Rajan as a Luddite. It's also at http://www.kc.frb.org/publicat/SYMPOS/2005/PDF/Rajan2005.pdf

[249] Brian Naylor, "Greenspan Admits Free Market Ideology Flawed" *NPR* 24th October 2008 at http://www.npr.org/templates/story/story.php?storyId=96070766

[250] Paul Krugman, *op cit*

[251] Paul Krugman, "The Malevolent Ex-Maestro", *New York Times* 30 June 2011 is an elegant summary of these issues.

[252] He continued to maintain this view in spite of Enron and WorldCom. WorldCom committed accounting fraud, which was missed by its auditors, the banks underwriting its new debt and the credit ratings agencies. Enron used SPVs, derivatives, disguised loans and accounting to shift revenues backwards and forwards, create phantom profits, hiding debts. We could not tell easily whether the transactions were indeed creative or fraud. Enron and WorldCom demonstrated the consequences of hyperactive financial *innovation* and the failure of self-regulation. Simon Johnson and James Kwak, *op cit*, loc 2867.

[253] Alan Greenspan, "Remarks" *Annual Conference of the Association of Private Enterprise Education*, 12th April 1997 at http://www.federalreserve.gov/boarddocs/speeches/1997/19970412.htm

[254] Alan Greenspan, *The Age of Turbulence: Adventures in a New World* (Penguin, New York, 2007) p52

[255] Thomas B Edsall, "Alan Greenspan: The Oracle Or The Master of Disaster?" *The Huffington Post* 19th February 2009 at http://www.huffingtonpost.com/2009/02/19/alan-greenspan-the-oracle_n_168168.html

[256] David Wessel, *In FED We Trust: Ben Bernanke's War on the Great Panic* Random House New York 2009

[257] Peter Goodman, "Taking Hard New Look at a Greenspan Legacy", *New York Times* 8 October 2008

[258] Thomas B Edsall, *op cit*

[259] Thomas B Edsall, *op cit*

[260] Alan Greenspan quoted in 2004 by Thomas Edsall, *op cit*

[261] Alan Greenspan, "Address America's Community Bankers" Washington DC, 2 November 1999

[262] Alan Greenspan, April 2005

[263] Alan Greenspan, "technological Change and the Design of Bank Supervisory Policies" FED regional bank, Chicago, 1st May 1997 at http://www.federalreserve.gov/boarddocs/speeches/1997/19970501.htm

[264] Alan Greenspan, "Consumer Finance" *FED* 8 April 2005 at http://www.federalreserve.gov/BoardDocs/speeches/2005/20050408/default.htm

[265] Anat Amanti and many others *op cit*

[266] Alan Greenspan "Regulators Must Risk More to Push Growth" *Financial Times* 27th July 2011

[267] Alan Greenspan, "Regulators Must Risk More To Push Growth" *Financial Times* 27 July 2011

[268] Anat Admati, et al "Greenspan's Reasoning on Excessive Equity Is Misleading" *Financial Times* 2 August 2011

[269] Peter Goodman, "Taking Hard New Look at a Greenspan Legacy", *New York Times* 8th October 2008

[270] Peter Goodman, *ibid*

[271] Peter Goodman, *ibid*

[272] Raghuram Rajan, "Has Financial Development Made the World Riskier?" *Symposium Federal Reserve Bank of Kansas City, Jackso*n Hole 27th August 2005 at http://www.kc.frb.org/publicat/SYMPOS/2005/PDF/Rajan2005.pdf

[273] Justin Lahart, "Mr Rajan Was Unpopular (But Prescient) at Greenspan Party" *Wall Street Journal* 2nd January 2009 in http://online.wsj.com/article/SB123086154114948151.html. Rajan's paper was presented at the conference: Rajan Raghuram "Has Financial Development Made the Work Riskier?" *Proceedings, Federal Reserve Bank of Kansas City*, August 2005 p 313 -69, and delivered at the FED's annual conference for central bankers and economists. It's also at http://www.kc.frb.org/publicat/SYMPOS/2005/PDF/Rajan2005.pdf

[274] This comes from a quotation in Justin Lahart, , "Mr. Rajan Was Unpopular (But Prescient) at Greenspan Party" *The Wall Street Journal* 2 January 2009 at http://online.wsj.com/news/articles/SB123086154114948151

[275] Brian Naylor, "Greenspan Admits Free Market Ideology Flawed" *NPR* 24 October 2008 at http://www.npr.org/templates/story/story.php?storyId=96070766

[276] Brian Naylor, *op cit*

[277] Alan Ross Sorkin, *op cit* P 85

[278] David Faber, *And Then the Roof Caved In* P 95

[279] David Luhnow, "The Secrets of the World's Richest Man" *WSJ* 4th August 2007

[280] Its all in Simon Johnson, "The Quiet Coup" *The Atlantic Magazine* May 2009 http://www.theatlantic.com/magazine/archive/2009/05/the-quiet-coup/307364/.

[281] Simon Johnson and James Kwak, *op cit* sec 1746

[282] Anat Admati and Martin Hellwig, *op cit* Footnote 60 on P 326, references information available on the Centre for Responsive Politics website at http://www.opensecrets.org/lobby/top.php?showYear=a&indexType=c

[283] Center for Responsive Politics www.OpenSecrets.org

[284] Simon Johnson and James Kwak, *op cit* loc 1770

[285] Simon Johnson and James Kwak, *op cit* loc 1791

[286] Adam Doster, "Durbin on Congress: The Banks 'Own the Place'" *Progress Illinois* 29 April 2009 in http://progressillinois.com/2009/4/29/durbin-banks-own-the-place

[287] Simon Johnson and James Kwak, *op cit* loc 3606

[288] Simon Johnson and James Kwak, *op cit* loc 210

[289] Frank Partnoy, *ibid* p167

[290] Enron Financials

[291] Ben Bernanke initially argued that the FED's interest rate policy was not a significant component in what lead to the housing bubble as there were also housing booms in Europe where there were much tighter monetary policies. This view however did not contemplate the relationship between the FED's interest rate policy and the expansion of real estate collateralized securitizations, a major culprit.

[292] Gretchen Morgenson and Joshua Rosner *op cit* p275

[293] Neil Barofsky, *op cit*, chapter 3 footnote 6

[294] Federal Reserve Board, *Federal Reserve Flow of Funds* http://www.federalreserve.gov/re;eases/z1/current

[295] The Financial Crisis Inquiry Commission, *op cit* 13 April 2011 P

[296] Charles Ferguson, *op cit* P 78 quoting from Greenspan, Alan and Kennedy, James "Sources and Uses of Equity Extraction from Housing" Federal Reserve Board, 2007

[297] Alan Greenspan, Speech America's Community Bankers October 2004

[298] Case Shiller US National Home Price Index at http://www.standardandpoors.com/indices/sp-case-shiller-home-price-indices/en/us

[299] Josh Rosner, "What" in *What* 29 June, 2001

[300] The Financial Crisis Inquiry Commission *op cit* P 7, The source is Richard M. Bowen III of Citigroup

[301] One was concerned with commercial real estate which targeted the small community banks, and the other for non-traditional mortgages which targeted the large West Coast S&Ls and non-bank lenders and options ARMS.

[302] Gillian Tett, *Op Cit* p 122

[303] Gillian Tett, *Op Cit* p 122

[304] Bethany McLean and Joe Nocera, *op cit* loc 4809

[305] Bethany McLean and Joe Nocera, *op cit* loc 5177

[306] Allan Sloan, "House of Junk", *Fortune Magazine*, 15th October 2007

[307] On 1 August, 2013 he was found guilty in an Securities and Exchange Commission civil suit of cheating investors out of more than $1 billion. Although he is guilty of violating federal laws and will have to pay hundreds of thousands of dollars in fines, what he eventually pays will be a drop in the ocean compared to what investors lost. And this was only one deal!

[308] Aptly named teams who went after customers to suck their blood

[309] Greg Smith, "Why I Am Leaving Goldman Sachs" *New York Times* 14th March 2014 at http://www.nytimes.com/2012/03/14/opinion/why-i-am-leaving-goldman-sachs.html

[310] Gillian Tett, *op cit* P 114

[311] Hank Paulson, *op cit* P 92

[312] Hank Paulson, *op cit* P 66. I am using slightly adjusted, more accurate numbers.

[313] Ben Bernanke, "Testimony before Congress's Joint Economic Committee", March 2007

[314] Ben Bernanke "Remarks delivered by satellite at the 2007 International Monetary Conference", Cape Town, South Africa 5 June 2007 at http://www.federalreserve.gov/newsevents/speech/bernanke20070605a.htm

[315] Ben Bernanke, "Problems in the subprime market seem to be contained", *New York Times*, 29 March 2007

[316] Asset bubbles are Ponzi schemes. Investors earn profits as prices increase. The profits attract new investors, whose funds add to the pool,

and replace withdrawn funds. More profits as prices continue to increase until there are no more suckers willing to invest.

[317] IMF "Financial Stress and Deleveraging: Macro Financial Implications and Policy" *Global Financial Stability Report* Washington DC October 2008. See also BIS *79th Annual Report* 1st April 2008 to 31st March 2009, Basel 29th June 2009

[318] Charles Ferguson *op cit* P 211

[319] Charles Ferguson *op cit* P 212

[320] Paul Krugman, *op cit* P 151

[321] Paul Krugman, *ibid* P 188 refers to *The Onion* Issue 44, 29 14 July 2008

[322] Ben Bernanke, *op cit* loc 653

[323] Alan Greenspan 2004

[324] Super senior debt is the highest AAA tranche, lowest risk debt in a securitization

[325] Derek Kelly, personal communication 9th March 2014, the HSBC shareholder announcement

[326] Charles Ferguson, *op cit* P 65

[327] Gretchen Morgenson and Joshua Rosner *op cit* P 187

[328] Charles Ferguson, *op cit* P 68 to 71

[329] Technically the ECB offered a fixed rate tender with full allotment, which meant that there was no upper limit.

[330] The LIBOR-OIS spread is explained in www.risktraffickers.com

[331] Bethany McLean and Joe Nocera, *op cit* footnote 17 at loc 7985

[332] New York State Office of the State Comptroller, *New York City Securities Industry Bonus Pool* February 23, 2010, at http://osc.state.ny.us/press/releases/feb10/022310.htm

[333] Goldman Sachs, *Proxy Statement for 2008 Annual Meeting of Shareholders*, 7th March 2008

[334] Lehman Brothers, *Proxy Statement for Year-end 2007*

[335] JP Morgan Chase, *2007 Proxy Statement*

[336] Merrill Lynch, *2007 Proxy Statement*

[337] Similar to a US S&L

[338] In fact in 1878 according to George Monbiot, "The Man Who Want to Northern Rock the Planet", *Guardian* 1st June 2010

[339] And on common equity, 85 to 1

[340] The agency was the Financial Services Authority

[341] Treasury Select Committee, Fifth Report, http://www.publications.pariament.uk/pa/cm200708/cmselect/cmtreasy/56/5603.htm 2008, quotes and comments in in George Monbiot, *op cit*

[342] Treasury Select Committee, Fifth Report, *ibid*

[343] Fallon, question 404 and Ridley response to question 406

[344] Mat Ridley, Power to the people: we can't do any worse than government. *The Daily Telegraph* 22nd July 1996

[345] Mat Ridley, *ibid* p 357

[346] Mat Ridley, *The Rational Optimist: how prosperity evolves* Fourth Estate, London 2010, p 357

[347] Danny Dorling, *Population 10 Billion* Constable, London 2013 p176-186

[348] George Monbiot, *op cit*

[349] FED at http://www.federalreserve.gov/newsevents/reform_taf.htm

[350] Neil Irwin, *op cit* P 132

[351] Alan Ross Sorkin, *op cit* p38

[352] Senator Christopher Dodd, "Panel I of a Hearing of the Senate Banking, Housing and Urban Affairs Committee" *Federal News Service* 3 April 2008

[353] This was a common expression. Trading positions were market to market. This involved finding market prices. The prices are then used to value positions. These prices are known as marks. For prices that are immediately observable in liquid markets, like foreign exchange rates for pounds against dollars, it is straightforward. But when we do not have liquid markets we rely upon models. So the issue for Lehman (and many others) was how reasonable were its marks. If the assets had to be sold, would they realize the prices claimed or implied.

[354] Neil Irwin, *op cit* P 164

[355] The G7, the Group of Seven is a regular meeting of central bankers and finance minister from US, Britain, France, Germanys, Canada, Italy and Japan

[356] It was Lehman, which was concerned about new accounting rules.

[357] Bethany McLean, and Joe Nocera, *op cit* loc 6683

[358] William Poole,

[359] Senator Jim Bunning, Republican, Kentucky

[360] David Einhorn, speech at the Ira W. Sohn Investment Research Conference

[361] Andrew Ross Sorkin, *Too Big To Fail* p116

[362] Those who deliberately sold the stock short expecting to be able to buy it back at a lower price

[363] Bethany McLean and Joe Nocera, *op cit* loc 3216

[364] In 2005, AIG FP profits were $950 million or $2.5 million per employee

[365] Gretchen Morgenson, *op cit*

[366] These amounts come from various sources, however, Simon Johnson and James Kwak, *op cit* is a good source: Société Générale $16.5 billion, Goldman $ 12.9 billion, Deutsche Bank $8.5 billion, Merrill $6.8 billion, UBS $4.3 billion, Wachovia $1.0 billion, Band of America $5.2 billion and Citigroup $2.3 billion

[367] Neil Barofsky, *op cit*

[368] Alan Ross Sorkin, *op cit* P 417

[369] Ben Bernanke, *ibid*

[370] BIS "A Framework For Dealing With Domestic Systematically Important Banks" *Discussion Paper 233* BIS, Basel 2012

[371] Financial Commission Inquiry Commission Report p 356 Interview 25th March 2011

[372] Anat Admanti and Martin Hellwig, *op cit* p256 footnote 9

[373] It announced the Money Market Investor Funding Facility, the MMIFF, on Friday 19 September. Another facility was also announced on the 10th, the Asset Backed Commercial Paper Money Market Fund Liquidity Facility, the AMLF to provide the funds liquidity.

[374] Sheila Bair, *op cit*

[375] Charles Ferguson, *op cit* P 62

[376] Sheila Bair, *op cit* Pp 93

[377] The details were published by Louise Story in the *New York Times* on 13th December 2011 at

http://www.nytimes.com/2011/12/14/business/ex-bank-executives-settle-fdic-suit.html?_r=0

[378] Sheila Bair, *op cit* P 95

[379] Douglas Fraser and Robert Peston, "HBOS Collapse: Ex-bosses face calls for City bans BBC Online 5th April 2013 at www.bbc.co.uk/news/business-22027664

[380] They were the TSLF, which enabled borrowers to collateralize loans with US Treasuries, the PDCF, which opened the discount window to the investment banks, the MMIFF, through which the FDIC guaranteed existing money market fund deposits, and the AMLF, which provided liquidity by lending for ABS purchases from the money market funds

[381] *New York Times* 21st September 2008

[382] The Emergency Economic Stabilization Act 0f 2008 and established TARP

[383] The clearing banks were State Street Bank and Bank of New York Mellon and Merrill although owned by Bank of America was still operating as an independent bank. The acquisition was still to be confirmed, and we said, both Goldman and Morgan Stanley had become commercial banks.

[384] Neil Barofsky, *op cit* p 77

[385] SIGTARP was the organization that the TARP act mandated to oversee the Treasury TARP operations

[386] Barney Frank, *Face the Nation*, CBS 21st September 2008

[387] James Fallows, *The Atlantic*

[388] Initial TARP allocation of $25 billion, a further bailout of $20 billion, and the AIG CDS payment of $2.3 billion

[389] Summarized in Bair *op cit* P 160

[390] Sheila Bair, *op cit* P 32

[391] ProPublica P 151

[392] Neil Barofsky, *op cit* P 195

[393] Neil Barofsky, *op cit* p93

[394] The Financial Crisis Inquiry Commission, *op cit.*

[395] Anat Admati and Martin Hellwig, *op cit* Footnote 60 on P 326, references information available on the Centre for Responsive Politics website at http://www.opensecrets.org/lobby/top.php?showYear=a&indexType=c

[396] Neil Barofsky, *op cit* loc 3289

[397] Better Markets, *op cit*

[398] Alan Blinder and Mark Zandi, "How the Great Recession was bought to an end", 27 July 2010 at http://www.economy.com/mark-zandi/documents/End-of-Great-Recession.pdf

[399] Andrew G. Haldane, "Regulation or Prohibition: The $100 Billion Question" *Journal of Regulation and Risk North Asia* 2 (2-3) pp101 to 122 2010

[400] Adapted from an article in www.tickld.com 12 January 2015. Doug McClymont drew my attention to it.

[401] "Trial of Iceland ex-PM Haarde over 2008 crisis begins" at http://www.bbc.co.uk/news/world-europe-17254544

[402] Simon Johnson, "The Quiet Coup" *The Atlantic Magazine* May 2009 http://www.theatlantic.com/magazine/archive/2009/05/the-quiet-coup/307364/

[403] Paul Krugman, "The Underserving Rich", *International New York Times* 19 January 2014 at http://www.nytimes.com/2014/01/20/opinion/krugman-the-undeserving-rich.html?_r=0

[404] Paul Krugman, "Zombie financial ideas, The Conscience of a Liberal" *New York Times* 3rd March 2009 at http://krugman.blogs.nytimes.com/2009/03/03/zombie-financial-ideas/

[405] Thomas B Edsall, *op cit*

[406] "Inside Obama's Bank CEOs Meeting", Politico, 3rd April 2009 at http://www.politico.com/news/stories/0409/20871.html

[407] Elizabeth Williamson and Damian Paletta, "Obama Urges Bankers to Back Financial Overhaul", *Wall Street Journal* 15 September 2009 at http://online.wsj.com/article/SB125292937349508441.html

[408] Elizabeth Williamson and Damian Paletta, *ibid*

[409] President Barack Obama, *op cit*

[410] By central counterparties

[411] Edward Luce, "Obama 'wasted' reform chances" *Financial Times* 29th June 2009

[412] Charles Ferguson, *op cit* p149

[413] Hank Paulson, *op cit* P 261

[414] Hank Paulson, *op cit* P 293

[415] Hank Paulson, *op cit* P

[416] Neil Irwin, *op cit* P 156

[417] Bloomberg, 2011

[418] David A Moss, "An Ounce of Prevention: Financial Regulation, Moral Hazard, and the End of 'Too Big to Fail'", *Harvard Magazine* September – October 2009

[419] Simon Johnson and James Kwak, *op cit* loc 277

[420] Tom Braithwaite, "Banks Turn to Financial Alchemy in Search for Capital" *Financial Times* 24th October 2011 quotes Jamie Dimon: "we will manage the hell out of RWA"

[421] Eric Rosengrad, "Flirting With Money-market Madness" *Wall Street Journal* 28th November 2013

[422] Paul Krugman, *op cit* P189. This is a reworking of part of what he is saying. He adds that if we do this during non crisis times, then we will limit excessive risk taking and but doing so limit the possibility of a crisis

[423] There is a list of them in www.risktraffickers.com. The Financial Stability Board plans to update it in November each year.

[424] Remember, the capital requirement is 7%: minimum common equity of 4.5% and a capital conservation buffer of 2.5%. Regulators can raise the requirement to 9% during a boom. We have Tier 1 which is mostly tangible common equity and Tier 2 to accommodate expected loan losses.

[425] Simon Johnson and James Kwak, *op cit* loc 4106

[426] Jamie Dimon, "No More Too Big Too Fail" *The Washington Post* 13 November 2009 at http://www.washingtonpost.com/wp-dyn/content/article/2009/11/12/AR2009111209924.html

[427] Joseph Stiglitz, "Too Big to Fail or Too Big to Save?" *Statement Before the Joint Economic Committee* 21 April 2009

[428] Paul Volcker, "Statement Before the Committee on Banking and Financial Services of the House of Representatives" 24 September 2009 at

http://www.house.gov/apps/list/hearing/financialsvcs_dem/volcker.p
df

[429] Mervyn King "Lecture to Scottish business organizations" 20 October
2009.at
http://www.bankofengland.co.uk/archive/Documents/historicpubs/sp
eeches/2009/speech406.pdf

[430] Sir John Vickers, *Independent Commission on Banking 2011,* its
recommendations protect depositors and segregates banking, all to be in
place by 2019

[431] Ring fencing will not increase retail banking costs, as some argue. The
profits from investment banking activities do not offset retail costs.
When retail activities are ring fenced there is less risk and the risk
pricing element falls, and compensates. Moreover, the High Street
banking sector as a whole becomes much secure, and attracts business.

[432] Simon Johnson and James Kwak, *op cit* loc 4179

[433] Danny Dorling, *Inequality and the 1%*, Verso, London 2014

[434]Andrew Cuomo, "No Rhyme or Reason: The 'Heads I Win, Tails You
Lose' Bank Bonus Culture" *New York Times* July 2009 at
http://dealbook.nytimes.com/2009/07/30/cuomo-report-blasts-wall-
street-bonus-culture

[435] Louise Story and Eric Dash, "Banks Prepare for Big Bonuses, and
Public Wrath" *New York Times* 10 January 2010

[436] Simon Bowers, et all, *op cit*

[437] Thomas Piketty, *op cit* loc 523

[438] Michael Lewis, *op cit* P 86

[439] Michael Lewis, *op cit* P 86

[440] Michael Lewis, *op cit* P 87

[441] John Reed retired Citigroup CEO

[442] Simon Bowers, et al, *op cit*

[443] The compensation legislation is a part of Capital Requirements
Directive IV that will bring all European banks to Basel III. To some
extent its based on the now extinct FSA's First Code on remuneration.

[444] Jenny Anderson, "Top Bankers in Europe Making Big Bonuses"
International New York Times, 8 January 015

[445] B. Wilkins at digitaljournal.com

[446] Joseph Stiglitz, "Inequality Is a Choice", *International New York Times*, 13 October 2013

[447] Joseph Stiglitz, *The Price of Inequality",* W.W. Norton & Company, 2012 quoted in Thomas B. Edsall "Separate and Unequal", *New York Times* 3 August 2012

[448] Angus Deaton, "What's wrong with inequality?" *The Lancet Volume 381, Issue 9864* P 363, 2 February 2013

[449] Angus Deaton, *ibid*

[450] Paul Krugman, "The Undeserving Rich", *International New York Times,* 19 January 2014

[451] Beall Sinclair Upton

[452] Jamie Dimon, "122 Minutes With Jamie Dimon" *New York Times Magazine* 12 August 2012

[453] Edward Wyatt, "Bank Lobbyists Sought Loopholes on Risky Trading" *New York Times* 12 May 2012.The quotations from Senator Carl Levin and Phil Angelides come from here too

[454] Again, we will go into the details a little later, but short-term debt is debt that is extended for a day, a few days, or perhaps a week or two. Short-term debt is almost always cheaper than longer-term debt, and typically, a lender extends the debt repeatedly and continuously. Thus, the debt is *rolled over.*

[455] Steven Gjerstad and Vernon L Smith, "Monetary Policy, Credit Extension, and Housing Bubbles: 2008 and 1929" *Critical Review* 21, no 2-3 (2009) on page 286

[456] Andrew G Haldane, "Why Banks Failed the Stress Test" *Lecture at the Marcus Evans Conference on Stress Testing* 9th and 10th February 2009 at http://www.bankofengland.co.uk/publications/Documents/speeches/2009/speech374.pdf

[457] Jill Treanor, "Tighter Banking Rules Will Drain £1 Trillion from the financial system *Guardian Observer* 11 July 2010 a PricewaterhouseCoopers study at http://www.theguardian.com/business/2010/jul/11/banks-economy-credit-warning

[458] Doug McClymont, Personal communication 10th February 2014

[459] Joe Nocera, "Subprime and the Banks: Guilty as Charged" *New York Times*, 14 October 2009 at executive suite.blogs.nytimes.com/2009/10/14/subprime-and –the-banks-guilty-as-charged/

[460] Elizabeth Warren, "Unsafe at Any Rate" *Democracy: A Journal of Ideas*, Summer 2007 at http://www.democracyjournal.org/5/6528.php

[461] Sam Pelzman observed that when we think we are safer we take more risks, for example we drive faster when we are wearing seat belts

[462] Quoted in Anat Admati and Martin Hellwig, *op cit* Footnote 86 p 313

[463] Tail risks are risks that happen rarely, but which can have disastrous consequences, and typically, they are not a part of the picture that models provide. Black Swans are similar. They are events that are not predictable given our current knowledge, like tsunamis and meteors that crash into the surface of the earth. They necessarily escape models, but can also have disastrous consequences.

[464] Charles Calomiris and Stephen Haber *Fragile by Design* Princeton University Press, Princeton New Jersey. 2014

[465] Charles W. Calomiris and Stephen H. Haber, "Why Banking Systems Succeed – And Fail" *Foreign Affairs,* Foreign Affairs Council on Foreign Relations, New York, Nov/Dec December 2013. They filtered the sample and excluded current and former communist regimes, those that could not report on private credit granted by their commercial banks for a minimum of 14 of the 21 years.

[466] The Riegle-Neil Interstate Banking and Branching Efficiency Act was passed in 1994. It opened up the doors

[467] By underwriting bonds including war bonds.

[468] Central banks hold reserves, conduct market operations and generally make profits which means that banks and not taxpayers pay for these protections. Sometimes banks pay fees too.

[469] Josef Ackerman, "Josef Ackermann im Gespräch: Ohne Gewinn ist alles nachts"(Talking to Josef Ackermann: Without profits everything is naught) interview Süddeutsche Zeitung, 20th November 2009

[470] Simon Johnson and James Kwak, *op cit* loc 4179

[471] Anat Admati and Martin Hellwig, et al "Healthy Banking System Is the Goal, Not Profitable Banks", *Financial Times* 9th November 2010. There were many notable signatories., *ibid* Footnote 53 p310.

[472] On revolving doors see Anat Admati and Martin Hellwig, *op cit* Footnote 56 on p325

[473] Congressional Oversight Panel, March Report, March 211 testimony by Alan Meltzer which proposes a minimum of 20% for the largest banks and testimony by Simon Johnson who endorses Eugene Fama's 40-50% equity

[474] We will use the term *fraud* to include *malfeasance*

[475] President Barack Obama, White House Press Conference 6th October 2011 at http://www.whitehouse.gov/the-press-office/2011/10/06/news-conference-president

[476] Charles Ferguson, *op cit* P 161

[477] Bob Diamond and Marcus Agius lost their jobs as CEO and Chairman respectively

[478] Fred Goodwin lost his knighthood and some of his pension and adjudged the worst banker ever, but that was it

[479] Louis Brandeis, *Other People's Money and How the Bankers Use it* 1914

[480] Joe Nocera "Credit Suisse Gets Off Easily" *New York Times* 24 May 2014

[481] Adapted from Julia Kollewe, Jill Treanor and Shane Hickey "Banks pay out £166bn over six years: a history for banking misdeeds and fines *The Guardian* 12 November 2014

[482] Professor William Black "System is Ungovernable, it has already largely imploded at https://www.youtube.com/watch?v=oUHS7TVVgww

[483] Sean Farrell, "The price of PPI: What the banks have set aside to pay for miss-selling", *The Guardian*, 3 February 2014

[484] Multiply by 10,000.

[485] House of Commons, "Treasury, Minutes of Evidence" 12 January 2009

[486] Ben Moshinsky and Lindsay Fortado "U.K. Lawmakers Seek Speedy Overhaul of Libor Following Review", Bloomberg, 28 September 2012

[487] The fuller story is that Barclays, Citi, JPMC and RBS paid $2.5 billion to the US regulators, then in addition, Barclays, Citi, JPMC, RBS and UBS paid $1.6 billion to the FED, then Barclays paid $1.3 billion, also to the regulators, an all of this comes to $5.4 billion.

[488] Angela Chen, "BNP Paribas to Pay $140 Million Fine in Sanctions Case", *Wall Street Journal*, 1 May 2015

[489] The European Savings Directive was put in place in 2005. It required the bank to deduct and pay taxes on balances held by the bank's European resident customers

[490] BBC, "Tax officials defended over HSBC claims", 9 February 2015

[491] Of the 6,800 accounts, after culling duplications, 3,600 were examined from which HM Revenue identified 1,100 individuals who have not paid their taxes

[492] BBC "HSBC settles mortgage case with US regulators for $550 million" *BBC News* 12 September 2014

[493] His nickname, Lord Five Hundred. He was accustomed to carrying only 500 notes.

[494] Dennis Kelleher, CEO, Better Markets reported in Reuters, "Big fine imposed on ex-Goldman trader Tourre in SEC case", 12 March 2014

[495] Matt Taibbi, "Why Isn't Wall Street in Jail?' *Rolling Stone* 16 February 2011

[496] Reworded from George Monbiot, "Hard Graft", *Guardian* 18 March 2015

[497] See Kate Barker, *Housing: Where's the Plan?* London Publishing Partnership, London, UK 2014, where Kate proposes a number of alternatives, involving both specific regulation and taxation

[498] See in this context Jay Winter and Antoine Prost, *René Cassin an Human Rights*, Cambridge University Press, Cambridge, UL, 2013

[499] Thomas Piketty, *ibid*